Home & Abroad

For Susie,
In memory of Dugald,
With love,
Marko

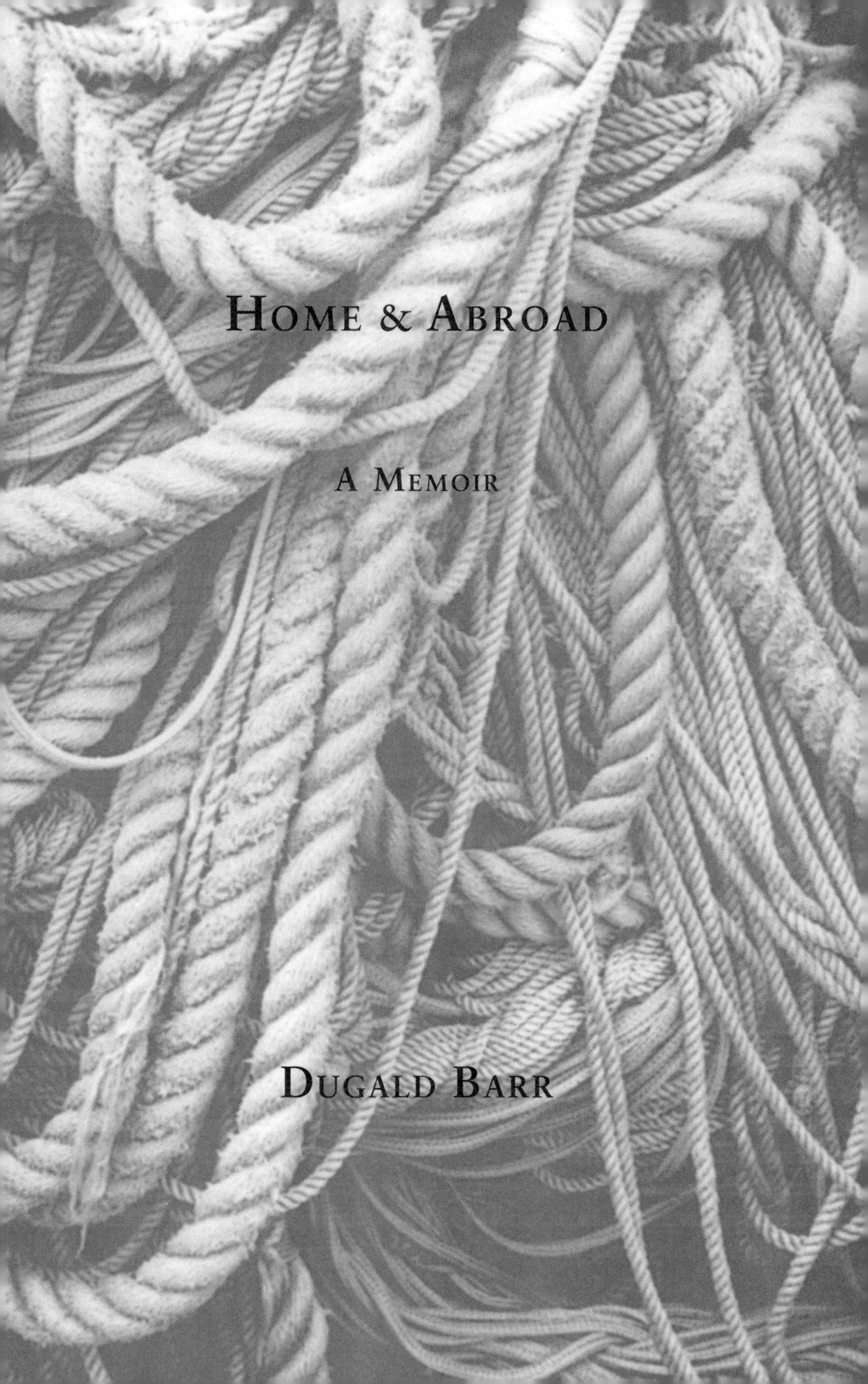

Home & Abroad

A Memoir

Dugald Barr

First published in Great Britain in 2025

Edited, designed and produced by Tandem Publishing
http://tandempublishing.yolasite.com

ISBN: 978-1-0687613-9-3

10 9 8 7 6 5 4 3 2 1

A CIP catalogue record for this book is available from the British Library.

Printed and bound in Great Britain by CPI Group (UK) Ltd, Croydon CR0 4YY.

Contents

INTRODUCTION

Dugald set out to write a *record* of his travels. He was emphatic that it was not really intended as a book for publication, but rather an aide-mémoire, trying to recall the many places visited across the globe

Dugald died of neutropenic sepsis on 3rd September 2023. In my great sorrow at his death, I thought I should create something from what he had left behind, as a way to overcome my overwhelming grief: this book is a part of that. Dugald's exceptional eye (both on the page and behind a camera lens), inspired me in this endeavour. Although not originally meant for wider publication, the sheer quality of Dugald's prose here, and his sensibility, range and humour, deserve a readership. Readers may think it self-indulgent on my part. But for me it is something to remember both his life and the long friendships formed with so many wonderful people who shared in the pleasures of his travels.

He loved travelling to the Continent, encouraged from a young age by his grandparents, and by his education and reading, steeped in the Greco-Roman tradition. But his natural curiosity and his sympathetic outlook on different cultures and peoples took him further afield. Everywhere he went he took innumerable photographs – another one of his major hobbies – some of which became the subjects of his paintings.

Dugald's death came unexpectedly, and so the record lay unfinished, and many trips are not covered in this book.

One special trip that, alas, was left unrecorded came in the spring of 2005, to South Africa. He had recovered from a liver transplant, and David and Chrissie Reid had the kindest thought to invite us so that, as they said, Dugald 'had something to look forward to'. Hospitality in their lovely home in the Bishopscourt district of Cape Town was unrivalled, and the drives Chrissie took us on to Stellenbosch and the famous wine estate of Vergelegen were enchanting. Down the coast road we went to Cape Point, where the Atlantic and the Indian Oceans collide: one of the most thrilling moments in all Dugald's travels. The backdrop of Table Mountain made our stay totally memorable.

He was able on this trip to see Cyril Drew (father of his first girlfriend Sarah, later Sarah Biffen) who was a great friend from his teenage years in Renfrewshire. Dugald cherished the memory of his only trip to sub-Saharan Africa. He very much wanted to go to Kenya and other places of great natural beauty and game parks to see the wildlife, but the transplant and its associated treatment excluded him from ever having Yellow Fever vaccinations (a live vaccine). There was also the long solo trip he made to stay with our dear friends Alok and Katy Agarwal in Bombay and with Alok's relations in Varanasi. Dugald made several paintings of the views of the Ganges at Varanasi, one of which he gave to Alok. On that trip he managed to go with them to the Ajanta caves to see the spectacular stone carvings. A couple of years after he went with Jacques Hennessy to Cambodia. Jacques had been for some years involved with the recovery of Khmer literature in a library near Angkor Wat, and Dugald asked if he could tag along on one of his annual visits with his colleagues. The painting of the ancient ruins that he made after this trip he considered to be one of his best, and we had it well framed. The two of them then went on to Borobudur in Indonesia. Dugald took the opportunity to follow this with a solo exploration in Vietnam.

Dugald took me to places I had never been to before and where otherwise I might never have gone. Some were en route to Tokyo on business, such as when we obtained a rare 'transit visa' to Peking from the Chinese Embassy, as described in the following chapters. It was only a year after Mao's death, a time when hardly any foreigners could enter the country for tourism.

He took me to India and Bangkok for the first time in 1975. We often visited clients in Hong Kong and Singapore. We sometimes then stopped for a short weekend holiday in Europe, and that was how I saw Venice for the first time; we were a little extravagant in those days and stayed at the Gritti Hotel on the Grand Canal.

Stopping in Athens on another return journey from the Far East, we then drove down to the Peloponnese, seeing ancient sites so familiar to him, and swimming in the Aegean for the first time at Tolon. He took me on holidays I would never have planned by myself, such as Istanbul, Bergama, Carthage and Dougga in Tunisia, Marrakech. He drove me along the southern Adriatic coast of Italy, stopping in Bari (then so crime-infested that the hotel insisted on keeping my handbag and Dugald's camera in their safe, much to Dugald's protestations!); Trani, from where St Nicholas of Santa Claus fame was thought to have originated; Bitonto – another 'dangerous' town – the lovely Baroque Lecce; the very dilapidated ancient town of Taranto; and the extraordinary Alberobello, where we bought handmade damask. Then it was up the Mediterranean coast to Naples.

Many times he would rent a car in France to show me his favourite places in Provence, Burgundy, Bordeaux, Dordogne and the Loire. We had many wonderful summer holidays in September staying at La Voile D'Or in St-Jean Cap-Ferrat; on one occasion we drove down in my open Jaguar XJS V12 Cabriolet and explored the Riviera. Sometimes friends joined, and one summer we visited my friends Derek Davies and his pianist wife Shizue at their home in Vence, where we met the well-known war correspondent Clare Hollingworth who was staying with them. Dugald enriched my appreciation of great cities like Rome and Paris, not just with historical and architectural knowledge, but with his favourite restaurants of the great cuisines (Prunier, Chez Pauline, Lasserre, Lucas Carton, Grand Vefour *et al*); he showed me the beauties of many early Romanesque churches of southern France, and further afield the ancient ruins of Fatehpur Sikri and Mahabalipuram in India.

Most importantly, it was he who showed me my own country – Japan.

I had never travelled in Japan when I was a child. I knew only the limited areas of Tokyo where we lived, and the summer resort of Karuizawa in the hills and the home on the beach in the Miura Peninsula, where my family had holiday homes. In Japan together, most often with clients, Dugald would show us different parts: places as far as away as the Shiretoko Peninsula in Hokkaido, from where one could see Russia through a telescope; Hirado, where the first Englishman to arrive in Japan in the early seventeenth century landed; Nagasaki, my father's birthplace; and of course innumerable visits to Kyoto, Dugald's favourite place in Japan. His knowledge of the many important temples, out of some two thousand, almost equalled that of Sir John Pilcher, Britain's Ambassador to Japan in the late 1960s/early 1970s, who had lived there to learn Japanese just before the outbreak of war. John knew the stories of almost every Kabuki play (as did Dugald) and mimicked the actors brilliantly, to everyone's merriment. Dugald was an exceptionally confident and competent driver, able to recognise road signs in Japanese by simply remembering what the characters looked like. He drove around Hokkaido and Tohoku with Alby Bowes-Lyon, as he did with Simon Nicholson and myself; he went to the UNESCO heritage site of Shirakawago in the depths of the Japan Alps in the snow with Dudley Dodd and Greg Walker; he drove Andrew Fraser to Kanazawa on the Japan Sea coast, he took Peter Thistlethwayte, Eric Elstob and myself around the north-west coast of Kyushu from Fukuoka to Sasebo (home base of the US Seventh Fleet) as well as the areas around the historic towns of Hagi and Izumo; and, as he writes in the later chapters, here he drove his mother across the Japan Alps to the Japan Sea coast in his Nissan Cedric, while stationed there with Vickers, da Costa.

His mother, Elizabeth, was a better traveller than I. Dugald jokingly once said 'I prefer to go on holiday with my mother than with you!' He was referring to my proclivity to complaining on those long car journeys: 'Shall we have lunch now, I'm hungry?'; 'Do we have to stop again to take photographs?'; 'Oh, more rubble-gazing?'; 'I am tired now; can we stop for today?' He gave me a book entitled *How to Complain*! Elizabeth was good natured enough not to say such things. But one day she confided in me that she found Dugald stopping to take photographs so frequently on journeys tiresome, and we had a chuckle together.

Elizabeth was a most warm-hearted person, with the loveliest welcoming smile. An only child, she showed no sign of *only child syndrome.* She was used to and loved travelling. Her parents engaged in the Edwardian and aristocratic habit of warm winter holidays, taking not only their daughter but their siblings and relations with them every year. The photograph of them on camelback in Egypt later in this book shows them on one of these winter sojourns that Dugald writes about. They went to the south of France often, but also to Turkey and to Egypt. Dugald writes that these holidays were interrupted by the Great War, but resumed by 1919. When Dugald was ten he was allowed to go to the south of France with them and each year thereafter.

The Macouat grandparents instilled in Dugald the pleasures of travel from a young, impressionable age. Skiing with his parents or driving holidays on the Continent, or indeed in the Highlands of Scotland, were very much part of his childhood agenda. When he was older he continued these with girlfriends, friends and of course also with his family. When his father died Dugald was stationed in Tokyo, and he asked his mother if she would like to come and visit. Elizabeth took to Japan like a duck to water. On the first day there she managed to find herself on the city train that went around Tokyo and took herself on a tour of Tokyo. In a provincial Japanese inn Dugald found her in the morning chatting away with the innkeeper's wife, showing her photographs of her family and having a jolly conversation. As he recorded, he took his mother on holidays every year, at least once, to the Continent and beyond; it was a family habit, not just filial devotion. But Elizabeth wrote him a special letter after one of those trips, in which she thanked him for 'being so good to me'. Dugald was devoted to her and loved her very much, saying after her death that he missed her. I liked her enormously and vice versa; she came to stay at Creems many times, including for Christmas. We spent many summer holidays together at Machrihanish, picnicking by the loch further into the Highlands, which she loved; we spread our rugs beside the car to enjoy her delectable mince or pheasant rolls.

This book has been edited and produced through the tireless efforts of Sam Carter. Having just successfully delivered my memoir, *My Families and Other Samurai*, he was probably a little reluctant to have to cope with my eccentric ways so soon afterwards! He generously agreed to look through Dugald's writings (of which there were duplicates and several editions of the same themes, with his own editing) and the monumental number of photographs to make sense of them. He spent a number of days and nights at Canning Place going through them and making selections for this book. I cannot thank him enough.

I learned so much from Dugald; he gave me his unreserved affection; he tolerated and forgave quietly my selfish idiosyncrasies. I dedicate this book to my real friend, life-long companion, love and my husband who gave me so much over half a century. It is hoped that his many friends will find it a memento of his friendships.

— Haruko Fukuda, 2025

Editorial Note

Dugald on his death left a wealth of memoir and travel writing in various forms and stages. All carried the hallmarks of his remarkable sensibility and attention to detail, and most pieces had been self-edited meticulously.

In attempting to assemble a permanent record of his writings in a single volume, we have been faced with some tricky choices, principally over repetition and ordering. All of Dugald's usages have of course been retained, and we took the view that allowing some repetition across sections was preferable to editing the text by cutting and shuffling his original words. The occasional explanatory note has been added in square brackets.

— Sam Carter

I

Unfulfilled Promise

or

My Academic Life

Early Days

Though in retrospect my reports from Mme. Jacquot's (kindergarten) and Dardenne (pre-prep; both in the neighbouring village, Kilmacolm) were good enough, I had no inkling then that I was considered any 'brainier' than my contemporaries. A brief word about these presumably formative experiences might, however, have a place in this tale. I believe I was already five when I went to Madame Jacquot's 'Mooi Hoek Bilingual School' in Kilmacolm. Helicopter parenting and competitive pressures, I believe, mean that these days children often start some sort of kindergarten or pre-school well before that age. However, I remember some studies – mainly from Scandinavia? – showing that a later start is if anything better for later academic progress. Anyway, it didn't seem to do me any harm. What 'education' I had at home I cannot really recall, though our nanny, 'Nana', Miss Clara Jane Cooper, was an intelligent Aberdeenshire lady from whom one learnt a lot including, I suspect, the basics of the 'Three Rs'.

Mme. Jacquot's, of course, was the only co-educational establishment I attended (until Oxford, which did contain some girls). Ages ran from five to twelve (the two Maclay sisters, who had three brothers nearer my age). Perhaps about twenty children in all, mostly from houses in Renfrewshire near Kilmacolm and Bridge of Weir. My mother, Mrs Jean Donaldson (joint master with her husband Fred of the local hunt) and a Mrs Gooch who lived near us took turns to drive some of us there and back. Mrs Donaldson was much the most popular: transport was either an open and very original and basic jeep (this was after all only a few years after the war's end), especially thrilling when it was refuelled at Hubert Duncan's garage into the tank beneath one's seat, or a vast Armstrong Siddeley where we sank back into the capacious rear seats and fought. I can't remember what Mrs Gooch drove, but think it smelt. My mother drove respectable and middle-of-the-road (not literally!) Rover 60s and 70s.

This was really the first place that I encountered 'other children' beyond my (younger) cousins. On day one I remember sitting at a round table and shyly asking the other boy opposite 'What's your name?' 'Joe' came the equally timid reply. Joe became Lord Maclay not that long afterwards and is not so shy now. The bonds made have I think endured for life, though distance means that meetings are few and far between.

I can remember little of the 'curriculum': reading and writing, between parallel ruled lines in exercise books; French, of course, perhaps rising occasionally above the piped 'Bonjour Madame' each morning. I suppose there was some maths. I didn't play a musical instrument but remember Mhairi Donaldson (my very first girlfriend) played the violin.

The school was in a little 1930s house beside the Birkmyre Park; though we tended to play outside more at the scruffier back, where interesting discoveries were to be made and we looked onto the wilder hills behind the river. Probably in my second year, when we had afternoon school, we used to run into the middle of the village to the Locarno café by the station for our lunch break.

I had been joined by my 18-month (to the day) younger sister Fiona, who was left there when my parents thought I needed a tougher, male-only environment to prepare me for boarding school. This was Dardenne, also in Kilmacolm, a much larger school housed in two (?) Victorian houses which we had run past every lunchtime. As with Mme. Jacquot's, I met contemporaries who have been friends ever since, though the social composition was perhaps more diverse. There was the usual collection of *Down with Skool* stereotype masters: one I remember was called 'Smithy' and could easily have been drawn by Ronald Searle. I cannot remember who the headmaster was.

I certainly started Latin there and have what is probably a false memory that I had begun reading Virgil before I left aged eight. I also remember really enjoying geography (especially, drawing in the course of the great rivers on blank world maps, etc.) and history. I think I was already aware that maths was not really for me.

While nowadays half-terms are the rule, and parents wait until then to fly their darling offspring off to exotic holiday places, this was not the case in mid-century. On the contrary, our parents waited until we were safely parked back at school and then sloped (pun!) off to Adelboden or Mürren to ski as travel became possible again after the war. I can't say I blame them. When I was at Dardenne, in the spring term we decamped with Nana (nanny *not* grandmother) to the now-vanished Kilmacolm Hydro up the hill: thus, I became a 'Kilmacolm boy' rather than a 'Bridge of Weir boy' for a while, with a shorter walk or more likely run up or down the hill to school. (From Bridge of Weir I had walked – or run – down to the station and from there taken the tank engine-propelled steam train the one stop to Kilmacolm. Sadly, that line has long since closed. Of course, my ambition was to become an engine driver 'when I grew up'.)

There were some other memorable and possibly formative sojourns away from Renfrewshire and parents. We went with Nana more than once to stay at the pretty Italianate private hotel Inverdon in Ayr (unaware that Fiona would spend her entire married life within sight up the hill). There I most remember coming across a most marvellous set of illustrated books of the Russo-Japanese War, with splendid cover illustrations of small, neat, fierce Japanese bayoneting hulking, bearded and above all surprised Cossacks – perhaps the first books I really remember. Another, not unrelated, early book was the *Wonder Book of the Navy* which I got when I went to Oban for a few days with my Granny Macouat. A perennial source of reading pleasure and information was Arthur Mee's *Children's Encyclopedia*.

Craigflower

I went to Craigflower in Fife to board in May 1952: starting in the summer term was then quite normal, though virtually impossible now with the 'school year' beginning in the autumn. The choice of school was made largely on the advice of one who will reappear in these pages, Freddy Macdonald, my father's old house tutor at Fettes, whom he revered. The alternative he had suggested was Cargilfield in Barnton, Edinburgh, where indeed many of my friends went and which perhaps (with little justification) considered itself socially superior. But Craigflower was definitely the right choice for me: an infinitely more attractive setting, a David Bryce Scots Baronial mansion in nearly 500 acres of varied land including a wild glen and running down to the Firth of Forth: ideal for 'outdoor leisure', and no comparison with a rather dreary, prim Edinburgh suburb.

Elsewhere I have written 'Random Recollections' on life and activities at Craigflower, which, leaving aside initial homesickness (very rapidly dissipated) and 'shades of the prison-house' on going back at the beginning of term I generally enjoyed, and from which I'm sure I profited. From now on this narrative will mainly focus on academic progress.

The criteria for entry to Craigflower seemed more to involve the ability to tie one's shoelaces and tell the time on a watch than anything else: though I imagine some more purely academic progress was reported. There was I believe an interview with my parents – each side sizing up the other – rather than any direct contact with myself. However, the fact that I had been speaking some French and had already made progress in Latin must have come up. So, my first sight of the place and of those henceforth to be *in loco parentis* was when I was left there after tea on the first night of term.

There were six forms in the school, Form 1 at the top and Form 6 at the bottom: the reverse of the conventional order where 'the Sixth' is generally the top form. I was in Form 6 for precisely two weeks: having come top in the 'fortnightly order' by a large margin I was moved up to Form 5 for the rest of the term. I suppose it would have been indecent to move me up again that term but for the autumn term – when many new boys ('babes' in Craigflower-speak) appeared – I was in Form 4 and then started the spring term in Form 3.

Form 3 was where one (everyone? – surely not) started Greek. I remember it took two whole days to learn the alphabet. I think I was there two terms, then started the new school year in Form 2, where I remained, I believe, for the whole of that academic year. This was a great step-up as we had as our classroom a high-ceilinged *piano nobile* room, probably the finest in the house; this was used for morning and evening prayers and all sorts of assembly, including 'silent reading' for half an hour after lunch before being told off for games.

My reports, still extant at Newark [Newark Castle, Ayr, home of his sister and brother-in-law Fiona and Archie Walker], will settle this but I think I therefore reached Form 1 after seven terms, leaving six terms for Form 1 before leaving in summer 1956. Accommodation was again much superior, being in the very classy Library (by David Bryce; very similar to the furnishings at Portmore [Portmore House, home of David and Chrissie Reid, in Peeblesshire] and no doubt many of his other country houses – not to mention Fettes). This was roughly divided into two parts. One was occupied by the half-size billiard table, with mahogany covers when used as a classroom, which were rapidly removed for billiards in free time (seldom snooker, which was considered *infra dig*). The other, beyond the 'frontier' of a huge sofa with frayed chintz covers, with two enormous and similarly decrepit armchairs facing a huge log fire, represented an agreeable and exclusive 'common room' equivalent. The seats in this area were usually occupied by two farting and incontinent spaniels and one chair by 'Stevo' (J H Stephens, headmaster and proprietor) introducing us to Damon Runyon, Saki, Para Handy, P G Wodehouse and similar boy-friendly but generally worthwhile tomes.

On the elegant shelves I mostly remember many mountaineering books – F S Smythe, Eric Shipton, though with Everest climbed in June 1953 *The Ascent of Everest* soon featured; also, the first generation of paperback classic Second World War books such as *Reach for the Sky*, *The Colditz Story*, *The Dambusters*, *The Wooden Horse*... these have all stood the test of time. There was also of course a wide selection of more general books: both academic, dictionaries etc., fiction (classics; but G A Henty and other purveyors of imperialist derring-do featured especially strongly). All these were read only in the Library. We also each had a capacious locker at the base of the shelves where our personal paraphernalia – textbooks, exercise books, items such as flippers and snorkels for the swimming pool – were stashed.

There were probably ten or so of us round the table. In each year there was one boy who was consistently top of the form – thus of the school – every fortnight: when I first got there it was Gavin Roberts, the next year David Mitchell (also of Bridge of Weir and a Dardenne alumnus). These were much older and when the way was clear I took over that unchallenged position. It had, however, been salutary to be third or second for some terms beforehand; in the lower forms I had always been top, except once or twice in the first fortnight after promotion.

The school term was punctuated by 'fortnightly orders' for which the whole school gathered in the 'Big Schoolroom', Form 2's classroom. On these occasions not only was academic prowess or lack thereof revealed, but also the balance of red or black marks gained over the fortnight. These were awarded by masters, matrons etc. – not least gimlet-eyed Mrs Stephens – not only for especially merit-worthy or underperforming school work (red or black accordingly), but also for conduct including punctuality, tidiness, insubordination, 'rabbling' and so on. A negative balance – how negative? – led to a wait outside Stevo's study for one's appointment with the cane. Plus, points accumulated and the leading balance over the term led to the award of the 'Individual Spoon', a fine silver teaspoon of classic design with the 'CS' monogram thereon. I won this in precisely half of the terms I was there. I must have been quite insufferable.

Already I suspect we must have been pretty classics-oriented, though I don't remember any overt specialisation. Charles Rodger, the classics master, irascible but kindly, with an especially pungent and picturesque turn of phrase, was a memorable character: at age eleven I wrote a couple of imaginary comic monologues, one on his taking our class ('Charlotte in Form 1') and one on his refereeing Game 2 (of three) in rugger, which I adorned throughout four winters without further promotion. When I unearthed them decades later – and put them on an evanescent Craigflower website – I was impressed how I had succeeded in reproducing this unique and creative vocabulary. George Roome, the maths master (and deputy head) was another memorable figure, quietly authoritative; he had fought the Japanese in Burma. Of an earlier generation, and thus a different war, was the previous proprietor and headmaster Frank Wailes: a compact, moustachioed man, handy with his walking cane, he was a perfectionist in drumming home absolutely exact French pronunciation – for which despite my linguistic deficiencies I have been grateful ever since.

While as for many prep schoolboys the *Eagle* comic, featuring the Mekon, Dan Dare and other epic characters, with its evocations of the recent conflict provided me an introduction to basic German: 'Achtung Schweinhund!' 'Gott im Himmel!' and so on, I realised that some command of German could be useful, not only for eventual travel and literary purposes but also because much work on the classics had been done by German scholars. So, I asked the modern languages master (for the moment I forget his name) to give me some one-on-one lessons after hours. I never subsequently followed up with formal German lessons, but these did form a basis to build on.

However, my father thought he must be a homo (he might have been: but neither he nor any other master ever did anything improper – perhaps in retrospect Rodger's invigilation of the communal bathing after muddy games might have been slightly suspect). However, the one-on-one sessions stopped before too long. This chap was supposed to know about thirty languages; and I suppose that once one has knocked off a few the next gets easier. I have always had some facility for languages, but it remains sadly under-exploited: Russian, Arabic, Hebrew, Mandarin being among those where I have little or no knowledge, of the 'difficult languages' only Japanese featuring much later and in an eccentric and partial form. A classical education of course greatly assists proficiency in the Romance languages, including oddities such as Romanian, but I am increasingly 'rusty' even in these – and find Italian and Spanish regrettably interchangeable, depending which country I was in last.

Of course, with nearly three years in Form 1 one was working towards an open scholarship at a public school, rather than Common Entrance. The *Public and Preparatory Schools Yearbook* in the library was eagerly devoured, and I became somewhat of an expert. Eton and Winchester appeared infinitely more interesting than the generality: I was more attracted by the former, but a Winchester scholarship was then considered the *ne plus ultra* of achievement and so that became the acknowledged goal of my efforts. (The last Craigflorian winner of an award there, a few years earlier, had been David Hannay, now Lord Hannay, previous head of the Foreign Office, and arch-Remainer.)

So, I practised on some old Winchester scholarship papers and even the occasional 'O' level and was duly entered for the Winchester exam in my last (summer) term. However, I fell victim, all unknowing, to a plot hatched, I am sure, by my father, who doted on his old house tutor Freddie Macdonald whom he thought would be mortally offended if he did not send me to Fettes also; by said Macdonald; and by Stephens who like all school heads seemed interested mainly in the number of 'awards' his school could chalk up, and never mind who awarded them.

So, I was told – and in those days you did what you were told and had no choice – that I was to go for a few days to

Fettes, close by in Edinburgh, and take the exam 'for practice' just before the planned trip down south to Winchester. I duly spent a few early-summer days boarding in the 'San' across from the hall where I sat the scholarship exams. I'm afraid the news came that I had come top and therefore would go there, and the Winchester excursion was cancelled. (In retrospect I would never have gone to Winchester, whatever the outcome at Fettes: had I succeeded in failing, I would surely have been scratched from the Winchester exam as having no hope, while since I succeeded, well, 'a bird in the hand…')

God knows, though, whether I would actually have enjoyed Winchester, or Eton, which had always rather appealed to me, more: one simply cannot tell. I have many good Wykehamist friends and a preponderance of Etonians – at most levels of closeness, around two-thirds. My father was rather put off Etonians by Ian Fleming whom he found insufferably supercilious – didn't prevent him buying his books; and Charles Rodger always said that Eton didn't expect its pupils to work – if true then, certainly not now! On such random prejudices does much hang…

Anyway: when it came to the Christ Church classical scholarship exam five years later, I came out ahead of both the top Winchester scholar of our year and the Captain of the School (roughly the same thing) at Eton. So, I can have no complaints about the quality of education at Fettes (of which more anon), which produced that result despite the allegedly superior teaching at these establishments. One of my father's prejudices from his time there had been an aversion to separate houses for scholars, as in his day and as in both the schools cited above; that they now had to muck in with everyone else he thought a good thing, and an advertisement for Fettes. Even today I am not sure which is right.

Fettes

The plan, however, immediately went adrift as I did not

immediately join my father's hero's house but as a last-minute entrant who had not been 'put down' for a house went for two terms to the reception house, Inverleith. The craggy but kindly housemaster, John Fairbairn, was also the Director of Music and my brief and inglorious music-making career stems from his pronouncement on day one: 'You've got big ha-ands; You'll play the chay-lo'. In the summer term I transferred at last to Moredun, Freddie Macdonald's house; but for precisely one term, as he gave it up (remaining Second Master, and incidentally my form master for the next year) and was succeeded by an awful man who might aptly be called King Stork following Fred's King Log. (Though a dear old thing, Macdonald was clearly losing his grip and a whiff of *ancien régime* laxity was succeeded by revolutionary terror.) I don't propose here to describe Stork's awfulness, but it was disappointing as I had known something of him beforehand: he had three nice if pint-sized boys at Craigflower, and a delightful (if, it turned out, thoroughly downtrodden) wife. Anyway, I was stuck with him for nearly four years.

As a scholar I started the autumn term in the Upper Fourth form (the numbering now more conventional) with a mixture of 'new men', all scholars, and second-year people. There I lasted precisely a week before being sent up a year to the Upper Fifth for 'O' levels the next June. It was very hard work; I remember in particular finding the antiquated English of Chaucer difficult, while in maths I was struggling with the calculus and other incomprehensible features of 'Add Maths'. There was no science for me, already designated (by some ineluctable process in which I had no say) a classicist: in that first week I had had one 40-minute period of physics, one of chemistry and one of biology – the sum total of my formal scientific training! One consequence of my promotion was that my working day was longer than my contemporaries', and especially in the Inverleith 'waiting house' I went to bed later than them. This I did not mind at all.

Anyway, seven 'O' levels were duly passed in summer 1957, spanning my 14th birthday. In those days one took only those papers strictly relevant to one's intended 'A' level course: there was no purpose in amassing passes for numbers' sake. I was told I had got 95 per cent in Latin: however, looking at my reports for that year, my best subject had actually been the mathematics which I scarcely comprehended.

Returning from summer holidays, I was now in the Lower Classical Sixth, under Freddie Macdonald. We were few, parked in a tiny but high-ceilinged classroom with a view down the west drive to the Western General Hospital. The staples were Caesar and Xenophon, both good martial stuff, and easy; introduction to Greek drama was Euripides' *Alcestis*; and we began composing verses as well as proses in both languages. For the next, 'A' level year we amalgamated with the higher year, in a horrid little windowless classroom on the way to the main lavatories, under John Robson, a very bright and rigorous individual who kept one's nose firmly to the grindstone as one's reading rapidly broadened and as one's capacity to write in the ancient languages improved correspondingly. Ancient history was studied with the amiable and distinctly more relaxed Mike Leslie.

As it happened, 'ancient history' was the only paper taken at 'A' level; in both Latin and Greek we took the supposedly year-beyond 'S' (for 'scholarship') levels, which were apparently more demanding. (No one nowadays has heard of these: the waters were muddied by the introduction of 'AS' levels which are intermediate between GCSEs – themselves supposedly less rigorous even than 'O' levels – and 'A' levels. Got that?) Rather to my surprise, I got 'Distinctions' in both Latin and Greek 'S' levels: there were no distinctions to be awarded in the ancient history 'A' level. Robson, who was now moving elsewhere, wrote a kind, brief card saying, 'there can be few who have done so well so young', to which I regret I may have replied rather flippantly.

Returning in autumn, our diminishing band had a new form master, Robert Philp, Sherborne and Pembroke, Cambridge: I believe his first job. A charming, quiet, civilised man. He had the dubious pleasure of overseeing my four successive efforts at winning an Oxford classics scholarship, the last of which was finally successful. (Message from John Robson: 'That's more like it!') The four efforts were, however, limited to two colleges.

The first attempt was Christ Church, in the December group of 1959. It was very exciting to go down by BEA Vanguard plane with two others from my house, stay a night with the parents of one of these (visiting Windsor and Eton – the sophistication of whose denizens amazed me – the next day) and then be driven up to Oxford for four (?) nights at the House. We wrote the papers in Wolsey's Hall, directly under the stern gaze of Mr Gladstone (as pointed out by the presiding – no invigilating of course necessary – don). Halfway through was the Interview in the Senior Common Room. After what seemed an interminable silence from the dons ranged on the other side of the long table a reedy voice piped up from the far end: 'Mr Barr, am I right in believing that next year, you will still be young enough to come back and *try again*?' So that was that.

The next attempt was Balliol, in March 1960. Balliol was generally considered the most intellectual college, and a scholarship there, especially in classics, the most prestigious of all. I must have done all right, as they later wrote that they would have given me an exhibition (one rung lower than a scholarship), but as I was still young, they thought it better to give that to someone else and expected me to come back in December and carry off the top scholarship. I would have given my eye teeth for the exhibition and leaving school for a year at a foreign university; all the more so as when I duly returned in December there was nothing for me. This was a low point. However, *nil desperandum…*

Now, of course, I am intensely grateful not to have gone to Balliol, though on occasion intrigued by wondering how its very different ethos would have shaped my Oxford and subsequent careers. In January 1961 I repeated the trudge south and this time did carry off the top classical scholarship at Christ Church. The exams were actually in the Christmas holidays (longer in those days before half-terms existed); the news came – in the approved way, via a telegram boy on a bicycle – on a rather special day, when in the morning I had passed my driving test in Paisley (first time of course: I had been driving since I was eight or nine), and in the evening found my first proper girl friend at the dance my parents held for my sister and myself at our house.

To my great disappointment my father said I must go back to school for a final term as he had paid the fees: I had hoped to go for a term or two to the Sorbonne, Florence or Grenoble to get up to speed in the languages and culture – and of course to meet girls and grow up in many ways. Alas, it was not to be. I was not pleased.

There were, however, compensations. I could temporarily abandon the classics and gain some exposure at a similar level to other subjects, principally modern history and English, with two inspiring tutors: Patrick Croker and Eric Anderson respectively. Patrick – 'Paddy' – I already knew well as second-in-command of my house: an eccentric, ebullient, enthusiastic Irishman, he introduced me to the concepts of the English constitution via Magna Carta, the Constitutions of Clarendon, and the Plantagenet era.

Eric was a more recent arrival, after a short period at Gordonstoun where he had practised on the heir to the throne for the various Prime Ministers and princes he was later to teach. His speciality was of course always Walter Scott and he coached and entered me for the essay prize of the Sir Walter Scott Society, for which the subject was *Rob Roy*. This I won. (Recently I read of someone getting the gold medal as the essay prize: I certainly remember no such thing!)

Both of these ended up, quite coincidentally, at Eton: Paddy not so long after I left school, with a long career there, during which I met him occasionally, either at Eton or in Oxford, finally cut short by illness; Eric, of course, following other head-masterships, as headmaster and later provost. Paddy, alas, died some years ago but a small group meet each spring to lunch in his honour at Winchester; Eric, after far too long I 'rediscovered' and enjoyed meeting for lunch now and then. Sadly, he too has now died. Bob Philp, also, I have much enjoyed corresponding with, and meeting, on a glorious May morning, still in Inverleith Place.

A few words may sum up Fettes for me. I did not feel myself ideally suited to it, nevertheless, am the first to be grateful to my parents for giving me an excellent education, there and elsewhere – even if I did pay my way to a certain extent through scholarships! Whether anywhere else would have suited me better, I cannot tell. However, I found the place in general conformist and rather narrow-minded. The worship of games, especially rugger, and automatically conservative thinking were of course typical of most public schools of the time. There was also a rather male chauvinistic and slightly brutal tinge to the place. Nevertheless, I would never say that I was actively unhappy there – it never occurred to me, it was just 'school', an episode to be traversed and survived as quickly as possible. Happiest days of my life, forsooth!

And there were several compensations. First of these I would put as being located in a capital city of great beauty (if insufferable climate): neither of the two aforementioned establishments could claim that. Only Westminster could really match this, after St Paul's went suburban; Highgate, City of London perhaps, or Channing for girls. When of sufficient seniority one could get a pass to go 'up town' after prep several nights a week, and I used often to run or take the bus up to the Usher Hall for unbelievably inexpensive concerts, being back before 'lights out'. And boys – or 'men' as we were called, even at thirteen – of any seniority could explore the museums, Castle, Botanic Gardens (close by) every Sunday. There were of course other opportunities for escape: rifle shooting at the Glencorse Barracks, sailing from Granton (my three or four day a week avocation, having presciently brought my own sailing dinghy), away games, internationals at Murrayfield – these rather a penance for me, since they were compulsory for the whole school: indeed, the sociability of the long walk there and back nearly made up for the tedium of the stadium. I did the Duke of Edinburgh's Bronze award the first year of its existence, 1957, involving among other things a weekend yomp over the Pentland Hills, and thus got my award from the Duke himself at the Canongate Kirk.

I was hopeless at games, except cricket where I was the 'go to' fast bowler of my year, playing for the Under 14 and Under 15 school teams; but eschewing dreams of First XI glory I gave it up as soon as possible to sail my boat on the Firth of Forth. (This elicited the memorable comment from my housemaster that he deplored that I had 'abandoned the manly sport of cricket, which leads to lifelong friendships, for the solitary pastime of sailing', etc. etc. With sailing, I have made so many deep and lasting friendships, seen so many exotic places around the world, and had so many adventures that even a life in an MCC tie at Lord's or on village cricket grounds would find it hard to match.)

Nautical interest was also displayed by my joining the Naval section of the Corps (CCF) after the obligatory preliminary period in the army section. Eventually I reached the dizzy heights of Petty Officer in charge of the squad. A perk of this was having a key – together with the master-in-charge as an RNVR Lieutenant – to the naval Nissen hut, a haven in the bitter Edinburgh winter where I could settle in of an afternoon before the electric fire with a book and a packet of Black Sobranies. Unfortunately, one afternoon this master had the temerity to use his key too: I was busted down to Able Seaman, but the demotion did not last long. The termly Field Days were also quite interesting, usually involving visits to warships on the

Forth, while the post-term 'corps camp' took the form first of a whaler expedition from Faslane to Bute, then down the Firth of Clyde on a destroyer – improbably giving rise many years later to correspondence in *The Oldie* on the subject of the Daily (rum) Tot.

Free at last, there was the wonderful news that my grandparents were taking us – myself, my mother, and my sister Fiona (who, irritatingly, was leaving school eighteen months younger than me) – to Athens, the Aegean and Rome. (Father alas was having to stay behind, working.) This was not only my first jet flight (Comet), when you had to scramble to get a window seat, but my first experience of Greece and Turkey, and indeed of Rome: though not of Italy, as I had spent much of the 1960 summer holidays on a Continental motoring tour with three schoolmates from my house who had just left. (We had had Rome as our objective but sadly decided to turn homewards after Florence – a decision camped above the Arno which I had strongly opposed. Both of these were marvellous experiences and opened my eyes in particular to the physical beauty of the classical heritage: first in Provence on the summer trip, then throughout the cruise and the great cities in the spring of 1961.)

Our first cruise stop was Troy – as I write I have just visited the British Museum exhibition for the second time, and it all remained vivid. Then to Istanbul and down the eastern Aegean, flipping between Turkey and Greek islands as one then could: Pergamum, Priene, Rhodes and of course Minoan Crete, before ending mainland Greece with Delphi. And of course, it was not all classical remains: on reaching Rome at last my eyes were opened to the Baroque and to the church (we were brilliantly served by a future monsignor (Scots) as cicerone; and I had an introduction to the venerable Cardinal Heard – Old Fettesian, Balliol man, Oxford rowing blue, an unusual combination). On the previous summer's whistlestop tour, as well as Venice and Pisa we had sampled much of the Alps, Salzburg, the Rhineland,

Alsace and Flanders. My taste for Continental touring has never abated.

Attempts to get away to a foreign university course for the rest of the summer failed on the rock of parental obduracy: I suppose I should recognise with gratitude their desire to 'have me at home' for a while, but the school holidays were then quite long. So, I had recourse to the usual stratagem of 'running away to sea' and spent a very agreeable summer in Scotland, mostly racing with John Grayburn on the Gareloch in the eponymous keelboat class ('Gareloch Goddesses' – no escaping the classics!) or cruising further up the west coast. With long stays at Machrihanish – the cottage had been bought only a couple of years earlier – this was indeed a very pleasant prelude to the next chapter at Oxford.

Oxford

I drove down to Oxford in Mother's scarlet Mini-Traveller (the first in Scotland), filled with kit for my rooms: with me also I took a Kilmacolm friend, Patrick Mitchell, also in his first term at Pembroke. In an M6-free era we reached Weedon in Northamptonshire (apparently the dead centre of England and thus site for a great arsenal as far as possible from putative Napoleonic invasion) and enjoyed a comfortable night in a hotel. The next day, an easy run to Oxford, park outside Canterbury Gate and unload everything into my new rooms. As luck would have it, they turned out to be just inside the gate to the right: a sitting room and bedroom, both almost perfect cubes, in Canterbury Quad and reached by the steps on which the notorious Bullingdon photos used to be taken. Though there is so much to be written about my Oxford life, here I shall concentrate on the purely academic.

I had four years at Oxford: 'classics' there is more than just languages and literature, which are covered in the first five terms, culminating in Honour Moderations in Classics ('Mods') in March. Then – often with some relief – one proceeds for the remaining seven terms to 'Greats', itself encompassing two different if interrelated subjects, ancient history, and philosophy both ancient and modern. ('Greats' is also the sobriquet for the full four-year course, known formally as 'Literae Humaniores'.)

Mods is undoubtedly testing. Without going into great detail here, it includes intimate knowledge of all of Homer and Virgil; unseen translation of prose and verse of both languages; detailed textual criticism and contextual knowledge of a selected work in each language; rendering of English prose and verse passages into a suitable equivalent in both ancient languages; and a 'special subject' from a range which included formal logic, Greek vase painting, etc. I chose the vases which proved a much harder option than I had expected. We were ten or twelve reading Mods and Greats in my year; and our tutor was John Gould, the very one who had asked the withering question at my first interview nearly two years earlier.

I got a second in Mods: probably rather unimpressive though I don't remember ever seeing my marks. (In those days, as Oxford unlike universities elsewhere could count from one to four there was no such thing as a 2:1 or 2:2.) In truth I had not worked nearly hard enough, the novel and liberating delights of Oxford after years of pounding round the same course at school in my two years of scholarship attempts having proved irresistibly distracting. More prosaically, the Mods term itself coincided with the Arctic blizzards of early 1963 in which the entire country, Oxfordshire and in particular my tiny bedroom froze solid, with the deplorable result that rising before noon became almost unthinkable. (I had changed rooms at the start of my second year: as senior scholar I had the choice of any free rooms in the college and had chosen ones with undoubtedly the best-situated, spacious and finely panelled sitting room, on the ground floor in Peckwater directly facing the Library. The downside, which I hadn't really appreciated, was that the bedroom was a poky little unheated thing at the back facing Bear Lane.)

Nevertheless, the college was very generous and gave me, unsolicited and not expected, a bursary of £20 – a lot of money in 1963 – to travel to Sicily in the Easter vac. I chose Sicily as Thucydides' account of the Athenians' Sicilian expedition had been my Greek special subject. So, the transition from Mods to Greats was even further enhanced by my very own Sicilian expedition. After a few days in Rome with parents and grandparents, I set off for Naples (luckily able to see *Tosca* in the San Carlo opera house while there), taking in Pompeii of course then overnight on the boat to Palermo. Arriving there and having located a modest city centre hotel, I found that the world premiere of Visconti's film of Lampedusa's *The Leopard* was taking place in the opera house that very night (and simultaneously in Rome). I was fortunate to get what I was told was the very last ticket. I had been fascinated by the book when it had appeared not long before and spent time in Palermo and inland Sicily, searching out places associated with the author and his epic.

The wondrous relics of the Normans in and around Palermo – the Cappella Reale and Monreale – were also a revelation. Then I set out, by train and bus, on a tour of the island which was more relevant to its Greek and Roman antiquity: Agrigento (where once more I bumped into a Christ Church contemporary earlier encountered in Rome); Piazza Armerina with its mosaics; and thence to Syracuse. I needn't describe its fascinations but the Latomie caves where Nikias and co. were imprisoned and the broad extent of the harbour brought my Thucydides reading vividly to life. The 'Greekness' of the place was evident, with the amphitheatre and on Ortygia the Christian cathedral incorporating the ancient Greek columns. Sicily has remained among my favourite places, though the Baroque towns of 'Inspector Montalbano' – of which I was unaware that first time – I now find as appealing as the antique.

I took the night train back to Rome, joined in my compartment by an enormous, caricature German scoutmaster type with *lederhosen* and bulging rucksack (from which he offered me a tube of condensed milk), who shut the window every time I opened it, said 'I go for Paestum; you vill vake me for Paestum' and snored off to sleep. In the middle of the night and out of nowhere he awoke with a start, exclaimed 'I go for Paestum' and with his rucksack clambered down onto the track. Some hours later we passed Paestum in the dawn…

Returning to Oxford for the 'final lap', Greats, in effect we were reading two different if closely intertwined subjects, philosophy and ancient history, and I now had three tutors instead of one. For Greek history I was 'up to' the impassive, pipe-smoking

David Lewis and for Roman history the more conventional but most thoughtful Eric Gray (it was he rather than Lewis, however, who had spent the war in caves with the Greek resistance). Philosophy was David Pears, with his welcome glass of vermouth accompanying tutorials.

'Great men' are in my experience either historians or philosophers: the disciplines and the mindsets are very distinct, I was (and still am) definitely an historian. I think I made a mistake in choosing for my special subjects, in both Greek and Roman history, the 'classical' periods with which I was already most familiar: exposure to later, hitherto unexplored periods – Hellenistic in Greek and later Empire in Roman – might with their novelty have aroused my interest more. Lewis had the more questioning approach; Gray had settled views on most problems, and I found that one got the most approbation if one found oneself agreeing with these.

Philosophy was somewhat schizophrenic, with three papers in Finals but two philosophical epochs about two thousand years apart. Plato, whose *Republic* I selected as my special subject, and Aristotle (*Nicomachean Ethics*) constituted the ancient: again, there might perhaps have been less obvious choices from the works of these two – let alone from the whole corpus of ancient Greek philosophy. The modern era in philosophy for Oxford's purposes effectively began with Descartes, and there, as at Harvard also, found its main focus in logical positivism: an area to which I had first been attracted at school by Ayer's *Problem of Knowledge* and *Language, Truth and Logic*, but which I feel ultimately verged on the arid. The Logic paper was essentially devoted to these questions. The third philosophy paper, dubbed 'Morals and Politics', required study of the mainly nineteenth-century philosophers whose work encompassed those themes.

I am sure I was preternaturally idle – and for example driving around 8,000 miles in Oxfordshire and Berkshire on beagling matters hardly helped – but in retrospect writing at least two essays a week did require a great deal of application. Nevertheless, going into 1965 I realised serious revision was required: research into the probabilities of various questions appearing in Finals papers led to my writing essays to myself on the most likely topics, rendered down until they became second nature, reproducible at will. Panicking shortly before Finals, I wrote myself a whole new set, as insurance; needless to say, the first selection came up just as predicted. There was no sleep during the week of exams, except for blissful oblivion from after (a well-earned Italian) lunch on the Saturday (a half-day for exam purposes) until late on Sunday.

After Finals there was much celebrating – fairly decorous in character and coinciding with Commem Balls and other entertainments. I asked my landlady, Mrs Hall, if I might hold a drinks party in the garden of 98 Holywell: 'I should hope you *will*, young man!' was her response. (So, I did.) I packed as much of my possessions as I could into my Mini-Cooper and took them up to Scotland, exchanging it for my mother's Bentley. This made a good sitting-out room for events such as the Beagles and Drag ball on Cliveden Reach and evinced not the slightest surprise from Norman and Fred in the buttery when I drove it into college to collect the champagne for my party.

Unfortunately, I had a blackout of sorts returning in the early morning from a dance at Hurlingham – ironically, I had left it early and had spent most of the night drinking coffee and chatting in London and was totally sober – and as an undergraduate in a dinner jacket and a Bentley had thought it judicious to drive slowly. I woke to find myself plunging towards the branch railway line to Cowley at Littlemore, sadly writing off the Bentley. I myself had just a cut to the chin but also a complex ankle fracture, which has plagued me ever since. (Both these would have been avoided had the Bentley had seat belts, not yet a normal feature.) An ambulance took me off to the Radcliffe where I spent a fortnight on a ward where the sun blazed through vast windows from around 4 a.m. and when I eventually managed some sleep the bikers alongside woke me with water-pistols improvised from syringes. Great fun. In retrospect I must have been extremely tired, deep down.

I was rescued and given wonderful care by the Blackwell family, spending the next fortnight at Tubney where I spent much of the time driving Miles, water-skiing behind his speedboat, on the Radley gravel pits. However, work also reasserted itself as in hospital I had learned that I was to have a viva, as I was poised between two classes on the basis of my written papers. I desperately hoped I had not sunk so low that it was to be a '3/2' but thought a '2/1' perhaps optimistic. Worry and work rather overshadowed this period of recuperation among dear friends.

Came the day, and I was driven in by Miles to the Examination Schools. Being encased in plaster and hobbling on crutches like Yossarian in the recently published *Catch-22* I had rather hoped for sympathy and allowances, but no such luck. Returning in the afternoon to read the class lists posted outside the Schools, I found my name among the Seconds (having superstitiously looked among the Thirds first). I don't remember much of the actual interview but a goodish mark on Greek history questions was brought down by a mere β+ in Logic, where the inquisitor was the late Mrs, later Dame Mary, later still Baroness Warnock. (One was examined at the viva on what had been one's best subjects in each discipline; in my case, on the philosophy side that had been logic, where in the written paper I had scored a respectable βα.) I was disappointed by my mark in Roman history, always my best subject, where the examiner was my tutor Eric Gray. I had accurately predicted the questions and believed my answers chimed with his theories…

My tutors wrote kind notes, straightforward and unreserved from Eric Gray and David Pears, quintessentially convoluted and enigmatic from David Lewis, which I have treasured. All, I think, felt I had exceeded their expectations. Nevertheless, the feeling of having come tantalisingly close has never left me.

However, when having tea that autumn with a Roman history don, Frank Lepper (father of a girl I knew) I was asked about my marks, he said 'But you should never have needed a viva: it should have been a straight First.' But a miss is as good as a mile: there can be no going back (Finals papers were always destroyed for that reason); and in all honesty I did not deserve better.

So, my degree, rather than a 'Desmond' was basically a 'Boris': perhaps with the difference that in my time only 8 to 9 per cent got Firsts in Greats, while now nearly half do: how far grade inflation (if such it be) counted when Johnson was gracing Balliol escapes me. (And did anyone suggest the viva, which he also fluffed, was superfluous?) Anyway, my supremely common-sensical but definitely unacademic father always pronounced that people distrusted a man with a First…

Later

With that concludes my formal education, the supposed subject of this part of the memoir, despite frequent barely relevant excursions and embellishments. I had not seriously considered reading for a higher degree, now almost obligatory to be considered 'educated' but then usually done with the aim of an academic career. Nor had I considered reading for the Bar, having an aversion to speaking in public. A few further episodes could perhaps count as 'learning' or putting learning to use.

Having given little thought to the vexed question of earning a living, about which I was totally confused – neither school nor dons having been of the slightest help – but having ruled out a career as either don or barrister, before Schools I had decided, with a keen interest in 'abroad', that the Foreign Office might be congenial. The exams and further tests would not come until the beginning of 1966 so there was a long period for recuperation at home and with friends. Adding to my foreign language capabilities seemed a sensible plan so, following Hamish Aird's example, I set off in the autumn to stay with Alastair

Boyd (later Kilmarnock) at the Casa de Mondragón in Ronda to learn Spanish. (Alastair was then running it as a summer school for debs and youth but in the winter would put people up and lay on tutors.) I was tutored in the late morning and early evening by someone with the pleasingly phonetic alphabet name of Andrès Sierra Bravo; and applied myself sufficiently to this not-hard language that after two months I was reasonably fluent and literate. Alas, easy come, easy go; and in later life I find Spanish and Italian all too interchangeable.

It had anyway been a most agreeable interlude. The Casa de Mondragón (generally called the Casa de Piedra, being one of the two stone-faced houses in the town, and later more pretentiously, after reverting to the Spanish state, the Palacio de Mondragón), perched on the edge of a cliff with a stunning view of the mountains to the west. Ronda was still an unspoilt, almost Victorian town; mine was one of the few cars in the place. Following *hora español* we got up late and retired late; before lunch around 3 there might be dry sherries at the Clube in town for about tuppence a glass: later, with the admixture of a minute quantity to gin bought in Gibraltar for 8 shillings a bottle they metamorphosed into dry martinis over which we played two-handed liar's poker. There were expeditions: to Jerez and Cádiz, following Alastair and Johnny Watson doing the journey on horseback, and to Morocco with my mother. Pre-dawn start on the steam express from Madrid to Algeciras, then Tangier, Fez and back to Gibraltar. Morocco appeared so prosperous in comparison to Spain. The Gib border was scarcely an issue (as the gin-buying expeditions had shown). The eternal sunshine of Andalucia turned suddenly to fog and cold well before Madrid, and through France to London.

There I sat the Diplomatic Service and Higher Civil Service exams, kindly put up at the Berkeley (in its old site opposite the Ritz) by my grandparents. There were three written papers: I can't quite remember what two of them were, but do remember that I came top, of the entire country, in the essay paper, despite or perhaps as a result of excoriating the Wilson government at length. I was then called, in the weeding-out process, to the two-day tests and interviews at the Civil Service building in Savile Row – the equivalent of the 'country house weekend' of legend. In groups we approached tasks, chaired meetings, did puzzles and were interviewed by a psychologist (who I thought might benefit from some analysis himself), the 'chairman', a retired colonial governor buffer, and a coming-man 'Young Turk'. This last was Ewen Fergusson who at one point said, 'It's not all just about becoming Ambassador in Paris, you know.' This I thought slightly unfair as one reason for applying was that I hoped to go to far more exotic places. (He of course ended his diplomatic career as – Ambassador in Paris!) Some research might have saved me from making somewhat caustic comments about my inglorious rugger career – he had been a Scottish international. Oh well.

Safely through this stage, I was called to the final interview before a panel of some dozen people – all or mostly men? – some weeks later. I suspect a large proportion of them were trade unionists. I don't recall much of the questioning: there was one about which theory of the Kennedy assassination I found most convincing, another where I revealed that I knew little of the difference between fiscal and monetary policy (I should have been mugging up economics as well as foreign languages, but it was a totally closed book). In any case my face clearly did not fit, and I fell at that fence. I was invited to take up some post in the Home Civil Service, but that did not appeal. I do of course often wonder how my life would have changed had I been successful – clearly, totally; also, who the others were with whom I had jumped through hoops in Savile Row, which of them had FCO careers, distinguished or otherwise. I remain proud of my essay prowess.

After that achievement we return to the realms of the absurd and bathetic. Having vowed never to sit an exam again (and making exceptions only for those for a private pilot's licence), and kept to that vow during employment in New York, London, and Tokyo in the 1960s and 70s, at the end of the latter I was invited to join the partnership of my City firm, James Capel & Co, requiring individual membership of the London Stock Exchange. Only a year or so before, the Stock Exchange had made membership dependent on passing four exam papers: Stock Exchange Practice, Interpretation of Company Reports and Accounts, Taxation and – I forget… (Irritatingly, this requirement was first watered down and then abolished, not long after I had become a member. At least, though, it provided the 'intellectual' qualification for Fellowship of the Securities Institute, which emerged as the professional body after the Big Bang.)

All this might have been relevant to a UK private client stockbroker but was almost wholly irrelevant to my field of international institutional investment in overseas markets. The experience itself was wholly depressing as it involved virtually shutting up shop and attending classes off Fleet Street, where one was coached for the exams. What was required was unthinking, parrot-like answers to formulaic questions, originality severely discouraged. As an example, one would be marked down for writing 'the Stock Exchange' (as I have done above) as against 'The Stock Exchange'. The antithesis of all the learning I had engaged in down the years.

In the event, I actually failed the Taxation paper. This of course had nothing to do with principles; merely working out some tax calculations (an important ability, without doubt, for accountants and tax practitioners). No matter how well one grasped the process, however, if one had wrongly entered one figure early on the result was inevitably wrong and one failed. And this is evidently what happened. Inconvenient in that the paper had to be re-sat six months later; infuriating in that it seemed so petty and was the first and only exam I ever failed – as well as the last I ever took! But I really could not have cared less…

LESSONS LEARNED

(in no particular order)

Without, really, any say in the matter I specialised all through my academic career: at any stage it seemed inevitable that I should specialise in classics. I would still maintain that if one must follow a narrow, specialised curriculum that of the classics is probably the best: apart from anything else it arouses interest in all sorts of other things and does inculcate a certain rigour of thought. However, the consequence is a total absence of, at least formal, training in the 'STEM' subjects, which are arguably more relevant to mundane modern employment. I suspect that at secondary school level the broader IBAC curriculum gives a rounder and more relevant education than the narrower 'A' level. Other serious lacunae included economics, which no one even dreamt of teaching at school.

That said, I would always support a curriculum – at school or at university – that developed critical thinking abilities and a broad awareness of culture, as opposed to purely vocational subjects such as appear now to feature so prevalently in newer universities. Nevertheless, it would have been nice to have had more of a choice: but that was the practice of the time.

Many distinguished (and fortunate) people write of having had an especially 'charismatic' teacher. Though I owe a lot to many kind and conscientious teachers I am not sure if 'charisma' ever featured. Did that really matter? Among those I might mention in despatches: at Craigflower the recently retired headmaster and former proprietor, Frank Wailes, was meticulous in inculcating scrupulous, exact French pronunciation; Stephens opened up the realms of literate comic writing; Charles Rodger was endearingly eccentric, enriched one's vocabulary and demonstrated how apparent gruffness can conceal much kindness. At Fettes my two classical tutors were excellent in rather different ways: John Robson precise and demanding, rather austere; Bob Philp much more easy-going, friendly, civilised, intelligent. However, neither quite instilled in me a real excitement or curiosity about the classical world: perhaps the demands of the exam syllabus were too austere, even Germanic, lacking the inspiration which even middle-of-the-road television documentaries can produce. Something nearer inspiration came in that final term when Eric Anderson with Walter Scott and Paddy Croker with English constitutional history devoted time to something much nearer one-on-one tutorials, opening up an introduction to university-style study patterns.

At Oxford, also, I can't say I was truly inspired by any of my tutors, though they were all formidably learned and civilised people. This is probably wholly my fault: tutorials seemed a weekly hurdle to be taken in one's stride, and for their part my tutors must have found them rather a tiresome interruption in a life of research. It was in fact a not disagreeable aspect of Oxford life that one was now left very much to one's own devices without too much tedious and intrusive 'pastoral' care.

Neither at school nor at university was there the slightest guidance given about future careers nor how all this expensive education might best be deployed in adult life. (There was a poky little cubbyhole under the back stairs at Fettes which contained a few out-of-date pamphlets about thrilling careers in municipal government etc.) One's parents were not a lot of help either: it was tacitly acknowledged that I was unlikely to be following previous generations in the family firm of chartered surveyors in Glasgow; otherwise, there was the mantra that 'chartered accountants never starved' and some references to how I would no doubt be welcome as an apprentice in a family friend's law office specialising in conveyancing… The prospect after the freedom of Oxford of some years at home in Scotland on an apprentice's pittance did not appeal.

At Oxford the one brush with the future was the visit of a Foreign Office official expounding the merits of that career (rumour has/had it that these visits were in reality about recruiting for MI5 or MI6); in fact, I fell for that one, as recounted earlier, but it didn't happen. (My grandmother, who had ex-ambassadorial friends, considered a career culminating in a prestigious embassy ideal for me.)

Of course, I blame myself for a lack of curiosity, self-awareness and preparedness for the wider world. Today's youth are infinitely more purposeful in directing their energies towards an appropriate career, researching carefully, and taking vacation jobs and internships, publishing their CVs, and submitting to gruelling interviews. I do admire them. In fact, it seems extraordinary now that so few of my Oxford friends seem to have thought much about what they would do when they went down: I remember even feeling quite scornful that one of my contemporaries had even secured a prestigious position before we took Finals.

Employers, of course, were far less vigorous in their selection procedures; internships were barely heard of, 'HR' unknown, and personal contacts and networking correspondingly important.

I obviously 'peaked' far too early, about age twelve, I should have thought. Of course, challenges and competition become greater as one moves into the wider world of public school and university: or perhaps I kept my end up reasonably well. There is a tendency to think that early successes led to complacency and 'taking one's foot off the pedal': but looking back there was a fairly constant application of nose to the grindstone (exams taken early, several attempts at the Oxford award, a rigorous curriculum there with two essays a week as well as unseens, proses and verses…). That said, Oxford seemed a liberation and I could and should have devoted many more hours to my studies.

There is little doubt that I tended to 'rise to the occasion' of exams rather than the ongoing 'coursework' (though perhaps consistently top fortnightly places suggest otherwise).

Chance, moreover, can play a great part in exams. This can obviously be mitigated with assiduous revision and also by the more cunning, through study of previous papers and application of probability theory. Nevertheless, it is hard to explain how one apparently successful scholarship exam attempt (Balliol March 1960) was succeeded nine months later by a failure (Balliol December 1960); and that after three weeks, all holiday, by eventual success (Christ Church January 1961). Another observation, which is surprisingly often borne out, is that if one thinks one has done well in a question, paper, or exam, one almost certainly hasn't; and vice versa.

The much derided 'essay crisis' culture of Oxford (and Cambridge, I believe) is in fact I think of great use in later life: the ability to assimilate information quickly and to work extremely hard, all night if necessary, to meet a deadline is priceless.

Research I have seen relating to the response to school and university closures owing to the coronavirus pandemic suggests that attending lectures in person may actually be counterproductive compared with online teaching or simply reading. Certainly, I attended rather few lectures at Oxford, mainly through sheer laziness but also because one could more easily assimilate what lecturers had to impart through reading their books or learned articles. There were some to which I was directed by my tutors where the lecturer had something novel or important to say.

They could also be a forum for meeting those reading the same subject from different colleges; and running (as one usually did) through the streets was an aid to fitness. There was also the pleasure of sitting in varied college halls or university rooms. What I do regret is not going to more lectures by distinguished dons in other Honour Schools: History, English, Modern Languages. The programme was listed there for all to see, and it was – is – a priceless resource. A missed opportunity given my earlier beef about over-specialisation.

II

An Overview of a Travelling Life

Introduction to a Travelling Life

This is an entirely self-indulgent memoir, meandering (with a capital 'M' in one early case) over various travel experiences down the years; in roughly chronological order but with diversions thematic as much as geographical as reflections emerge from the corpus of memory.

I am writing largely of overseas travels here: a following section reveals the different traditions of the two sides of my family, and there is little space here to describe or reflect on a childhood and youth largely spent in Scotland and my enduring love for that most hauntingly beautiful of countries. It has been as great a privilege to spend so much time, mostly in the West Highlands, and to possess a small house within yards of our own bay with unsurpassed views to the islands of the west – Tír na nÓg. My regret is that I cannot get up there – or beyond, to my first and real love of Ardnamurchan and Moidart – enough these days (and not at all in the past two years).

I cannot claim to be in any way an adventurous explorer – a mountaineer, or cohabitant with exotic tribes; nor to write with the aplomb, humour and charm of our great travel writers, who valiantly maintain that tradition to this day. Nevertheless though meekly following their paths in (and on) the main my travels, whether holidays pure and simple, solitary roamings (often by car) or incidental to work and business, have been one of the most meaningful aspects of my life. Discussions on that 'meaning' are thus likely to recur as diversions from a geo-chronological narrative.

One most important constituent of travel is of course one's travel companions. I have been immensely and almost invariably lucky in these. (These may or may not be mentioned in dispatches later.) Sometimes one loved or congenial other; sometimes cheerful groups; sometimes a boat crew in exotic and far-flung places; sometimes even clients or work 'associates', those mainly in Japan. Reactions to new sights are almost always stimulated and enhanced by the company of congenial others – both the 'fresh impressions' and sometimes even the perils and traumas.

In many of these episodes, it is the 'first impression' that is the most important and testing. Often that has been so far at odds with my preconceptions as to have jolted me into a quite different experience of the place in question. Examples might be the great walls of Constantinople and Rome, and the quite unexpected colouring of the latter city; the scurrying uniformity of the Japanese first viewed *en masse* on a May morning at Haneda airport; the vast size of the North American continent exemplified by the trucks on the Quebec quayside one November night. I could go on (and shall).

However, I am at least equally happy with my own company: essentially, this gives the opportunity to roam, to use time and space as I will, for serendipity to intervene and often cause drastic changes with any 'timetable'. Hence some aversion when touring to booking ahead, at least until there is reasonable certainty how far one might reach. Likewise, an *étape* might stretch for two or more days, for its own merits or as a base for local exploration. On a higher plane, despite the contribution just described, to appreciate new places, often by those far more expert than I – one can decide where to divert, tarry or linger without influence from or consideration for any others: this is a great freedom. I have never minded dining (and sleeping!) alone. As photography has become more and more insistent, the constant recording is apt also to irritate companions. 'For lust of knowing what should not be known, we take the Golden Road to Samarkand.'

Perhaps this sums up the essence of a compulsion to travel. Nevertheless this is just one element. The formalities, and repetition year by year, and the companionship of one's oldest friends are just as important. Argyll and France – and further afield Japan – are constants and in years other than 2019 and 2020, blighted by myeloma and pandemic, have accounted for sizeable parts of the year. In earlier times I always experienced a certain *frisson* when meeting friends – sometimes most unexpectedly – in foreign parts, ranging from Paris to Sicily to Saudi Arabia.

I never yet got to Samarkand, or Bukhara or Khiva, despite devouring the accounts of Robert Byron, Fitzroy Maclean and earlier intrepid travellers: there were plans for an overland expedition in the 1962 summer vacation, but they came to naught. One day, I swear… Necessarily, though, there are other unexplored areas which I would dearly love to see – the 'bucket list' in somewhat banal modern terminology. Since they won't feature in actual accounts, I should perhaps mention, as well as Central Asia, essential Russia around Moscow, and Ukraine; the Grand Canyon and the national parks of the American West; Rio; Patagonia, Cartagena and more Mayan ruins in Latin America. The Amazon and sub-Saharan Africa are 'out of bounds' for medical reasons – Timbuktu as well as East African game parks. Of course, there are many large countries which I know well, but where there are many areas still unexplored: India, Argentina, and of course the USA.

Two Family Traditions

I am one hundred per cent Scots: British certainly, but not ever English. Much of my genetic inheritance, however, is probably Viking: indeed a 'Dugald' or Dubhgealleachd is a 'dark stranger' or Dane, as opposed to a Fingal (like him of the cave, a 'light-haired stranger' or Norwegian).

Thus I grew up in the west of Scotland, though educated from eight in the East: holidays were principally in the West Highlands, reflecting perhaps the principal elements of my family background, more Highland than Lowland until more recent generations.

Excursion #1: my father's and my mother's families had very different traditions and habits concerning holidays and travel. Notwithstanding that, quite coincidentally, both my grandmothers' maiden name was Maclachlan; though they were of different branches and only my maternal grandmother's family were truly Highland residents in recent times (Ardnamurchan), though Great-Grandfather Maclachlan on the Barr side had descended to Dunbartonshire, presumably from the clan HQ in Strathlachlan on Loch Fyne.

The Macouats were a sept of the Buchanans who inhabited – and still largely do – the area of Stirlingshire north of Glasgow where the Highlands begin and which was the subject of such dread by Glasgow folks in Sir Walter Scott's *Rob Roy*. They were prosperous farmers around such places as Buchlyvie and Killearn; very much intermarried with families such as the Colvilles and Bilslands who prospered greatly after moving to Glasgow ('Second City of the Empire') and the wider world (iron and steel and bakeries respectively). Public service, of a Liberal persuasion, was natural to them and peerages and other honours came: indeed my great-grandfather Robert Macouat was apparently offered a barony by Asquith but was peremptorily told by his (Drummond) wife to refuse it as being too grand for the likes of them. Pity: my mother might have rather liked it, though I could not have inherited. My grandmother certainly would have enjoyed it.

No reflection on a genuine sense of service, but there might have been a tiny element of nepotism: Robert was appointed a Deputy Lieutenant of Glasgow by his brother-in-law and indeed also first cousin who happened to be Lord Provost and Lord-Lieutenant for many years. His principal business in the world's leading centre of shipbuilding and railway engineering was the poetically named 'Rivet, Bolt and Nut Company' which my grandfather, a chartered accountant, manfully carried on (though failing to diversify among the challenges of welding – see Japan's Makino Milling – but investing in a number of diverse concerns). The Rivet Bolt was eventually bought by GKN and is no more.

Granny Macouat maintained very strong links with the Highlands and with Ardnamurchan in particular. There they stayed at Acharacle at the inboard end of the peninsula (I shall come to that shortly, or eventually), where she was the 'grande dame' and Lady Bountiful. A great many clan relations, often distant and of relatively humble estate, would be visited and patronised, in the nicest possible way: we were dragged around many of them each September.

Her father, Dugald Maclachlan, had been one of seven brothers, sons of a 'tacksman' (sub-laird) on the north side of the peninsula, known apparently as 'the handsome Maclachlans'. Every Sunday they walked seven miles to church in Kilchoan (over Ben Hiant) in the morning, seven miles back, then repeated this for the evening service. My great-grandfather took the boat from Kilchoan to Tobermory every week to board for school there; thence to the Glasgow Academy and Glasgow University (BL), and a prosperous career as a city solicitor. He was closely involved with the great St Columba's Church in the city: it is perhaps remarkable – or is it – that my grandmother retained a very strong Christian faith. (My grandfather's was perhaps of a more restrained nature: I well remember his disdain when we first visited St Peter's in Rome together for all the flamboyance of Catholicism and popery – I was of course entranced.)

The Barrs were the only truly Lowland family of the 'quartet' of my grandparents' families. It is a Renfrewshire and Ayrshire name. In the late eighteenth to early nineteenth century they seem to have settled in Greenock, where a Miss Barr married Robert Train, another solicitor and son of Joseph Train, the celebrated writer and antiquary (and exciseman following in – well, the train – of Robert Burns, mainly in Galloway), who was known as 'the antiquarian correspondent of Sir Walter Scott', to whom he sent numerous antique and historical objects for Abbotsford, as well as stories which the great man used for plots of his novels, gratefully acknowledged in his somewhat prolix prefaces. (Some of these which came down through the Barr family I now possess: an ancient carved oak cabinet, in which my grandmother used to keep her gin, a few feet from me as I write in Suffolk; and Old Mortality's – Robert Paterson's – 'mell' or mallet is currently lent to Abbotsford.)

In Greenock the intermarriage was largely with the sugar families, the Lyles and Speirses (the Lyles of course joined up with London's rather better known Tates). The sugar industry was devastated by German bombing in 1941 – I well remember the ruined factories in my youth, rivalling Clydebank – I am not sure even now if all is restored. Anyway with the building of the second railway route from Glasgow to Greenock by the Glasgow and South Western through Bridge of Weir and Kilmacolm, salubrious commuter villages grew up, and the Barrs decamped to Bridge of Weir; more exactly Ranfurly, occupying the hill above 'the village' lower down, whose main industry was – and still is – the leather tanneries on the banks of the River Gryffe. (To this day the Bridge of Weir leather may support one's bottom in a Rolls or Bentley or Aston Martin.)

Indeed Robert's descendants did also now make Glasgow their focus: James Barr and Son was the leading chartered surveyor in the city for several generations (now also amalgamated and disappeared: unlike myself my young cousin James stuck it for a while but left it to others and now lives abroad). Grandfather Barr worked especially tirelessly in and after the war on damage estimation in particular, was President of the RICS and was knighted: unfortunately he died prematurely of cancer in 1952 and I mostly remember visiting him as an invalid in bed in Ranfurly House up the road. He was – like all the family men, except me – a large and imposing man: the story goes that when he was on a London Underground platform in the war, when they had 'Speak Your Weight' machines, the following exclamation from one urchin to another took place: 'Ere, Alf, come quick: 'ere's a bloke wot weighs a blinking ton!'

Sir James was both the oldest and the only survivor of four brothers in 1914–18: as the eldest he had to carry on the firm as a vital reserved occupation. The other three, named inevitably Lyle, Speirs – and then Fred – were all killed in France. I have visited their graves. In the first two cases the name they were called by was a surname, but at least the parents put that second. My father was called Lyle after his recently deceased uncle but was given, first, a family name from his mother's side, Allison (his uncle also bore it, which was confusing to us as children – 'Uncle Allison'? – especially as his granddaughter was christened 'Alisoun' – I could go on). This apparently caused great mirth when first read out at public school. Why then my parents, intending always to call me Dugald, preceded it by 'James' as a presumed compliment to both my grandfathers I cannot imagine: in the days of credit cards and indiscriminate use of forenames by strangers it causes many problems.

Finally, then, Granny Barr. She again was, in the nicest and kindest possible way, the 'grande dame' of Bridge of Weir from her eyrie of Ranfurly House at the summit of the village, whence the two superb golf courses head off into the hills. She had a long widowhood, supported by Belle the cook and Waldie the chauffeur/gardener (universally known as Touchy, which he was). She lightened this existence with a succession of gentlemen 'admirers', no doubt perfectly innocent: we never met any; but she took long trips, mostly on the Union Castle Line, to South Africa and other places. She was fun: had a neat way with her walking stick (cane) and made our weekly or so visits to her in her sitting room most enjoyable. She kept her gin in the aforementioned Joseph Train cabinet with its carved griffins.

Inevitably she was patron of village activities such as the Flower Show. On one occasion the compère or whoever introducing her, in his broad Scots accent, said 'We urr maist grateful for

Mrs Barr furr opening the show…' (Dig in ribs from colleague: '*Lady* Barr!') 'Oh aye, Missis Lady Barr…'

Sadly, she, like my Granny Macouat, died while I was in New York for a couple of years, and I could not say goodbye to either of them. Not only did I love them but they loved each other: there is a wonderful colour photo of them both in their matching finery at Ranfurly setting off for my sister Fiona's wedding at Paisley Abbey in early 1967, for which I did come back, and which was before they both got ill. (Grandfather Macouat had died the year before.)

So with my parents' marriage a perhaps rather unusual bond of affection was cemented between two families which, having become pillars of the professional classes in Glasgow, definitely came from the same milieu and shared traditions and interests. (As a final example, the great Glasgow Empire Exhibition of 1938 was largely overseen by the Barr firm under the political leadership of the Bilsland/Macouat clan. Second City or not, it was a smart place in terms of 'connections', of which the older generation spoke incessantly.)

However: we now return to the main theme. Though there were, inevitably, shared interests with unequal emphasis between the two families, there was a distinct divergence when it came to holidays and travel. '*Un peu d'histoire*' again. Despite common membership of what could be called the Glasgow '*gratin*' one family – the Macouats – had been familiar with 'abroad' as a matter of course from their early days: the Barrs on the other hand were faithful and constant stay-at-homes, mainly in Scotland.

Great-Grandfather Macouat's riveting business had taken him to places like the then Fiume (now Rijeka in Croatia via Yugoslavia), then a major Adriatic shipbuilding centre, and no doubt other such places. In the early twentieth century the habit of spending much of the winter on the Côte d'Azur was established; and there are photos of him and the family at the pyramids outside Cairo. No doubt there were other

Mediterranean excursions: some old negatives seem to indicate the Amalfi coast, and there are photographs of Bruges and Zeebrugge very shortly after the 1914–18 war.

The sad thing of course is that these – before being augmented by my very young mother, born 1917 – were without their elder son John, killed in France also, on the Somme in 1916. My mother and I visited his grave, literally under the crossing of the A1 Lille-Paris and A26 Calais-Reims autoroutes near Arras. So both families were grievously depleted – like most of the country – by premature bereavement. One consolation was that his fiancée, 'Aunt Ella' who did later marry, settled in Beaconsfield and was so kind to me at Oxford, often featured on a post-war trip.

In fact both Granny and Grandfather Macouat (and his lost brother) had undergone some late-stage education on the Continent. Granny was 'finished' at Mme. Manilève's in Brussels; while the Macouat boys after Glasgow Academy went on to the Moravian School at Neuwied on the Rhine (this of course being before relations between Britain and Germany somewhat deteriorated). So there was familiarity with Europe and with the French and German languages. My grandmother was a terrific Francophile and fond of using the language – in moderation and usually in interjections ('*Tiens, chérie…!*').

So it was shortly after the war that trips to the south of France resumed, by now featuring my very young mother. They normally stayed at the Winter Palace at Cimiez above Nice, with many excursions to the Promenade des Anglais (*ou bien écossais*?). At Cimiez Grandfather used to play tennis with the King of Sweden, until one day an obsequious equerry came along and suggested that he let the King win for a change: at which point the encounters sadly ceased, this not being my grandfather's style.

Also in winter (from photographic evidence) were stays for 'winter sporting' – skating and sleigh riding – langlauf rather than downhill – usually at St Moritz. This may have been in the 1930s, judging by photos of my mother. That was also when they took up La Baule on the Atlantic coast, where they met the Langsdorff family from New York who became the greatest of friends over the years. The matriarch, 'Aunt Martha' (another 'aunt'), an inspiring figure in voluminous black after widowhood, at the same time outclassed both my grandmothers in grande-damehood but could also have held her own at the Round Table in the Algonquin (maybe she did: she lived just round the corner in Park Avenue). After the war she came over to Europe on the *Mauretania* each year to stay for a month at each of the Hassler in Rome, the Lotti in Paris and with my grandparents in the West End of Glasgow. Many of her grandchildren came to stay with us over the years.

The one family member I had yet to meet was her son-in-law Bruce Friedlich (of whom more later), who in response to a letter gave me an intern's job in his advertising agency in New York, which only ended two years later when I was nominally 'Director of Research'. During that time Martha was exceptionally kind to me, giving me tickets to the Metropolitan Opera and Carnegie Hall to which she subscribed, letting me and others spend weekends at her glorious house by a lake in Connecticut, and more.

Back to the Macouats. As mentioned they visited Belgium (several times?) not long after the war, and my mother had memories of Knokke-le-Zoute seaside and so on. But this does not mean they neglected Scotland (or indeed England, especially London and the south coast). As mentioned, Grandfather's main sporting activity was fishing, and this fitted well with Granny's attachment to Ardnamurchan. However, he also enjoyed (though not on a Barr scale) playing golf, and would often on a summer's evening take the train down to the Ayrshire coast – Troon or Barassie – for a round in the long light evenings. There were also longer stays on the east coast – North Berwick and Lossiemouth come to mind – principally for the golf.

Highland Holidays: Acharacle and Machrihanish

September was Ardnamurchan. Acharacle is just north of Salen at the beginning of the peninsula and is at the south-western end of the freshwater Loch Shiel, a long loch running up to Glenfinnan and the railway to the north-east. A mere three miles of the River Shiel debouches into the sea at Loch Moidart, by Castle Tioram. Thus there is a mix of salmon fishing (now pretty defunct) in the river and sea trout from a boat on the loch. Grandfather was, to my delight as I enjoyed rowing the boat rather than wielding a rod, much more interested in the loch fishing.

They – and later we – stayed in the Lochshiel View Hotel, a marvellously unreconstructed place owned by the Cameron family and their son-in-law Morton Smith from Oban.

(I should mention that before idiotic redesignation the River Shiel divided Argyll, where most people were called Cameron and were Protestant, from Inverness-shire where most were called Macdonald and were Catholic. These distinctions have now I believe been largely eroded, as trans-Linnhe Argyll was subsumed with Inverness-shire into 'Highland Region'.)

Granny spent happy hours with the Cameron family and the two devoted helpers, Neil (Neil Maclachlan, undoubtedly some remote clan relation) and Lachie (Lachlan Macneil, just to differentiate!). Mother remembered Neil's beautiful singing voice with Gaelic songs on picnic excursions out to Sanna Bay, at the western edge of the British mainland. I much enjoyed hanging out with them in the hayloft with rat-catcher cats, at the antiquated petrol pump (now you have to drive nearly to Fort William to replenish the fuel you have just used driving there!) and suchlike ways of passing the time. The main excitement though was running down to the pier after breakfast to see off 'the Clan': the ancient steamboat powered by paraffin engines which were often reluctant to start. The Captain 'Angus the Clan' and the mate Sam roared in on motorbikes from Kinlochmoidart and Arivegaig respectively, clad in black oilskins. In the afternoon, especially if on the loch, one would look out to spot the craft returning past Dalilea.

The 'big house' at Acharacle was Shielbridge, a rather ugly Scots baronial edifice in a superlative position: at the front looking up to the loch and Ben Resipol, while at the side lovely gardens led down to the vast salmon pool, its whirlpools fed by the surge issuing from below the old arched Shiel Bridge. Thither one sad July day in 2003, as requested, I fed my mother's ashes to the water she loved the most.

Shielbridge had been owned by the Paisley thread magnates, the Clarks, and Kenneth Clark the art historian cordially loathed the place. It and the whole of Ardnamurchan were later owned by Lord Trent, Jesse Boot of Nottingham pharmaceutical fame; he left the estate divided between his two daughters, and I remember visiting the Hon Mrs Holman, who had inherited the eastern half and Shielbridge, there. In around 1950 my grandfather was offered it to purchase; but in the difficult post-war period felt he could not possibly take it on. (The nearest big house, Dorlin on the Inverness-shire side opposite Castle Tioram, was one of many first to lose its roof and then to be demolished – only the stable block is left.) I would love to have had the Shielbridge estate in time – different times – but it would not have worked for an 'expatriate' – even a small house in Kintyre is woefully under-visited.

After this scene-setting, back to the central theme: my travels. I know far less about the travelling and vacationing habits of my father's family. Certainly Scotland and in particular golfing venues formed the larger part. Eastern and north-eastern resorts such as North Berwick, Lossiemouth and Dornoch were certainly favoured: but the palm was undoubtedly taken by Machrihanish. This village at the southern edge of Kintyre, with long beaches and machair (sea) turf, and marvellous views across to Islay and Jura (and Northern Ireland), had been made accessible with the opening of daily steamer services to the previously hard of access whisky and herring town of Campbeltown – to the extent that even day trips from Glasgow or Gourock became possible. Thus in the 1880s 'Old Tom Morris', the leading golf course designer, laid out a course of championship standard and great beauty, which inevitably attracted Glasgow businessmen and professionals for their summer retreats. A row of substantial and elegant Victorian, and later Art Deco, villas grew up facing the course and the sea and families such as ours would take them for the summer, the 'breadwinner' often returning at the weekend after a working week in the city. An imposing hotel, the Ugadale Arms, made briefer visits practicable, especially once the road transport was improved.

For the first ten years of my life, therefore, I never left Scotland. Acharacle as a constant until late teens has been covered; my first, indistinct memory is of my third birthday in 1946 when we had taken a house called Lochshiel View where I nearly suffocated in an iron bed (vivid early memories!). Also in these early years Machrihanish featured: we stayed in the Ugadale, and one visit involved my first ever flight, in a De Havilland Dragon Rapide biplane.

There was then a rather long hiatus – perhaps the one holiday at Acharacle was deemed sufficient. In the mid-1950s we bought a caravan (I was asked whether I preferred a boat or a caravan, said 'boat, of course' so the caravan was bought and we enjoyed rather free-range holidays, principally near Lochinver in Sutherland, where we parked on the machair (sea turf) by a beautiful bay of white sand. This was rather more informal than the somewhat dismal fishing hotels which were the main alternative in the Highlands.

One year, however, I suggested we return to Machrihanish for a change: did so with the caravan, but within a short time my parents had been offered a small 'fisherman's cottage' at the edge of the ocean on its own little bay by our great friend, the local laird Hector Macneal. Allegedly the price was three bottles of gin: however, the Edinburgh lawyers considered this 'most irregular' and said there must be 'a pecuniary consideration' – I have no idea how much. Anyway it was extended in two phases shortly after, and my sister and I still own it. Mother used to spend from June till October there; I try to manage two to three weeks in May and June (when the weather is often marvellous), though this has been more difficult of late.

Abroad at Last

France

So much for early days in Scotland. My first trip abroad came shortly after my tenth birthday, in August 1953: to France of course. In fact a few days were spent in London first, my earliest experience of England. By a strange coincidence we stayed at the now-rebuilt-as-flats Kensington Palace Hotel, a few hundred yards from the house I have lived in for forty years. Granny Macouat, Mother, Fiona and I boarded the *Royal Scot*; great excitement at interviewing the engine driver before leaving Glasgow Central, a distinct memory of the Euston Arch before what seemed an endless drive to Kensington. Unsurprisingly it was the sheer scale of London that most impressed me. I remember that we were in Chelsea and that our main 'sight' was the Tower, reached by what seemed an interminable Tube journey. We must have 'done' Buckingham Palace and the rest, but I have no recollection. I was amazed that the buses numbered into the hundreds: Glasgow I think could just manage nine.

Meanwhile Grandfather and Father had been bringing down the Rover 75 on which we would embark in France. Again, we others took the train – this time the *Golden Arrow* to Dover: then there was Customs, formalities, embarkation, the Channel – abroad!

We were to stay a night in Le Touquet before the drive down to Brittany, but this was the introduction to that quintessential French practice, *la grève*. A general strike for some reason kept us in Le Touquet for three days: agreeable. We peered into the quaint timbered houses from our attic window and observed the antics of some French children who Granny labelled 'chipmunks'. Fiona and I walked by ourselves along the seafront boardwalk, were photographed and handed a ticket, which terrified us – until we learnt that this was just a pro photographer's attempt at a sale.

We set off very early one morning: still dark as we drove down the straight RN 1 lined with poplar trees and containing little but horse-drawn carts. (Curiously, my first experience of Peking in 1977 – dusk rather than dawn – was immediately reminiscent; and, coming from island Japan, I felt I had regained the same great land mass that stretched to the Channel.)

We were peas in a pod: with bench seats, three males in the front and three females in the back. A jam-packed luggage rack on the roof. Yellow bulbs in the headlights. So, we proceeded in decorous fashion: croissants for breakfast in a café on the long pavé hill down into Neufchâtel, then into Normandy passing names already redolent from war books – Rouen, Falaise, Avranches – and into Brittany after Dol. (For Father, these names would have meant even more: scarcely nine years had elapsed since a very different sort of visit.)

Our destination was St Lunaire, a somewhat faded resort just west of Dinard. The imposing hotel – long since apartments, of course – commanded a wide and splendid beach; the headlands either side showed the remains of Rommel's Western Wall in various states of disrepair; at night a myriad of winking lights ahead testified to the many jagged rocks and islets awaiting the careless navigator. This was bucket and spade and in our striped Breton T-shirts we spent most time on the beach. The patisserie – another novelty – ran it close and eclairs were another discovery of note. We were introduced to very watered-down red wine, in those days thought a suitable rite of passage for sub-teen children. I imagine the food was more than passable by 1950s British standards.

Apart from the beach, there were two excursions that I particularly remember. First, up the Rance to Dinan, whose half-timbered charm and dramatic river gorge enthralled me. Then St Malo; I had hurt my foot stupidly jumping off a rock and my mother nobly carried me round the ramparts. There was also a picnic on the sand by the causeway at Mont St Michel; I could not believe how hot it was in comparison with, say, Argyll, with the butter melting in short order. I think the Mont may have been quite impressive too.

We did later spend a night at la mère Poulard's establishment there, but that was on returning to Cherbourg on the next Breton holiday in 1958. Of course the highlight was the ceremony of the 'renowned' omelette beaten out in a vast copper bowl: I am not sure if the result justified the expectation.

That first time we stopped for the night at the Chaîne d'Or at Les Andelys: happily revisited twice in recent years, when of course it is much modernised but retains its great riverside charm. In 1953 the furnishings were plain. I presume we returned via Boulogne and Dover: the final leg, excitingly, for the non-drivers was a flight from Northolt to Renfrew on a BEA Vickers Viking. When the Captain walked down the aisle this obsequious if observant boy said 'I see you have both a DSO and a DFC', and was promptly invited into the cockpit to pretend to fly the plane.

Easter holidays 1956 saw France again: the first visit to Paris (and Versailles), Mother taking Fiona and myself. We stayed in a large hotel on the Boulevard Haussmann and 'did the sights' – most involving climbing things: the Eiffel Tower which we walked down after lunch 'up top', and Notre Dame where it was exciting to clamber right up the tower pyramid (perfectly safe!). We went to the Opéra to see Prokofiev's *Romeo & Juliet*: amazingly, I found looking at the programme after all these years that the Ballets Russes lived on, as the Friar had been Serge Lifar. Afterwards we had *baguettes au jambon* at the Café de la Paix: I found it too garlicky. Our one splash-out dinner was at Prunier in the rue Duphot: a revelation.

The subsequent Breton holiday was in 1958. This time it was a two-centre affair. As usual, without Papa we motored down with a stop at Oxford and another where we met up in Salisbury (the latter especially enchanting to one as yet unfamiliar with England), and had the open Ford Zephyr put into the belly of the Silver City air freighter at Southampton bound for Cherbourg. Taking off from a (then) grass runway in a downpour was interesting.

It must have been that night we stayed at the Lion d'Or at Bayeux (again, revisited quite recently: many photographs and memorabilia of Churchill, Ike, Montgomery *et al*). Caen was still essentially a pile of rubble and of course the whole journey was for Father a reminder of very recent events, with his commentary on the landscape (bocage) features and more than a few war wrecks still to see. (His MC citation especially mentioned the Battle of the River Odon but, though it lies between Bayeux and Caen, I don't think we stopped for a look. When I did quite recently, I found it a most insignificant stream.)

The first week we spent at the resort of Perros-Guirec, further west on the Breton peninsula than we had been the previous time (when Cap Fréhel had been the limit) beyond St Brieuc. Driving was enjoyable in the open convertible we then had. The Hotel Printania was perched high up above the bay, with a fine view of the broad and wide crescent of the Plage de Trestraou where we enjoyed the usual beach activities. The 'mini-golf' caused much merriment, especially from my father. After the week there was a cross-country drive down through places like Morlaix – I remember the great viaduct – and near Brest to Quimper and our next week, at another hotel, this time shoreside, in Bénodet at the mouth of the Odet. While the south-facing aspect there was open, the nucleus of the village was round the corner in the estuary proper: we went round there quite a lot and Father enjoyed a *fine* or two – my first hearing of this term for a brandy. There was a certain amount of fishing activity and the bit by the jetty and little ferry was picturesque: I did an early and rather primitive oil of the scene, at Newark to this day.

We went up to the fine old city of Quimper once or twice, and I recall a longer drive for a picnic on the very long beach south of Audierne and Douarnenez, where we were plagued by wasps. Memory fails me as to the exact route back to Cherbourg: there was a night in Dinard and then the names of Pontorson, inevitably Domfront with William the Conqueror's vast castle, Mortain, Avranches come to mind. Not just Norman keeps but the detritus of a later Normandy campaign was still ubiquitous and pointed out by Father the 'veteran'. It may even be that the Bayeux night was on that return rather than the outward leg.

Skiing in Norway

So far, 'abroad' had meant France; and of course I had hardly touched on England. Diversification came in the next spring with a skiing group to Norway featuring the flower of Renfrewshire youth and led/chaperoned by my uncle David Buchanan (expert skier and mountaineer) and Aunt Pauline, with Mother coming along. Train to Newcastle, then along the Tyne to the docks where despite familiarity with post-war Glasgow I had never seen such desperate slums. The *Leda* took us across to Bergen with the first stop at Stavanger. Bergen for a night was pretty in the evening sun and the funicular provided an impressive view. Next morning, we took the train on the Bergen-Oslo line up to its highest point, the diminutive ski resort of Finse (essentially just one hotel, half-buried in snow).

The hotel, rust-red, was set back just behind the railway platform: a few yards uphill was the single T-bar taking one up the hill (not very far). This provided good nursery slopes for the tyros learning Christianias and other near-obsolete techniques from the virile ski instructor Cort ('Bend ze knees!'). For the more confident it was more a matter of a schuss straight downhill, culminating in a jump right over the railway line: the fact that there was but one train in each direction each day made this a pretty risk-free pastime.

Finse was where the film *Scott of the Antarctic* had been made, and we arranged to be towed up the Hardanger glacier in echelon behind a tracked contraption, then skied down. I suddenly got a kind of snow-blindness (everything went red), then langlaufing across the lake at the end it cleared, to a vision of my elders imbibing happily on the hotel terrace.

A feature of the warm, dark, womb-like interior was old Arthur Waley, the great Chinese and Japanese scholar, who was in solitary residence there for long periods: alas, I knew little about him or his studies aged fifteen.

The next milestone was formed by my return the following year, accompanied this time only by another Bridge of Weir boy (at school with me but younger and not of my cohort). So this was the first time I had effectively been abroad on my own. I can recall very little of this trip – same route, same destination – I presume all went off well. I was just sixteen and having done 'A' levels the previous summer was buckling down to Oxford scholarship exams beginning in the winter.

First Proper Tour: Florence and Back

A much more ambitious expedition, my first real European road trip, however, took place the following year, in my last summer holiday from school. Three slightly older boys had left or were leaving at the end of term, and much planning had gone on. The father of one, Niall Maclean, was (amazingly) willing to lend us his large Austin Cambridge saloon. Niall was in fact now at Grenoble University so Johnny Watson from Edinburgh and I took it down the A1, picked up Ian Macleod in Bromley, then spent an hour or two visiting Canterbury before it was time to get the ferry (specific time booked in those days).

In Paris we had had hopes of camping in the Bois de Boulogne but this was not possible: so carried on down the famous N7 into Burgundy. It poured. Eventually and excitingly we got to Grenoble and picked up Niall; then I remember a wonderful al fresco evening high up on the precipitous col above the Isère as we headed into the Vercors.

After the verdant Vercors (sorry) with its *colonies d'enfants* scattered in the valleys, one goes through a short tunnel and emerges onto a 'balcon' overlooking the Drôme and the hills of Provence, ranged in ever paler blue into the southern distance. This, my first sight of the Midi, was a revelation I have never forgotten: the contrast so extreme, the promise so great.

Despite a green Michelin and a classical education I had not perhaps realised quite how many Roman edifices remain in Provence. We spent several days – and a dramatic night in the car in the *garrigue* between Nîmes and Avignon in an ultra-dramatic thunderstorm; then I was anxious to get down to the coast and see the fabled Côte d'Azur, playground of (among others) my forebears in the past. Also to see and immerse myself in the Mediterranean at last. The N7 took us – inland – to the coast at La Napoule where this ambition was realised.

The ambition had in fact been to reach Rome and then turn around for the return. However – having passed along the French and Italian rivieras – camped on a hillside above the Arno between Pisa and Florence a council was held at which a three-to-one majority decided to turn back after Florence (I need hardly say who was the dissenter!).

Florence of course was hardly a disappointment. My initial memory is of my first experience of a 'squat toilet' in the Piazza di Santa Maria Novella (the only church I have ever been thrown out of – 'Fuori de la chiesa' – for, inevitably, the mortal sin of taking a photo. We certainly went to the Uffizi but of course could only scratch the surface of Florence in a limited time. I did buy some nice small leather things with fleurs-de-lys.

Then it was over to Ravenna on the Adriatic. Easier to view in a hurry: so there was time after seeing the sights for a long bathing session at the beach. Being guileless about the sun's power I managed to get extremely sunburnt and this began to hurt like hell on the drive up to Venice. We pulled in at a campsite (again) near Chioggia and took the passenger ferry (celebration of Visconti's *Death in Venice*) over to the city. Thus my first Venetian experience was being sick into the canal beside the Piazzale Roma car park.

After an evening and a day 'doing' Venice we had an al fresco 'wild camp' between Venice and Trieste, where, I recall, star-gazing after supper we espied the very first *Sputnik*. The next day marked the true turn northwards, up over the Brenner Pass and the Sud-Tirol to Salzburg. This appealed to me greatly, as a Mozartian in particular. Going in and out of Germany (for the first time) we tried to find Hitlerian remnants in and around Berchtesgaden but with no success: there was just an undistinguished resort town.

I don't recall much of the rest of the return journey: Heidelberg was the high spot between autobahns (and very impressive), and I remember the Atomium from the recent World's Fair on the outskirts of Brussels. Then, with much too early an arrival for the ferry at Boulogne, whiling away the time on the Cap Gris-Nez cliffs and inspecting the massive detritus of Rommel's Western Wall. And so back to Dover.

I left my companions in Edinburgh after another A1 stretch and took the trains to Glasgow and then down to Bridge of Weir and trudged up the hill home. Apart from some sort of luggage and a suntan, I had some money left from the £30 cash I had taken with me for three weeks! And many happy and useful memories.

Classical Initiation: Turkey, Greece and Rome

Having got my Oxford award but being required to stay on for the Easter term at school, a welcome and compensating surprise was that my grandparents were taking us – Mother, sister Fiona who irritatingly left school at the same time as me though eighteen months younger! – but as usual not poor Papa – to Greece and then Rome.

We flew to Athens in a DH Comet – the first jet I had encountered. No assigned seating so I rushed to the plane to get some seats, bagging the window. Looking out of aeroplane windows has been an enduring delight and I followed the route avidly (even the Tyrrhenian Sea, scene of recent Comet disasters, from a Comet window didn't faze me!). At Fiumicino I was amused to see the phalanx of young priests on the viewing platforms, with the wide-brimmed black hats they wore in those days. Then it was on to Athens. Lord Poole had most kindly lent us a large American car and genial chauffeur George for our stay. George duly drove us to the Grande Bretagne in Syntagma Square: very distinguished. However, on entering their room my grandparents found a party of Athenian gentry on its balcony, waiting for the procession to come down from Lycabettus hill – it was Orthodox Good Friday. An initial humph from my grandfather was followed by the most cordial relations and invitations to stay, and we benefited from explanations of the ceremonies and participants.

On Easter Day George drove us to Delphi. On the way lambs were being roasted with the most delicious aroma; and all the boiled eggs were dyed scarlet. Earlier we had stopped to view the beautiful little Byzantine church at Daphne; and had of course been thrilled by a near-deserted Delphi and the vast bulk of Parnassus behind and above ('Gradus ad Parnassum').

Then to Piraeus to board the Typaldos Lines *Kriti* for an Aegean cruise. The *Kriti* had been a Hull–Rotterdam ferry and had a distinct list to port. Luckily it was the first cruise of the season and the passengers were few: an elderly couple from Ayrshire, and a pair of American college students were those I remember. The latter, affable and handsome young men, paid great attention to Fiona.

Heading for Istanbul we stopped first at Çanakkale for Troy – then much less 'opened' and explored than now. Then through the night and the Sea of Marmara to Istanbul. There my first surprise was to discover, on a tour, how much of the ancient city wall remained: I had not been exposed to Talbot Rice activities at that stage. Of the great mosques I remember the Blue Mosque the best, though on subsequent visits I would undoubtedly award the prize to Sinan's Suleyman (Hagia Sophia is perhaps *hors concours*: and despite its undoubted architectural brilliance I find its Islamic despoliation pathetic and weep for the lost mosaics: while the exterior has always seemed to be lumpy, brutalist and confused).

In 1961, despite some tensions, it was easy to pass between Greece and Turkey. The *Kriti*'s itinerary took us to Ayvalik for Pergamum (where listening in on an Italian group I found I could understand the woman tour guide very well), then past Samos to Kuşadasi: this time a choice between Ephesus and Priene. My earnest new classicist friends from Yale recommended Priene, perhaps the best example of a Hellenistic planned town, against the more obvious Ephesus. In no way do I regret Priene, which was most interesting – especially the view of the meandering Meander from a terraced site – but I am sad I have never yet been to Ephesus.

Then it was Rome: the Flora at the top of the via Veneto.

Again, many surprises which showed how unprepared I had been among textbooks for the reality. As in Istanbul, again, the massive Roman city walls: the Flora lay right beside the long stretch separating the old city from the Pincio gardens. Also, that the city stones were orange, red, yellow and ochre (where Florence had been green and grey).

The monuments of course were stunning – the sheer number of pure Roman remains if nothing else, but also of course the proliferation of churches, from the early ones to the Baroque of the Jesuits. We had been entrusted to the care of the lovely Father (later Monsignor) McEwan, late of Cardross, who acted as cicerone – a most erudite one. We went down into the recently explored and partly opened depths below St Peter's to view the reputed site of his burial. I visited the Scots College, of which he was (I think) Deputy Rector and was charmed to hear that it was compulsory for the ordinands to have a glass of wine with every meal. Alone, and following some correspondence before the trip, I went to the English College to pay a call on Cardinal Heard, not only an old Fettesian but a former Oxford rowing blue (Balliol). He was an ascetic, polite, distant figure: Dean of the Holy Roman Rota, the ecclesiastical court. I forgot to kiss his ring.

All this Catholicism – I was rather intrigued by it already through reading at school – was inevitably put in its place by my grandmother who naturally had an introduction to the minister of the Scots Kirk on the via XX Settembre. This of course led to tea there with him and his wife, pretty well indistinguishable from Kelvinside despite the exotic setting of Baroque churches and the Quattro Fontane. They were most hospitable and kindly.

We passed that way also to visit Tivoli, where I remember we perhaps spent more time down at Hadrian's Villa than up in the town and at the Villa d'Este. Another excursion from the city was to the ancient, now landlocked, port of Ostia just by Fiumicino airport. Excavations there were at an early stage and vastly more has been uncovered and learnt since then.

Summer Interlude

That had been a marvellous introduction to the classical (and mediaeval, Islamic and Renaissance) world, and opened my eyes to experiences unimagined in book learning. It was some time, however, before I was to set forth abroad again. I had hoped – and had done much research – to spend some time before Oxford in the autumn on a course at a French or Italian university – the Sorbonne, Grenoble or Florence the front-runners – to learn the language properly, and if I am honest perhaps to meet some girls and 'grow up'. However, this was vetoed by my parents and I reverted to the Barr tradition of what would now, regrettably, perhaps be called 'staycation' in Scotland till Oxford in October. In the event this was quite agreeable and even, arguably, useful. I spent most of it sailing – driving over to the Royal Northern YC at Rhu for the evening races of the Gareloch class on the Gareloch every Tuesday and Thursday, followed by late supper at the club and home after midnight (long light evenings); and on Saturdays a further day out on the Firth. (The Garelochs, lovely 24-foot racing keelboats designed by McGruer and dating from 1924, were carefully regathered after disposal and are going strong still.) We went to Rothesay on Bute for the Clyde Fortnight (as it was in more spacious days) and won our class the following year. The experience marked a step up from my teenage dinghy sailing towards even larger craft as I aged and gave me valuable experience for a lifelong pursuit (more, indeed, anon).

Beyond that I was able to spend long periods down at Machrihanish (the dinghy still featured, moored beside the pier in Campbeltown). My father the surveyor was expanding the house and it was good to get to know the place and the people properly.

Easter 1962: Switzerland and Paris

At the end of Hilary term 1962 – the only term when I did not have a car at Oxford – I met my mother and the Mini-Traveller which I had brought with all my stuff for Oxford for my first term, off the train from Scotland at (curiously) Paddington, *en route* for France and Switzerland to collect Fiona who had been definitively 'finished' at Vevey and do a bit of skiing. On the way to the Channel the car packed up, with a defective oil pump: amazingly, it was soon mended with some roadside assistance, and we were on our way: now to be loaded into the hold of a Silver City Bristol aircraft at Lydd, for Le Touquet (those were the days).

Emerging, a metaphorical milestone was reached as this was the first time I had myself driven abroad. It did not seem a problem. We reached Reims and found an agreeable hotel: then on through eastern France. This also was not without its automotive hiccups as on a particularly dreary stretch near Langres or Gray we suffered a puncture: wheel changing easy in those days on a small car, but a few miles further on – we had another one. Somehow, we were rescued with some repair made, and carried on. I recall the extreme contrast between the endless dark woods of the Jura and emerging over the pass to look down on the brilliant, twinkling lights of the shores of Lake Geneva – almost a wartime feeling. We sank with pleasure into the Trois Couronnes in Vevey and opening the curtains in the morning I was thrilled to see the mass of the Alpine mountains across the lake. (It was not of course the first time, and especially in the 1990s I was to become extremely familiar with that area: but this was a special moment.)

We had a good few days in Villars and Zermatt – blizzards and slush driving up the Rhône valley – then back through France for another short Paris visit, stopping first at the Chapeau Rouge in Avallon and experiencing proper *premier cru* burgundy in a proper 'balloon' glass. My then girlfriend Sarah was being introduced to civilisation at the Sorbonne, so we made the most of the brief time: a trip out to Rambouillet, Versailles, museums and quite a lot of bohemian hanging-out in the Quartier Latin with the friends she had made. I suppose we then drove home to Scotland. A good introduction, anyway, to 'driving on the right'.

Hilary Break 1963: Italy and Sicily

Twelve months later a foreign travel-free year had taken me as far as Classical Mods, the exam bringing the first part of my Oxford years to a close. Rather to my surprise, despite an undistinguished Second, Christ Church gave me the then quite substantial sum of £20 as a travel bursary. A mainly Italian trip with parents and grandparents was already planned and after days in Lugano, Milan and Rome I headed for new horizons, i.e. Naples and the south. Having 'done' Thucydides on the Athenian expedition to Sicily as my special subject, Sicily was a natural lure. In fact, however, an even greater one was Lampedusa's *The Leopard*, not long published. I had revelled in it and looked forward at least as much to discovering that world as to inspecting the ruins of classical antiquity.

The overnight ferry to Palermo led me to the Quattro Canti where a pleasant hotel was found. An even more pleasant surprise was that the Visconti film of *The Leopard* was to have its premiere simultaneously in Palermo and Rome – that very night. I got, I was told, the very last ticket. The Principessa attended. It was interminable, magical, and I even understood some of it. (Later cinema showings were something of a travesty; dubbed into atrocious American, abbreviated, sequences changed. Fortunately, the original version has been resuscitated and is now available as a DVD.)

In Palermo I sought out the Lampedusa Palazzo and the crumbling Baroque locations of the story. I hired an Alfa Romeo Giulietta sports car – not something I imagine an 18-year-old could do today – and blasted it around the old Targa Florio course in the hills. Mondello and of course Monreale with the marvellous mosaics were also visited (not I think by Alfa), and the palace and duomo 'downtown' revealed the wonderful Norman legacy of which I'd been scarcely aware.

I left Palermo to begin my 'Giro di Sicilia' first by train to Agrigento. Here there is the contrast between a dark mediaeval hill town with distinct mafiosi vibes (perhaps unfair), and the set of classical Doric temples in the valley below. The *passeggiata* in the evening showed the strictest segregation of sexes. Next morning, I rode the bus down to the temples and for the second time (the first time having been in Rome) saw an intrepid Christ Church contemporary, John Lake, plodding down the hill. (These chance encounters were to become surprisingly frequent.)

From Agrigento it was bus all the way; via Piazza Armerina with the amazing Roman mosaics an earlier (and pagan) contrast to those of Monreale and Palermo, and eventually to Syracuse, epicentre of the ill-fated expedition. One surprise in central Sicily was the number of people with red hair: the Norman genes clearly still hang on.

Syracuse was delightful: the rather faded Grand Hotel on the Ortygia waterfront an ideal location to imagine Nicias and his fleet battling it out in the bay. (Sadly, like the Palermo opera house it was closed for another thirty years or so, and when I revisited Syracuse in 1992 it had to be the rather banal Jolly Hotel up the hill.) The Latomie caves where the Athenians were incarcerated were appropriately spooky.

What I had not seen in that first visit to that island of so many civilisations was the great Baroque zone of Noto, Ragusa and Modica. But that was to come in future years – as also vicariously experienced through 'Inspector Montalbano'. Nor Taormina and its spectacularly sited theatre overlooked by Mount Etna, though that too became familiar some decades further on. The Syracuse train passed close along that coast – at times almost in the sea – heading for Messina, loading onto the ferry and then across – Scylla and Charybdis – to the Calabrian mainland.

That far I had shared the compartment with some genial Italian squaddies. On the boat they were exchanged for a caricature (but equally genial) German scoutmaster type who, after offering me condensed milk from a tube hanging from his rucksack (declined with thanks), turned to the wall commanding 'I go for Paestum: you vill vake me for Paestum!' The train rumbled through the night. The German awoke from his stertorous sleep, rushed for the exit, exclaimed 'I go for Paestum' and disappeared onto a pitch-dark railway track. Some hours later we passed Paestum…

Rome was by now seeming very familiar, almost mundane. I have been there countless times since and find it (together perhaps with Kyoto – a very different experience) the most inexhaustible of cities. I was to get to know it much better the following summer, of which more shortly.

Riviera Deckhand

In that summer of 1963, it was the French and Italian rivieras that were to occupy much of the summer, again laying the foundation for a lifelong acquaintance. My uncle David had suggested to a friend who owned a pre-war twin-diesel motor yacht, the *Thelma VI*, based at Antibes, that I might join them as a deckhand. It sounded ideal, combining nautical activity with Mediterranean glamour. So, on a filthy wet early June day I sold my old MG TC for a paltry sum (£35, as against the £25,000 it could now be worth!), to raise funds for the train to the south. A night spent in the corridor by the door broke to the colour and sunshine of Provence after Marseille. I found the way to my new ship, met my new fellow crew members, Stevie or Stelios the Greek cook and Willie, older, from Aberdeen, deckhand, with whom I would occupy the forepeak.

The skipper, known only as 'the Skipper', was a dour and humourless little man from Dunoon; his wife, who looked after the guests, was a kind dear woman. The boat had been chartered by Dundonian friends of the owner, inevitably from the jute business: with another Dundee couple they were a quartet, and though I kept to my place there was the occasional gin on the 'quarter deck' and even a 50-franc tip for my twentieth birthday – kind thought.

We moved up and down the coast between La Seyne west of Marseille and Alassio in Italy: I became very familiar with the early-morning markets of all these places, going with Stevie to select the most delicious ingredients every day, and most days trundling back huge blocks of ice (no refrigerator on board). We ate well. Willie smoked incessantly and did the *Telegraph* crossword every day. Long siestas at anchor after lunch: the Lérins off Cannes and Port-Cros and Porquerolles islands further west were especially magical. In the evening after mooring in the ports of Cannes or Nice, Stevie and I often went ashore rounding off our early-morning swims with a promenade and a beer and totally unsuccessful pursuit of girls.

When this idyll ended – Mother kindly came down to meet me at Oxford, to collect my belongings from my Christ Church rooms as well as myself – I was a deep brown, after several ill-advised peelings (melanoma in later life). For weeks I had worn little more than the tiniest 'budgie-smuggler' bathing briefs, even – inconceivable now – in places like the rue d'Antibes in central Cannes. This tan was much admired back home.

Coming at the end of my second year at Oxford, that 1963 long vacation was an episode of simple immersion (literally, in the delectable Med) in another culture and milieu which has featured so much in my life – in villas, staying with friends, in the poshest of hotels as well as in simple places in the hinterland. But the next visit, the following summer, was just a brief passage early in a much more ambitious expedition.

The Next Grand Tour

The final summer vacation is always the last respite and the last chance for a seriously long period away – holiday or employment – before the final year and the imminence of Finals followed by a lifetime of travail. It was no different for me in 1964.

I had just turned twenty-one and with some proceeds bought

an Austin Mini-Cooper. Phase 1 was to drive with my girlfriend Sarah Drew from Scotland to Rome – thus completing the unfulfilled aim of the 1960 trip: then when she had to return, meet up with Hamish Aird my fellow-classicist and wander down to Greece, a much more ambitious plan than 1960's (but with much more time to accomplish it). All came to pass.

Once again, the car was driven into the maw of the Silver City Bristol Freighter: from Le Touquet we drove down to the Loire, for my first (comprehensive) tour of the châteaux; then by Bourges through the most *profonde* France to Le Puy, then the Rhône and Provence. I vividly remember being stopped by the gendarmerie near the bottom of the long and winding descent through the Ardèche, on a boiling hot July day, to await the Tour de France which still had this blistering ascent before them.

Avignon, Antibes and the Côte d'Azur were by now familiar: into Italy we tarried less, eager to get to Rome. Suddenly we were driving past the Bernini colonnade of St Peter's: we had been recommended a small, basic but perfectly adequate *pensione* nearby. After a few days Sarah had to return to work in London and I was left to explore alone, awaiting the arrival of my friend Hamish.

The Mini-Cooper had to be started each morning by giving it a shove down the steep, narrow cobbled street, then jumping in; after which most mornings I drove to the Borghese gardens for an al fresco breakfast of orange juice, coffee and croissants before setting off on whatever I'd planned for the day. One expedition was to Tivoli, another further up into the Apennines to Sulmona and Ovid territory. In the evenings I often drove up to the via Sardegna, off the via Veneto, where Giovanni's trattoria was: unassuming and entirely family-staffed in those days. It moved several times (the family generations evolving too) before its current more sophisticated incarnation in via Marche. Great interest in the Mini-Cooper parked at the kerbside beside me and its, to them, amazing performance: '*Cento sessanta all' ora*!'

I had arranged with Hamish that from a certain date I would be sitting in Doney's café on the via Veneto from around 6 every day. Several days passed, with epic consumption of Negronis, before, lo, one day there Hamish was. So, after dinner it was back to the *pensione*.

Despite his classical education Hamish had never been to Rome; so, the natural first stop was the nearby St Peter's. We took the lift up to the roof and to the internal gallery of the dome; from which we were treated to the sight from directly above of a cardinal processing, garbed in the *cappa magna*, the long scarlet train held up by numerous boy minions. This I thought a suitable introduction to the splendours of Rome. (Sadly, the *cappa magna* was abolished fairly soon by some depressingly egalitarian Pope.)

We spent the next few days 'doing' the compulsory sights; I remember a delightful outing to the lakes and Castel Gandolfo south of Rome. Eventually it was time to move on in the general direction of our ultimate objective, Greece. We lunched in Perugia, and I believe stopped in Padua before reaching Venice: I cannot remember where we stayed there – was it in Mestre on the mainland?

After Venice and a brief stop in Trieste, we started on the long drive through Yugoslavia. For the first fifty miles or so, on a good, well-surfaced road, there were perhaps nine German-registered cars for every one British, French or indeed Yugoslav. After the road abruptly changed to rough and unsurfaced, the Germans gave up. Over the next few days, we were to have a duel with one Citroen 2 CV; every time there was a tolerable surface we shot ahead, overtaking it; then when an appalling surface reduced us again to 5 mph, I would see it bouncing along behind, gradually nearing then overtaking again in turn… But I am getting ahead of myself.

Our first night in Yugoslavia was spent encamped on a barren bit of land on the Zadar peninsula. Around 5 a.m. I peered out of my tiny tent to find a soldier with a red star on his forage cap aiming a rifle at my head. However, the situation was soon defused with a conversation in sort-of Italian with the elderly peasant accompanying him. The soldier left and the friendly peasant revealed that he had a brother who was a waiter at the Savoy!

Until the pretty coastal town of Makarska the road was generally good. After, I saw a small wooden sign for 'Dubrovnik' pointing left to a very minor road ascending a steep and unpromising mountainside. As that could not possibly be the main coast road to Dubrovnik I carried on, on the good road, which, however, shortly ceased abruptly, just before a cliff above the Adriatic. So, it had been the main road after all.

Two or three days were spent as described above sparring with the Frenchmen in the 2 CV. Honour was restored when in the far distance ahead I saw what I immediately knew was an AC sports car belonging to an American from Oxford (I forget his name). As he was slower even than us, I eventually caught up ('a stern chase is a long chase').

Dubrovnik, eventually reached (though two punctures just before it called for a lengthy process of 'vulcanisation') was delightfully empty and unspoiled: nowadays I gather so swamped with tourists that access is rationed. From there we drove down to the breathtaking Gulf of Kotor and thence up the dizzying mountain road into inland Montenegro. From a viewpoint we gazed onto the lake in Albania, of course totally mysterious, sinister and inaccessible in those days. Montenegro gave way to Kosovo where we orated from the pulpit of the diminutive Patriarchate in Peç, then down into Macedonia. The terrible earthquake at Skopje had occurred the previous summer, but much clearing up had been done. The road was unspeakable and mud-blocked. Thence the final leg down to Greece.

Not for the first time, the car broke down near Lamia and for the first time ever I hitched a ride pillion on a motorcycle into the town, whence I emerged with mechanic and (I think) new fuel pump to get us on our way again. Cars were simpler to repair in those days! A simple *pensione* was found near Omonia just off the main drag, which suited us well for the next few days.

A rendezvous had been arranged long since with a quartet from West Downs preparatory school at Winchester: Tristram Jenkins, reading Greats also at Oxford, two 'matrons' (names forgotten) and Gerald Potts or 'Potto', last encountered as a new master at Craigflower in my last term almost ten years earlier. This was to take place in Marathon – none other. 'The mountains look on Marathon'. Marathon no longer looked on the sea, but there they were in a roadside café: happy reunion. It was planned that we would tour the Peloponnese more or less in convoy: they recommended a place called Tolon near Nauplia/Nafplion, suitably furnished with Mycenean antiquities and, more importantly, beach.

A few days later we did indeed arrive there. We found an agreeable place to camp on an eminence above the bay and settled in. Promptly a policeman showed up and suggested we move as this was the site of a Mycenaean acropolis. It did not look like it to our practised classical-scholar eyes (who had never heard of Asine anyway) and we demurred. Only when he changed his line and spoke of the many snakes infesting the site did we pack up rapidly and move down to the Hotel Solon, solitary on the shore below; where we found the others.

The Hotel Solon was to be a frequent étape over the coming years and decades: in 1964 it was alone on the beach, behind it the road and just olive groves, with the small village and its fishing boats about half a mile in. Back home I suggested an investment in some land to my parents; no takers, but very few years later new hotels had sprung up all around and Tolon had the making of a mini-Benidorm. Parents should listen occasionally.

The Peloponnesian tour continued by endless twisting roads through the centre (Andritsaina; Bassae) and down to Pylos and the Ionian. Homeric thoughts of Nestor, Menelaus and

Helen. Olympia of course and a camp by the long sandy beach fronting the Ionian. The next day we parted, and Hamish and I took the ferry across the Gulf of Corinth and the switchback road up to Delphi.

A few days later we were breakfasting in a café reading newspaper headlines saying 'Ο Πολεμος εν Όψει' – 'War in Sight' (against the Turks of course). September was moving on and we thought it politic to move for home. There is a photograph of me the next morning at 6 a.m. asleep in a sleeping bag with Mount Olympus in the background: 24 hours later I was again asleep, this time under the Grossglockner in Austria having driven straight through Yugoslavia, 1,100 miles in 22 hours (including lunch).

Said lunch was in Belgrade, *djuveç* (stew) and disgusting. Asked the way out of town to the *autoput* (motorway), an obliging chap jumped into the nearest car and led me through a maze of mediaeval streets to said motorway. We drove on and on through the night; wasted another hour in Slavonski Brod trying to find a bed for the night, with no success; so, on past Zagreb and eventually into Austria. To my surprise the quite acceptable Yugoslav road was succeeded by a very poor one on the Austrian side. I turned into a clearing in a forest, parked and we slept – briefly. It was raining.

The brakes failed on the long descent of the Grossglockner pass but double-declutching into first saw us safely to the bottom and eventually to Salzburg. A really comfortable *gasthaus* by the river, large beds, duvets, delicious coffee and *küche* – it was a quite different world from the Balkans and the Aegean. Mitteleuropa can seem comfortable. I had of course been in Salzburg four years earlier, but I think it was new to Hamish.

We didn't, I think, stop in Munich or Bavaria but headed for home on the last lap: another rainy early night in Alsace, then the Channel. Hamish's diary if ever released to the public may provide greater detail: did we stop in Nancy? (I have old maps somewhere.)

Moving On: Ronda and Morocco

After that traditional 'last long vacation' of almost two months in Europe, it was down to the slog of the final year at Oxford. In truth the imminence of Finals didn't really dawn on me until the spring, when after a rather brisk excursion to Deeside with parents I devoted myself to relentless and rather apprehensive cramming. Finals safely over, however, I had that car accident, which kept me immobile for several months with a smashed-up ankle. This didn't prevent me from some domestic travel – notably Dorset with dinghy sailing which had a curious melting effect on my whole-leg plaster. But most of the later summer months were spent at Machrihanish or in Northumberland.

I was becoming conscious that it was by now time to fix on some occupation for life. Earlier in the year I had encountered a recruiter for the Foreign Office and thought this would do well enough (the fixation with travel again!). Too late to have sat the exams during my final university year, I decided to do so when the process restarted in the coming January. This left some months still which could usefully be employed in combining some relevant preparation with agreeable recreation and travel. I determined to learn another language – Spanish.

The means of doing so was to spend a couple of months in Andalucia, at the Casa de Mondragón in Ronda. This was another Hamish introduction as he had spent some time there in previous vacations with Alastair and Di Boyd, who ran a rather debby summer language school there: in the winter they were glad to have the occasional PG and lay on the services of a tutor – the wonderfully phonetic alphabet-named Andrès Sierra Bravo.

The journey in the Mini-Cooper down to the south of Spain was not without incident. It being the first time I had been abroad in more than a year I was singing to myself on the N1 down to Paris. Next day I was off early for the long drive through the Massif Central – to become so familiar a touring territory in more recent years – and to Rodez for the night. Then the

Languedoc and to the border for my first experience of Spain. It was to be somewhat different from that expected.

Arriving late – but not perhaps by *hora español* – in Barcelona I parked directly outside the main police station in the Ramblas, and – famished and weary – sought some comfort food and a simple place to rest for the night. Both accomplished, I returned to the car and found the windows smashed and all the clothes and everything in the interior gone. (Ironically, being dubious of the lock on the boot I had put the less valuable things like underwear there, but suits etc. in the interior – presciently as I thought – as I had fitted Yale double locks to the doors. I had not reckoned with urchins skinny enough to be able to crawl through a Mini's sliding windows.)

Next morning, therefore, my introduction to Spain consisted of a visit to the Palacio de Justicia to make endless reports in the Spanish I had not yet learnt to sundry bored and unshaven *funcionarios*. The atmosphere was greatly enhanced by the sight and sound of chain gangs of convicts clanking along the stone-flagged floors. Probably on their way to be garrotted.

Spirits improved as I left Barcelona and headed south along the Mediterranean coast. Only as far as Tarragona (of which I remember little) that day; but had a wonderful full day along the El Cid coast, passing through a sleepy fishing village with a few houses whose name I surprisingly remember: Benidorm. Many other places I wish I had had time to see: Cartagena, Murcia. I can't remember where I spent the night but was in Ronda in reasonable time the next day.

Having located the Casa de Mondragón, I found no one was expecting me despite letters. However, I received the warmest of welcomes, and soon settled into the routine, which was roughly along these lines (*hora español*, again).

Not early: rise, breakfast in room – hot chocolate or coffee, 'churros' pastries. Then an hour or two with Andrès or 'revising' on my own. Towards, perhaps, one o'clock Alastair and I would perambulate into the town, destination El Clube, an establishment as resolutely all-male as anything in St James's. There we would down numerous glasses of fino sherry at a minuscule price, before wending our way back to the house for lunch at about three. Being winter, siesta not indicated, and I often took a drive into the surrounding countryside, full of Roman aqueducts and suchlike. Then an evening 'work session': by then it would be seriously cold, and we would sit at a low table with its cloth reaching down to our laps, our feet round the brazier underneath; very cosy. (Even cosier when the pretty young assistant – daughter? – stood in for Andrès.)

After the evening's 'work' Alastair and I would sit by the roaring fire upstairs and play liar's dice for two, or occasionally backgammon, to the accompaniment of numerous Ronda martinis (gin obtained from Gibraltar at eight shillings (40p) a bottle, well worth it taking the minimal petrol cost into account, and a dash of aforementioned fino, whose cost would have been infinitesimal). Then supper and bed – no nightlife!

The Casa de Mondragón, commonly called the Casa di Piedra as it was one of the two mansions in the town faced in golden stone, and more pretentiously now that it has reverted to the Spanish state known as the Palacio de Mondragón, stands in a stunning position on the edge of the high cliff on which the old town is built. Besides a minute garden, complete with minuscule swimming pool (care needed to dive in the right direction), the house has several courtyards, the Patio Romano and the Patio Arabe the most notable. From the main rooms on the first floor, one looks straight across to the Sierra de Grazalema, whose jagged silhouette was especially marked at sundown.

There were two mini-expeditions during my stay. Johnny Watson, a great hunting man and friend of Alastair's, had come out for a few days and the two of them set out on horseback to Jerez (a tale which is told in a *Country Life* of April 1966 with accompanying photo of the two of them on the Mondragón balcony, taken by myself). Johnny was the horsey correspondence of *Country Life*. Giving them a good start, Di and myself and another chap called Charles (not James) Fox motored down and met them there: the horses having been safely stabled in the *posada* (or caravanserai). While the horsey people went to the cockfighting, for which I had little stomach, I chose to take the boat across from Puerto de Santa Maria to Cádiz: a place of great historical resonance. More contemporary resonance was provided by a visit to the Gonzalez Byass sherry establishment in Jerez itself.

The next expedition was further afield. My mother had come out to visit and we planned a trip to Morocco and Gibraltar. One morning long before dawn we were up at the railway station waiting for the overnight Madrid to Algeciras sleeper, which came impressively roaring, hissing and steaming: no dreary diesels in those days. We settled in a compartment with several very comatose Spanish gentlemen.

The Straits were pleasingly rough and the voyage westward to Tangier along the coast with the Atlas mountains behind us exhilarating. Tangier itself seemed surprisingly dull, even the Kasbah; dreary weather didn't help. The train to Fez was a revelation: the countryside green and fertile, a total contrast to the aridity of Andalucia; a plush compartment shared with a genial large and evidently prosperous Arab gentleman in full white djellaba and – what else? – fez, well supplied with oranges and sweetmeats which he offered us.

Fez itself was a revelation: first the abrupt distinction between the French colonial town, where we stayed, with spacious boulevards and Art Deco buildings; and the old town reached through a spectacular gate, after which one went down into what is effectively an indoor space. (It must be unusual that a walled city is a depression rather than an eminence.)

The various trades and crafts all had their own 'quarters' – coppersmiths, potters, weavers, tailors. Laden donkeys and a milling crowd jostled in the confined space; appetising aromas arose from the multifarious food stalls or spice emporia. One sensed that to the inhabitants this was the entire world and that the

Srinagar floating garden.

Selling the produce of the floating gardens.

Nigeen Lake, Srinagar, Kashmir, 1972. 'The young persons paddling held wide hats of giant lotus leaves above them against the constant downpour.'

Sonamarg, Kashmir.

Rajasthan.

Inside the Diwan-i-Khas Red Fort, Delhi. Showing the beginning of the Shah Jahan high Islamic decoration.

Eastern scenes.

Opposite, top: Dome of the Rock, Jerusalem.

Opposite: Mysore madrassah.

erleaf: Rajasthan.

Sheikh Lotfollah Mosque, Isfahan, Iran.

Peking, 1977

'Everywhere we were the object of great if rather cautious curiosity... I don't remember seeing another foreigner.'

'When Haruko and I went in, one among the Chinese who had been intently studying the pandas' table manners noticed the arrival of a far more exotic species. As word spread the entire room turned to gawp at these exotica – the pandas quite forgotten…'

expanses 'outside' would be totally alien. Only the malodorous if picturesque tanneries, of necessity outside the walls, effectively bridged the two worlds.

Returning to Tangier, we flew back to Gibraltar, landing in the dark at the airport squeezed between the border fence and the looming Rock. The morning was bright and sunny and made for relaxation on the terrace of the Rock Hotel, before a peregrination of the town. It struck me then, and no doubt would today, how anglicised this enclave at the extremity of the Mediterranean was: a sort of Catterick-sur-mer with all the banal but reassuring props of fish and chip shops and telephone boxes and of course squaddies.

Mother having returned home – flying from Malaga I presume – I set off on the homeward journey, timing it to be back in Scotland by Christmas. The first evening I arrived in Granada and found a room in the Parador – not a place one can just turn up at nowadays. Sightseeing of course of the Alhambra and the Generalife: gloriously warm, verdant, free of any tourists. Setting off northwards again, there was an almost instant change as I climbed up towards La Mancha, the warmth was replaced by chilly mist and the first frost of winter.

In Madrid what was most noticeable was how different the tapas culture was from the relative austerity of Andalucia: large portions, great variety, red wine not sherry, and of course the hubbub of the nocturnal crowds in the densely pub-populated zone around the Gran Via, late into the night.

The Prado was if anything more impressive than I had imagined: the order and spaciousness in which the great masterpieces of Spanish art were displayed seemed absolutely right. Of course, I also looked around the old town and the Plaza Mayor: a brief enough introduction but if anything enhanced by the midwinter atmosphere of market day activities, tourist-free amid the chill grey air.

I had found myself talking to one English girl in front of some Prado masterpiece and when it transpired she was also returning home I offered her a lift: which worked very well as I enjoyed some company and we shared the petrol cost. An overnight stop in Burgos and brief exploration of its superb cathedral and impressive old town was the finale in Spain before the long haul back through a wintry France and cross-Channel to Dover and finally London.

I had learned quite good Spanish very quickly; but found that one is just as quick to forget it again, while there is always the problem of confusing it with the near-relation Italian. But the trip had opened my eyes to the charm and variety of Spain, thitherto not explored but later to become very familiar.

New Horizons: the New World

Several months at home followed a term teaching (French!) at Bradfield while I took the Foreign Office exams, only to fall at the final hurdle (my face, I suspect, not fitting an interview board seemingly composed of trade unionists). At least I could console myself that I had come top of the entire country in the essay paper of the exams. At that point I turned in another direction and decided it was time I exposed myself to the North American continent, as well as to regular working and earning a salary. A letter to our family friend Bruce Friedlich (mentioned above, but whom in fact I had never met) elicited a warm invitation to come and work with his eponymous advertising firm in New York.

I should say here, no doubt to the profound relief of every reader, that I do not propose to narrate in detail every overseas journey between 1966 and 2021. There have of course been various motivations or reasons for travel, the main categories being business, both residential sojourns abroad and intermittent visiting trips, often with clients; and pleasure trips or holidays, varying as to whether alone, with a friend or two, with my mother, or with a group. Other categories would include sailing, which has sometimes taken me far afield. Thus, I may describe some examples in the various categories in some detail, while merely enumerating others (if that!).

So it was that I embarked on the Canadian Pacific's *Empress of England* off the Tail of the Bank at Greenock, bound for Montreal. It was a glorious cloudless autumn evening as we sailed down the Firth past Arran's mountains. A friend from Kilmacolm and I viewed this from the first-class deck until summarily expelled. The contrast below was striking: she and I were probably alone among close to a thousand emigrants, and I shared an inside cabin with three of these: one was an agricultural worker, one a German ex-prisoner of war from Birmingham, and I can't remember the third. One asked on about the third day 'Is this the Atlantic or the Pacific we're crossing?' We seldom met as for some reason they seemed to be up all night and in their bunks all day. I met my friend – our doctor's daughter – at the dining saloon every day.

A day or two out we ran into a storm which apparently briefly reached Force 12. I spent much of my time on the bridge where gins and tonics were routinely consumed… I enjoyed the storm immensely: I was amazed to think that small boat transatlantic sailors could survive in such gigantic waves. One morning, taking my daily exercise round the wildly rolling deck, I saw the back of a man gripping the rail and gazing out to sea. Assuming that like me he was exulting in the wild seas, I greeted him with a hearty 'Good morning!' He turned to me slowly and in the broadest Glaswegian said slowly 'Do ye think wur gonna sink?'

It was cold and clear by the time we sighted Cape Farewell, the southern tip of Newfoundland and my first sight of the New World (so in fact Cape Hello!). However, 24 hours later steaming up the impossibly narrow-looking St Lawrence it had become dark and drizzly – more like the recently left west of Scotland in fact. There was a late evening stop at Quebec city, where the ship tied up in the centre below the scene of General Wolfe's triumph on the Heights of Abraham. The Citadel and Château Frontenac rose imposingly above the quay: equally imposing was my first sight of North American road transport, with gigantic trucks moving back and forth at the port. Then on to Montreal.

I stayed for a few days with my father's cousins, the McMartins. I was following in the footsteps of sister Fiona, who had spent some time in Montreal a year or so earlier, working in the Royal Bank of Canada before touring the States. I became familiar with the city, in particular McGill university quarter (a number of school contemporaries had gone there). Bizarre licensing laws entailed a drive across state boundaries to Ottawa where there were liquor stores. Soon, though, it was time for the USA.

I took the 'express' (which was unbelievably slow and ran infrequently) and entered the United States at an insignificant place called Rouses Point. The long day was spent trundling down by Lake Champlain and the Hudson River Valley, past resonant names such as Ticonderoga, Schenectady and Poughkeepsie to Grand Central Station. An infinitely more stylish way to arrive than the arrivals hall at J F Kennedy airport (as it had only just become). In fact, I first set foot on American soil precisely 28 floors below my future office, which I was going to meet the next morning, after my first 'working breakfast'.

I had arranged to meet Bruce at the 'parking garage' in W 43rd Street: this happened as planned and we drove out via the Midtown Tunnel to Verona, New Jersey where I was going to spend the next three months or so chez Friedlich.

I don't propose to go into any detail about my work, nor the 'family' or social side of my American stay. Suffice it to say that while I had expected to stay a few months for 'work experience', we got on so well that I stayed very nearly two years. It was both the first and last time in my career that I had an office to myself. However, the settings and sundry excursions are perhaps worth a mention. The company occupied a floor – the 28th – of the Graybar Building, 420 Lexington Avenue and essentially part of the Grand Central complex. The Pan Am building seemed just a few feet from my window: in those days Chinook helicopters regularly took off and landed from its roof, connecting with JFK – an infinitely easier airport transfer than now, and which I used many times. Bruce's office looked north, straight up Park Avenue: it intrigued me that the traffic lights were so efficiently synchronised, all the way up to Harlem. On the 28th floor, we were able to boast that 'now we are above J Walter Thompson'.

Grand Central became almost the centre of my universe; I still love it for the unspoiled grandeur of its central hall, its art deco period details, its multiplicity of shops and services (Oyster Bar; bookshops; shoeshine 'boys' and so many more). I learned how to walk underground for perhaps 20 blocks, from the high 30s, to the 50s – most useful when it was pouring. The trains seemed an afterthought and of course many were on the lower level.

After New Jersey and the New Year – and a brief, but most enjoyable skiing trip in New Hampshire – I moved into a delightful little studio apartment on the 12th floor of a good block on West 12th Street in Greenwich Village. Now I could really explore the Village as well as midtown and the rest of the city. This was a sublet from a friend of a colleague – after a year unfortunately she needed it back, so when in June 1967 I returned after a couple of months back in London (coinciding with the Seven-Day War, a great success in New York), I moved up to another sublet on the Upper East Side. This I hardly bothered to furnish – it was much more basic – but rather surprisingly found the supposedly classy Upper East Side far less enjoyable and even less smart than the West Village. However, there were compensations: the Metropolitan Museum and Central Park were very close. Both these places were an easy commute to the office via the Lexington Avenue subway.

At times, especially at weekends in the city, I could find New York a desperately lonely place: I think it was the sensation of being a tiny ant among these precipitous skyscrapers. Most friends had homes and families in the suburbs or surrounding states. Nevertheless, I also had 'urban' and single friends; and one great friend, Robin Garton (sadly now lost on a Glencoe mountainside) joined in all sorts of activities and cheered me immensely. (He was Christies' No. 2 man in New York and shared the grandest of Belle Epoque rooms with his boss, Charlie Allsopp – now Lord Hindlip – their desks about twenty yards apart.)

Though the world seems full of vacationing Americans, they

actually seem to take very little time off. Thus, apart from weekends I had relatively little time to explore the East Coast. There was another, longer skiing trip the next New Year, again in New Hampshire (I have never been colder than on a chairlift ascending the White Mountains: though when in the evening after bath I went up the road, lightly clad, to view the 'alpenglow', though getting chilly I was amazed to see the temperature was now 30 degrees below zero – whether Celsius or Fahrenheit.)

I had a wonderful sailing trip from Connecticut along Long Island Sound, to Nantucket, Martha's Vineyard, Cape Cod and eventually Gloucester, Mass on a fine old John Alden schooner, at the kind invitation of Charles Coffin and his wife Eileen who had befriended my parents in Antigua. Also on board was a Pan Am Captain whose navigation from buoy to buoy in dense fog was truly spectacular. Mrs C cooked wonderfully and bourbon and cookies started the process quite early in the day.

That was summer 1968: I should have mentioned that in the spring I had joined the parents for a few days in Antigua – a most welcome interlude of warmth and colour after months of dour and dreary weather in New York among drifts of half-melted snow. There was swimming and sailing there (English Harbour): in a 'sailfish' I beat the man who had just won the America's Cup at the start of a race but being new to this strange craft capsized several times later. We made good friends with Charles Cunningham, Lazards' man in Canada, and his wife Leilia, who were kind to me in Toronto when I was 'winding down' for home.

Business trips had taken me up and down the coast to Philadelphia and Washington, as well as occasionally upstate. In Washington once I stayed (on the floor!) with a pair of Robert Kennedy's secretaries who gave me a great tour of the Capitol; highlights were hearing Senator Fulbright's speaking of 'the arrogance of power' in the Senate chamber, and a Saturday morning session visiting RFK's office where I sat in JFK's famous rocking chair. Sadly, 'Bobby' had only weeks, if that, to live, and down in New Jersey for a wedding I remember waiting with thousands along the railway track as his funeral train passed slowly by.

Whether this time or another, I hired a car for a weekend drive through Virginia: Mount Vernon, Monticello, the Blue Ridge Parkway, Appomattox and Gettysburg the highlights. I had read rather more about American history, and this brought the years of the American Revolution and the Civil War vividly to life – augmenting all I had absorbed from *National Geographics* and Christmas books from 'Aunt Martha' in my boyhood.

Omnipresent in these two years were the Friedlich family and cousins. The matriarch, Martha Langsdorff, aforementioned, was immensely kind in giving me tickets from her, largely unused, subscriptions to the Metropolitan Opera and Carnegie Hall, as well as lending me her Park Lane apartment on occasional weekends when I was living in New Jersey – a useful opportunity for investigating city rather than suburbs in the early days. More special perhaps was 'the Lake' – a splendid rustic house by, indeed, a lake in wooded country in Connecticut, where I often went with family and friends – Judy Greenebaum and Bill Friedlich especially, cousins and my nearest contemporaries (they had all come to stay with us in Scotland over the years). In the winter there was an ice yacht and skating; in the summer I did not fish!

The Tame West: California and Mexico

Fortuitously, I had bumped into an old Oxford friend, (then) David Douglas-Home, son of course of the most recent Prime Minister and 'transitioning' between being Lord Dunglass and (now) Earl of Home. This was in Central Park: an unmistakable figure. We met often in midtown for gins and tonics and lunch. He, on secondment from Morgan Grenfell to J P Morgan, had a rather more select social life than I, including trips to Newfoundland with the Duke and Duchess of Windsor – I was quite glad, though intrigued, not to be going on that.

For both of us, our time in the USA was coming to an end in summer 1968, and we decided on a trip to 'the Coast', i.e. California, which we had not yet visited. After a final stay with the Montreal cousins, then the Cunninghams in Toronto, I met David in Chicago whence we flew to Denver to start the 'Wild West' journey. In the Denver hotel we viewed on TV Richard Nixon being adopted as the Republican presidential candidate at the convention.

Starting in our hired Chevy we broke down just before the Continental Divide in the Rockies but were soon on our way again through that dramatic landscape and down to Salt Lake City with its Mormon temple, past the Bonneville Salt Flats and through endless Utah and Nevada. Surprises included mile-long trains and being stuck at a desert 'gas station' for hours when a freak storm had put the pumps out of action. Also, the extraordinary lack of places to eat or stay – in Sacramento we were unable to find a single restaurant!

This was after we had passed through Reno, Nevada ('Greatest Little City in the World', self-proclaimed), and past the stunningly beautiful Lake Tahoe into the California wine country. San Francisco, however, was vibrant enough. We stayed somewhere 'midtown', visited Alcatraz, Fisherman's Wharf and of course the Golden Gate. We drove over the bridge to see the amazing redwood forests beyond Sausalito. I loved San Francisco and have been back since, on the way to Japan (which I visit regularly).

Also fully rising to expectations was the drive down the west coast to Los Angeles on the Pacific Coast Highway: stops at Monterey, Carmel, the dramatic Big Sur and Randolph Hearst's Castle: a night in a motel (San Luis Obispo) and past Santa Barbara to LA.

There we parted as David had been invited to stay with a mega-rich packed meat baron at his gracious home in Bel Air. We found the place – a sprawling, elegant white Spanish hacienda-style mansion, and were greeted by our burly, affable host.

First drinks were in a highly elaborate pink and gold room in which every painting was a Rubens. Then our host suggested we went outside to the 'Loggia'. Here every painting seemed to be a Manet. Our host approved of Nixon's choice of running mate, announced earlier: 'That Spiro Agnew, he's going to be vurry, vurry good!' He wasn't. Soon though it was time for me to leave this opulent zone.

I had a pleasant night in a place on the beach at Santa Monica, then stayed a few nights in a spa resort, a kind gesture by New York friends, then stayed briefly with my ex-colleague Ray Hernandez, recently assistant art director at Bruce Friedlich, before crossing down into Mexico. It was good to see the US Navy up close, and to see my old colleague – who had been my first 'mentor' in early days at BF.

A cab ride to the Mexican border, right beside San Diego at Tijuana, was revealing. After the formalities we seemed in a totally different world of shanty-town squalor. Luckily, I spent no time in Tijuana but went to the airport for the flight to Guadalajara. Guadalajara was and presumably is a fine city with numerous excellent, mainly ecclesiastical buildings. A good atmosphere of bandstands, flowers, mariachi and pervasive equine culture. Nevertheless, there was a somewhat sinister feeling especially at night – characters hissing '*Que estas haciendo*?' when one was merely walking in some of the more picturesque parts of town.

I made an expedition to a beautiful lake in the hills, visiting an estancia, then departed for Mexico City. I have little new or original to say about this awesome city (then I believe with the largest population in the world). Of course, the museum was quite marvellous, as was the vast space containing the cathedral, the cathedral itself, and the Aztec ruins at Teotihuacan.

Next after the big city was the very different scene of the Yucatan. I flew to Merida and had a couple of nights in a most agreeable colonial-style hotel in the golden Baroque centre. Then I took a miniature plane to the diminutive airport at Chichen Itza, where the terminal was a thatched hut. Hotel pretty thatched too but I think probably adequate. Of course, I crawled all over the great temple ruins and noted the very distinctive Mayan features of the locals – exactly as featured on the stone bas-reliefs.

With a girl I'd met there, I took a day trip the twenty miles or so to Uxmal, a temple more ensconced in the jungle than Chichen Itza in its near-parkland, and perhaps more unspoiled and evocative: the temple steps were even steeper than those at Chichen Itza!

Returning to Merida the next day (I assumed) I waited for the little plane at the thatched terminal, only to see it drive over about 2,000 feet above. 'Maybe mañana?' the operative said. So, it was back to the hotel and mañana did in fact bring me to Merida, for a flight the next day directly to New Orleans and back to the known world. I had really enjoyed Mexico and have always wanted to expand my acquaintance with the Maya civilisation; unfortunately, have never got to Guatemala (Palenque) or Nicaragua. Americans know pre-Columbian civilisation, especially of Central America, in a way that we don't seem to. It's much more than Acapulco!

Arriving hot, dusty and scruffy at New Orleans airport, I telephoned my recent Oxford friend Jim Coleman who had lately started as a lawyer in his family's firm. Jim instantly invited me to come and stay the night and I found myself transported to a different world: a magnificent Audubon Avenue house where I was given a berth in a lovely pavilion at the bottom of the garden. A bath, change, several gins, lunch, siesta, reminiscences, dinner – wonderful. Then Jim suggested we should go sailing during the night on Lake Pontchartrain! A few friends were summoned, and we arrived at the dock where his boat was waiting: sailed through the still night to the small hours with a magical whisper of breeze accompanying quiet conversation. Next day was back to reality with the flight to New York for the final few days before returning home. So ended my two-year North (and Central) American sojourn.

Back in Europe

After nearly two years in North America, I was naturally longing to reacquaint myself with the continent of Europe. However, with much of late 1968 and early 1969 spent jobhunting in London and southern England this didn't really happen till late in the year apart from one winter cultural weekend.

Early in 1969 dear Robin Garton, his steady girlfriend Juliet 'Aylmo' Aylmer and myself travelled to Harwich one Friday evening to take the overnight ferry to the Hook of Holland, lured by the great Rembrandt exhibition at the Rijksmuseum in Amsterdam. With early decanting from ship to train the landscape was duly wintry: light snow fallen and freezing and to our gratification occasional long-distance skaters speeding along the trackside canals. A scene Avercamp could have painted, leaving us avid for the museum's other treasures too.

I hadn't been to Amsterdam, or indeed any of the other historic Dutch cities before, merely crossed the southern salient near Maastricht in 1960. We stayed in a nice little hotel round the corner from the Rijksmuseum with an impossibly steep staircase: rather convenient. Obviously, the exhibition was the main draw, and it was magnificent – I believe the first for a long time after careful curating and restoration. 'The Night Watch' was inevitably the high point of the whole show, but it was I suppose the most comprehensive exhibition of his works yet. (I still have the catalogue and must check to see if any of the exhibits have not survived the hyper-critical scrutiny of recent years.) We naturally toured the rest of the building and at one point bumped into two great friends, Liz Floyd, colleague from Christie's whose father 'Bunter' was its chairman, and Susie Wigan now Bonsor.

Amsterdam also has the Stedelijk for modern art and the Van Gogh museum: we 'did' these too. Beyond that it was fun to explore the city, atmospheric with its frozen canals, and eat and drink in cosy and (then) smoky dens. We learnt about Dutch 'genever' and the right way to drink Bols and Wynand Fockink – the glasses filled to surface tension. In the snow we went down to the Marktplein and Rembrandt's house and learnt of his unfortunate financial ineptitude. It was to be the first of many quick trips to Amsterdam, a convenient and congenial nearby destination for weekends.

There was one further tantalising glimpse when, having joined the crew of the celebrated One Ton ocean racing yacht *Tina*, the course of the Channel Race took us round the buoy off Cherbourg – but no stopping!

Two Tours to Habsburg Lands

In fact, it was not until the autumn with my first holiday leave as a fully employed stockbroker that I had a prolonged return across the Channel. This was a two-week motoring tour accompanied by Miles Blackwell to Austria in my Lotus Elan. He came to the City and we set off after work for Southend Airport and the Silver City freighter: two quite large men wearing British Warm overcoats in a small open car on a late October evening (the roof was never up in the next fortnight). From Ostend we swept along the Jabbeke Straight of XK 120 record-breaking fame and, having disposed of one country rather fast, found a berth for the night in Aachen.

A quick look at Charlemagne's cathedral on a glorious morning and we traversed Germany at speed, autobahns all the way and probably averaging around 120. *Tankstelle* stops seemed alarmingly frequent. It was well and truly dark by the time I stopped under Salzburg's Hohensalzburg Castle, magically floodlit. Miles who had been fairly taciturn on the road uttered an awed appreciation of the sight: his first time in Salzburg. And so to bed.

No need to detail our few days in Salzburg or through Austria to Vienna (new to both of us); we turned south to Carinthia then Innsbruck, Liechtenstein, Switzerland, and Alsace homewards: it was an exhilarating autumn al fresco drive with a goodly share of Alpine passes and scenery. One particular highlight I remember was the Wachau stretch of the Danube: the great abbey of Melk, Dürnstein where Richard the Lionheart had been imprisoned for ransom; river barges, vineyards, *gemütlich* inns.

I fast forward here to the late autumn of 1971, two years later, when some of the same ground was reprised, with the same travel mate and one important addition. I flew to Orly to meet Miles who was already in Paris, this time with the Blackwell Bristol. No sign: then I found *a* Blackwell, but the wrong one, Nigel, who I had no idea was in Paris (nor had he that I was). Eventually we found Miles, unsurprisingly asleep (on an ashtray), and went our various ways. The motoring party reached a village signed 'Colombey-les-Deux-Églises' and thought there could be no better place to stop – especially seeing a really inviting roadside inn. Before the *steak-frites* though we felt it important to make the short walk up the road and visit the church with de Gaulle's grave. Standing silent in the dark, Miles said, 'I feel an enormous fart coming on' and obliged. Immediately several gendarmes leapt out of the trees. '*C'était un grand homme*' pronounced Miles solemnly; at which there was much nodding of heads, proffering of cigarettes and general *fraternité*. We slept well.

The road to Vienna and Vienna itself was now familiar. We met up with 'the Guv'nor', Miles' father Richard Blackwell, and stayed in a charming little hotel near the Stephansdom. But the target this time was Rome where, as in Vienna, there was then a Blackwell's bookshop. The excitement after Vienna was the first breaching of the Iron Curtain for any of us: all our papers in order, there was a pleasurable *frisson* in the leisured crossing of the border into Hungary. Lunch at the lovely Esterhazy palace of Fertöd (previous haunt of Haydn, favourite composer of us all) and towards dusk a stop to see the imposing cathedral of Esztergom above the Danube, where a fully scarleted cardinal conveniently appeared.

For the few days in Budapest, we naturally stayed at the historic Gellért hotel, enjoyed the castle, cathedral and old town of Buda up the hill above; also the more modern and spacious attractions of Pest over the river. No opera alas, but much *zigeunermusik* in pleasant restaurants. One night the Guv'nor and I decided to cross the river by walking up the suspension cables of the chain bridge, but were quickly grounded by an amused gendarmerie. The weather had turned wet by the time we got into Slovenia (Yugoslavia of course in those days) and drove straight through Ljubljana along the river quays. Back in Italy it was fairly dense fog for the final stretch along the coast to Venice. Minder drove well. The Piazzale Roma was familiar even in the fog: which greatly enhanced the vaporetto journey up the Grand Canal, again something new to Miles who was enthralled. We stayed right by the Fenice at the charming little hotel of that name (again, though, alas no opera). It was wet most of the time in Venice, and even wetter on the way south where we had a brief stop and lunch in Siena, viewing the obligatory (wonderful) sights.

The skies had brightened in Rome, and we enjoyed several days of 'Indian summer'. We stayed in a smart little hotel recommended by one Blackwell's colleagues just off the Borghese gardens; I can't remember which of the innumerable attractions of that inexhaustible city were visited that time. We went, as was becoming routine for me, to Tivoli and had an atmospheric and lengthy lunch with the most amazing, enormous mushrooms. I do also remember – I think on my last day (I was flying back) a jolly al fresco lunch at Ostia with the two 'Lionesses' – the formidable ladies who ran the Blackwell's bookshop. Ostia being convenient for Fiumicino, I think I took the plane back straight after that.

Two French Trips

It has been natural to take these two Blackwell road trips together, despite their being two years apart. In the meantime – i.e. in 1970 – there had been other Continental excursions. Each of these was a prototype of a holiday category that was to become more frequent: one, a motoring tour with my mother, and the other a summer (usually late summer) seaside relaxation, usually in a rented villa.

In May, my mother and I took a quick trip, in the Lotus once more, down to the south of France and back. Down through Burgundy – I remember a delicious lunch at the Greuze in Tournus; the Imperator in Nîmes, then to Marseille and reacquaintance with the Côte des Maures to the east. The next stop at Cassis (*Thelma VI* had not got that far west) and St Tropez revisited. The harbour – as I can see in my Kodachrome slides – was full of beautiful old sailing yachts, long before the invasion by hideous motor mega-yachts cramming the quayside.

I was back there a few months later when a 'team' villa holiday took place in mid-September. Miles and I again crewed the Lotus while Nigel and Andrew Fraser drove in Nigel's BMW, NSB 444. First night at Compiègne, next at Tournus (again) where the Romanesque abbey laid on a splendid concert; next in Avignon. For room-sharing we swapped 'partners'. After several breaks at propitious places such as Châteauneuf-du-Pape we made it to the Mas de Basloup up the hill by the entrance to St Trop where the rest of the team duly foregathered.

The cast of characters comprised – of course – the Guv'nor and Mrs B, who presided with amused and unruffled equanimity over our antics; Dudley Dodd; Adrian Fort; and our quartet above. It was very much a late-season beach holiday and after a leisurely croissant-session we would drive over the hill to the Tahiti-Plage and settle in for beach umbrellas, pastis, swimming, lunch… The visual scene was enhanced by this being the apogee of toplessness: the Guv'nor took the award for critical appreciation, benignly watched by Mrs B. Dudley displayed an unexpected talent for power-swimming far out to sea. Ugly gin palaces – 'dommers' – anchored off and the denizens came ashore for lunch, then cleared off again. In the velvety night we usually ate outdoors somewhere in the town and enjoyed endless games of boules under the plane trees and lights of the boulodrome.

One day – 17th September – a telegraph boy came up the hill bearing the news of the birth of my niece, Rosamund Margaret Elizabeth. But this welcome news was soon overtaken by more sinister developments. I drove back alone and arriving early on the Channel coast (one had to book a specific ferry time then), stopped for refreshment outside the Westminster Hotel in Le Touquet, immediately finding John and Jean Wood, great friends of my parents, having tea on the terrace. (Living near Deal they would pop over as if to the next village.) They asked anxiously how my father was: nonplussed, I asked if there was anything wrong? I heard – quite new to me – that he had been having tummy pains and was going to have some investigation in hospital.

I was, of course, up in Scotland straight away and driving down from Glasgow when my mother heard that the investigation had shown that he had liver cancer – incurable. There were no transplants then. Over the next three months he was in and out of hospital, steadily becoming more emaciated. Naturally, I visited every weekend; but alas, was in London at work on the Tuesday that mother rang to say he was going fast. The race to Heathrow and the shuttle did not get me home quite in time. He was just fifty-three. That quarter had seen the arrival of a new generation, followed so closely by the departure of one, older but really in his prime, who deserved to have lived to enjoy the young.

Consolation in Portugal

This was mid-December: an amazingly well-attended funeral in Paisley Abbey on a dark day pouring with rain and a somewhat subdued Christmas at Newark. We thought a total change of scene was necessary, especially for my mother. Alex Bridport had kindly offered a stay at his Maniace estate in Sicily (once Nelson's: Alex had inherited as Duke of Bronte – sadly, the Mafia later relieved him of it so that was the only chance). Anyway, by then we had arranged a brief trip to Portugal. We stayed first at Estoril – a favourite of my grandparents – visiting Sintra, Cascais and the unexpectedly beautiful pink Rococo Queluz palace. Then we moved into the city of Lisbon and explored it thoroughly. A little restaurant near M. Eiffel's vertical construction produced perhaps as good a bottle of red wine as I have ever drunk.

I was at the station very early one morning to catch the train to Oporto: my friend David Orr was working in the port business with Cockburn's and living some way north of the city, and they had invited me to stay for a day or two. It was a different aspect: I remember mostly freezing cold (in contrast to Lisbon and the shores of the Tagus), alleviated by glowing log fires. Unfortunately, I had no chance really to see Oporto either coming or going.

Departure from Lisbon was not as planned: we went to the airport but there was fog, and the BEA plane could not land. Eventually there was nothing for it but to be carted off to some anonymous hotel. Next day, up early, a day at the airport, same thing – a different hotel. By the next morning, the fog had moved to London; however, late in the day we were at last rescued by an Aer Lingus plane (whose interior was decorated with holy saints, no doubt responsible for our deliverance) and we finally made it to London.

It had I think been a very worthwhile trip for my mother, to take her mind off things, and she displayed admirable composure and cheerfulness throughout. Going to a 'new place' full of discoveries probably helped: aforementioned Queluz, the spectacular site of Lisbon, the dramatic monument to Henry the Navigator…

Travels in the Seventies

It seems remarkable, from the perspective of 2022, that so much travel abroad was possible in the 1970s, when we were restricted to a foreign currency allowance of £50 a year (and a mere £25 before then). This, however, did not apply to business travel: which nevertheless was strictly controlled with much marking of passports and other bureaucratic paperwork. Thus, having a job which took me to the other side of the world twice or three times a year, I was often able to 'tack on' a weekend or so on the way home, in some salubrious, novel or interesting place.

Another means of circumventing the currency restrictions was to book flights or stays in advance: the 'charter flight' came into its own even for very short-haul journeys (these, however, were often at highly antisocial hours). Before Ryanair there was DanAir: these were the precursors of the low cost, no-frills airlines which really opened up air travel when scheduled flights were seriously expensive.

Charter flights also generally flew from London's second-line airports – Gatwick or Luton, Stansted then not featuring – and often flew to the second airports of major European cities: Ciampino rather than Fiumicino for Rome, Orly rather than Charles de Gaulle for Paris. This was only mildly inconvenient: in general, one checked in at a town terminal (Place des Invalides in Paris), as indeed one did for BEA in London (Cromwell Road).

Thus, they provided an easy, affordable means of spending a weekend in European capitals: Amsterdam, Paris and Rome featuring most. Invidious to mention particular trips, many of which I took solo: but one which especially stays in my mind is when in January 1972 Aubrey Lawrence, Nicky Talbot Rice and I made an expedition to Rome. Apart from the historic city centre 'rubble-gazing' (© H. Fukuda) I recall a day trip out to Tivoli: as usual visiting Hadrian's Villa below the town and the Villa d'Este up top, but what I most vividly remember is a long lunch in a hillside trattoria before a roaring log fire, with the most impressive giant mushrooms ever experienced, and more than one bottle of aged Barolo or similar. Lunch indeed seemed to provide the high spots: another day – of balmy winter sunshine – we lunched in the Piazza Navona, outside. Successive photographs show us among the other lunchers at tables on the pavement at the far end; then ourselves still going strong but everyone else having left, tables and chairs still in place: finally, at a solitary table with a large space between us and the restaurant entrance…

Mariage à la Mode

In May of that year, however, it was my own car rather than any aeroplane that transported my mother and myself to France, for the wedding of my Bridge of Weir friend Geoff Fairbairn to Mlle. Ariane Ramolino at Linières-Bouton in the Maine, north of the Loire. They had met through a mutual love of golf, at some up-market Paris establishment where Geoff was practising accountancy. We spent the first night at the Domaine de Beauvois at Luynes, a most civilized old-established château-hotel (*'une impression d'élégant classicisme'* – Michelin): a delicious dinner and unbroken sleep and the next morning we drove over to Azay-le-Rideau to meet Bobby and Betty Headon-Smith, friends of my parents also from Bridge of Weir, for lunch. I hadn't seen the château before and could quite see how it had been an important source for David Bryce at Fettes: a very 'petite' château, self-contained within its moat, perhaps the most perfect of all the Loire châteaux. Outside it was a rally of vintage French sports cars: interesting for the Amilcars,

Talbot-Darracqs, Hotchkisses, etc. as a change from Bentleys, Alvises and SS-Jaguars!

I remember little of the marriage ceremony, more of the reception at the surprisingly intimate château or *gentilhommière* of the Prince Napoléon, a relation of the bride (Madame Mère, *the* Napoléon's mother, was *née* Ramolino). I snooped as much as possible at all the fascinating memorabilia in the interior, but on a lovely day the action was outside. Though only May, it was blisteringly hot and my car, the Ferrari 330 GT, proved an ideal 'sitting-out room' for the mother of the bride to take a siesta. Meanwhile the festivities were in full swing. As befitted an Auld Alliance alliance there was a simultaneous competition going on between a scarlet-clad brass band from the local hunt (this being *terrain de la chasse, par excellence*) and some tartan-clad Scots pipers. Much importance was attached to simultaneous performance, with the huntsmen, their splendid horns backed into the garden wall, vying to outperform the skirl of the pipes. The result was interestingly cacophonous and I couldn't say who 'won'!

Then there was dinner and dancing. I found as partner an attractive *cousine* of the bride's but alas around 1 a.m. I was prised away by my poor mother, who had decided that we should be on our way: we had in fact yet to check in at our overnight stop! So, we drove through the forests and the fog, the drive enlivened by the Ferrari's steering column emitting blue flames: this somewhat alarming development, I found, could be suppressed by turning off the headlights. Though this made navigation no easier, somehow we found our way to the grandiose if somewhat (visually) chilly Château d'Artigny where the front desk seemed to be totally unsurprised at our unconventional check-in time. And so to bed.

The Château d'Artigny had been the property of the Coty *parfumier* family: René Coty had been President of France, for quite a long term, only a few years before. However, we spent but little time there – I suspect we rose not too early – before setting off for lunch at the somewhat more modest but equally refined Domaine de la Tortinière, also at Montbazon nearby. I recall little of the journey home except that it clearly didn't involve night driving.

Our next motoring tour together was to be the next spring, but in Japan: I shall soon revert to why that should be.

Asiatic Initiations

Principally Business, Partly Pleasure

1971 now brings into play another category: business-related travel. I have of course written of the (relatively few) leisure travels during my two years working in New York. As then, I don't propose to describe journeys taken in the course of my work: but there are 'grey areas' where in the course of looking after clients, weekend trips, for example, could be classed as purely pleasurable (especially when the clients were already good friends, or the trip was exploring new ground). There were also stops on the way to or back from Japan: mostly brief, but some were prolonged. And while the great majority of my business-related time abroad was in Japan, there were also frequent visits to clients in Europe, the Middle and Far East and America, which might also be combined with a little 'recreation'.

By the summer of 1971 I had been rather dubiously pontificating about Japan for two years, without having ever been there. I could read and write a certain amount of the language, but neither speak nor understand any but a minute fraction of the spoken word – ideograms, which I had been studying, giving no clue as to pronunciation. I was longing to rectify this with, at last, some direct experience. So, it came about that I was finally permitted to join my then boss and one agreeable client in May.

With the inadequate range of the aircraft of the day (principally Boeing 707s), the trans-Siberian route to Japan had to make a refuelling stop at Moscow. This was to me an even more enigmatic destination than Japan: so, I took the Friday off to travel by BEA for a 24-hour stopover in Moscow. The tall Intourist Hotel in Gorky Street (long since demolished) was, shall we say, utilitarian. Seeing a television, I couldn't resist seeing what was on, before going out. Of course, it was Brezhnev, addressing the Nth Party Congress. I turned it off. On a long walk I could hardly believe that I was now in Red Square, the Kremlin etc. without let or hindrance. The cathedrals of the Kremlin with their many gold-plated domes were wonderful but also oddly lonely. One speculated what was going on behind the walls of the palaces. Out in the square again, a visit to GUM which had hardly any merchandise and was quite ignorant of the concept of window-dressing was rather depressing. After deliberately getting lost in numerous back alleys I arrived back at the hotel extremely footsore. I put the telly on again: Mr Brezhnev seemed to be approaching his peroration, but that might have been some way off and I was disinclined to wait; anyway, it was time for dinner.

Seated in the vast dining room I was impressed by the comprehensive and delicious-sounding menu (the Russian Tea Room by Carnegie Hall in New York had left me with a great appreciation of Russian cuisine). After a very long time, giving the opportunity to choose from the manifold delights, a portly little waitress appeared. 'I'll have this – and this', I said. '*Nyet*!' Try again. '*Nyet, nyet, nyet*'. A kind East German gentleman asked if he could help: I said that if he could ask for something they actually had, I would have it. It was disgusting.

There was a cacophonous sort of 'oompah' band and acres of dance floor. When the band struck up, as of one mind, the company rose and stomped up and down on the wooden floor, almost drowning out the musicians. The uniform of royal blue polyester suits for men and shapeless 'sack' dresses in huge floral prints seemed wholly appropriate. I slept well.

There was time for further exploration the next morning with my plane to Tokyo not until late afternoon. Places of ill fame such as the Lubyanka were just up the road and were, well, just ordinary. The Bolshoi was almost next door: I don't think I went in (nor to the Lubyanka!). I did have some rather better lunch at the National Hotel: quite different from the Intourist, small and intimate and really rather cosy feeling. Perhaps Lenin and his associates were not quite so cosy. At the airport I sought to be reunited with the six bottles of Johnnie Walker Black Label, which I had been enjoined to bring as presents for Japanese brokers and suchlike (Red Label would never do, apparently): they had been taken off me on arrival and I had doubted I would ever see them again. But no, I was taken down into the subterranean regions, left by myself and eventually found them all alone in a sort of strange cubicle. Armed with these – if not broaching them – I settled down for the long flight on Japan Air Lines, squashed in the middle seat of an economy row beside an entertaining American businessman who kept me awake all night with his tales of Japan.

Japan at Last

Arriving at Haneda in the morning, I recall various impressions. First, the light – astonishingly bright, and perhaps 'pearly' in character. Second, that all the (male) Japanese airport workers and staff seemed identical; same height, black hair, white shirts, neat beyond belief. As was to become wearily familiar, immigration spent ages 'correcting' my writing on my entry card. And having made the mistake of wearing smart new shoes for the flight, then the further mistake of taking them off for the night, I couldn't put them on again; so, made my first step to the '*genkan*' (entrance) of Japan in my socks – appropriate perhaps.

Before, as promised, 'going silent' over my working fortnight, I must describe the 'overture' of my first evening. Having met up with Jeremy, my boss, and our suave and delightful client John Huntsman, we went to dinner at Hannya-en, a high-class Japanese restaurant which sadly no longer exists, in its lovely gardens in Shiroganedai. Though I was no stranger now to Japanese food, whether in New York or London, this was my first experience of a proper *kaiseki* formal dinner. Thus, it was also my first experience of a great number of exquisitely presented dishes, few of which I could eat. But the most astonishing feature of the evening was the sudden appearance of two geisha: however much one had read about the culture, the complete shock of the dead-white faces will live with me forever.

Next morning it was down to work visiting Nippon Electric (NEC). As I mentioned, I am not going to write of any travels purely in the course of work. However, apart from interviewing Japanese company management a substantial part of my time in Japan was spent looking after clients, some familiar with the country and some visiting for the first time: often with both groups the weekend might be spent as a recreational/relaxing visit to some other area of Japan. Some of the more notable weekends might be mentioned, as falling within the 'leisure' category. There tended, however, to be a certain repetitiveness as, especially with first-timers, it was often difficult to suggest going elsewhere than must-see Kyoto – which luckily is a quite inexhaustible city. On this first visit, for John Huntsman as well as myself, Kyoto of course was a given. It was our first experience of staying in a ryokan and appreciating the fusion of garden and interior: again magical. A second weekend was in Shikoku where we had been visiting companies: memorable were the Ritsurin garden, (officially) one of the three best in Japan, and the memorable comment of John when invited to join Jeremy and me in the scalding hot bath: 'I'm not in the habit of bathing with my broker!' (Straight face…)

It was a nice Vickers, da Costa tradition to allow those visiting Japan for the first time a week's free time in Japan 'on the firm'. Stipulations were that one should travel as far in the country as reasonable in a week and should not travel first class. These seemed entirely acceptable conditions. So, I planned a trip to Kyushu, the western island. After taking off from Osaka the aircraft described a wide circle before descending again: the flight attendant immediately announced 'Radies and gentermen, we are shortly randing at Osaka Intaanational Airport'… So, there was a considerable delay before we took off again for Kagoshima in a different aircraft. It was perhaps twenty miles in a taxi in the dark to the hot-spring spa of Ibusuki where it was long past the ryokan-keepers' bedtime. However, they kindly insisted on producing the full works for dinner, some of which I could actually eat. It poured relentlessly. The next morning rather than 'enjoy' the traditional buried-in-hot-sand experience in the pouring rain I headed back for the urban bustle of Kagoshima. I enjoyed the views of the smoking volcano Sakurajima and bought a vivid scarlet wedding kimono for my sister.

Thence a combination of trains, buses and taxis took me up the west coast of Kyushu. First to Kumamoto, on the way to Nagasaki and eventually back to Tokyo. A pleasant prefectural capital with a largely restored castle, woods, hills and gardens: in particular Shizenko, in my view just as good as Takamatsu's Ritsurin. From Kumamoto the ferry took me over to Shimabara, site of the massacre of Christians in the seventeenth century: memories remain, also the vast castle which like Kumamoto's is almost entirely rebuilt. Interesting nevertheless, with an old samurai district surrounding it. That night though was spent in the spa town of Unzen, under the volcano which was to erupt with devastating effect some years later. No sand baths but much evidence of lava and a most distinct sulphuric smell: the soil seemed also to support an inordinate amount of azaleas, in full bloom even in May.

From Unzen it is no distance to Nagasaki. Apart from its recent unsought notoriety Nagasaki is interesting for its memories of the Dutch trading enclave during the Tokugawa period, Dejima; echoes of unfortunate Madame Butterfly evoked by the Glover mansion linking the Edo and Meiji eras; for the harbour and Mitsubishi shipyards; and for myself a curious perception that right at the epicentre of the atomic bomb there were many wooden buildings which appeared to be of much greater antiquity but had survived. Evocative both of early Christian believers, of Edo-era trade and Meiji international development, and of the rise of Japanese shipbuilding prowess,

Nagasaki would be an interesting destination even without its winding, hill-encircled harbour.

Leaving the coastal route by Sasebo, Hirado and the potteries of Imari and Arita for another time, I flew back to Osaka from Fukuoka – the little YS-11 seemed to take an age – for a further brief look at Kyoto, this time staying at the venerable Miyako Hotel, before returning to now-familiar Tokyo.

Thence to Hong Kong – which was basically work, visiting clients, but with some sightseeing of course, and an excursion on the Vickers junk from Aberdeen. This was the first of many sojourns in the wonderful Mandarin Hotel, enjoying the world's best Chinese food 'up top' and the *gwailo*-frequented Captain's Bar by the entrance. In contrast, I was kindly invited by the office manager to lunch at his flat halfway up the Peak and found that they subsisted exclusively on British food (mostly tinned) – admirable refusal to 'go native'!

Then, given the stopover possibilities on the 'southern route', Bangkok beckoned. It was not then the city of tall buildings it has (partly) become: the new tower of the Oriental Hotel had not yet been built, though supplementing the original colonial-era building an edifice of medium height had been constructed. It was a surprise to see a gecko lizard crawling up the wall inside the lift. Apart from enjoying river trips, floating markets and palaces, shopping for silk in every imaginable shade kept me busy.

Next stop on what was proving to be a lengthy trip was Iran. Teheran from the air looked absolutely enormous, brightly lit, and stretching as far as the eye could see. I was staying with Anthony and Sarah (née Drew) Wood: he being now First Secretary at the Embassy. Their house was in the salubrious northern suburbs: waking in the morning I was astounded to see the precipitous Elburz mountains practically overhanging the house. A spacious pool made for welcome relaxation after visiting the town, palace, Peacock Throne, and all.

I flew in a rather ancient Douglas plane with smoking engines down to Isfahan: across endless desert criss-crossed with the ancient subterranean water channels, fascinating to view from the air. Staying in a pretty little garden hotel recommended by Anthony, I ate once or twice in the more glossy hotel made from the ancient caravanserai in the centre. The Shah Mosque was enormous and impressive; Sheikh Lotfollah more refined, also in the great rectangular Naqsh-e Jahan Square, and the more ancient and perhaps more evocative Friday Mosque was north of the square. South of the city, I visited the Pul-e Khwaju bridge, up there with the Ponte Vecchio or the Pont du Gard in its multi-arched impressiveness. There was perhaps also a feeling of Córdoba – another great Islamic city – with the shallow river, gardens adjacent, the dun-coloured desert and hills rising beyond.

Asian Holidays

I was due to pay my second investment visit to Japan in September 1972: but had taken no holiday so determined to use my entitlement to increase my knowledge of Asia, after a taste the previous year. The first week was for India. Arriving at Srinagar it was of course pouring with rain, as it did incessantly for the next two days. I was staying at the Oberoi, which had been a residence of the Maharajah: a sprawling complex of low-built courtyards, rooms open to view with Indian families, to my surprise, cooking their evening meal inside. I had plenty of time to observe my surroundings, quite fascinating. I was glad I was not staying in one of the celebrated houseboats which were popular with British travellers at the time (even for ducal honeymoons): they were moored very close together and one could see that the water around was being used for every purpose… But the lake was beautiful, the floating gardens growing all sorts of vegetable produce fascinating, the rhythm of the paddlers hypnotic. Ashore, I did also explore the rather scruffy town of Srinagar: again, perhaps the most interesting feature was the floating markets, this time on punt-like craft. I took a cab along the lakeside to the Mughal Shalimar Gardens, perhaps the prototype of their genre; luckily, the weather had improved by then and the sun came out.

A longer car journey was up in the hills to Gulmarg ski resort and Sonamarg, to the foot of the pass which leads to Leh and Ladakh, full-blown Himalayan lands. There was a certain frisson in coming so close to Tibet and China. Nanga Parbat could occasionally be glimpsed through the clouds in its pure whiteness.

Leaving Kashmir, I flew first to Agra and then at last to Delhi. Agra was of course for the Red Fort and the Taj Mahal. The former impressed me greatly, for its site on the Jumna (with excellent view of the Taj), its massive red sandstone walls and in counterpoint the exquisite white marble of the little mosque and pavilions. But if I was pleasantly surprised by the Fort, I was simply struck dumb by the beauty of the Taj: one of those places, perhaps *the* place, where however much one expects to be enthralled its beauty far exceeds all expectations.

Then Delhi: a schizophrenic city and it is not easy to express a preference between the spacious avenues, villas and lawns of New Delhi and the ancient Mughal city to the north. My hotel was in southern New Delhi, and I found the scale of Lutyens' Viceregal Lodge (that was now the Rashtrapati Bhavan, the presidential palace), the Rajpath, the India Gate etc. so impressive. Not that that area is without its older monuments, and I found and find Humayun's Tomb a very close runner-up to the Taj: indeed, in many ways I rather prefer it as the less showy predecessor.

Scale, again, is perhaps what first hits one about the older town. The Red Fort is at least the equal of Agra's, again with the combination of monumental walls (no river close by, however) and delicate pavilions of white marble inside. Truly ugly barracks buildings erected by the British Raj merely serve as a counterpoint and reminder of India's mixed history. Across the way, the Jama Masjid (Friday Mosque) is truly awesome: the ascent up broad steps to the vast courtyard again stunning in its impression of scale: the elegance and symmetry of the domes and minarets; the beauty of the carved stonework. It is a haven of peace right beside the turmoil of Chandni Chowk and the congested streets of Old Delhi.

After getting used to the omnipresent poverty and squalor of India (a necessary corrective to any sense of First World complacency), there was the usual shambles of baggage reclaim at Bangkok's old airport dispelling the sense of arriving at an infinitely more prosperous country. I stayed at the Erawan in the middle of town, thus exchanging the fascinating scenes of river traffic by the Oriental for the shrine and a different urban scene. However, it was still the monsoon and poured relentlessly: the streets around the hotel were largely flooded. Soon I drove down to the much-hyped Pattaya in search of much-anticipated flopping on the beach. It was not to be: the rain continued, now enhanced by near-gale force winds: the beach was impossible and for the few days I was there the hotel was my refuge. Luckily in an otherwise-deserted hotel there was a very pretty and very nice young Lufthansa air hostess on her own.

... and Unexpected Residence

In Japan at last, three of us had two clients from Edinburgh for company visits and of course for a weekend expedition. This was to Hokkaido, where we enjoyed the bears in the Sapporo Zoo, then flew down to Hakodate at the southern tip. However, this being September we were overtaken by a typhoon. The Sunday night Hakodate-Tokyo flight was cancelled: Jeremy had an unbreakable Monday morning appointment with the Ministry of Finance in Tokyo to apologise for his temerity in denominating the new Nippon Fund in Japanese yen, so we had to re-book a very early flight from Sapporo and take a couple of taxis back there for the night, a long 200-kilometre journey in a typhoon, with the clients in one taxi while the three of us sorted out who was to take on the task of setting up an office in Tokyo which had suddenly become urgent. The lot fell on me: so, within a week I had been back to London, settled my affairs and returned to Tokyo to embark on the next posting of my career.

My role was now very different as I was resident and '*en poste*' and looking after visitors rather than visiting myself. Naturally, this brought a quite different rhythm to life in Tokyo and Japan generally. I was preoccupied with establishing the office – furnishings, staff, as well as looking for somewhere to live (for the first few months I had to slum it in the Hotel Okura, a 'second home' where in all I have spent well over two years). The office was in the Kabutocho area – specifically Koamicho – of Nihonbashi, close to the stock exchange. This is the ultimate 'shitamachi' or old-fashioned 'lower town'. It was mercifully rare to meet a *gaijin* or foreigner: indeed, when I went further uptown to Ginza or Marunouchi I was usually rather affronted to see such a thing. My Japanese speaking improved somewhat as I had to arrange many matters with monoglot Japanese; though both my second-in-command and my secretary were fluent in both, and the pressure eased. I was mostly consorting with Japanese brokers (of whom we were the clients) rather than with visiting British clients. So, both function and atmosphere changed notably in these altered surroundings.

Fortunately, a good friend, Robert Woods, was also in Tokyo for around a year on behalf of P&O (of which rather later he became Chief Executive). We had a number of memorable outings at weekends. In no particular order: we flew up to Sapporo, were hauled off the Olympic ski jump, drove (on some pretty poor unmade roads) to Lake Shikotsuko and the mini-Mount Fuji and overnighted in a ryokan by spectacular cliffs at Otaru: very Russian influence in all the old wooden buildings, and for a moment we fancied we could see the Russian coast across the sea – a mirage, however. Lakes and sea both had a complement of decrepit but picturesque fishing boats long since abandoned. The October colours were magnificent.

Another October trip was to Nikko, just for a Sunday. Again, the colours of the maples and cherries were spectacular, especially viewed from Lake Chuzenjiko where we went for a row: at the Toshogu Shrine, by contrast, the vast evergreen cryptomeria induced awe. The Irohazaka (= alphabet) drive of endless hairpin bends up to the lake was solid with trippers' cars: returning later, we estimated that we wouldn't be able even to board the last bus back to Nikko before the last train to Tokyo left. So, we commandeered a very sporting young couple who drove us down at speed on the hard shoulder, passing all the stationary traffic.

Other weekends were spent relaxing in Tokyo (Saturday morning chess with Bloody Marys in the much-missed old Orchid Bar of the Okura) or around, to Enoshima and Kamakura, Atami, or Yokohama for curry lunch on P&O ships. In midwinter we braved the night train from Shinjuku up to the Japan Alps to ski, trudging at midnight through a deep snowfield. Kyoto of course received several visits, mostly accompanying colleagues or clients: one especially memorable one was with Robert's mother and aunt, in the aftermath of my opening party at the Okura and shortly before Robert departed for home in the spring.

There were other friends and new acquaintances around, notably a group around Colin Chisholm and Chris Buttery who were Jardine Matheson 'cadets' stationed for a while in Japan. These two and myself had a trip to Taipei at Easter 1973: this was an interesting change after six months in Japan. (The informality of the Taiwanese/Chinese, especially at tourist sites and the superb National Museum, contrasted with the stiff formality of Japanese tourists photographing each other in grey suits.)

Mother Visits

Before that I had had a week off when my own mother came to visit. She arrived after a long flight with an overnight stop in Singapore, settled in at my Palace View (no such view available) apartment, and the next morning was sent off to explore Tokyo while I went to work as usual. In the evening she recounted how she had had a marvellous time going right round on the Yamanote line ('Circle Line') and was clearly becoming *au fait* with Tokyo's geography. We were entertained to lunch and dinner by kind friends and explored Tokyo further together. Then we set off in my Nissan Cedric to Nikko, picnicking on the old road between the ancient cryptomeria trees and spending the night in the historic old Kanaya Hotel. In contrast to the autumn, there was almost no one there. The wind howled among the mighty trees. Next day we could drive up to Chuzenjiko but it was definitely still winter in the Japan Alps and we found the road we had intended to take closed. Reversing our tracks and somehow finding a route through the mountains we emerged through the 'snow country' to the Japan Sea coast near Joetsu. The coastline between there and Toyama is spectacular, with the mountains as with Marathon 'looking down' upon the sea. We found a very subfusc-looking old ryokan perched on a cliff-ledge: they had probably never seen a *gaijin* before, especially unreserved and uninvited: but accepted us with equanimity and we dined and slept well on our futons in our shared room.

Through Toyama, next étape was pretty old Kanazawa with one of the three most famous gardens in Japan (official), and a charming district of samurai houses by the river, after which the country is flat until one reaches the coast of Fukui, then Kyoto prefectures. This has that indefinable 'west coast' feeling that has struck me in so many parts of the world: perhaps it is being a West Highlander... Kintyre, South Island New Zealand, north-west Spain and Portugal: somehow – not just the sunsets – they just could never be facing east. That Japanese coast had been much 'improved' the next time I drove along it a decade later: but in 1973 it had an air of forgotten, fading decrepitude – old fishing villages and fishing boats – which I found most seductive. Nearing Tsuruga, the scenery became more conventionally beautiful as we moved up Tsuruga Bay: a surprising amount of unspoilt sandy beaches among the pine forests. Tsuruga was another fine old town for a night's stop.

By this time, we were already in Kyoto prefecture and our final destination was calling. After climbing from the Japan Sea coast, it seems a long descent through picturesque old villages and then steep cryptomeria forests to the familiar northern outskirts of Kyoto itself. We stayed in the rather smart Japanese annex of the Miyako and so were well placed for the sights of Higashiyama... The last lap was a day-long trip along the Meishin and Tomei expressways back to the familiarity of 'home' in Tokyo. It was so good that my mother, not long widowed and 'abandoned' by her temporarily expatriate son, could make the long journey to the other side of the world, and really get to know what had been until then the abstraction of Japan. In the event this was her Japan visit No. 1 and a sequel was to come about some years later.

Expeditions with clients, colleagues and friends in my remaining months expanded my knowledge of the country: I remember those to the Inland Sea and Kyushu, to the lakes around Mount Fuji, to Kanazawa and the Japan Sea coast again. Cedric and Japan's brilliant railway network were kept busy. The Taipei gang had a weekend expedition to Shimoda, where Commodore Perry's expedition landed, at the end of the Izu Peninsula.

Way to Go Home: Birthday in Hong Kong

Unsurprisingly, my return to London was prolonged by a couple of stops, essentially for pure pleasure (it would be a shame to miss a stopover opportunity). First, to Hong Kong: there of course I was still among colleagues and indeed clients and friends (the categories are easily mixed). There was, however, no 'work'. I had my 30th birthday party on the Vickers junk, out of Aberdeen on the south side of Hong Kong island: my main memory is of being driven in an open MGB back and forth from the Indian restaurant in Central whence came all the goodies; and of a lovely evening cruise with much consumption of champagne, jumping overboard and frivolous warnings of sharks.

I had been conveyed to Hong Kong, appropriately enough, by BOAC VC10: the first leg of its Tokyo to Johannesburg flight, the next stops being Colombo and the Seychelles. Time, I suppose, did not run to an investigation of Sri Lanka; but a few days of sand and sea in the Seychelles had irresistible appeal. It was a brilliant interlude: the informality an enormous change from Japan. I stayed on the west coast of Mahé (the main island) in a 'cabine' at the Vista do Mar high above the shore. (There is a distinct difference, again, between the east coast, where the capital Victoria and the airport are, but which loses the sun early, and the west.) The form was to hire an Austin mini-jeep, a superbly simple and informal means of getting about wearing few clothes. So, I toured up and down the coast with its multitude of little sandy coves, from time to time leaping into the inviting water.

One activity I felt impelled to try was scuba diving. I heard of an Australian who provided introductory classes at a French-owned tourist hotel nearby: so, signed up. There was just me and a Jesus-bearded beatnik-type Brit: after an introduction, we donned our breathing apparatus, entered the pool and solemnly walked down from the shallow end to the deep end: where we sat, breathing rhythmically and feeling foolish. Looking up, I saw a group of just-arrived French tourists in 'normal' clothes peering down at us in utter mystification.

The next day (or two), it was time to try out new skills in the sea. We drove to a nearby cove and repeated the procedure: this time walking down the sloping sand until we were swimming (underwater). Being a sandy beach, there was not the magical transformation one experiences when immersed above and within a coral reef: but there were some rather magnificent-looking silvery fish. When we emerged our tutor (who had swum alongside) exclaimed 'Did you see the barracuda?'

Alas, there was no time or opportunity to visit some of the lesser islands such as Praslin, La Digue or Silhouette, which are warmly recommended; but pottering around Mahé in the little Mini-Moke was extraordinarily pleasant. The succession of little sandy coves with their huge boulders simply invited jumping in for a quick dip. Every day it rained on schedule between 3.00 and 3.15 p.m. – an alternative to bathing for the lightly clad.

However, it was time to return to the UK. Reintroduced to London office life (if in a different office and different role), it was not long before I and a few friends returned to the Côte d'Azur for a short villa sojourn near St Tropez: a 'cut-down' version of

1970 with some of the same participants. I do remember an awful lot of mosquitoes. Tahiti-Plage and boules by lamplight again featured strongly. There were to be further such south of France stays, whether villas or hotels, over the next two decades: it would be otiose to describe every one, but it has remained a constant love. In late 1973, however, I was preoccupied in negotiating a change of firm, and with the responsibilities of starting a new department in another firm opportunities for such leisure vacations disappeared for some time.

Sundry Trips

Another mini-tour with my mother was nearly three years later, in Greece, in 1975. In fact, I flew out alone to Athens, to meet her and extricate her from the British India Line's old SS *Uganda*, which for some time had been used for educational cruises for young people, but which carried a few conventional cruise passengers as well. Mama had been around the Levant visiting Cairo, Jerusalem, Beirut and other places: I was highly envious, and it was to be many years before I was to visit any of them. The ship was familiar to Mother as she had sailed to Kenya in 1954 on her sister ship the *Kenya*. I arrived at Piraeus and talked my way aboard; leaving for the Grand Bretagne after the drinks party she gave on board, it was with some difficulty that we explained to the port officials that she was now for the first time officially entering Greece, while I had already entered (with much bureaucracy of currency declarations etc. which were promptly binned by the Immigration officer) even if I was now coming from an extra-terrestrial (so to speak) ship! It took some time for officialdom to get their heads around that.

So, we drove straight back to the Grande Bretagne, for both of us reminiscent of our first visit nearly fifteen years before. I had hired a little Renault whose first outing hardly promised well, when the steering column-mounted gear lever came away in my hand on the Lycabettus hill. Quickly reinserted, however, it performed adequately over the next few days, spent mostly in the Peloponnese. The first phase inevitably took us past Corinth to the Argolid and the marvels of Mycenae, Tiryns and Epidaurus, heading for the Hotel Solon at Tolon – of course. The development of the village has indeed proceeded apace, as foretold to my parents a decade earlier: the hotel seemed in a time-warp and thus distinguishable from its upstart neighbours.

Through Argos, we penetrated into the mountainous Peloponnese heartland above: climbing into mist and fog, it became seriously chilly. With romantic evocations of the Wars of Independence and of the Peloponnese respectively, the temple at Bassae in its rocky fastness lost nothing by being enveloped in swirling cloud. The night was spent at Andritsaina, a picturesque little old village clinging to the hillside; then the descent to sunnier and warmer climes as we approached the Ionian around Pylos. Thucydidean and Homeric evocations seemed curiously absent, though the scenery was good. Rather than the classics, however, I was thinking more of Patrick Leigh Fermor and his descriptions of the southern extremities of the Peloponnese, where Byzantine and mediaeval memories predominate. We spent the night in the hotel at Methoni, by the beach, and in the morning roamed over the vast extent of the ruined castle, occupying the southern promontory, its surrounding walls reaching right to the seashore. Methoni is at the southern tip of the western 'finger' of the Peloponnese: by contrast with the evidence of past glory the present town seemed a collection of nondescript dwellings struggling northwards from the shore.

The following day took us deep into the Mani, archetypal Leigh Fermor (and feuding) country. Passing through the main town, Kalamata (of the olives), one is soon at Kardamyli where Leigh Fermor lived (when he was not at Pratt's). It's a pleasant little village on the hillside above the gulf, which one follows for a while until the distinct change to the wild 'Deep Mani' before Areopolis. There one sees the celebrated fortified towers in the very town centre from which families could pursue vendettas against each other (not unlike those of San Gimignano in Tuscany, though on a much smaller scale). The stony little town presages the arid mountain country as one drives south to the little cove of Yerolimin near the southern extremity of the peninsula, the mountainous spine louring over the road. Yerolimin itself had that 'end of the world' rather Cape Horn feeling, the seas surging in past steep cliffs to the tiny settlement.

Retracing our tracks, we passed by the slightly more substantial port of Gytheion before turning north and inland to Sparta. Despite its heroic name Sparta is a very ordinary little town on the plain, appositely reminiscent of a Roman legionaries' outpost in its square, grid-pattern arrangement. The hotel was itself unremarkable, though I remember a very nutritious moussaka. The main point of staying in Sparta, of course, is its handiness for visiting Mistras, which we did the following day.

Mistras (or Mystras or Mistra or Mystra) is perched on a ledge of the Taygetus mountains above Sparta: though wholly ruined now the city site is sufficiently dense, with around half a dozen major churches, palaces, fortifications all crammed together on the narrow site, climbing steeply to the castle at the summit. First built by the Franks, it was subsequently conquered and occupied by Byzantines, Turks and Venetians: the main impression remains Byzantine.

The same could have been said of our next stop, Monemvasia (= 'One Entrance'), the Gibraltar-like rock connected by a narrow causeway to the east coast of the third Peloponnese 'finger' (or toe?), which when we were there on a grey, distinctly Novembery day slumbered almost deserted, ruined and full of 'the last enchantments of the Middle Ages'. A melancholy place of deserted houses, fig trees growing from buildings, a shadow of the past (and future?) glory, it had not yet been tarted up and invaded by hordes of tourists. Now, however (I have not been back), it seems to have been woken from its slumber and reinvented as a tourist trap with restaurants, cafés and souvenir shops within the steeply ascending mediaeval walls: houses re-roofed, paths paved; and beach resorts sprung up on the mainland opposite. And all looks very attractive: but the press of tourists in summer must be considerable. We returned to Athens with a quick stop at Corinth and the canal: then flew back, two of us this time.

It was little more than a year later that I was back in these parts with Haruko; somehow it must have been fitted onto a return from the Far East. Again, after Athens we went down to stay at Tolon and it being June it was glorious to swim in the pellucid sea from the Solon's beach. We took a boat the short distance across the strait to Spetsai, a handsome little island town above its indented harbour with fine neoclassical houses. Together with Hydra, Spetsai had a reputation for shipbuilding and sea captains and played a vital part in the Greek War of Independence against the Turks. (Hydra, perhaps more trendy among international travellers, I have never yet been to.)

Endless Summer – 1976

After these relatively brief Greek experiences we immersed ourselves (in both literal and metaphorical senses) more fully in the summer of 1976. With the exception of the tour with my mother the previous spring we had had no holiday since moving to James Capel in spring 1974 and decided that even at the cost of virtually closing our department we would take no less than three weeks off in July. We found the Villa Agrambeli on the outskirts of Mytilene in Lesbos to rent for the three weeks and planned for a few good friends to join us at various points.

So it was that after weeks of the hottest summer yet known in England, Haruko, Jimmy and I took a charter flight at some ungodly early-morning hour from Gatwick to Athens. With several hours to spare before the connecting afternoon flight to Lesbos we took a taxi into central Athens and settled down to breakfast in Syntagma Square. It rained! However, it was not raining on arrival on the island, and I don't think ever did again. We found the *ΒΙΛΛΑ ΑΓΡΑΜΒΕΛΗ* or Villa Agrambeli easily enough and it looked ideal – capacious enough for a succession of good friends to arrive, duly spaced out with what overlaps there very congenial: nicely shaded on a quiet street, a balcony stretching all around the first floor. Rooms were chosen and we settled in and began to explore the town.

The villa was in the southern part of town, essentially a pleasant suburb separated from the town centre by parks and promenades: the old town starts at and circles an inner harbour area (with just some small fishing boats); the main drag, Hermes Street, winds north and uphill to another residential area overlooking a bay to the north. Thus, there is a quasi-isthmus leading to the castle occupying a spacious coastal site to the east, with the modern ferry port below it. Even in 1976 there was much evidence of a garrison presence both at the castle and in barracks elsewhere; and a destroyer used to come in every day from patrolling the strait between Lesbos and Turkey to tie up for a very long lunch break and siesta at the naval quay.

We found a rather battered pale blue Opel saloon to hire and explore the island: it didn't break down too often and we felt happy enough with it on pretty poor roads.

The team arrived in various stages, not all at once: Peter Mangold I believe early on, Hamish Aird shortly after and then Aubrey Lawrence; so, the road down the coast to the little airport became quite familiar. Lesbos is an island of remarkable variety: not too big, not too small, so it could all be taken in over the three-week period, though some places became favourites, mostly for beach and taverna-type activities. Mytilene lies in the south-east corner on a projecting peninsula, effectively the eastern side of a large inlet or lagoon separating it from the western parts of the island. Thus we frequently drove around through glorious beech woods to perhaps our favourite daytime place, Agios Ermogenis, a pretty sandy cove backed by pine forests and with the obligatory taverna. Further west along that south coast, but reached by a quite different road, was a larger place – a proper village – Plomarion, with a more open aspect and a long slightly pebbly beach, and notable for its ouzo. It was extraordinarily hot there. The hinterland to both was deep forest of beech and pine with deep ravines, in one of which lay the more sizeable town of the area, Agiassos: the guidebooks spoke of its 'calm bustle', and one would have to take their word for it.

The east coast was quite different, open country sloping down to the shoreline and with views of Turkey startlingly near to the east (and eventually north). Our day trips there were to a little village called Nea Kydonia, again with taverna beside an adequate beach, and itself an archetypal village sloping uphill where the men's principal occupation seemed to be sitting at tables in the street outside the cafés playing draughts and cards (no women visible).

The west and north of the island of Lesbos were quite different again: flat cultivated land with cypresses around the Gulf of Kalloni – the second huge 'bite' out of an otherwise triangular island, and a vast lagoon with the narrowest of exits to the sea, reached by more open cypress-fringed roads surrounded by endless olive groves. Northwards again led to the most arid part yet, leading to Petra on its wide bay and, at the northern tip of Lesbos, the small resort of Molyvos and at the very tip of the island the higgledy-piggledy town of Methymna crowned by the mini-acropolis Molyvos citadel standing guard over the narrow strait separating Lesbos from Turkey. We had an expedition there – fairly late on in our sojourn, and I believe it was only Aubrey who was with us; it was a few days earlier, after a celebratory (and quorate) farewell lobster barbecue in the villa garden, that I had seen Hamish depart on the rather smart *Arion* ferry for Piraeus (*Arion* alternated with *Sappho* on successive days) and remember sitting on the quay and watching it (can't say 'her'!) sail away.

Our most ambitious expedition, much earlier as it was only Haruko, Jimmy and myself, was in fact to 'Turkey-place' (as the Greeks called it). With Anatolia almost on the doorstep and relations somewhat easier in those days, a day trip across the strait beckoned. So in Mytilene harbour we boarded a little green vessel with an awning above an open deck for the short crossing to Ayvalik. Less quick though (easier relations or no) than the sea voyage were the customs and immigration formalities on the quayside. Eventually, however, we could board some contraption for the drive to the ancient ruins of Pergamum (now Bergama), one of the completest and most dramatically sited ruined cities of the ancient world: a stunning acropolis site with copious monuments, the better for not seeming over-restored or preserved – as tends to be the case in Turkey. The theatre is especially – well, dramatic. Drinking our fill of antiquity, we descended to the 'modern' town far below which had much charm also, and enjoyed sitting in the café in the square, taking in the scene of modest mosques, kebabs and general Turkishness. Then back to Greece after a full and enjoyable outing. I suspect such an informal day trip between the two countries might not be easy or agreeable today.

It had been a marvellous break and instilled the feeling that three weeks is about right for a proper summer holiday! However, only a month or so later I found myself using a further tranche of holiday 'leave' to spend a week or so in Nice and Corsica.

Summer Continues: Corsica

Rather like Hamish to Lesbos, but the other way around, I took the boat from Nice to Calvi but flew back. Calvi is an attractive place combining an old town on a promontory, inevitably housing a massive fort, with a long beach (ten miles or so?) with the usual accoutrements of beach bars and restaurants, and fine sand. There was a very adequate hotel there, so I had much swimming, but was anxious to explore, so hired a car and was off down the west coast. This has some of the most stunning scenery imaginable: deep *calanque* inlets guarded by impossible pinnacles of red rocks, as memorably and accurately portrayed by Edward Lear. Pine forests and lone pines clinging to the sheer cliffs provide a certain Chinese scroll quality also. After the most spectacular bit the scenery calms down (slightly) and one arrives at the little bayside settlement of Porto (not really a port, though a more recent development, Marine de Porto, has appeared below the fort guarding the bay). A wide but very shingly beach, reached by crossing the river, made for rather moderate bathing. The hotel was all right.

My scenic tour reached new heights with the dramatic hairpinned drive, inland but with sea views, to Piana and thence down to Cargèse and Sagone. Frustratingly one can't follow the coast by car – it would be wonderful by boat. Interestingly (in view of some earlier pages) Cargèse was settled by Greeks from the Mani escaping the Turks (and each other, with feuding). A Greek Catholic (not Greek Orthodox) church was built in the mid-nineteenth century, which was seen and painted by Lear: it faces directly opposite the 'Latin' Catholic church, of the same period. All this above a small fishing and pleasure harbour. Sagone, further down the coast and not far from Ajaccio, lies on a much more extensive bay and has become a well-developed resort. Thence I struck inland over mountainous terrain to Corte, a more important, central town with a highly improbable fortress which looks as if it could topple off its rock, and down to the coast at l'Ile-Rousse and thence to Calvi, Nice and home.

In Andalucia, 1977

After a long summer stint in the office September 1977 presented another Continental fortnight of both beach and culture, this time to Andalucia. Haruko, Jimmy and I were joined by Nigel Blackwell to make up a congenial foursome. Flying to Malaga, we were based at the modern beachside hotel at Fuentebravia on the west coast: the long beach stretches from Puerto de Sta. Maria up to the naval base at Rota, and its fine sands made for wonderful bathing, so that aspect of a summer holiday was well taken care of: it was hot! There was, though, much culture too. El Puerto is a delightful and (certainly then) unspoilt little town of mainly grid pattern streets of fine town houses with enclosed balconies, a Moorish/Reconquista castle with the appropriate 'toytown fort' battlements and towers, cathedral, bullring, sherry bodegas… We enjoyed spending time there and drinking in the atmosphere as well as the sherry.

Not far, conveniently, are both Sanlucar de Barrameda, the home of manzanilla, and Jerez that unsurprisingly of sherry. As recounted earlier, I had been to Jerez before, in 1965, and was delighted to see it again: it looked very much as it was. Again, we visited the Gonzalez Byass bodegas which are always welcoming. Sanlucar I had not seen before: a much more modest place – no domed and buttressed cathedral – but with a fine site as the Guadalquivir debouches into the ocean. I recall mainly vast dishes of seafood at a roadside restaurant one night, giving great pleasure – to others.

Of course, we also took a trip across to Cádiz, which had lost none of its charm. No cockfights seemed to be on offer, mercifully (the reader may recall my visit to Cádiz a dozen years earlier). However, retracing that 1965 excursion we did journey inland to my old haunt of Ronda. I found that very much changed: a sleepy little town with only a few vehicles had become a tourist centre. A *parador* had appeared – about time – beside the Tajo gorge and the main drag was pullulating with mainly tourist life. We visited Spain's most venerable bullring and 'El Jimi' (sobriquet by Nigel, in Andalucian accent) did an excellent imitation of a bull evading the matador, Nigel. In the old town, my former home the Casa de Mondragón had reverted to the state, was open to the public and had been absurdly promoted to Palacio. The once virtually empty streets had filled to overflowing with cars. Ronda had been polished and 'civilised' with modern commerce supplementing old-fashioned sleepy charm.

Driving back down to the coast through the Sierra de Ronda, I found the little hill towns, Grazalema and Zahara, much changed also: where there had just been a handful of small white houses in cobbled lanes around a little church, there were now banks, bars and other appurtenances of modernity. Their picturesque appearance from afar, huddled below sheer mountains, remained as before. We stopped for a while in Arcos de la Frontera, perhaps the most prominent of the Pueblos Blancos; the 'white town' sits on a high ledge, west-facing, the last before the descent to the sea, its natural fortifications of high cliffs reinforced by an impressive array of walls and watchtowers.

We left the principal towns of Córdoba and Seville, new to me so comparisons with the past not possible, to last, leaving the coast to begin our journey home. This stage was not without its complications. We stopped on a hillside not far from Córdoba – for the view? – but on arrival in Córdoba found that Nigel's 'handbag' in which among other things was his passport was missing. So, it was back to the exact layby where we had stopped and where Nigel knew he had taken the bag out of the car and exactly where he had put it. It wasn't there – or anywhere nearby. Thieves seem to work fast in these parts. There was little we could do that day as we settled down to enjoy Córdoba, which I find the most attractive of the Andalucian cities. We were staying at the Maimonides, an historic and not too grand hotel perfectly placed in the square almost next door to the great cathedral/mosque and gave a pleasing aura of one of the great figures of the Middle Ages and of the Spain of the Caliphate.

This has to be one of the world's most extraordinary buildings: the great square area pillared with innumerable double-arched Moorish columns, then inserted in the centre this quite incongruous elaborate Gothic-Renaissance-Baroque cathedral – the only 'indoors' cathedral I can think of. The combination and the contrast in fact work marvellously well. Outside also is the contrast between the Islamic walls and gateway and the Christian bell tower – itself owing much to the minaret. From the higher vantage point of the Alcázar gardens, however, what had seemed an entirely enclosed or interior edifice shows its verticality, soaring, supported by flying buttresses and crowned by a pyramidal tower, above the acres of *mezquita* roof. The gardens are an enchanting paradise of greenery, palm, and orange tree terraces above the Guadalquivir, whose waters through an ingenious system of conduits supply its extensive pools, and which look down on the massive Roman bridge recalling Córdoba's first origins.

Seville, of course, was the final lodestar and we somewhat reluctantly followed the river downstream: we had business there anyway to obtain a temporary document from the British consulate to replace Nigel's passport. This was eventually achieved, and we were free to explore. The cynosure, naturally, was the cathedral which astounds by its sheer size – in fact the largest Gothic cathedral in the world. In contrast to Córdoba the Islamic mosque was demolished with the Reconquista and a wholly new Gothic cathedral built; the spectacular Giralda bell tower, built as the minaret of the great mosque, found itself topped with a Renaissance construction for the Christian bells to replace the muezzin. More than anything, its mass is comparable to the great Koutoubia minaret at Marrakech. The whole cathedral complex is completed by the superb Patio de los Naranjos, its symmetrical rows of mature orange trees providing an intimate yet grand frame for views of the cathedral and the Giralda. The overwhelming impression is of great size, but also of great delicacy of ornament.

Evocations of the Islamic period persist in Seville, as also of the Christian reconquest, the exploration of the New World and even the nineteenth century of Carmen and the tobacco factories and bullfights. Unlike in upstream Córdoba, there is also a real whiff of the sea with a much broader river and genuine workaday docks, guarded by the solitary multifaceted Torre del Oro: thirteenth century but even in its name hinting at the riches of the New World and the shades of Christopher Columbus.

We walked quite a lot around the centre, a much more spacious affair than Córdoba but perhaps less atmospheric, with the exception of the Juderia Jewish quarter. I don't recall where we dined or stayed, but petty crime returned when the next day we found our hire car had been stolen. Luckily with few people in a smallish car we'd taken most of our luggage indoors, though I believe Jimmy lost some artworks he had been creating: there may have been more. So, more office visits and explanations, and instead of a replacement hire car we took a taxi to the airport. Remembering my first experience of Spain in Barcelona in November 1965, it seemed somehow appropriate if unfortunate that this latest Spanish excursion should be signed off with another automotive heist!

Weekending at the Ends of Japan

I shall write shortly, compressing the chronology, of how we visited China on the way back from Japan: in 1977, 1978 and 1979. In 1978, when we had Simon Nicholson with us, we also spent the weekend before in Kyushu. We hired a car in Fukuoka and drove along the north-west coast: first to the porcelain centres of Imari and Arita, then to Hirado island and town, crossing by the dramatic new scarlet suspension bridge. First the Portuguese, then the Dutch and (for a short period in the seventeenth century) the British East India Company used Hirado as their base for trading with Japan: eventually the Dutch too were evicted by the shogunate to the smaller island of Dejima in Nagasaki bay.

Christianity introduced by these pioneers survived even in 'hidden' form under the persecution of the Tokugawa shogunate, and remains relatively strong in this area, evidenced by some prominent churches (St Francis Xavier Catholic Cathedral looks almost poised to take off from Cape Canaveral!). Of course, there has been considerable restoration, including of the Dutch warehouse area: nevertheless, the legacy of the former trading enclave can still be sensed.

Now in Nagasaki prefecture, we passed through and briefly stopped at Sasebo, of similar memories and now one of Japan's major naval ports: many destroyers and frigates could be seen in the near-landlocked harbour. A further short drive beside the even larger and even more landlocked Ōmura Bay brought us to Nagasaki.

Nagasaki of course is known the world over as having been devastated by the atomic bomb; yet just as on my previous visit in 1971 I was surprised by how much that is, or at least appears, old remains. It again is very much a port city and with its orientation towards China, Korea and places West has always been cosmopolitan and outward looking. It has very personal connotations for Haruko as her father's boyhood was spent there, his father being chief naval architect at the great Mitsubishi shipbuilding yards (still there). We paid a respectful visit to the monument to her aunt who died in infancy: though she herself was Baptist this was erected by the priests of Shuntokuji Buddhist temple, where she used to go to play, who loved her greatly.

Another weekend expedition with Simon, after a week of gruelling company interviews, was to the extreme other end of Japan, northern Hokkaido. We flew up to Kushiro near which we could see no great number of its famous cranes, picking their way stealthily across the grasslands. Thence we drove inland to the Akan-Mashū National Park, wherein lie the two volcanic lakes of Kussharo-ko and (the much smaller) Mashū-ko. The latter in particular is quite remarkable, almost circular with sheer cliffs from the viewing spot all round the lake, itself in a deep woodland setting. Kussharo-ko's site is much more open and has good views of volcanoes on either side. By the lakeside could be found tastefully placed groups of indigenous Ainu people in their 'native' dress. The lakes themselves contain an even rarer inhabitant: *marimo*, curious spherical dark green 'moss balls' (actually algae) – like velvety tennis or ping pong balls.

Having gazed on these wonders we set off the next morning for the far north. Not far from Teshikaga the main road stretched far into the distance, flat and straight as a die. The speed limit was 60 kph or 36 mph; there were few if any other cars. I persevered within the limit for what seemed an age until with the end of the restriction in sight I put my foot down a bit. Almost immediately I was waved down; the surprised cops saw that this was a *gaijin*, who could not be expected to understand Japanese highway codes, and issued no more than a mild reproof.

Arriving at the coast, a very 'northern' sea presented itself with chillier versions of the Japan Sea fishing hamlets I had known further south. A stop was immediately made to purchase a gigantic spider crab whose 'leg-span' must have been at least four feet. This was avidly consumed by Simon and Haruko with much crunching (and expressions of pleasure) while I drove on impassively. We followed the coast of the Shiretoko Peninsula to the point where one can go no further – the national park, off limits to cars, occupies the extremity. (In fact, Shiretoko is the north-eastern rather than northern extremity of Hokkaido, Cape Soya near Wakkanai being the northernmost, with Russian Sakhalin little more than twenty miles away and clearly visible on a fine day.)

Not being able to see anything so exotic, we retraced our steps, sad to leave this lonely and evocative coastline (I should love to see it in winter when the sea is frozen!). The haunting melody of 'Shiretoko', my favourite together with 'Hana', may have rung in my ears as night fell and I drove on thinking of evening meal deadlines at our destination hotel at Teshikaga. But it was not from inattention that I slowed rather than stopped as our road joined a more major road at an angle: I could see perfectly well that nothing was coming from any direction. However: almost at once a policeman with a scarlet illuminated baton jumped out and I was invited into the van. I had to admit that yes, it was us they had stopped in the morning, apologise profusely, and play the dumb foreigner ('Oh, I thought it was just advisory...'); during which Haruko the fluent Japanese speaker remained concealed lying down in the back of the car... Anyway, the cops clearly thought one was a lost cause and we were on our way again.

Back on the Continent

These late years of the 1970s, mentioned earlier, saw a number of quick add-ons to Europe following trips by me or others of us to Japan. 1978 was a good year: first, in May, I stopped off very briefly in Vienna on the way back. It was just a weekend but the *gemütlich* flavour was as ever enticing and a pleasant reintroduction to Europe's quintessential culture. I stayed in the Hotel Bristol – just affordable for a night or two – extreme though discreet luxury directly opposite the Staatsoper: alas here was nothing to go to in the time I had. Having 'done' Vienna fairly comprehensively in 1969 and 1971 I was fairly familiar, and I think stayed in the centre gently strolling. The main difference of course was that this was May not November and the city's greenery was startling.

Two months later we were visiting clients in Milan and after a fairly brief look-around decamped to Venice for the weekend. Staying at the Gritti opposite the Salute was glorious, especially eating outside on the projecting deck as the luminous twilight fell and the gondoliers glided past. The room was equally splendid. We went to the nearby Accademia as well as to churches and palaces; and for the first and only time took a gondola trip around canals grand and minor – a possibly overrated experience, though the perspective of the canals was from canal level perhaps better and more 'genuine'.

We also went together to Munich, to see clients in the Bavarian banks, but also to see the sights, most notably the Alte Pinakothek but also places like the cathedral (Frauenkirche), the Rathaus, many other churches and palaces and the Englische Garten by the Isar, a haven of greenery apparently larger than New York's Central Park. Then we drove south towards the ever-looming Alps into the land of fantastically ornamented Baroque and Rococo churches and abbeys, and of course of the castles of Mad King Ludwig. We spent a night at Garmisch-Partenkirchen, a perfectly pleasant little town which exists now principally for the skiing in winter. It's not far from Oberammergau which, so far, I have avoided visiting at Passion Play time, and never will, though I have a sneaking curiosity and interest about doing so.

In their different ways, which is mainly a matter of scale, the church of Wies and the abbey of Ottobeuren are simply superb. The Wieskirche is a pilgrimage church, alone on an eminence; lovely in its setting, the real glory is revealed in its Rococo splendour with every surface painted or sculpted: white and gold predominating and a well-populated painted ceiling substituted for the sky, with the heavenly host. Ottobeuren, by contrast, occupies (again on an eminence) much of the centre of a small town, the Baroque successor to a twelfth-century abbey which burnt down and struggled on for centuries half-ruined. The present abbey church was built only in the eighteenth century and though indubitably Baroque does not have quite the Rococo confectionery aspect of the Wies. Inside, however, is decorated and colourful enough for anyone. The crowning glory is the organ – actually more than one – and its music programme is world-famous.

We drove fairly quickly around the Bavarian alpine foothills and stopped to see Ludwig's absurd but rather imposing castles, but only from the outside, perhaps mercifully... Both have hilltop sites, among woods but with good views of the lakes, the Hohenschwangau nearer the village. Neuschwanstein is more attractive and peculiar in its verticality, emphasised by its totally absurd turrets. The views from a distance are good too, whether from above (with lake) or below. Then it was back to Munich and the airport and home.

Family Skifests – Three Years Running

Alpine visits of a different variety took place over three Christmases and New Years over the turn of the decade, 1978, 1979 and 1980: skiing with Archie and Fiona, Jamie and Rosamund and my mama. The first year was at La Plagne in the French Maurienne: flying to Geneva, there was a long bus drive up past Moûtiers and Aime for the resort. This was a newish purpose-built resort and entirely soulless – no matter. I had a room in a largish block of flats with, of course, a restaurant and bar, and rooms for ski storage and boot-onputting. First of course was the ski hire performance and then essaying the slopes, of which there was a good variety from easy to extreme (black runs). For the children it was ski school on the nursery slopes: they very soon picked it up and Jamie was soon hurtling down in typical fashion. Rosamund learnt quickly and like her mother became a stylish and accomplished skier: she still goes skiing every year. Fiona and I accompanied each other: though outclassed (I had done very little skiing since Norway – just the occasional mad, heather and rock in Glencoe, Zermatt and Villars when collecting Fiona from being 'finished' in 1962, Connecticut and New Hampshire in 1966–68, and a rather snow-free Gstaad in 1974–5), I at least managed to catch up most of the time. It was exhilarating to be up high with the extensive views over the Vanoise mountains, towards Tignes and Val d'Isère. Of course, there are trails across to these various resorts, but we stayed at La Plagne – apart from anything else there was meeting up at lunchtime, much vino and hearing how the young had fared. Mother too had donned skis and was happy pottering on the lower slopes. Being midwinter, it was dark early, and the hotel was somewhat gloomy (a place where all the lights turned off automatically): nevertheless, we had cheerful evenings of fondue, wine, liqueurs…

Next year was Isola 2000, much further south and very near to the Italian border at that point. I flew on Christmas Day 1979 to Nice, where it had snowed: the one time I have seen it under snow and very attractive it looked. I stood myself a night and Christmas dinner at the Negresco and in the morning set off for the bus station and the winding journey up the Tinée to Isola, where I found the family. I was suitably attired in the blue padded cotton Mao coat which I had bought in Peking the previous month (and still have, though not worn in recent years!). I remember that this was just the time of the fall of the Shah of Iran. Isola accommodation was not so different from La Plagne, but the place generally seemed sunnier and more 'southern' than La Plagne, if not quite 'Mediterranean'. I think we all made progress in our varied skiing abilities.

Then we move a year on, to December 1980, this time to Verbier in Switzerland. Again, I had to meet them out there, presumably for work reasons. This time I was in a different hotel from them (it being of course 'no room at the inn' season), at least as nice as the one the others were in. Switzerland (which I knew quite well but was to get to know extremely well) seemed indefinably different from France, at least as far as ski places were concerned: perhaps older money and more established chalets. There were long queues for chairlifts, stunning views when one arrived 'up top', somewhat fearsome descents (I think I may have tried at least one 'black run'). In the evenings we often met up with the Harvie-Watts, great friends (Roselyne in fact is Swiss) who have a lovely chalet there. That I think was the last skiing until some expeditions from Montreux up to Villars in the 1990s – and more since. Again, I returned earlier, without them, as I was shortly to visit Japan etc. and had to finalise arrangements.

China in the Seventies

1977 saw the eventual realisation of the long-standing dream of visiting the People's Republic of China. Scrolling back a bit, we had in fact caught a glimpse in 1976, shortly after Mao's death. We had had no success in getting visitor or tourist visas, but I discovered from the invaluable ABC (these were the days of fixed timetables and prices for all airlines) that Iran Air flew on Friday evenings from Tokyo to Teheran via Peking (as I insist on calling it in English usage). Though we could not stay in Peking, at least we could get a glimpse of the airport; whether we could 'deplane' to the terminal we couldn't know.

In the event the answer was 'no'; but in the fog of a November night it was still rather eerie to see the vast image of the Chairman gazing at us from the terminal building. The People's Liberation Army (or Red Guards?) in the form of a troop of little bespectacled girls in green fatigues and gym shoes came aboard and engaged with the crew in what looked suspiciously like black market negotiations. Then we took off for an interminably long flight to Teheran, most of which I spent trying to sleep on the floor across the three seats of economy class.

The flight ended in anti-climax and disappointment: while Haruko passed immigration without any problem, I was met with a definite negative 'yok' (cf. Robert Byron). This was apparently because my passport had been renewed in New York with a C prefix, so I could not be a pukka Brit and allowed in. Protestations and explanations were in vain. A counter-productive interjection by a rather languid Foreign Office man in the queue behind sealed my fate. An interview with a swarthy unshaven official produced a concession that we could stay if within 24 hours the British consul in Shiraz – where we had hoped to go – would vouch for me. It was not hard to refuse this. If indeed there was a British consul in Shiraz, on a Saturday afternoon he was likely to be on the golf course and unsympathetic (I may be unfair, but the FO was suffering severe cuts). Neither the airline nor the hotel had replied to my booking telexes of weeks earlier, so the chances of being left stranded seemed high.

The question therefore was: where was Iran Air flying in the next few hours? One answer was 'Rome', which suited us fine for an agreeable weekend, even if we were passing up Hafiz and Omar Khayyam for Horace and Ovid. But first there was the considerable hassle of retrieving our luggage, re-booking etc; mostly done by Haruko who was legally 'in' Iran, and had the dubious pleasure of racing to and from the 'other' terminal to change the ticket. I met the Catch-22 that in order to leave Iran I had momentarily to enter it, somewhat alarming with a man pointing a rifle at me.

The flight seemed unsure of its whereabouts over a snowy Yugoslavia, reporting an identical position after an interval of an hour, but did get to familiar Rome where we had an enjoyable if unscheduled weekend at the Eden.

Returning to China after this 'overture': somewhat later the Chinese chargé d'affairs came to lunch at Capels and said we must come and visit China. We said we had been trying to do precisely that but were not allowed visas: at which he said the way to do it was to get a transit visa, possible if one had arrived at Peking to change to another airline whose flight was not leaving for a day or two. So having consulted the invaluable ABC again, I found that on Friday evenings a PIA flight to Karachi stopped at Peking; there was then no other westbound flight until Swissair to Geneva on the Monday evening. Perfect: of course, we needed to visit our Swiss clients after an investment trip to Japan. And so it came to pass.

Mao looked down impassively as we entered the curiously

old-fashioned terminal. Forms were filled in on benches with antimacassars and handed to officials in high wood- and glass-panelled eyries. We boarded the inevitable pale grey-green 'Shanghai' car and trundled down the straight poplar-lined road to the city. In the dusk there was little traffic except for horse-drawn carts crowded with people in quilted khaki coats and fur hats. There was a weird flashback to my first ever experience of northern French roads before dawn in 1953. I had reflected that, no longer on an island, one was at one end of a land mass stretching to Boulogne and could – at a pinch! – walk it.

In Peking we stayed, of course, at the Peking Hotel ('Beijing Fandian'): strictly off-limits to most Chinese, but open for 'foreign guests' and the cadres, for whom the different classes in the vehicle hierarchy – the 'Red Flag' Rolls-Royce rip-off, the Shanghais, the khaki jeeps – were arranged within the gates. We were allocated a spacious room each on different floors: I remember the fine fawn-coloured cashmere blankets. On the corner, the view was down Chang'an avenue: precisely the same viewpoint as for the famous film of the sole protestor and the tank at the Tiananmen Square incident in 1989.

We could hardly wait to walk along the avenue to the Forbidden City. Motionless soldiers with bayonets fixed lined the dimly lit avenue, just a few feet apart. At the Tiananmen gate Mao was again shining down through the mist. Unexpectedly, we could pass through and walk up to the massive and awe-inspiring Wu Gate. At night that was as far as we could go. The whole experience was overwhelming and somewhat sinister.

In the morning of course we lost no time in repeating the walk. On a bright but cold morning the atmosphere was transformed. Bicycles, trucks, and jeeps sped along the avenue: just the occasional car. Tickets were had from a little wooden hut in front of the Wu Gate: when my turn came, I said 'Er…' to the old woman who immediately produced two tickets without looking up: I was ridiculously proud of my prowess in Mandarin.

We proceeded through the vast courtyards and imposing halls.

The former was limited to the central strip as replacement of the paving stones was proceeding. The latter were pleasingly faded and had not yet suffered the 'improvement' of being garishly repainted. There were remarkably few people about: men and women dressed in shapeless baggy trouser suits in combinations of grey, blue and khaki-green, sometimes combined and sometimes overall. There were clearly acres of unopened halls on either side, and very little in the way of objects except at the altars in the halls on the central axis. The marble ramps up to the halls with their dragons and clouds were especially memorable.

Everywhere we were the object of great if rather cautious curiosity. I was certainly the only person there who did not have (or had had) black hair: Haruko the only one in 'non-standard' dress (the Moscow airport-bought fox tippet a matter of especial curiosity to little girls who came up to finger it). I don't remember seeing another foreigner.

Exiting by the northern gate looking onto Drum Hill, there was the question of how to get back to the hotel. The few Shanghais parked there were clearly not for hire; there were no taxis. Luckily, I had a map of the city – not something obtainable in China, and itself a thing of great curiosity to the locals: it showed that the no. 3 bus went down the east side of the Forbidden City then turned left along Chang'an straight to the Peking Hotel. After a bit of a wait, lo and behold an ancient single-decker bus appeared, exhibiting the number 3 and clouds of evil black smoke. We boarded it – I don't remember paying – and fascinated, timid but essentially friendly passengers backed away to give us adequate space.

Inevitably, we took a car up to the Great Wall (at Badaling) and the Ming tombs. The road was full of horse-drawn carts, often crammed, and mainly military traffic of jeeps and trucks. A superb Ming gateway is the precursor to the short stretch of the wall which was open, permitting a surprisingly steep climb up to a watchtower. From there I was surprised to see stretches of wall marching off in several different directions. Looking north, we had a sense of the immensity of the Mongolian plains from which the Manchu eventually succeeded in breaching the wall(s).

It was on this first occasion that our (not very skilled) driver skidded on an icy patch and left the side of the car millimetres from a precipitous drop to the river far below. Nevertheless, we made it to the relative safety of the valley of the Ming tombs. Fewer, I believe, were open or even excavated then: the upside was that the whole area was left as natural, without the paraphernalia of railings, notices, and tourist infrastructure. Thus, for example, children could clamber over the camels or other beasts in the long, then unpaved, approach – to my mind the most charming feature of that site.

We returned in each of the two following years, with Simon Nicholson in 1978 and Peter Thistlethwayte in 1979: naturally, we repeated these 'highlights' each time, though I become somewhat hazy about which we saw in which order. What was very noticeable though was that the sense of 'pioneering' of 1977 was quickly reduced in subsequent years as more foreigners appeared in Peking. One might not necessarily have expected to bump into a friend on the Great Wall, but in the second (?) of these years we encountered Mr Shintaro Sakata, of Daiwa Securities, and a special friend. By 1979 there were even some Americans! The homogeneity of communist dress was diluted by vulgar casual outfits of foreign tourists.

It was certainly in 1977 that we explored Liu Li Chang, the antiques district just south of Tiananmen Square, and made some modest purchases. Beyond the shopping, the back streets were still the old grey 'hutongs', single-storey and full of atmosphere: the vast identical apartment blocks were already looming, and I believe have almost entirely obliterated them.

We managed to make an appointment for dinner at the Peking Duck restaurant in that area, south of the Drum Gate. Our reservation had to be for 4.30. For a very few yuan we had I think fourteen courses, all duck of course (I persuade myself that there was even duck ice cream). There was no one else there except for a small group of Canadian military attachés – after all it was late! After dinner we went down to the kitchen to see the ducks, in a row of course, in their oven. Two years later we were paying twice as much for half the number of courses.

Non-antique shopping meant Wangfujing, round the corner from the hotel: there was 'the department store' and 'the supermarket'. Beautiful and heavy silks were to be found in abundance: Budd made up lovely white silk shirts and Henry Poole a black cashmere overcoat as a result. We had lunch at the supermarket: we had to wait behind to be seated at a large round table while the seated diners gobbled down their lunch.

Of course, there are many marvellous things to see in Peking and I am unsure how many times or in which year we visited each. Certainly, in the first year, 1977, Haruko and I went to the Peking Zoo to see the pandas (greater and lesser). The former has an enclosure in which they can munch bamboo all day, observed by the zoo visitors from a covered structure looking on to it, and of course entered from the rear. When we went in, one among the Chinese who had been intently studying the pandas' table manners noticed the arrival of a far more exotic species. As word spread the entire room turned to gawp at these exotica – the pandas quite forgotten (I don't remember that the pandas showed especial interest in us). We also saw the 'lesser panda' (not really a panda at all) – a handsome chap in reddish brown rather like a more vivid fox.

Further out to the west was the Summer Palace, as notoriously looted and burnt by the British and other Westerners putting down the Boxer Rebellion. The site is picturesque, the lake pretty, the ascent to the tower gives an excellent view of that and the western hills; but my principal feeling was that Chinese taste had deteriorated considerably during the nineteenth century.

My strictures on the repainting of the most iconic structures, applied to the Forbidden City, are even more applicable to the Temple and Altar of Heaven. In 1977 they were pleasingly shabby and subfusc, but by the 80s had become lurid and 'jazzy'. (That is, of course, as they would have looked originally; one might make a comparison with brightly coloured pre-Reformation English churches, now mercifully 'toned down'.)

It is sad to think of the great walls of Peking, now wantonly destroyed: some remnants remain, one of them the old Observatory with giant, weird orrery-and-armillary-type instruments of wrought iron or bronze. A great eminence is the Drum Hill immediately north of the Forbidden City, which also we have visited more than once.

In the last of these three years, 1979, we also visited Shanghai. We did not have the stamps in our passports permitting this, but we did have the air tickets; so we turned up at the airport fully expecting to be told 'No Go'. However, we were allowed to board the Russian airliner (Peter with a first-class ticket, oddly, in the middle section and the two of us in business equivalent at the front). Arriving at Shanghai was another hurdle: told we were not supposed to be there, we feigned surprise and bowing to the inevitable (there were no further flights out that day) the officials amiably let us in and booked us in the Jin Jiang skyscraper hotel.

Arriving there it was of course the usual pretence. We were told that the hotel was chock-a-block: there remained only three corner 'suits' on three successive floors. As with the Peking Hotel, we were fine with that; from the sole high-rise building there were fine views down the Nanking Road to the old single-storey suburbs stretching into the far distance. There was of course hardly anyone else staying in the hotel.

Obviously, we were keen as soon as possible to get down to the river, to the Bund and the old pre-war buildings such as the Peace Hotel and the Hongkong Bank building. They stood solid and grimy; the streets were virtually deserted. We lunched at the Peace (ex-Cathay) Hotel: there were a few ideologically pure-seeming Eastern bloc or Third World diners too, and a wonderful time-warp jazz band featuring a saxophonist, exact clone of the one at the Marine Hotel in North Berwick *circa* 1950. Lunch was fine, though dinner that or another night in the Shanghai specialist restaurant in the Confucian sage's garden was especially delicious.

We had discovered that this was the first week in which foreigners would be allowed to travel on the excursion boats which plied the Whangpoo River from the quays on the Bund to the confluence with the Yangtze: so naturally bought tickets to board. Especial interest was provided by the Chinese navy whose ships – few larger than corvettes or patrol boats – lined the far bank, all painted in a fetching tone of palest duck-egg blue. A loudspeaker warned anyone against photographing these: naturally that served as a challenge. There was a very obvious security man who stood on the upper deck surveying everyone from behind blank dark glasses. However, our tickets included the use of a cabin on the 'promenade deck' to which, it having no front wall, one could retreat and unobserved click away. Rather like a Japanese ryokan, the space by the rail contained wicker table and chairs at which one could sip delicious tea. And so, the river slipped by.

Eventually we did reach the confluence: the far shore seemed an infinity away, until one realised that that was merely a mid-channel island, which was not even halfway across! As with other major confluences – Ganges–Jumna, or Rhône–Saône for example – there was a complete and sudden change in colour and clarity as one body of water met the other.

These visits in three successive years already showed enormous changes as China began to grow up after the Mao era: however – I am getting ahead of myself – that was nothing to the transformation seen in my two more recent visits, in 1987 and 1999. The most obvious changes, it goes without saying, were in traffic – by 1989 the streets, sparsely populated in the 1970s by military and official vehicles and carts, and over-populated by bicycles, had become a tangle of flyovers choked with traffic, a good deal of it taxis; buildings – a steady encroachment of vast apartment blocks and destruction of the 'hutongs', and of course a transformation at street level with shops, restaurants and above all with advertisement hoardings; and in the dress of the people, drab Mao suits exchanged for Western dress, often rather garish. This was perhaps the point at which it was easiest to fall for the observation that China was becoming essentially similar to the West. How wrong we were!

Venice and Palladio, 1980

In May 1980 I managed to escape with my mother for about ten days to Venice and the Veneto. One main theme of this trip was to hunt down as many of Andrea Palladio's creations as possible. In Venice itself, where we stayed in the Luna at the western corner of the Piazza (and very convenient for Harry's Bar!), the great churches, the Redentore and Sta. Maria Maggiore, were the prime examples (nor were the Basilica, Doge's Palace, Accademia etc. ignored). Picking up a car and venturing onto the mainland the first of the *terrafirma* villas to be 'knocked off' was the Malcontenta (Villa Foscari); though others' villas along the Brenta Canal were taken in too. A brief visit to Padua naturally counted Giotto's marvellous frescoes in the Scrovegni chapel as the highlight; the cathedral of St Anthony of Padua also is highly impressive with its multitudinous domes and vaguely oriental air. (Rather to my surprise, I recently found that a quick prayer to St Anthony resulted in soon finding whatever it was I had lost!)

Westward took us to the Palladian city *par excellence*, Vicenza. Here his genius is shown in diverse forms of urban architecture: some imposing (the Basilica, the Palazzo Chiericati, of a notable elegance); some quirky or incomplete (the two bay-wide Palazzo Porto in Piazza Castello, or the Palazzo del Capitaniato, narrow, tall, ornamented); or again the side-street palazzi which endow the streetscape with an indefinable elegance and originality: palazzi Valmarana, Thiene, Schio, Porto (again). The Teatro Olimpico is an extraordinary one-off: what spectacles and *divertimenti* it must have seen! We stayed at the Jolly Hotel in a park nearby.

The Palladian jewel of Vicenza must of course be the Villa Rotonda, on its eminence overlooking the city. One of these buildings which can only be described as simply perfect and inspired, its four-ways façades are deceptive in their simplicity, almost austerity. Walking around shows the three-dimensionality with the transition from one façade to the other immaculate, much aided by the prominent classical porticos. The interior also is so perfectly pure and unadorned, the spaces and columns the true definition of architecture. No wonder the Rotonda has served as the prototype for so many imitators, in England and the USA above all.

Indeed, a peregrination through the Venetian *terrafirma* provides the introduction for so much of the country house culture we are so familiar with in England from the eighteenth century. Even more perhaps than here, the country villas of Palladio are expressive of working estates: the wide-reaching wings of such as villas Maser, Emo and Pisani given over to agricultural or estate uses. Despite its rural setting and purpose, the simple architectural spaces of the Villa Barbaro at Maser are rendered indescribably grand by the stupendous series of frescoes by Veronese, covering every wall and surrounding every pillared doorway: quite breathtaking in their *trompe l'oeil* virtuosity. Yet Palladio's signature is also visible in several more urban settings: again, often with a frontage on a piazza, but substantial park or garden behind. Palladio's 'take' on classical prototypes, again, shows his inventive and inspired genius, paving the way for a whole new language of architecture.

From Vicenza we moved on west to Verona, a larger if less architect-monopolised city which I was to get to know much better in later decades. Roman evidence such as the bridge and the amphitheatre gives it an atmosphere both more antique and more picturesque. 'Juliet's House' is perhaps more avoidable. What we did find unmissable was the Basilica of San Zeno a little way from the centre: not just the impressively striped nave, interior and exterior, and bell tower but a most beautiful cloister and, above all, perhaps the most dramatic set of sculpted bronze doors I've yet to see – Florence included.

Verona set us on the road towards a brief encounter with the lakes – Garda in this instance. The plain between Verona and Sirmione is criss-crossed with little waterways enabling the fertility of local agri- and horticulture. Sirmione I was interested to see at last as being the site of Catullus' villa, and the subject of several poems. It's almost absurdly romantic, on its narrow peninsula or spit pointing up to the lake and the mountains, entered through the drawbridge and machicolated defences of the Scaligero castle. We went on by the precipitous western lakeside road – corniche – and came to rest at a very nice hotel at Riva del Garda at the head of the lake. There were probably many smart 'Riva' speedboats in the marina – there certainly had been in the moat before the castle peninsula at Sirmione.

Until after the First World War that area had been Austrian: in fact it was the only bit actually captured by the Italians, but of course a much greater area to the north (Sud-Tirol) was given to Italy after that war. I remember being somewhat surprised by that when first coming that way in 1960; and still there is a distinctly German-language culture. Starting on the fast valley road past Trento and Bolzano towards the Brenner Pass, we diverted to the most astoundingly scenic Dolomite zone with the objective of Cortina d'Ampezzo for lunch. I found the dramatic shapes of the Dolomites quite thrilling, and the alpine meadowscape beneath these awesome pinnacles the epitome of pastoral charm. We had a splendid repast in the lovely Hotel de la Poste, luxurious and historic in equal measure. I have never been back that way but would love a sojourn in that beautiful setting.

Moving down from the hills, where the plains begin, close together are Bassano del Grappa: notable not just for its eponymous and ubiquitous spirit but for a most picturesque galleried wooden bridge over the river, and Asolo, clinging with equal eye-appeal to the hillside. Not just Robert Browning but Freya

Stark too had houses here: the latter was still very much alive, and her house identified, but since her death I gather the house and garden have become a museum.

Downhill again, there were those villas and towns still to see nearer Venice. The Villa Barbaro at Maser has not only the eponymous villa but also Palladio's spectacular little Tempietto: its building – wide dome and dramatic Corinthian-columned portico seemingly parked at a bend in the road – in fact effectively creating one. In a quite different idiom, the now quite extensive town of Castelfranco Veneto has at its centre the perfectly square, moated and walled mediaeval town, with a magnificent tower to its church. Castelfranco was Giorgione's birthplace, and the church contains a Madonna (with St Francis), arguably one of his best. And to complete the mixture, the nearby Villa Cornaro is an interesting and good example of a Palladian villa in a town centre, its façade on the piazza contrasting with the more informal garden behind.

And with that and return to Venice, what had been a very satisfying brief trip, taking in fantastic cities, the varied oeuvre of a great architectural genius, lakes and precipitous mountains, came to its close.

Into the Eighties: Japan and Europe

1980 before Christmas at Verbier had seen a number of quick trips added on to business trips. In late January Haruko and I drove over to Paris to see our good friends and clients there: though at less than alpine altitude there was still snow on the ground. We stayed in the Marais for a change, at the Hotel Henry IV, and enjoyed a renewed acquaintance with that old quarter, including the Musée Carnavalet, the museum devoted to Paris' history. Driving back to the Channel, with a diversion through Normandy, it was very noticeable how the snow diminished and the last bit from Beauvais to the coast was in driving rain.

In May, again, we were visiting our clients in Munich and Zurich, and as usual enjoyed these two fine cities. Zurich was becoming especially familiar: we almost always stayed at the Hotel Storchen, right on or almost with its embarked terrace in the river, beside the zig-zag bridge linking it to the 'Old Town' to the east; though the Storchen's environment is just as venerable, with old, cobbled streets like the one the hotel entrance is in. Across the river there is a great view of the twin-towered Minster. The Storchen's cosy restaurant introduced me to the delights of *geschnetzeltes kalbfleisch mit rösti*, also to be found in Kronenhalle just up the hill by cobbled street and many other places throughout Switzerland.

We spent our weekend in Salzburg, new I think to Haruko but hardly to myself. Again, I have described the main places seen in Salzburg on earlier occasions, but this time in particular remember visiting Mozart's birthplace in the Getreidegasse, also Schloss Hellbrunn, the elegant pale yellow seventeenth-century palace of the prince-archbishops of Salzburg, sitting in slightly Villa d'Este-style gardens and park (though less precipitous) with inventive fountains, lakes, ponds, pavilions and above all trees and flowers just springing into vivid life in May. Hellbrunn lies well south of the Hohensalzburg Fortress and the cathedral and centre of the city, which may be why I hadn't visited before. It was well worth it. (It must have been quite a commute for the prince-archbishop – though designated only a 'summer palace'.)

A January visit to Japan was unusual for me at that stage and one rediscovered Tokyo in the snow, and an unusually picturesque journey on the *shinkansen* to Kyoto when there were long pauses in the mountainous bits between Nagoya and Kyoto. For that weekend expedition we had both Sarah and Peter Thistlethwayte with us – Sarah's first visit to Kyoto (and Japan). Both Sarah and Haruko looked terrific in their fur coats (it was very cold – Kyoto like Oxford is in a basin, in its case surrounded by mountains – well, Oxford has the Chilterns and Cotswolds, not quite the same thing – and traps the cold air). We stayed in our usual old Anzai ryokan, which sadly now has closed, opposite the pagoda of the Yasaka Jinja at the end of the steep cobbled street leading down from Kiyomizu. We warmed out feet on the *hibachi* heater under the quilted table as we sat on the tatami floor.

One evening we went down to the historic Gion entertainment quarter and were entertained by Mr Uramatsu, president of our close friends Sanyo Securities, and his colleagues, to a very special dinner in an old-established restaurant. At one point no less than four *maiko* ('apprentice geisha') appeared and did their singing and dancing, pouring saké and conversing. Mr Uramatsu said this was a half of all Kyoto's maiko contingent, but I think this may have been erroneous. Anyway, it was a memorable evening. Again, with limited time at a weekend, we tried to fit in as many of the main sights as we could in that inexhaustible place. Haruko's mother had also most kindly shown Sarah around Tokyo while the three of us were visiting companies and factories in and around Tokyo and Kawasaki.

Of course, there were many other occasions over the next couple of decades when we both travelled around Japan with clients and/or colleagues, for weekend diversions, and in Tokyo were royally entertained by our brokers to dinner (and sometimes lunch): too many to mention now, though I may bring up any especially memorable times later. The same effectively goes for visits to Hong Kong, Singapore, the Middle East, and the Continent – basically work.

A couple of months later, in April, it was 'family' again when mother and I took just Jamie and Rosamund for their introduction to Gallic civilisation in Paris and Versailles. We stayed in the little but soigné Hotel de l'Elysée near the eponymous presidential palace and the Madeleine. In Paris of course we fitted in as many of the obvious places including the touristic but young-person-friendly Eiffel Tower and the *bateaux mouches* along the Seine, enjoying all the bridges and buildings. At some point we visited Notre-Dame and of course had to climb the southern tower – from which a rather more meaningful view of inner Paris was to be found than from the top of the Eiffel Tower. Naturally Jamie – closely followed by self – had to climb to the top of the shallow pyramid surmounting the tower. Mother was having kittens but of course it was perfectly safe.

There was then an expedition, by train I imagine, to Versailles for the day: the main palace, of course, but also the Grand and Petit Trianons, and much walking in Le Nôtre's splendid fountain-rich park. I don't remember that by then one's palace tickets restricted one to limited 'visits' to different areas of the palace, nor that for each there was a different guide, far less the supercilious, sarcastic and above all Anglophobe guide I was forced to suffer in 2016.

Relaxation in the Eighties

With the arrival of a Conservative government in 1979 and removal of exchange controls, foreign travel became infinitely easier from the 1980s on: also, our business was going well (although any money was needed for buying into the partnership, buying houses and flats etc.), and with more staff we could both spend longer away ourselves and also take them on visits abroad; and we had more offices overseas.

India and Arabia

An early return to India came with a flight in December 1981 homeward bound via Singapore: we flew across the Bay of Bengal to Madras (now officially Chennai), my first visit to that eastern part redolent of the early East India Company days when the French were still in the game. Madras was pleasant, chaotic and low-rise. Broad green spaces and a garrison church with evocative memorials. We were driven down the coast to the ancient structures of Mahabalipuram, with the pyramidal Shore Temple and the gigantic rock carvings of elephants, warriors, and the rest. The sky was grey and the water greyer: with the waves breaking on the shingle beach it could have been a dreich day at Machrihanish – except for the idiosyncratic little outrigger boats and the palm plantations.

From Madras, a night flight across the subcontinent to Bombay (OK, Mumbai – but all our Indian friends still say Bombay). Of course, we stayed at the Taj, with its wonderful view of the Gateway of India and the harbour beyond. In those days India was really flirting with the Soviet Union and there were a number of rakish Russian warships anchored in the roads, as well as some superannuated British ones the Indians had bought. In the naval dockyard, which was also just on our doorstep, was a Town class cruiser similar to HMS *Belfast*. I did wander round and got into the dockyard, but apart from spending some time around the Gateway of India that was as far as we explored beyond the immediate hotel grounds. The waterside below the great arch was busy with little ferries and excursion boats going to and fro across the harbour, with groups and families often in most exotic bright-coloured saris taking the evening air. Otherwise, we spent time either inside in the excellent shopping arcade, or by the pool in the garden, where we were accompanied by the England Test cricket team, probably recuperating after yet another defeat by India.

There were a number of Middle Eastern visits around the turn of the decade: a brief client visit to an Abu Dhabi which was almost entirely low-rise and 'village-like', then a somewhat longer and altogether more rewarding one to Oman, together with Ian Perkins from our gilts department and his wife Melissa. Muscat itself is tiny, the Sultan's palace occupying almost the entire space of the waterfront between the twin forts on the promontories either side. I was pleased to see that the painted names of HM ships which had visited in the eighteenth and nineteenth centuries were still to be seen on the rock face: just one reminder of those close bonds with Britain which one feels more in Oman than elsewhere in the Gulf. Beside the Sultan's lawn – which boasted an anti-aircraft gun – was the residence of our friend Anthony Wood (of the FO), so visiting him we were really at the heart of things.

In fact, we stayed at a large modern hotel by the beach some way out of town. As Muscat is so constricted, the main commercial centre is the adjacent Muttrah; then further out, mostly on the western shore, are hotels and residential areas. The pool was half roofed-in against the blazing sunshine: it was quite fantastically hot and an attempt to walk across the wide sandy beach to the shore proved very painful!

We took a car to Nizwa, the ancient walled town in the hills to the south. I was amazed at the perfect state of the road, wide, fast, and smooth and almost entirely bereft of traffic: one could have gone any speed (not even any Ferraris or Lamborghinis to be seen!). We stopped a few times to view locals in their elegant white dressing gowns with daggers in their waistbands. Nizwa itself is not large: fortified, white, ancient. With less humidity already the heat was more bearable.

Another 'stopover' returning from the Far East was in 1983: from Hong Kong I flew to Dubai to stay with my great friends Robert and Georgie Woods, he being posted there for a while representing P&O (of which he later became CEO). They had a little house in a small modern development near Jumeirah Beach, some way out of town. With three small boys the pool there was a blessing. We also went down to the beach and the sailing club there; and Georgie and I went into the town to visit the souk and generally look around. The Creek was still little changed and there were few tall buildings yet. As on the Oman trip, we piled aboard their rather large American car and headed up into the hills to an oasis: emerging from the air-conditioned car, again we found the insufferable humid heat of sea level had been replaced by pleasant dry heat. I cherish a photo of myself holding my two-year-old godson in my arms beside sign saying 'WADI'.

The same phenomenon of humidity – or absence thereof – was apparent a few years later (I am getting ahead of myself to preserve thematic consistency) when I found myself playing badminton on a hotel flat roof in 130F heat, in Riyadh. I was one of a team of four pitching to the Saudi monetary authority (again this is strictly 'business' rather than 'travel', but there was also an excursion). We were staying in the Hilton on the airport road and every day went into the centre patiently to wait at SAMA to be called in. After two or three days eventually we were able to make our pitch, to a fearsome-looking army general (like a bad-tempered sea eagle). What was gratifying was that a delegation from the much better-known Merrill Lynch had been waiting before us and were still waiting when we left. Less gratifying is that nothing I believe came of our visit.

It was good to see and dine (alcohol-free) with my old friend David Reid Scott, seconded there for a while by his American investment bank (and sadly now dead). The expedition was down the dead-straight desert road to the south to see the extensive and deserted ruins of King Abdul Aziz's palace. Pushed aside off the road, what seemed like every few yards, were the wrecks of fairly new cars: some burnt, some clearly accident victims, some perhaps whose ashtrays were full…

On being dismissed from SAMA there was little left to keep us in Riyadh. We had already viewed downtown, including the gold souk where a policeman laid a cane on my shoulder – gently – for daring to take a photograph, and the notorious main square/car park where they behead criminals. We were booked on a Saudia flight to London around 9 p.m., so had a long wait ahead: and so, no extension being allowed, paid for the coming night as well before eventually checking out. Arriving at the airport we found that the flight was delayed as the plane had to cool down. When it was eventually cool enough the crew were out of hours: so, the flight was postponed until early the next morning. Accordingly, we returned to the hotel and asked for our room keys. 'Ah, but you have checked out' said the desk clerk. 'No, we have paid for tonight: keys please!' Sleep of the just disturbed only by the operatic and synchronised wailing of several score muezzins at some ungodly – or all too godly – hour, an excellent alarm clock for early departure to catch the flight in a now-cooled aeroplane with a now rested or relief crew…

[The India visits are covered in greater length in the later section 'Three Decades of India Visits'.]

Japan, Hong Kong, Bali 1982

The next expedition with Mother was played out over a much wider area and much further afield: to wit, the Far East. This, in spring 1982, was nearly ten years after she had first visited Japan. The previous time, it will be remembered, took the form (after some days in Tokyo) of a drive north to Nikko, then, after some frustrated attempts at closed mountain passes, down to the Japan Sea coast, to Kanazawa, Eiheiji and Tsuruga, to Kyoto and then in a day along the expressways back to Tokyo. This time was also to concentrate on the Japan Sea side, but now striking north with a hired car from Kyoto to take up where we had left off, westward along the San'in coast.

Past Miyazu and that steeply descending coast of Kyoto prefecture, we spent a night at Japan's officially second most beautiful spot, Amanohashidate. From the hotel high above the sea, we could see below us the famous pine-adorned spit of sand enclosing a lagoon. All very picturesque: what I remember most was the vast quantities of ghostly looking octopi displayed and drying on every wall. The waters surrounding must be full of writhing limbs. The north-west coast of Honshu (called Chūgoku, with the same characters as China) is remarkably varied: from the deep indentations and steep wooded hillsides of Wakasa-wan past Obama, Maizuru and Miyazu to the strange sand dunes stretching some fifteen miles east of Tottori. Inland, the hanging woods were draped in wisteria to the treetops: wonderful sight.

Just outside the historic old town of Matsue, redolent of Lafcadio Hearn (more ghosts), is the sprawling and equally historic Yakumo Honjin ryokan, where we had an atmospheric night. I think we missed Matsue city, a shame as the city castle looks most interesting, and is one of the few original survivors. But we had to press on to Izumo Taisha, one of the pre-eminent Shinto shrines of Japan: perhaps equalled only by Ise (which I did not visit until many years later). Like the latter, it has the combination of grandeur and simplicity which wooden structures, of imposing size, among tall cryptomeria forests convey. Though entirely ignorant of Shinto practices and observance, I have great sympathy with a religion which can see the divine in nature and endows trees, mountains, rivers with supernatural qualities; and respect for ancestors can't be bad either.

The final overnight stop on this tour was Hagi: an old castle town, of no great size but considerable charm. The castle area is still surrounded by old samurai residences in narrow streets, with evocative old earthen walls; of the castle itself, not unusually, only the moat and walls survive. A temple in the forest nearby contains many tombs of the Mōri family, the feudal lords of old. Hagi was intimately involved with the Chōshū samurai who played a major part in the Meiji restoration: Hirobumi Itō, a leading light in the restoration and Japan's first designated Prime Minister, was a Hagi man. Of course, the town's other claim to fame is as the producer of Hagi ware, simple and undecorated and one of the main Japanese pottery schools. Next day we drove across Yamaguchi prefecture at the western tip of Honshu to reach Shimonoseki, where from beneath the narrow Kanmon Strait separating Honshu from Kyushu the *shinkansen* arrived to whisk us back to Tokyo.

Back in Tokyo, we shortly took flight for Hong Kong. Mother had never been there (though passed through Singapore on her previous visit to Tokyo): for me of course it was very familiar – as was the routine, as I was basically working, telling our clients there what exciting things I had discovered in my interviews with Japanese companies. (In many cases though this involved long and delicious lunches at the Man Hwa restaurant at the top of the Mandarin.) However, there was a more serious side: the Falklands reconquest was in full swing, not necessarily going very well – the news of the sinking of the *Sheffield* I remember watching in our office. The conflict dragged on during this and our next stop on the itinerary.

This was Bali, and definitely pure holiday. We stayed in the south of the island, not far from Denpasar at Sanur Beach: near but not, mercifully, too near the Kuta 'strip' in the extreme south favoured by backpackers, hippies and Australians. It was low-rise, atmospheric (the culture new to me, omnipresent in the hotel's décor) and highly relaxing. Lovely to swim a lot: but pool only as the beach proved highly disappointing, a coral reef with water only about nine inches deep (and the bottom very scratchy) for hundreds of yards out to sea.

While mother relaxed in the hotel grounds, I had one 'cultural' expedition: a nice French girl we had met and I took a taxi one day up to the north of the island. We visited one temple in the middle of the island near Ubud and found the atmosphere, both intimate and exotic, very enticing: ancient sandstone walls, enclosed courtyards, curved *garuda* birds and other mythical sculptuary. There and on several other occasions on the trip processions of garlanded young girls in long, tight skirts (cheongsam?) and silk blouses, bearing offerings to who knows what deity for what purpose were encountered. Rural life among the terraced rice fields looked deceptively idyllic. The high point after this low-key rustic bliss was also our goal and turning point: Lake Batur and its volcano and temples. This is probably *the* iconic view in Bali: the slender ten-storied pagoda of the temple on its promontory, with the volcano in the background across the lake, is a travel photographer's dream.

Twentieth-century Garuda – the Indonesian national airline – did the hop from Bali to Jakarta, where the air terminal was pleasingly cottage-like and al fresco in those days, thence to the somewhat more up-to-date Singapore and back to London on wonderful Singapore Airlines.

Berlin and the Baltic Shores – Again

With the unfolding saga of the dismantling of the Berlin Wall and the imminent demise of the Soviet Union, somehow Berlin seemed to have a magnetic attraction in 1989–90. After that first incursion behind the Iron Curtain to Czechoslovakia in late 1989, I paid a brief visit in May 1990 to Berlin, solo. I had enjoyed my previous visit of little over a day when the two halves were completely separated: now that the Wall had been breached, I was keen to see how things were moving and to get to know a city I already found exciting. This time I stayed in the old 'West' in Kreuzberg near the canal. I was anxious to see more of the East German countryside beyond Berlin, after my previous drive down from the Baltic, so after picking up a hire car set off north again, for the Baltic shores east of Rostock. This is flat and somewhat dreary country dotted with little lakes, heading past Neubrandenburg: but pleasant enough. Somewhere before the coast the road gave up entirely and *Umleitung* signs led me a merry dance over the fields till it was rejoined.

I reached the sea at Greifswald, a fine old Hanseatic town with very typical old buildings prominent: it had housed several different abbeys and one of the earliest universities – it's very much a university town still. The buildings were still pretty shabby and neglected, but the town suffered relatively little in the Second World War thanks to a timely surrender. Most spectacular was the fortified cathedral with its tall spire culminating in the mini-onion shapes to be seen also in places such as Riga and Copenhagen. The Baltic seemed very close. The broad market square contained a fine assortment of buildings with high pointed gables.

I drove along the coastal road towards Stralsund and the island of Rügen. Stralsund is another old Hanseatic town, with unsurprisingly a rather more maritime feeling than Greifswald. Like Greifswald, it was for a long time part of the Swedish empire, later of Prussia. The town has a couple of enormous brick churches with the usual embellished towers/spires, a Lübeck-like city hall, vast market square and an historic centre with what, when I was there, were very neglected old gabled buildings.

With shipbuilding activity, docks and a marine esplanade one is much more conscious of the open Baltic and the bridge over to the island of Rügen summoned. I didn't penetrate all that far

'By the summer of 1971 I had been rather dubiously pontificating about Japan for two years, without having ever been there… I was longing to rectify…'

Below: Matsumoto-jō and Shirakawago, 2010.

Odori, 2010.

Opposite: Fuji Goko in the autumn.

Ginkakuji, Kyoto.

Pachinko parlour.

Going up the Tokyo Tower.

Bagan, Myanmar.

Farming in Myanmar.

Humayun's Tomb.

Opposite: dancing in Bhutan.

Bagan, Myanmar.

Opposite, above: Dhammayangyi Temple; *below*: dancers in Bhutan.

Daibutsu in Japan.

Angkor Wat.

into Rügen, as time was slipping by, but far enough to get some idea of the scenery: not alas quite reaching the 'white cliffs' made so famous in the paintings of Caspar David Friedrich (native of Greifswald).

Returning towards Berlin (with no further agrarian diversions), on a quite different wavelength I felt impelled to visit the notorious women's concentration camp of Ravensbrück, about fifty miles north of Berlin. Were it not for the connotations the site would be idyllic, beside the Fürstenberg/Havel lake. Any such illusions are dispelled as one passes into the camp. In fact – mercifully perhaps – there was not so much to see: the main emphasis is on the high brick wall with many moving memorials, plus the main admin building with cells and crematorium – curiously 'minimal'. The true revelation came by standing on tiptoe and peering over the wall to the much greater acreage of the camp behind. Much to my surprise many or most of the old huts remained: the difference was that they were now the living quarters of the Soviet Russian soldiery. Grim. I was glad to have seen this place, but much gladder to be back in a thriving West Berlin for the evening.

With the car, I had a more limited excursion the next day, down the Havel to the south-west towards Potsdam. The inner suburbs of Grünewald and Zehlendorf seemed very pleasant. Soon I was parked by the Wannsee enjoying the sight of many small boats, rowers etc. making the most of the weekend. I saw but didn't go nearer the infamous villa of the Wannsee conference which kicked off the Holocaust. Past Babelsberg of the film studios, I crossed the Glienicker bridge of spy-swapping fame into Potsdam, for a good wander in the park.

Bavaria and the East – Still 1990

Later in 1990 – October – it was back to Germany with my mother, or rather to collect her from another Danube cruise. I flew to Munich and hired the usual VW to drive over to Passau to collect her. On the way, I stopped briefly in Landshut, an attractive Bavarian town with an impressive castle. At Passau I found the vessel at the quay and went aboard to inspect it and find my mother and her new friends. Then we left for Regensburg, the ancient city also on the Danube, a mediaeval wonder. We checked in at the Bischofshof am Dom, a delightful old hotel in an old courtyard/beer garden overlooked by colonnaded windows, adjacent to the cathedral: very comfortable. The cathedral is the only truly Gothic one in Bavaria, which otherwise tends to the Baroque: it is similar to many French Gothic cathedrals of the era (begun 1275), rather comparable to León in northern Spain. It shares with them a fine array of stained-glass windows, notably in the apse, and elaborate Gothic font and chapels. From the twin-towered Cathedral streets led a short way down to the Steinbrücke (stone bridge) across the Danube, even older than the cathedral, being Roman. Regensburg is a very ancient city, having Celtic origins, being effectively founded by the Romans as an imperial city, maintaining that status under the Holy Roman Empire, and so through many vicissitudes to the present. It's a World Heritage Site and the old town contains not just some Roman relics and Romanesque chambers pre-dating the cathedral, but fine merchants' houses, and warehouses by the river.

We drove a short distance down river to Wallhall (Walhalla), the mock-Parthenon standing on the hillside above the Danube in whose interior cold white busts commemorate the heroes of Germany (up to the nineteenth century). As might be expected an aura of classical scholarship and seriousness permeates the place, which is nevertheless impressive – to one whose schooldays were spent reading of Mommsen and other obsessive German classicists, rather intimidating. The view down to a long curve of the river is impressive too, a good choice of siting.

Before turning east and north for our ultimate destination, Berlin, however, we took a tour westward into Franconia to spend a night in Würzburg, stopping in picturesque Rothenburg (ob der Tauber) on the way. Würzburg, heavily damaged during the war, had made great efforts of restoration. The town lies beside the river Main and from the quayside, featuring a remarkable crane, one looks up over the steep vineyards to the Marienberg Fortress overlooking the city. We were content to view it from a distance. However, the later, Baroque residence of the prince-bishops who ruled Würzburg demanded full attention. This imposing building features a most grandiose staircase, the ceiling of which has the largest fresco in the world, painted by Tiepolo (and no doubt a legion of assistants). The palace – for such the Residenz is – lies among beautiful formal gardens, rising up a slope and giving plenty of opportunities for flights of stairs as well as formal pools, statuary etc.

After Würzburg we stopped in Bamberg, not so far away, and now heading back towards our objectives in the east. Bamberg is supposed to lie on seven hills – as with Rome it is rather difficult to distinguish or count them. But it is definitely hilly. The cathedral, with high spires, sits above a broad square and flight of steps descending to the lower town. The 'Bamberg Horseman' statue, mid-fourteenth century, stands at the entrance and is the best-known symbol of the town. Inside, the cathedral is spacious and austere. Beside it the 'new Residenz' is a massive and uncompromising L-shaped block. Down by the river (the Regnitz) the town is more attractively jumbled, the main focus being on the old town hall on its own little island – in fact, no island is visible other than the Rathaus' buildings, so it appears to be swimming… A bridge leads through a central arch to join it to both banks. At the 'prow' the triangular plain is matched by the steep triangular roof of the projecting edifice. The river is lined by handsome old houses with extensive windows, bedecked with geraniums and overlooking small boats moored by the riverbank.

It was time to move on, on a late autumn evening: we still had the old frontier to cross. We passed in the dark through Coburg (still in the West), where at least the schloss was illuminated; then found ourselves in old East Germany, Thuringia. We were staying in Erfurt, as I recall in the station hotel (not a lot of choice). It seemed fine: the public rooms rather soulless. In the (bright and sunny) morning we took stock of our surroundings, conspicuous were many soldiers, both East German and Russian: most carried briefcases, somewhat incongruous beside their short-jacketed brown uniforms. Erfurt also has a great twin-spired cathedral up broad flights of steps, and some pleasingly mediaeval-looking old streets down by the river, including one enclosed bridge. In contrast to the West, however, façades were peeling and shabby, and shop signs and the like antiquated. Alongside the cathedral the Severikirche boasts triple spires, punctuating the sky like needles.

In fact, from Erfurt, we retraced our steps westwards, to visit Eisenach and Gotha, neither to be missed in that part of the world: Eisenach of course largely for Johann Sebastian Bach and his modest hillside birthplace and childhood home. Martin Luther also lived in Eisenach, apparently during his schooldays at the end of the 15th and beginning of the 16th centuries, before later translating the New Testament in the Wartburg castle nearby. His house is a much more impressive building than Bach's, tall and half-timbered but relatively low in dormers in the high gabled roof; it is one of the oldest in Thuringia, dating from mid-thirteenth century. It's a museum but despite Presbyterian antecedents we really didn't have time on a packed day to visit it.

We did, however, make sure not to miss the Wartburg. It's on a precipice overlooking the town, with extensive views over the Thuringian forest. From below, the high towers of the oldest, Romanesque fortress dominate; but on a long spur from the entrance gate one passes through a succession of newer, i.e. fourteenth–fifteenth century, houses and secular buildings. In one is Luther's room: simple and spare (probably not originally so to judge from most scholars' and academics' quarters!), but extremely evocative of the Reformation's beginning. Two little paintings by the also ubiquitous L. Cranach the Younger.

Next in what was to be a long and action-packed day was Gotha (after all, we had passed through Coburg). Again a town on a hill, lined with quite substantial but very grey-brown and dilapidated houses, with a broad green space between, leading up to the Friedenstein castle, itself already pretty smartly restored. This is a U-shaped Renaissance/Baroque edifice of imposing if relatively low-built construction: white with ochre decorations. On the 'port' side as you look at it entering the courtyard, facing south, the corner tower has a rounded roof, and on the 'starboard' a pyramidal one. The connecting hall between them has the most extraordinary Baroque plaster ceiling. There are the normal appurtenances of Baroque opera house or court theatre and chapel also – no doubt a library or somewhere where the eponymous *Almanach* was composed. Down the hill the lower town was inexpressibly dreary with long lines of flat-fronted apartment blocks, peeling and rusty: though in the usual market square is the fine high-towered St Margarethen church; and there are several fine municipal or aristocratic palaces.

But the day was moving on and it was time to see Weimar, settling in at the celebrated Elephant Hotel, which since its inception in the seventeenth century has hosted more or less appreciative guests from Lucas Cranach to Adolf Hitler (not excluding us, not put off by the list, who found it most agreeable): rather more character than the station hotel in Erfurt, spacious public areas and dining rooms, a longish, plainish building on the marketplace with garden between the wings behind. The Elephant stands by the entrance to this historic square, irregular in shape and climbing gently from the town hall at the bottom, in mid nineteenth-century red-Gothic, past various former ducal and current municipal buildings, up to the high level bordering the riverside park where the schloss and, more interesting to me, the beautiful Duchess Anna Amalia Library are to be found. The other 'must see' for us before we had to hurry on for our return 100+ miles journey to Dresden, an even more vital objective, was the Goethe-Haus: quite a substantial residence with many interesting exhibits. Goethe and Schiller being the literary lions of Weimar, there is of course a Schillerhaus as well, but I don't think we saw that. We did, however, go for the 'downtown' to view the National Goethe-Schiller memorial statue in the square before it: a remarkable piece. None of this of course is far apart: but I found, both on first arrival the night before, and on second arrival from Dresden that night, that it seemed virtually impossible to drive to the Elephant on the Marktplatz: 'No Entry' signs whichever street one tried! But managed it in the end. The streets were full of Russian soldiery.

We said a temporary 'Auf Wiedersehen' after our first Elephant night and got on our way for the longish drive to Dresden. I don't think we went into any of the churches nor the plethora of other museums Weimar boasts – leaving aside anything to do with the Weimar Republic. I know we did not go the short way up the hill to Buchenwald. It is really impossible to believe the inhabitants of Weimar did not have any idea what was going on there: something which tinges one's view of the very charming people, of a later generation, one meets there. Though a year earlier I had thought Ravensbrück north of Berlin an essential stop, I was not going to take my mother to a concentration camp: in April or May 1945 my father had been sent as second-in-command to Belsen to clear it up, days after it had been discovered and liberated (an Argyll, he had been transmuted into the Royal Artillery for the actual fighting from Normandy on). He never once spoke of this to us; but I am sure his letters and private words with my mother must have been devastating.

Bypassing Jena (famous as the home of Zeiss-Ikon) and Gera we went on into Saxony and found we could park with relative ease in the centre of Dresden. It still looked pretty bashed about. First call was for the Zwinger, that marvellous palace/museum round a spacious courtyard, whose walls are in turn surrounded by a wide moat. And what arched walls, prominent gateways and pavilions of the most delicate Baroque exuberance – foretelling all that Dresden had to offer. The Zwinger is a major art gallery with Raphaels galore (highlight the Sistine Madonna), but also Rembrandt, van Eyck, Vermeer – all the great names of Italian, Netherlandish, Spanish art (not too many Brits, it seemed). A special word of course for Bernardo Bellotto, masquerading sometimes as 'Canaletto' being the nephew of the 'proper' one, who made several paintings of Dresden and the Elbe on his visit there.

The gallery lies to the Elbe river side of the great garden square, and from there the main sights are all within easy reach – as is the sense of the river itself. Nearest is the Semperoper – I believe, unsurprisingly, one of the first major buildings to be repaired and reopened. It also fronts a sizeable piazza with several remarkable pieces of bronze statuary, notably a large mounted king of Saxony waving his wand. On the other side one sees the beginning of the Hofkirche – church court – perhaps the real (Catholic) church of Dresden. Though its tower was complete the nave was not – much daylight to be seen – and it was closed. Leading along from it is the street to the north of the royal palace, where there is a hundred-yard long mural of princes on horseback, in black and gold Meissen porcelain tiles, along the palace outer wall. The palace itself was again Renaissance leading to Baroque, though largely destroyed during the war: when we saw it there was a highly romantic roofscape of pointy towers, belvederes and high gables with sky behind – all blackened. I was to see it in much better condition in 1997. As one moved eastward the scene deteriorated further, with the place around the almost totally destroyed Frauenkirche near-covered in its rubble. Only a chunk of (?) apse remained standing, but totally ruined. The Frauenkirche also was well on the way to rebuilding a little while later and has now been completely restored and reopened – thanks, one is glad to say, largely to British money.

Life returned to something more like normality as we moved to the Brühl's Terraces looking over the river. Here were moored the old excursion streamers which cruise the Elbe, often on the brief stretch to the palace at Pillnitz which I was also to see in

1997. These elegant craft are very like those to be found on the Swiss lakes: long-waterline narrow ships with extensive open or glazed saloons; white, cream and apple-green. They belong to the rather wonderfully named Sächsische Dampfschifffahrt. On the curve of the river below the terrace esplanade, they provide a fitting foreground to the scene of, in turn, the castle, the Hofkirche and the Semperoper. Nearest in the castle complex is the Grünes Gewölbe or Green Vault: this was, at least partially, open then but has since relocated in parts, I understand. Nevertheless it seemed pretty complete and comprehensive. Second oldest museum in the world after the Vatican (and just pipping the BM), while started by some earlier Electors it owed its pre-eminent collection – of jewellery, precious stones, gold- and silver-smithery, bronzes and a multitude of other treasures and objects of virtue – to the presciently named Augustus the Strong in the early eighteenth century, who made it into a public museum. Unfortunately, his spirit was unable to prevent further depredations: first by the Red Army in 1945 – some items but not all were returned; then by a daring robbery (echoes of the film *Topkapi*) only a few years ago of some sets of 'crown jewels', presumably now broken up for the gemstones, and irretrievable.

Leaving the historic centre, a most concentrated area of Baroque wonders in course of transformation, we crossed the Elbe to the Innere Neustadt suburb: a long straight thoroughfare leading remorselessly up the hill through rather uninspired mansion flats and government buildings, in the direction of our next stop, Moritzburg Castle. This is a quite extraordinary Baroque palace standing on an artificial island in its own little lake a few miles northwest: a massive structure approached by a low causeway, with four massive dome-topped round towers at each corner extending from the central range: cream and red-roofed. It was nearly sunset so of course only viewing from across the reed-fringed lake was possible, before moving on to catch Meissen before total darkness fell.

We were just in time to catch the view of Albrechtsburg Castle and the Gothic cathedral with its amazingly tall spires rising on their eminence above the old town and the river before us: good silhouettes against the fading light. (Again, a proper visit, in particular to the porcelain factory, was to come a few years on. I love Meissen porcelain and have a few pieces.) Then it was dark for the long, long slog back to Weimar and the Elephant. (Appropriately perhaps, my main Meissen pieces are of a sultan and sultana on their elephants…)

Leaving Weimar in the morning, we were on our way to Berlin at last. First stop was Naumburg where the rather pretty main street – of shabby but essentially fine houses – wound down and gave tantalising views of the wonderful cathedral with its four tall Romanesque corner towers. Dating back to the thirteenth century, the 'cathedral' is almost symmetrical with Gothic choirs at either end. (The inverted commas are the consequence of the Catholic cathedral becoming a Protestant parish church with the Reformation.)

The Reformation was also prominent in our next stop, Wittenberg, where Luther famously attached his 95 theses to the door of the castle church (Schlosskirche). Today that door is of bronze, and it is difficult to see how one could have nailed anything to it – but it's a nineteenth century replacement. The other main church, the Stadtkirche, is twin-towered and impressive – as often in these parts (cf. Prague's Old Town Square), it is actually hidden behind a row of buildings facing the marketplace. There are fine memorials to Luther and his associate Melanchthon in the market square. A relatively small town still, Wittenberg has some nice old streets in parallel leading back from square and church: the outskirts were in 1960 extraordinarily grim, with factories with high smoking chimneys and extensive communist signs and placards.

In aiming for Wittenberg, we had bypassed both Leipzig and Dessau: so I have not yet seen either the Bach memories of the former nor the more recent Bauhaus ones in the latter. So, soon we were in Berlin again. We drove through the now-redundant Checkpoint Charlie up the Friedrichstrasse to Mitte and installed ourselves in the Grand Hotel on Unter den Linden: ideal for the centre of old East Berlin. In the morning we could see how much had already changed since my previous visit: where the wall had been towards the west was now just a vast glacis with traces of old foundations, tramlines, variegated surfaces the only clue as to what had been East and what West: *pace* Rudyard Kipling, the twain had met. The Brandenburg Gate, Reichstag and neighbourhood, however, were still fenced off and impenetrable; nor could one drive from West to East along the main axis. I did discover, however, that by going a short way north to the banks of the Spree one could drive straight through to a street running parallel into Unter den Linden, used thenceforth. Much rubble and detritus of superannuated border checkpoints lay around. In the central Mitte area, we could visit the Gendarmenmarkt square with, this time, Schiller alone memorialised by a fine marble statue in front of the former court theatre, now concert hall, one of Schinkel's best. The north and south sides of this elegant and symmetrical square are occupied by the French and the German cathedrals respectively: tall columned and domed towers top elegant equally symmetrical classical churches. The whole ensemble is immensely elegant.

The 'German cathedral' is not to be confused with the Berliner Dom, the vast edifice on the right as one moves towards the Museumsinsel and the great museums there. Dom by name and indeed dome by nature: I personally find it overbearing, over-decorated in *fin de siècle* Hohenzollern taste. The museums are something else and come a a relief. Schinkel's Altes Museum, long, low and classical; the not-to-be-confused Alte Nationalgalerie, conversely standing high on its podium and inevitably preceded by flights of steps and bombastic mounted statue; the Neues Museum (of course); the domed Bode Museum serving as the 'prow' to the island; and above all the Pergamon Museum form an incomparable (and highly convenient) complex, much enhanced by the waters dividing around it. We did I believe see the rotunda inside the Altes Museum, but most of our time was devoted to the Pergamon (several galleries in fact were still closed for restoration). Here the principal sight of course is the great Hellenistic altar from Pergamon; scarcely less impressive is the Roman Gate of Miletus, and a number of sizeable Egyptian constructions – as well as a world-class collection of Greek, Roman, Egyptian etc. treasures. Nineteenth-century German archaeologists were busy indeed!

After some more exploration of the centre of old East Berlin, including an excursion further east past the Alexanderplatz and the television tower to see how quickly the townscape deteriorated, we took an evening drive westward down the Havel to see the lake towards sunset and indeed briefly to cross the bridge into Potsdam. Thither in fact we returned the next morning to take advantage of a beautifully sunny autumn day in the park. By now the principal buildings were all visitable. Parking at the 'town' end (redolent of garrisons) we could stroll gently through the enchanting Sanssouci Park. Perhaps the most romantic building is the Chinese tea house – the epitome of chinoiserie in architecture, which never ceases to delight. The little Charlottenhof – Schinkel again, of course – is by contrast the purest neoclassicism, inside and out. Sanssouci itself had now reopened (though Frederick the Great had not yet been restored to his simple grave outside); it is I suppose the main 'attraction' of the place, both for its flawlessly simple-yet-ornate single storey design with a low cupola and for its setting on top of a small hill terraced with vines either side of the central steps. In fact the vines are placed vertically in planted squares, facing a series of gravel strolling paths. I discovered that this has its problems as one cannot from various aspects see who is on these paths. I became quite worried when my mama and I had become temporarily separated – not in itself at all unusual – and I could not see her anywhere. (No mobile phones then!) However, we did eventually rediscover each other. The final visit was to the Neues Palais – again for me – where there was a very nice, definitely non-Chinese, tearoom in a high-ceilinged, chandeliered and tapestried setting. Leaving aside the individual buildings, the whole walk in the park had been lovely with the usual eighteenth-century array of lakes, sculptuary etc. at its best in the golden autumn light.

That brought to a fitting close our brief visit to Berlin; we were not so far from the airport and it remained but to take in the scenery of obsolete wall and abandoned frontier posts to the west of the city as we made our way in late afternoon to the airport and home.

Three Decades of India Visits

I first visited India in August 1972. I had a fortnight's holiday owed and managed to attach it as a preface to my second investment trip to Japan. So I had arranged a week in northern India followed by a further week in Thailand: thus aiming to add to my fairly limited acquaintance with Asia.

I flew to Delhi but did not (yet) tarry there, the plan being to 'do' Kashmir first. So several hours were spent at Palam Airport, used first to send a telegram (as one did in those days) to a great friend getting married that day in Scotland, secondly to start on *War and Peace* which I had never read (though attended the New York world première of the marvellous Sergei Bondarchuk film a few years earlier). Arriving in Srinagar I stayed at the Oberoi hotel, a sprawling two-storey former royal residence up the hill above the town, with (had it not been pouring with monsoon rain) an extensive view over the Dal Lake and up to the Himalaya. To reach one's room one walked along a series of walkways bordering an internal garden courtyard giving views of the rooms through open doors. I was surprised to find that in most the occupants were sitting on or near the floor and cooking their supper: I rather hoped I should not be expected to exhibit my own lifestyle in similar fashion when I got to my room. But all was normal.

I had arranged with a Mr Butt (everyone in Kashmir is called Butt) to go for a day-long tour of the Dal Lake on a *shikara* (open wooden vessel with a – vital in the downpour – canopy and paddled by two, from the bow and the stern respectively. Despite the incessant downpour this was a lovely trip. We paddled our way past the houseboats, so popular at that time with affluent or even aristocratic Western honeymooners (regardless or heedless of the all-purpose stagnant water in which they were moored) and emerged to make our way through the 'floating gardens' which produce vegetables, flowers, etc. for the equally water-borne markets in Srinagar. The young persons paddling held wide hats of giant lotus leaves above them against the constant downpour. Eventually the vegetation thinned and gave way to the open lakes – first the small Nigeen Lake, then the great expanse of the Dal Lake stretching north. One could at last see the shores, and features such as the small island with its four huge ancient deodar trees. I was getting on well with *War and Peace*. The paddlers were occupied stirring up pots of curry.

Crossing to the opposite, east, bank, we could see many of the beautiful, if somewhat decayed, Mughal garden estates, and stopped to explore perhaps the most celebrated, Shalimar Bagh (what a lovely name!). It rained. I remember a quiet evening making great progress with Tolstoy, and no doubt with Kashmiri curries.

The next day was spent exploring the city. A rather ramshackle place, inevitably. A very Muslim feeling but the mosque was modest, of brick. Many buildings, however, were of corrugated iron or aluminium so familiar to habitués of the Scottish Highlands – including the optimistically named Institute of Mathematics and Science: a rather small corrugated-iron hut but with its imposing title written along the gutter line. For me, the most interesting, however, was the riverside and the commerce being carried on between the boat people and the stallholders in or above the 'quays'. Their elevated level suggested frequent inundation by the river Jhelum. Photo opportunities abounded, as they had on the lake.

On my last day I took a car up to the ski resort of Gulmarg – as desolate and uninviting as such places are in summer, even in the smartest ski venues in Europe – and on higher up to the border with Ladakh at Sonamarg. This was high – genuine Himalayas – and one could sense the propinquity of Tibet and thus (now) China. Then at some point it was the plane back to the plains. From the window I remember my main impression was how rapidly and steeply the mountains rise from the flatlands. But thereafter that was where I was bound.

From Srinagar I flew back to Agra, this time staying for a couple of nights. The Taj Mahal was the obvious first target: it would be otiose to add any description to perhaps the best-known and best-loved building in the world. Suffice it to say that it is undoubtedly true that, however marvellous one's first experience might have promised to be, it exceeds all expectations. Also, the supporting sandstone buildings, the nearness of the shallow Yamuna River, and the view upstream to the Red Fort and the tomb of Itmad-ud-Daulah had not been foreseen.

The Red Fort was almost as worthwhile. Though smaller, it compares well with its namesake in Delhi, principally because of its location right beside and above the river. The fort itself is similarly sandstone with several palaces of white marble – mosque, halls, etc. – of exquisite adornment.

Thence, a brief but interesting car journey westward into Rajasthan. On the way, two main stops: the deserted city of Fatehpur Sikri, before Jaipur; and the Bharatpur Bird Sanctuary on the way back the next day. Fatehpur Sikri was once the designated capital of Mughal Rajasthan and contains some truly impressive palaces, mosques, walls on a high acropolis reached by broad steps: from there the view reveals a vast expanse of further ruined buildings spread across the countryside: truly Virgilian, I have to say that the deficient ornithologist in me has difficulty in remembering what exact species were found at Bharatpur – storks, flamingos, hoopoes. Many migratory species from the lands of the north. The park was extensive and pleasant – with some larger animals also present.

In Jaipur, I had hoped to spend a night in the leading 'heritage' hotel, the Rambagh Palace, but it was either full or shut: so stayed in a very pleasant more modern establishment. My time in the city was relatively brief: though it was already a large place, the main attractions are grouped close together in the centre, the City Palace, the Hawa Mahal – that extraordinary near-triangular pink façade with its multi-storey windows for the harem: and opposite the Jantar Mantar. This last was the great astronomical observatory serving the scholars of the Mughal and Rajput empires in their world-leading astronomical studies. The various 'instruments' are enormous, mainly of stone, standing in their own park at ground level opposite the Hawa Mahal. There is a similar set-up in Delhi; also (visited a few years later) in Peking, this one at roof level along Changan Avenue.

From Jaipur I flew back to – at last! – Delhi. Again, there is little point in any full description of such a well-known and historic city. Its area, a fraction of that now, did already surprise me. I was staying at the modern Oberoi International on Zakir Hussain Marg, not far from the Lodi Gardens and Humayun's Tomb. From the higher floors of the hotel there are extensive views over a vast expanse of greenery: several much-touted golf courses hidden among the trees, but also rising like islands a number of earlier ruined or near-ruined edifices attesting mostly to the period of Mughal Islam supplanting Rajput Hinduism in the area. Most prominent also is the immensely high Qutb Minar minaret – to my shame I've never been up close, let alone climbed it – with its gigantic complex of mosques. Otiose to mention in detail the landscape of tombs and mosques in honour of various imperial worthies: but as one moves east the transition to the later rule of Humayun is apparent as the gigantic Purana Qila fort gates appear, nearer the river. Inside the fort (which I have visited), the structures and pavilions testify to the refinement which Humayun brought as Islamicisation proceeded both in architecture and in government.

Humayun's tomb I personally found one of the most congenial buildings in Delhi or indeed India. While the Taj must remain the *ne plus ultra*, this is a softer, less perfect forebear owing little to Italian marble mosaics and floral decoration. Unusually it was built some time after Humayun's accidental death (from a fall). But its sandstone redness erected as usual with pearl-white outlining and panel infill seems spot on. The approach to its site on a square central platform is through a larger square garden, having four quarters, divided by rivulets, parcelled into eight smaller squares. In the evenings, the promenaders – often couples taking their leisure – make a pleasant scene. There was a broader canal forming a central cross under the tomb: and floral delights everywhere. The interior – Humayun's tomb at the centre and subsidiary tombs in the four core pillars – is somewhat austere – but I rather like that.

There are many more relics from the past: Humayun expansion north and west of the Yamuna, before one is suddenly crossing the vast expanse of New Delhi on the way to Old Delhigarh. After the court moved to Agra under Akbar, the founder of that incomparable town, Shah Jahan returned to Delhi but built his city further north. The transition is abrupt. The Red Fort built above the Yamuna looks across a lower area to the Jame Masjid (Friday mosque) and the Chandni Chowk bazaar area. The fort is immensely impressive and normally entered from the west through (appropriately) the Lahore Gate, the upper part behind, then with four chakris and pierced screens by the central delicate towers. I shall not comment on the ghastly Victorian barracks architecture to the north, testifying to the – perhaps inevitable – tastes of the engineers and squaddies of the Raj: but unfortunately, independent India has not yet seen fit to blow them up.

The inside of the palace/fort shows wonderful examples of the 'marbled halls' of the great Diwan-i-Am (Hall of Public Audience) and the more intimate Diwan-i-Khas (ditto Private Audience), now standing alone in an open garden setting. Both show the beginning of the Shah Jahan high Islamic decoration with cusped rather than pointed arches and much coloured *pietra dura* decoration – presaging perhaps the Taj. A particular jewel is the Moti Masjid (Pearl Mosque), built by Aurangzeb for his private devotions. These 'pearls' provide a perfect punctuation for the sometimes austere sandstone architecture of the Red Fort.

Opposite, one climbs up towards the old city aiming squarely for the Jame Masjid, Delhi's principal mosque. This is as impressive as any in the Islamic world and to my mind the harmonious simplicity is even preferable to, say, the very elaborate major mosques of Persia. Having climbed the hill, there is still some way to go: the great sandstone walls on three sides rear up with ceremonial gates at the centre of each. Entry is now from the (side) north gate, and a massive flight of steps must be ascended to reach the courtyard. Then what is revealed is a place of perfect symmetry and harmony. The west side facing Mecca opens onto the mosque proper, with a large central dome and one more each side. The proportion and regularity of the arcades are wondrous: while emphasis on the russet stone façades give appropriate solemnity. In the centre of the courtyard is a large rectangular 'tank' or pool for ritual ablutions, seldom without colourfully sareed ladies performing same. Dusk seems the most magical time there, and I have painted the scene at that time for the golden glow behind the cupolas.

Next morning, I was off on the next stage, to Bangkok. Bangkok airport at that time was primitive in the extreme and baggage reclaim shambolic: instead of a carousel, a hopeless youth stood on top of a pile of luggage, called out names, at which point everyone shouted their own name and demand, then the youth abandoning the previous one would start afresh and at random, with equally little rhyme or reason. After a very long time I was in a taxi heading down the airport road to the centre and the venerable Oriental Hotel.

Approached by a rather nondescript street of silk shops etc., the Oriental has a superlative position on the banks of the wide Chao Phraya River, Bangkok's principal artery of trade and waterbound traffic. Curving around to the right can be seen the façades of the city centre. Almost straight ahead is the elegant if massive structure of one of the innumerable Buddhist temples: I was amazed on inspecting it more closely the next day to see that the exterior, so venerable- looking from a distance, was almost totally clad in cheap nineteenth-century Chinese blue-and-white porcelain fragments – of the sort sold in vast quantities to the UK, Europe and the US!

One arrives at the front door of the original smallish buildings so reminiscent of Somerset Maugham and other Orientalist writers. It now contains two lounges, dining room etc. But being of inadequate size it was followed by a larger more impersonal structure to give adequate infrastructure as well as room space. So that was where I would lodge for a few nights. I was somewhat taken aback in the lift to see one or two gecko lizards impassively if athletically – and silently – climbing the walls. Arriving at the room one had a superlative view of the whole curve of the riverscape – including small naval craft, innumerable ferries and of course the spires of the pagodas.

As in Srinagar, one's early priority in a place so reliant on intensive commerce and communication was a trip in a gondola-style boat. I was paddled through what seemed miles of teeming traffic, with some excursions ashore. Later was devoted more to terrestrial shopping as I searched for just the right shades of silk for curtains or for presents. This took me ever more 'downtown' where there was an incongruous mix (already) between modern skyscrapers and flyovers and very basic low-rise terracing in-between. What had been a sunny morning had turned for the worse, and rain beckoned. This was not as bad as the next time, when I stayed at the more central Erawan inundated by floodwater. (But this is supposed to be about India, not Thailand or SE Asia in any detail!)

Nevertheless, the next day I set out for Bangkok's fairly close seaside resort, Pattaya. This nowadays has innumerable hotels but then there were just two by the beach – one a rather boring-looking and more modern one, eschewed in favour of the other, older and more characterful. (I cannot remember the name of either now.) It rained. There was just one other guest, a pretty Lufthansa stewardess: so we spent some time together perforce, both in the garden, the pool and walking along the beach to the other hotel. At the end of the stretch was what existed of Pattaya town – a rather sleazy 'drag' of bars and bargiris whose inducements one was quite easily able to repel. Haruko and I went back (in a Mercedes) some years later and though vastly more developed nothing much of the essence seemed to have changed.

It was good to have had a glimpse, though, of a prettier and more 'proper' Bangkok. Naturally this involved a visit to the Royal Palace and its many ultra-decorated temples and halls: I was to get to know them much better in later years. Emerald and golden Buddhas of every size, reclining or upright, abounded. The amount of gold used was stupendous, matched perhaps only by Rangoon's.

Thence to Tokyo for what should have been barely a fortnight; but thanks to decisions made in a taxi in Hokkaido in a typhoon (it rained, and how!) I was back in barely a week to start up an office in Tokyo, a stay lasting almost a year. But that is another story...

The next Indian visit, by Haruko (whom I had met for a mere, if auspicious, half hour, before finding myself in Tokyo) as well as myself, occurred somewhat fortuitously when her appointment in the Shah's Iran was cancelled at short notice. This left several days free before our joint visit to Japan. India called.

Several days were spent in Delhi where we spent some time with Haruko's friend Bina Agarwal – I remember a particular stroll in the Lodi Gardens. Another introduction was to a delightful lady who had been Mrs Gandhi's social secretary: it was most interesting to meet her in her house in New Delhi's Civil Service zone, redolent of the Congress administrative culture. The next day, exploring the great Rajpath and India Gate up to the Rashtrapati Bhavan (presidential palace, Lutyens, previously Viceregal Lodge), we were able to enter and wander at will. Not now. Thence naturally to Agra: again, it need not be described a further time, nor Fatehpur Sikri which had not changed a lot in a few years after a millennium and a half of slumber. Later in the day our car took us on to Jaipur. An abiding and rather marvellous memory is entering the city from the east at nightfall, climbing a hill to the centre with wonderfully atmospheric lit-up market stalls, food places, shops: a sort of brilliant caravanserai scene.

Again, the attractions of Jaipur, close together, were fairly quickly 'taken in'; we should have liked to know it better (I still don't), but time and Singapore pressed. So this time we flew south to the unique Udaipur, revelling in staying in a most elegant suite in the incomparable Lake Palace Hotel. From there one obtains a perfect view of the City Palace complex and other massive structures lining the waterside of Lake Pichola from on high. Next day these had naturally to be explored. The City Palace (museum now) is enormous and the number of – often smallish – rooms, pavilions, etc. to visit uncountable. There is a tendency towards over-elaboration, even fussiness, and in some bits a plethora of lurid stained glass. From the palace a main shopping street leads down to the commercial centre with some excellent jewellery, silk, etc. emporia: here it is a (rather smart) modern Indian city. More congested and picturesque areas are found in the narrow bazaar street to each side. Many cows wander. I bought the textile hanging which to this day serves as the curtain to my garden door.

The next visit to India was also with Haruko and this time was westbound. We had been in Japan together and were making our way back by the 'southern route', the business element finishing in Singapore. There – abbreviated account – the high spot was perhaps the Changi Beach restaurant with its prawns, joyfully consumed by Haruko and A P Rajah, if not by me. (A P, a wonderful man, had been Chief Justice of Singapore and indeed invited to be President. A Tamil, and father of our friend Mala in London.) Raffles Hotel, however, disappointed, with a noisy smoky air-conditioner in the room and other inconveniences. The general atmosphere was 'obsolete colonial' with many references to 'tiffin' and all that. So the next morning we departed in favour of the much more modern, if less 'storied', Shangri-La further inland.

There might have been something of a 'double-take' by the Raffles people when we turned up for lunch with A P, who was being given an award for his faithful support!

From Singapore we flew to Madras (now of course Chennai). I remember a somewhat bumpy stormbound flight over the Bay of Bengal. Madras indeed was where the British engagement with India really began, and the centre felt older than, say, Calcutta: the church and its monuments evidencing the old East India Company days. Extensive grassy lawns extending from church to fort and beyond give a spaciousness to the scene which is completed by the beach, extending out of sight both north and south. We were headed south and in fact made our base at the excellent Fisherman's Cove (Taj group) for both Madras and Mahabalipuram. The hotel is set right on the shore above a private beach: alas when we were there the weather was grey, even cool, and the sea uninviting.

Mahabalipuram is undoubtedly the most fascinating ancient site near to Madras, with the great temple cities of Tamil Nadu further to the south – Madurai, Tanjore etc. But these are newer and the temples built, rather than as at Mahabalipuram largely carved from the rock. First one comes to the Shore Temple – as its name would imply built right on the shore, in fact on a small rocky promontory. It's an 'iconic' sight, an elegant multi-storeyed slender pyramid: not unlike some in comparable lakeside positions in Bali (also Hindu of course). Towards the centre and inland is an extraordinary array of bas-reliefs cut from the rock and illustrating scenes of Hindu mythology. The free-standing elephants are a much-loved feature amid all the warriors.

An intersubcontinental flight took us west to Bombay (as all my Indian friends still call it – it being left to the politically correct foreigners, the bureaucrats and the computers to adopt 'Mumbai'). We stayed, naturally, at the celebrated Taj hotel overlooking the Gateway of India, erected for the Durbar of 1907, the apogee of the Raj. There's now a high-rise addition but the character of the hotel remains unique. From a high-up room one has a brilliant view of the Gateway from above, on its little 'cape' surrounded by a melée of tourist boats to take punters across the bay to the island. On the shores the colourful saris of the womenfolk astound. By way of contrast, to the left stretches the huge naval dockyard; a berthed feature was an old British county class cruiser, somewhat outclassed by the instantly recognisable streamlined shapes of several Russian warships anchored in the roads.

The Taj is noted for its very high-class shopping arcade – jewellery, textiles, tailoring, etc. – and considerable time was spent there. Some lovely things, mainly silk, were obtained. Haruko was in fact disinclined to venture outside the hotel precincts; I did make one or two walks around the immediate neighbourhood, Colaba, which in fact is rather an up-market residential area, leading down an ever-narrowing peninsula to its own little cape.

After a brief period in Bombay we went our separate ways. Haruko having finished her business there was headed back to London for more; meanwhile as a leisured person I could fulfil a long-held desire to see more of southern and western India than I had encountered before. Thus Haruko headed for the international terminal and a by all accounts untroubled flight back to Heathrow. It was a very different story at the domestic terminal. A whole gallery of 'delayed' or 'cancelled' signs testified to Indian Airlines' habitual punctuality. The Bangalore flight, on which I was going, seemed to suffer more postponements than most. At least I could have a comfortable seat, alone, in the business class lounge. However, late in the evening a functionary came along to throw me out as the lounge was closing for the night. I adamantly refused to move and stayed until, amazingly, the flight was called in the early hours.

Arriving at Bangalore with the first glimmerings of daybreak, I found my car outside and the driver fast asleep in it. He rapidly bounded to his feet and drove me to the Taj hotel where I had booked a room. Shuffling of papers, whispered consultations, embarrassed avoided glances. 'You have given my room away, have you not?' I said. They admitted they had but said they had re-booked me in another Taj hotel across town. In fact the early-morning drive through the cantonments gave me an atmospheric sense of Bangalore which I would otherwise have missed. Arriving there not in the best of moods, I gave strict instructions that I was not to be woken or telephoned before I myself had made contact with the switchboard. Needless to say, after about an hour of fitful sleep a perky female voice rang, 'About your schedule for today sir…'!

But not too late that morning I was ready and eager to be off. First a rather perfunctory tour of Bangalore: already a large and major city mostly because of its new computer – and science – based industries. A contrast was provided by an extensive stroll through the Botanic Gardens, very fine. Then we were off to Mysore, with a stop at the evocatively named Srirangapatna – otherwise known as the Seringapatam of Tippoo (or Tipu) Sultan, 'taken out' by Robert Clive to consolidate the Company's control of eastern India. Situated beside the sprawling Cauveri river, Srirangapatna has a plethora of historic and architectural sights. We visited Tipu's summer palace to the north of the town, with its broad lawns and imperial memories; the fort stormed by Clive and a madrassah where unfortunate but well-schooled boys were automaton-like nodding their heads as they (allegedly) committed the entire Koran to memory.

Mysore was barely twelve miles away and from the first impression delighted. I was staying at the Lalitha Palace, a residence of the maharajah now converted to a hotel, which stands aloof on an eminence above the city. Imposing as the building is, it suffers from a not-unusual defect of having far too small lower rooms inside: my bedroom certainly was nothing special. But the marble has a certain elegance and presence.

The grandiose palace of the existing maharajah is the main feature of 'downtown' Mysore: an amazingly complex structure of Victorian metalwork (product of McFarlane's in Glasgow!) strung with, it is said, over 100,000 light bulbs. Alas I was not there to see the evening ceremony of them being lit, with 'oohs' and 'ahs' worthy of the most ambitious firework displays from those assembled to watch.

Mysore I thought was one of the most agreeable towns I visited in India: just the right size, with a super focal point in the palace and a vibrant town centre of colourful teeming markets, with ample parkland and spacious avenues contrasting with the bustling marketplaces. One salient feature was the 'multi-storey' tank of considerable size, gradually reducing in size towards the bottom. Another, some way out of town and indeed beyond the Lalitha Palace, is the hill on which a gigantic Nandi bull can be seen from far away. We went up to inspect the awesome animal at close quarters.

The long journey northwest through Kapurthala began quite early in the morning. It was notable how many young persons were already limbering up with bat and ball on any spare piece of land. No wonder they tend to outclass the England elevens! Leaving the outskirts, there was a long and rather lovely road ahead. Cattle herders and buffalo wallowers were ubiquitous. By this time my driver and I had struck up a good and useful friendship including my specifications for photographing from a moving car – occupy the whole back seat and – slide from left to right as photo-opportunities showed themselves. (We did stop more than just occasionally.) The landscape is truly Virgilian with lakes, woodland, cattle and brightly attired villagers.

We reached a nice modern hotel – nice apart from the mosquitoes – near Chikmagalur, with an extensive view over the lake/reservoir. The sunset was glorious, and peace reigned. This was a good starting point for a quick visit to the twin temple towns of Belur and Halebid nearby. Successive capitals of the eleventh-century Hoysala empire, Belur was abandoned to the invading Mughals but remained and remains a sizeable town both mercantile and religious; Halebid, however, was destroyed by the Muslims some centuries later, who were by then perhaps tolerant enough to have left the temples, if not the secular buildings, in place.

All these Hoysala temples are very evocative of their past era: immensely complicated friezes cut into the stone in multi-layered tiers, some below and some above walkways (polished smooth by pilgrims' feet!). As usual, gods, goddesses, elephants, dancing girls and musicians crowd the scene. Unlike most regional temple complexes, these temples are relatively low – two-storey – and there are no tall *gopuram* towers around. The whole two ensembles have an intimate and evocative look. The interiors were dark and atmospheric, redolent of strong incense surrounding the flower-bedecked religious idols.

It was either before or after then that my lovely driver – perhaps the nicest man I've ever known – kept softly intoning 'Belur, Halebid.' Clearly they had made their mark on him too. At last I got round to asking his name: 'Boopati, sahib' he said, 'John Boopati'. This was so appropriate for navigating the bumpy Karnataka roads that I have used it descriptively ever since! Alas I was to lose him after Hospet (for Hampi) for a far less agreeable driver, and a hopeless car which had to be exchanged, to the coast at Goa.

The highway north with the objectives of Hampi, Badarni and ultimately Goa was uncluttered except for numerous huge, gaily decorated and certainly over-manned trucks making their inexorable way towards us; skilfully avoided by Boopati. Much blaring of horns. It is amazing how drivers find their way as there are very few signs or maps; and stops to enquire of passers-by are frequent (whose knowledge is necessarily limited). The scenery becomes more open and indeed Deccan-like (I imagined): several large lakes.

On the way we had stopped for a brief but somewhat testing visit to Shravanabelagola. The town itself seemed unremarkable – if unnavigable – but from everywhere the steep hill containing one of the main Jain temple complexes, and certainly the largest nude statue, was visible. This was the 'testing' bit and the very large number of steps to be – gallantly – climbed were duly taken. The statue was astounding – if somewhat indelicate, though perhaps presaged on a smaller scale in early Crete and Greece; unfortunately much of the surrounding temple halls were closed for redecoration. Naturally there was no shortage of Nandi bulls and lesser statues. The views were astounding.

It's time to describe the main object, perhaps, of this Karnataka phase: the ruined and once enormous city of Hampi. In the Middle Ages, according to some, the largest city in the world Hampi was built by the Vijayanagara empire as the so-called 'dark eyes' and remained such for almost a millennium. All except the major monuments, spread over a great area, have gone: but what monuments!

It takes a long time, mostly 'hopping' by car, to visit everything (to be described later). Most amazing to us, perhaps, though no doubt with extreme sacred importance, is the huge stone cart on its great stone carriage and wheels, at the end of the running field. The area of rather isolated ruins runs basically downhill towards the Tungabhadra river, where the small town of Hampi is found, and further upstream the finest temple complex, the Vittala Temple.

There being no adequate accommodation at Hampi – just one or two hotels for backpackers – it was necessary to go the dozen or so miles to the unprepossessing town of Hospet for the night. The Malligi Tourist Home was a rather windowless dump on the corner of a busy street. Despite the fallacious claims for its restaurant, the main feature was a concentration of mosquitoes the like of which I have never encountered. Somehow I survived.

Escaped from Hospet, there was one further group of sites to visit before leaving the Deccan plateau for the coast. The main one was Badami, old-established capital of the Chalukya dynasty in the sixth to eighth centuries. It occupies an extraordinary site at the end of a narrow lake overlooked by high sandstone cliffs on both sides: on these, cave temples were carved out. There are also free-standing 'built' temples, projecting in some cases onto the lake. As well as the art-historical interest of these very early temples – including a few wall paintings from the sixth and seventh centuries – the setting with the lowering cliffs is extremely impressive, if not romantic, comparing favourably with most sites on the flat, dry Deccan plateau.

These include the final two: Pattadakal and Aihole, both slightly later than Badami and lacking its dramatic setting. Ten surviving temples have both northern (Chalukya, Vijayanagar) and southern (Dravidian) Indian influences; and are of both Hindu and Jain observance. In contrast to rugged Badami, the Pattadakal temples stand on flat lawn-like ground, looking almost like giant beehives with tall, tiered domes in several cases. Nearby Aihole was built earlier and in many ways served as the prototype for the Chalukyan architecture of Pattadakal: in fact the hundred-odd known temples reach along the river-bank (Tungabhadra again) between the two.

There was a very pleasant hotel just outside Badami, where in the morning the journey down to the sea at Goa commenced. Several fairly unremarkable but quite major towns such as Hubli and Belgaum were successfully navigated, after which it was a long and scenic descent from the plateau through the densely wooded Western Ghats to Goa.

It now seems ancient history that Goa was 'absorbed' into India, but of course the contrast is immediately striking. Instead of temples and mosques (though there are some), great Baroque churches testifying to the missionary vocation of St Francis Xavier. A population still evidently of Portuguese antecedents; and above all the presence of the ocean, a refreshing if (for me that time) brief change from the high inland plateaux.

Thus, Goa being endowed with endless miles of pristine white sand beaches, my own respite from inland India (memories of Hospet still fresh – if that's the word!) saw me ensconced for a few days in one of the smart beach hotels, where swimming and sun could be interspersed with a little light sight-seeing. First stop was unsurprisingly the little riverside capital, Panaji. The main sight is the mid-sixteenth century church of the Immaculate Conception, with its twin Baroque towers within easy distance of the Mandovi River. But the larger concentration of these impressive Baroque (Jesuit) churches is found in Velha Goa a short way to the east, the original Portuguese capital. Impressively fortified against attacks from seaward in particular, the inner port contains several large and impression religious buildings: the Basilica of Bom Jesus, containing the tomb and shrine of Francis Xavier; the larger cathedral: and several other churches of the late sixteenth to early seventeenth centuries. A day with a knowledgeable guide gave a good idea of this conveniently concentrated area of architectural splendour.

After my beach R & R, I took the plane to a very different part of India: Rajasthan. I flew to Jodhpur (where I had been, briefly, before), this time for a few more days. I stayed in the Umaid Bhawan Palace, up a steep hill from the city, which is at once the main residence of the maharajah and (in part) a hotel of the inevitable Taj group. Built in the mid-twentieth century, it is a vast, sprawling place of traditional Indian design under an imposing dome with lesser towers delineating the different quarters of the palace. From the broad lawns in front a stunning view of Jodhpur over to the enormous Mehrangarh Fort is presented. The interior is equally spectacular, the atrium beneath the dome featuring an impressive array of stuffed animal heads – tigers, antelopes, whatever.

The current maharajah, Jai Singh (known to all as Bapji) I had known vicariously for some time as featuring as a contemporary of numerous Etonian friends in house photographs: in fact he had also fagged (being a few years younger) for one of my closest friends. So on arrival I took the liberty of sending him a brief note introducing myself and hoping to meet him. I received a most prompt and gracious reply, welcoming me and inviting me to lunch that day, to be followed by a visit to the polo ground where Jodhpur was to take on Kenya. The lunch – outside with a view of the town and the desert stretching away into the distance – was a delightful occasion: I sat between two very senior Air Force officers who were most informative (if obviously somewhat partial) about the Indo-Pakistani situation. There were also two or three other maharajahs – the only one I can remember was Udaipur.

After lunch we all went down to watch the polo: this is a mystery to me but was exciting to watch, and one could only marvel at the horsemanship shown. I have no idea who won nor how the goals were counted. The home crowd's hero was clearly the Yuvraj (son and heir to Bapji) as constant shouts testified.

Successive days were spent in the city itself: in particular of course the great Mehrangarh Fort. This is largely given over to a museum now but inside or out is hugely impressive: the scale is tremendous and looking up from (spacious) courtyards the *zenana* (harem quarters) tower above like a cliff. Moving to the western end it is a long way down to the city level: again, stunning views to the west especially. From on high, looking in the other direction, Jodhpur's moniker as 'the Blue City' is entirely borne out as at least two-thirds of the houses are painted in this vibrant light blue. To that area I descended to view the street scene more closely.

The final destination – in many senses – after Jodhpur was Jaisalmer, about 180 miles to the west and an unmistakably desert outpost. From the flat wasteland stretching away into Pakistan there suddenly rises this amazing fortified eminence, massive round bastions in succession along the high walls. Once breached a crowded, vibrant city reveals itself. Apart from the inner fort and the palace, the main interest comes from the narrow but richly endowed streets of merchants' *haveli* or town houses: these themselves have a superabundance of carved decoration, while inside all is cool and dark.

Of course the city has spilled over outside the great walls and it was along the straight road to the west that I found my lodging: in a pretty little 'villa', formerly a royal dwelling but now made into a hotel. In fact the distinction is somewhat blurred: I found that the staff and the few guests were on friendly and almost equal terms, exemplified by the impromptu cricket game in which I joined. Held on a wicket of tarmac (a fast bowler's delight!) it was refreshingly and amazingly informal. I can't remember who if anyone won, or indeed whether there were sides – I rather assume not. I do, however, remember that one of the team, undistinguishable from the generality (staff or other), turned out to be the maharajah of Jaisalmer, who clearly felt very much at home there rather than in any palace.

One evening I was driven out – together with a few of my new friends – to a little village with quite a concentration of Jain temples and tombs – a few miles west of Jaisalmer. From that, relatively elevated, site we could look across the broad expanse of the Thar desert stretching hundreds of miles into Pakistan. Totally flat, this was more extreme than the scrub to the east of Jaisalmer. As the sun set the spectacle was marvellous. Then the next day it was back to Delhi for the flight to London.

My only other experience of southern India was when Haruko and I had a free weekend in Bombay between appointments and had decided to take a flight down to Cochin and explore a little of the very different Kerala surroundings. I enjoyed the flight, parallel to the coastline with the Western Ghats behind: very sparsely populated it seemed except for a few large towns (principally Mangalore): a beautiful near-deserted coastline of mountains reaching to the ocean, cliffs and little sandy coves alternating, not dissimilar to the Russian or Chinese coast as one leaves Siberia for the Japan Sea.

On the (quite long) drive from the airport to Cochin city the cultural landscape changed completely from that in the north: most evident was the amazing number of churches of 'new religions', mainly of evangelical character; some quite substantial, others little more than sheds. The town itself, sitting on the top end of the little peninsula, was charming: old-fashioned in many ways but also prosperous-seeming, and cosmopolitan. There remains a sizeable Jewish population (it used to be much larger) and one of the main sights is the splendid synagogue in the old Jewish town across from the island. A spacious hall lit by great windows; chandeliers, silver, gold and brass objects glitter, while blue-and-white tiles covering the floor complete the brilliant effect.

These tiles were also a main feature of the St Francis Church inside the fort on the island: a fairly simple and Baroque frontage (1503), as its name suggests it was at first a Catholic church built by the Portuguese. If its current Anglican denomination comes as something of a surprise, the reason is that it was 'repurposed' by the Dutch when they took over Cochin. In turn the English supplanted the Dutch who graciously (force majeure?) presented it to the English with their own Protestant church. The church is simple and attractive, with its single curved-gable frontage and inside the roof clad in exquisite blue-and-white tiles between the rafters.

Moving southwards, the main item of interest is the little 'colony' of Chinese fishermen sitting above the beach in their complex constructions of nets. We were headed further south for a day booked on board the celebrated rice barges of Alleppey and neighbourhood, on the island lagoons of the area. This was a most tranquil and enjoyable experience: gliding through the palm groves on a sturdy, handsome teak? mahogany? boat.

BHUTAN

A dozen or so members of the group (but not Peter and Caroline [Stanley] who were already in Calcutta after wanderings elsewhere in India) were foregathered in the departure lounge at Heathrow; introductions made where necessary, though several of us knew each other, from earlier tours or otherwise. Then we clambered aboard and BA whatever began its long flight over Eastern Europe and Central Asia to Calcutta.

This being BA, with its long-established policy of punishing those who spend most with it (see H. Kissinger and self, Miami, October 2003, page 344), while most happily collected their kit and disappeared into the Calcutta night, Malcolm and Kate Colquhoun and myself from business class were left with no baggage appearing on the eventually stationary carousel. An hour or so of form-filling and similar entry bureaucracy saw us at first light bumping through the already-stirring street life to the Oberoi Grand Hotel.

A brief sleep: then down to the verdant courtyard for breakfast and to meet Peter and Caroline and the others. I had to go out and buy a somewhat naff shirt and some pants: BA's next flight into Calcutta was for two days' time, when the missing baggage, it was solemnly sworn, would be returned. Then we embussed for a tour of central Calcutta: the great grassy expanse of the Maidan with its aspirant cricketers everywhere, and the cricket and football stadia on a rather different scale. On the other side the huge commercial palaces of the nineteenth century range along the great north–south artery of Chowringhee: culminating in the triumphant approach and then vast edifice of the Victoria Memorial closing off the south end of the Maidan. In white marble, with cupolaed towers at each corner, the

Memorial sports a truly massive central dome owing not a little to St Paul's: likewise, the great hall under the dome.

After promenading to the extensive gardens with their statues of the heroes of British military and viceregal achievements in India – Clive, Wellesley, Dalhousie *et al* – we soon found ourselves in the sharply contrasting, teeming district to the south. Predominant colour seemed to be orange or red whether of apparel or shops and stalls, or of lurid powder being thrown around. Among the noise and bustle in a slightly larger street is Mother Teresa's house, to which due homage was paid. Various intriguing little temples inserted themselves into crevices or corners of the business or market quarters. A more congested, colourful, seemingly chaotic neighbourhood would be hard to find anywhere.

At the other, northern end of the Maidan are the principal buildings of Calcutta as the eighteenth- and nineteenth-century capital of British India: the law courts, garrison church, and the remnants of Fort William, site of the infamous Black Hole. No evidence of this last remains, but a tall column with memorial inscriptions was erected and stands near the site. Though the street-facing façades are grand the inner courtyards and the churchyard are surprisingly intimate.

A little further north is the great Howrah Bridge over the river leading to Calcutta's principal railway station. Staying on the east bank the mud flats were active with people engaged in tanning and other riverine occupations. At increasing intervals were the grandiose houses of the colonial merchants, more often put to other uses. In fact, we were bound for the self-contained settlements of other colonial powers, notably the French and the Danish, each with their own distinctive character.

We visited the Danish settlement Serampore and the French Chandernagore, both on the west bank of the Hooghly, with Chandernagore the further north. Though both became industrial towns when eventually ceded to or bought by the British, much of the original colonial character remains: in particular, broad riverside esplanades backed by churches, schools and colleges, and municipal buildings characteristic of their original founders. By now the industry (mainly jute) is almost gone: to be replaced by tourism and commuters from the crowded and polluted city. As always, it was agreeable to wander along the esplanades before boarding our bus back to Calcutta: itself a most interesting drive with aspects of quotidian Bengali life – more logging now than anything else.

On our final day in Calcutta most of us arranged to have lunch at the revered Tollygunge Club, perhaps the world's original country club, in its spacious grounds beyond the melée of downtown Calcutta around the Kali temple and other exotic and pullulating places. The Club sits among many acres of beautifully kept lawns, with tennis courts, pools and all the other appurtenances of its genre. We were, I think, all there bar Malcolm Colquhoun who had gallantly agreed to stay at the hotel until the missing luggage was delivered as promised.

Malcom arrived: so, has it come? No, it had not. The disappointment was total. The Colquhouns and I would have to go on a bazaar shopping expedition on this last afternoon: a cruel twist being that we would miss visiting the Park Street cemetery (in the same street at the Oberoi), which evidently had a most amazing collection of funerary monuments – pyramids, obelisks, grottoes and more – from the olden times in Calcutta, allegedly rivalling Paris' Père Lachaise or perhaps the Glasgow Necropolis. Returning to the hotel then, we asked the concierge to confirm that no delivery had been made by British Airways: he concurred.

Back in my room, a red light was winking on my bedside phone. It was the front desk. 'Sir, some baggage was delivered some hours ago, by British Airways' – shall we bring it up to you? Well, yes… But I still never got to the cemetery, though compared with the relief that was a small price to pay.

Druk Air, Bhutan's national airline, flies Boeing 737s between India (Delhi and Calcutta) and Bhutan's only airport at Paro.

The plane was smart and the flight northwards spectacular beyond imagination: it seemed that once we had climbed to altitude over the Bengali plain the ramparts of the Himalayan foothills rose up to embrace us, until it seemed we were flying below their peaks. As indeed we were: the first approach to Paro follows a winding course of the Paro river, far below the surrounding forested hills. It was a virtuoso feat of flying.

Disembarked from the aircraft parked on the tarmac a hundred yards or so away, we had our first encounter with a modest-sized terminal built – like everything else in Bhutan – in traditional Bhutanese style, of wood with bright painted decoration. Inside we were greeted by most civilised officials from the Court, dressed of course in the equally traditional (and compulsory except for evening leisure) 'gho' – a sort of dressing gown in striped or chequered cloth, almost tartan, gathered at the waist and tied by a belt, with deep white cuffs. Somewhat incongruously, below the knee the ensemble tends to be completed by woollen stockings, often black, then football/hockey/hiking boots – the case for which is soon apparent.

The terminal being pleasingly informal and 'open-air', Malcolm and I went to sit outside and watched the flight crew leaving the aircraft and walking towards us. Both of us had (lapsed) private pilot's licences and were in a position to appreciate their airmanship; and told them so. 'Ah', said the Captain, 'You should have come up into the cockpit with us.' Well, of course, we didn't know: however, we jumped at the possibility of doing so on the return, which in any case would be a longer and more scenic flight, along the line of the main Himalaya from Paro to Kathmandu. So we put in our bid; but he said that it depended on the crew that day, and some captains were not as accommodating as him. We bore that in mind.

Off we went eventually in the bus into Paro town. First visit was to the remarkable bridge over the Paro River.

[Dugald's account of Bhutan ends here – ed.]

Westward Ho!

The chronology resumes with some mid-1980s excursions. First, in September 1984, is a westward journey via America to Japan. The first leg was the one and only time I have been on Concorde. It was like a noisy, bumpy sports car (? Aston Martin) compared with a 747's subdued spaciousness. The seat back would not stay upright but slid back to full recline the moment one leant back against it. The roof rack would not accept an ordinary briefcase, nor the restricted legroom allow it to be placed on the floor other than diagonally. It being mid-September a partridge arrived for lunch (? breakfast), but the contortions needed to reach and consume it were extraordinary. The small windows were low-set so more bending contortions were required to look out: in any case all that could be seen was a blue sky much darker than the norm as usually seen from 35,000 feet. Nevertheless, I found it thrilling and it was fun to arrive before one had left.

I stayed as often at the Knickerbocker – very classy apart from the world's least comfortable bed – and saw quite a few old friends (my third breakfast that morning I seem to remember with Richard Bonsor). Then a little turboprop plane from LaGuardia along Long Island Sound to Providence, Rhode Island for Nigel Blackwell's wedding to Eliza Mauran. The entirely predictable 'team' of ushers, best man, relations and in-laws stayed at the wonderful Hope Club on Benefit Street and Benevolent Street (what better auspices could one have imagined?). Many 'rehearsal dinners', drinks parties, lunches and other preliminary festivities were arranged and enjoyed before the marriage ceremony itself. This took place at the Unitarian church directly across the street and I seem to remember timing it at 17 minutes, which must be something of a record. Then it was off to Philmoney, Eliza's parents' lovely rambling house in the country near Exeter, RI, for a glorious afternoon and evening of reception, refreshments, swimming, dinner, dancing … and back to the club, probably for some more of the same… Goodness it was hot, if not quite Riyadh.

Providence itself is a delightful and civilised city: though its industrial quarters had seen better times with huge and decaying mills 'on the wrong side of the tracks'. It's an old-established New England city founded and re-founded from the mid-seventeenth century on with a reputation for tolerance of dissenters and minorities (if also, unfortunately, deriving much of its wealth from the slave-shipping trade). In the same area as the two august institutions already mentioned are world-famous cultural and academic institutions such as the Rhode Island School of Design, the (Ivy League) Brown University, and a host of others.

Back in 'the city' briefly then Kennedy airport to fly on to Honolulu. It was a long, long flight; no stopping on 'the coast'. Through the night I was afflicted by a great and tender nostalgia for the years I had spent in New York and the eastern seaboard. But Honolulu showed up bright and exciting and these feelings soon passed. I was staying at the Okura's Halekulani – so a very familiar ethos – on Waikiki Beach and I think it might just be the best hotel at which I have ever stayed. It is elegant and modern, right on the beach which is extraordinarily narrow: from room to sea, virtually instant (though I had an upper-storey room, with a great view along the shore to Diamond Head). The water was lovely.

Soon enough I made my way along to Pearl Harbor, visited the 'visitor center' above the wreck of the *Arizona* and took in the whole geography and aspect of that fateful scene. I believe there have been many improvements and additions since, in particular the arrival of the battleship USS *Missouri* on which the Japanese surrender was signed in Tokyo Bay – I should very much like to see that. I also tarried in the town, bought lurid

Hawaiian shirts, and visited the 'iconic' Royal Hawaiian Hotel: a charming, colourful flower-bedecked low-rise building redolent of the decades both before and after the war. I may have had a meal there.

I made a day trip to visit my second cousins Bill and Bob Dart on the smaller island of Maui: 'raised' in Montreal, they had migrated via British Columbia to this sunny spot, where they ran a steak and seafood restaurant by the beach in Lahaina. Lunch duly consumed there and a brief visit to the golf and country club just up the way at Kaanapali, then a swim. Without exception, I can say this was the purest, clearest, softest, gentlest sea water in which I have ever swum.

The 'day trip' had been enabled by a flight on a small twin-engined prop-jet: much of the route involved flying past the cliffs on the northern side of Molokai, between Oahu and Maui. These dispute with those of the Faroe Islands the distinction of being the highest sea-cliffs in the world. At any rate, the plane flew along them at not much more than half their height. As to the record claims, I have seen both, one lot from the air and one from the sea, and declare it a draw. So there!

Tuscany, Umbria, Rome

Pure holiday this time, but for poor Haruko rather abbreviated as work called back in London; almost exactly a year later we flew to Pisa and up to Florence for a few days in the Hotel Medici (now Cavalieri) some way along the westbound via della Scala from the Tornabuoni/Duomo/Signoria/Uffizi *centro città*. But it was elegant in that demure Italian city way with a lot of quiet character. Walking or taking a cab further away was not a problem. Pointless to 'review' the Duomo or San Marco or Sta. Maria Novella (just round the corner), but we did walk a lot. Santa Croce is of course marvellous for its church and Giottos (among so much else), but its broad piazza contains arcades with great shops – books, albums, paper, bookbinding especially notable. We spent some time across the river both at the Pitti and higher up at the classic if clichéd viewpoint below San Miniato al Monte and looking down across the Ponte Vecchio to the centre. In fact, we also spent some time around the bridge itself and I bought a fine tie with signs of the zodiac near the southern end.

With the car we could drive further out: on the southern outskirts to Galileo's haunts, to see (from the outside) the Villa Gioiello or Villa Galileo where he was confined for heresy until his death: but not visitable except in groups at vast expense. Lovely gardens though all around. It's easily reached driving south from San Miniato and is a pleasant neighbourhood on the reverse side of the hill above the Arno. Turning north again, we had lunch at the terrace restaurant of Michelangelo's Villa San Michele above Fiesole: a great experience on all fronts: gastronomic, architectural, panoramic.

Florence had really been at its best in the early autumn with the heat turned down a bit and much of the tourist crowd gone. We queued for only a short time at the Uffizi and Haruko set some sort of record by having us out again not half an hour later in the approximate direction of the handbags and similar of the via Tornabuoni, though having spent a respectable few minutes in front of Botticelli's 'Primavera'. (To be fair, we had spent rather longer in the Pitti, as well as in San Marco with the Fra Angelico cells.) These apart, one of the best things about San Marco is the view as one returns southwards down the street to the awesome mass of the Duomo and its great dome: here I think Brunelleschi 1, Buonarroti 0; though the Medici chapel in San Lorenzo in my view is quite peerless, both architecturally and sculpturally.

It was time for Haruko's return to London and I embarked on my quick tour down through Tuscany to the Etrurian coast, Rome and back. I found – with some difficulty – a nice hotel in the country near Siena and visited that excellent city in somewhat more clement weather than on a wet November with the Blackwells, *padre e figlio*, over a decade earlier. St Catherine and the great Pinturicchio frescoes in the Piccolomini library were revisited: good to see Pinturicchio giving due space to the shipwreck off Arbroath of the Piccolomini who was to become Pope Pius II. (They got around!)

My journey took me down the main road from Siena, past Grosseto, to the sea, the Orbetello lagoon and the spit leading across to Porto Ercole on the Argentario peninsula. There had been some thought that Nigel and Eliza B were still in a villa around there, but I could not get in touch. I think they had left. Anyway, I booked in at the celebrated Hotel Pellicano, on the south side and a stone's throw from Porto Ercole. However, with plenty of time in hand I thought it would be good to circumnavigate the Argentario anticlockwise, via Porto Santo Stefano and Monte Argentario on the north coast, then by the rocky west coast looking across to the islands of Giglio (near) and Elba (further). As it happened most of the rocks seemed to be in the road which rapidly degenerated to river bed status. I pressed on: it was just possible. The scenery made the whole exploit worthwhile – and it was fun. Eventually I mounted the last steep incline to an unconventional approach to the hotel. I must have looked, in my dust-shrouded hired Alfa (or Fiat?) rather like a member of Graziani's army in full desert retreat from Benghazi!

The Pellicano was wonderful. It sprawls down the hillside from the reception, restaurant, pool, etc. centre with scenic views down the coast, with villas or cottages spread around in the gardens under ancient pines. I had one adjoining the tennis courts where future Federer-style hopefuls were limbering up, all of course correctly dressed in whites. I wandered down with my kit to the waterside where – something I always enjoy – we could bathe off the rocks (with ladders where needed, of course). I particularly love when trees are growing right down to the shoreside rocks. No pesky sand or shingle to get into one's toes and crevices.

A nice dinner looking down to the twinkling lights of the Tuscan coast, then it was off next day to follow that coast briefly before turning in to the Etrurian heartland: Toscania, Tarquinia, Lake Bolsena, Montefiascore and finally some time in Viterbo. Though that is the heart of Etruria and a pleasant little town I did not tarry very long – it does not seem to have much in the way of museums – so left for Rome and (on the way home, but not alas with the time to visit) Volterra. All these places have rather Macaulay-reminiscent names (Tarquinia, Toscania). I returned seawards to Civitavecchia, not somewhere I believe I had been before, pleasantly villa-endowed as well as a port for Tyrrhenian Sea ferries; thence the Via Aurelia takes one along the shore past endless beach resorts to enter Rome. All of a sudden one is descending the hill and passing St Peter's with Bernini's colonnade thrillingly on the left-hand side.

I remember little of that quick 'turn-around' in Rome, or

indeed where I stayed – probably the Flora. Evening almost certainly around the via Veneto, anyway: probably discovering where in the via Sardegna/Sicilia/Marche zone the family had moved Giovanni's restaurant to this time! Though far more imposing since the early 1960s days Giovanni's has lost none of its charm – though of course the generations have now changed completely.

I set off north on the autostrada for a first overnight stop in Orvieto. A tiresome incident was when a threesome of thoroughly evil-looking young men in a khaki Alfa saloon took exception to me for some reason, tailgated me, flashed, hooted, then overtook and slowed to about 20 kph, repeating several times. I believe I may have addressed some disobliging gesture to the occupants one time they passed, at which they fell back with murderous signs and tailed me even as I speeded up. (Presumably, they were mafiosi with a carful of Berettas if not AK-47s.) However, I was counting on overconfidence on their part and as we approached my autostrada exit for Orvieto I first speeded up further – followed – then at the very last moment swerved down the slip road: they had no option but to continue straight ahead. I gave them a cheerful wave.

The approach road eastwards towards Orvieto gives a wonderful view of the city and the cathedral on its 'acropolis'. This was layered in September mist and was most photogenic. The stripey cathedral is a real star, inside and out: horizontally banded round columns, mosaics, frescoes (notably Luca Signorelli), stained glass including front rose window: the whole thing a complete vision of early and extremely elaborate Gothic. From the cathedral terrace there is a stupendous view of the surrounding Umbrian rolling countryside, through which I was to drive back the next day (no mafiosi in evidence), past Siena to San Gimignano.

Again, San Gimignano is sufficiently world-famous that I don't need to describe it in detail. The views from round about of the skyscraper-crowned hill are inevitably spectacular.

Nearer, in the town centre, they loom massively in mute and mutual competition. I had not realised how many steps one had to climb to arrive inside the cathedral – one of these wide-fronted brick constructions which become more evident from here north towards Lombardy. The long street descending from the centre to the west contained much of interest, and I bought beautiful embroidered linen napkins and tablecloths.

Interludes

America

The next year saw a number of shorter trips, many of them 'add-ons' to business trips. In late autumn I had been in Japan and this time flew back via New York, where our erstwhile department member Peter Green had been stationed and was proving himself an excellent salesman. It was December and frighteningly cold – the contrast when one left the overheated interior of my Park Lane hotel into the freezing outdoors was breathtaking. I most vividly remember one evening when I had gone uptown to the Carlyle, for a drink with my old friend Judy Greenebaum (niece of Bruce Friedlich, see earlier); I hadn't seen her in ages and the drink went on very much longer than planned. But I was due down in midtown, on 46th between 2nd and 3rd Avenues, to dine with Peter and his wife, and was very late. So, I marched rapidly downtown, turned into 46th street, saw the street was roped off with a police line and unidentifiable objects besides many cops (as usual in New York then): I stepped around if not over it, entered the Greens' apartment block and made profuse apologies. Only then did I hear that what I had seen was the 'hit' by John Gotti on the mafia 'capo di tutti i capi' Paul Castellano, who was very dead. Truly, mafia encounters seemed to be ubiquitous.

It must have been a year or two earlier that we were both in New York for the wedding of Peter and Darcy. This took place at St Patrick's Cathedral on 5th Avenue – obviously, New York's premier venue – and the reception was out at a country club in New Jersey. Country which had been well known to me twenty years earlier. It was a happy occasion, much helped by the balmy weather of early summer.

... and Dutch

After an uneventful 1986 in 'leisure travel' terms: I remember mostly an expedition early in the year to Amsterdam to view the collection of Chinese porcelain which had been recovered from a wrecked Dutch East Indiaman in – where else – the East Indies (Indonesia) and was to be auctioned at the Hotel Okura. We were as usual staying at the Hotel d'Europe on the canal side. The Okura, however nice its parent, seemed unremarkable. So was the pottery. We did, however, hire a car and make a tour of Holland proper, new to me, around the Zuyder Zee (or what little is left of it): Volendam, Hoorn, Medemblik – a great centre of boats and boatbuilding, this of especial interest to Tom and Ellen: Hoorn and Monnickendam perhaps even more so. Though the land is unsurprisingly dead flat and boring the little towns had much charm: mini-Amsterdams all with vintage boat-lined canals, seventeenth-century ornate canalside houses, impressively towered churches and some good waterside castles. All still very reminiscent of the great age of Dutch painting. We probably bought some cheese in the markets in the cobbled squares.

Summer holidays (abroad) waited until a brief villa stay at Grimaud at the head of 'Loch' St Tropez. Andrew Fraser was with us, and I think Nigel. We were mostly in St Tropez and beyond at Tahiti-Plage: it was very much a late (September) beach holiday.

China Changing

I mentioned some way back that we were to revisit China, after a gap of nearly a decade, in early 1987. This came, yet again, after an investment visit to Japan which included our friends and colleagues from Foreign and Colonial, Nick Talbot Rice, for whom it was his first visit to Japan, and Eric Elstob, for whom the umpteenth. As Nicky was a Japan neophyte he and I flew down to Kansai for a couple of days in Kyoto: then a few days later all flew to Peking. It was indeed greatly different in appearance after more than a decade of Deng Xiaoping's economic reforms. Vast new dismal apartment blocks obliterating ancient 'hutong' neighbourhoods, greatly increased traffic including some private cars as well as taxis, colourful clothes beginning to be seen, garish advertisements even if much was still exclamatory Party sloganeering. Yet this was to be but a preamble to Tiananmen Square two years later.

We stayed at a more modern but rather characterless hotel west along Chang'an nearer the zoo, rather than the more atmospheric if antiquated Peking Hotel. The obligatory sightseeing itself was largely aligned along Chang'an's west–east axis: Tiananmen, and of course the Forbidden City, then on east to the Observatory with its incongruous metal armillary spheres and other curious devices testifying to Chinese astronomical interests pre-dating Galileo and Newton, all simply placed on a low roof overlooking the street. Not so far away was the Temple of Heaven and Altar of Heaven complex, disimproved now with somewhat garish restoration compared with a decade earlier, but sombre reminders in the evening light of China's geocentric pretensions. Nick and Eric took the ride up to the Great Wall and the Ming Tombs, but we felt we had 'been there, done that' and probably went shopping.

From Peking we diverged, Haruko and Eric to Korea for investment reasons, Nicky and I to Hong Kong, where we also rather went our separate ways for business reasons.

The Costa Smeralda and the Maddalena

In August 1989 – funny how we choose the hottest time to visit the Med – we decided on a part-land part-sea visit principally to the Costa Smeralda on the north-east side of Sardinia, with an important component the charter of a beautiful large sailing yacht. Haruko and I flew to Olbia and up to the 'Costa Smeralda' zone with its Aga Khan-owned hotel complex. First, we stayed at the Pitrizza, supposedly the choice 'boutique' hotel. It was charming but ultimately unsatisfactory: mostly because our accommodation was in one of these poky little beach cabins. The beach was pretty but isolated bits of nice sand were separated by rocks dotted around. We did in fact desert it after a day or two for the much larger Cala di Volpe, at the top of its own *golfo*. This was much more spacious: a lovely big room and all the facilities – lounges, restaurants, arcades of a larger and pretty up-market hotel. The arcade provided me with a Breguet wristwatch, and the dining room seemed to be populated by hedge-funders and their like, with families. The beach was some way along the shore, and one was ferried there in launches: this was fine.

After a day or two – we had more preliminary investigations of Porto Cervo and I had inspected our vessel and crew – Nicky and Wiggy Talbot Rice came to join us, and it was soon time to join the boat. My 'preview' had introduced me to the skipper, 'Filthy Phil', a professional rigger whose failed 60s rock-star appearance did not immediately impress me, but who turned out to be expert and very nice. So were the other two: a handsome blond young South African, and a petite Australian cook/hostess. They had of course done all the provisioning and the girl had filled the freezer etc. to bursting (space is tight on any boat): whether it was that or her unfamiliarity with the ingredients, when Haruko arrived leading a few live blue-black lobsters on a string, she was more than discomfited.

The charter boat was a beautiful Swan 65 ketch: a classic of all time, 65 feet overall of course, with main and mizzen masts, spacious cockpit, main saloon, and cabins forward (and forepeak for the crew), and a very special 'ensuite' cabin aft for Haruko and me. She has classic lines, with quite a pronounced sheer, and a very easy motion through the water. Steering through an enormous wheel at which both Nicky and Eric tried their hand – the former with immediate effectiveness, the latter perhaps less so…

We set off in uniformly glorious weather of sun and light winds into the scattered, rocky archipelago of the Maddalena islands between Sardinia and Corsica: anchoring both for the night and for daytime lunch/swims/siestas in isolated coves. Speedboats sometimes zoomed around; not so many other yachts: but in general, it was extraordinarily peaceful. There are some strange structures: of fortifications from times of Franco-Italian tension in previous centuries, or prisons on the Alcatraz model. The main town, the port of La Maddalena, is lively and has a naval presence: but the most historic is the neighbouring island of Caprera, whither Garibaldi was exiled for a long period and whence the Risorgimento was essentially conceived. After many further adventures Garibaldi bought a property and retired to Caprera in later life and died there.

We crossed the straits into Bonifacio and therefore France, at the southern tip of Corsica. A most spectacular site, Bonifacio has a secluded but spacious harbour below its remarkable clifftop castle and ascending old town: like Edinburgh right beside the sea, perhaps? After we'd tied up at the quay the Talbots managed to talk on the telephone – quite a feat then – to their son Harry who had just arrived for his first night at Eton. We explored – more climbing, good exercise after days at sea. After Bonifacio we sailed but a short way up the south-west coast and stopped off a long white beach for the usual activities (or inactivity).

Back in Sardinia, after saying farewell to our nice crew we also saw the others leave at different times, with some shoreside eating and visiting, and drives to Olbia and the airport. Haruko and I now transferred for the final phase to the third hotel, the Romazzino, larger again than Cala di Volpe, less smart but really very nice, and overlooking from above its own wide beach. There were marvellous views across to the offshore islands, notably the booming presence of long, cliffy Tavolara, like an aircraft carrier or container ship parked offshore. Another mainly holiday and pleasure port centre towards Olbia is Porto Rotondo – recently of Berlusconi fame – while we also explored the indented and rugged coast west of Porto Cervo towards Palau, noting the remarkable 'elephant rock' on one cliff face.

Some Rivers of France

Haruko and I had not finished with Continental touring by October that year and flew to Bordeaux for a leisurely trip to culminate in flying home from Marseille. It was now definitely autumnal and a great change from the balmy late summer days in the Mediterranean. From the Médoc we headed inland through the St Emilion vineyards into Périgord's black, white, and green. We drove up towards Bourdeilles and Brantôme and stayed at the delightful little Moulin du Roc beside the river Dronne a few miles on at Champagnac-de-Belair. Possibly slightly too twee? Then down past Périgueux into the 'Dordogne' proper with its châteaux looming in the increasing gloom, to Sarlat, Souillac and then further into upland *causses* territory to Gramat and a rather forbidding château-hotel. Standing alone in its grounds on the rather bare hillside, it was a distinct contrast to the Moulin. Gloomy but atmospheric.

We must have wandered around a bit, as there was both a need to find a Michelin-starred restaurant for a long lunch in Cahors and a stop in Florac, where it was now dark and non-stop raining. However, things had brightened up by the time we got down through the Languedoc and into Provence. We stayed at Fontvieille near Arles, scene of Alphonse Daudet's windmill, visited the castle ruins there and pottered around the lower Rhône by Arles, Beaucaire and Tarascon till it was time to drive down to the airport at Marseille. I remember we sat by the river experiencing a remarkably vicious mistral wind and discussing how stock markets seemed improbably high and due for a correction.

When we arrived at the airport, we duly found that the plane had been delayed for several hours in London because of the hurricane there. Eventually we got back: but driving along the Cromwell Road saw that many if not most of the plane trees had blown down. Next evening coming back from dinner in the West End we heard that the New York Dow Jones had fallen 690 points, an unheard-of crash. So much for premonitions!

The Mezzogiorno

Following our southern French tour of the previous autumn, we explored the south of Italy in May of the next year, 1988. We had been in Switzerland as so often and stayed briefly in Lugano to see Andrew and Jojo Grima there, a Ticino foretaste of Italy. From their hillside eyrie the lake was misty and evanescent: the town was drizzly. Not much had changed since I was there with grandparents in Oxford days. From nearby Milan we flew to Naples and hired a car for the tour of the heel and toe.

We didn't stay in Naples itself but after the usual baggage/car rental preliminaries set off across the peninsula, rapidly climbing up into the Apennines on the autostrada (no mafiosi evident despite it being prime Camorra territory), and regrettably bypassing such ancient cities as Benevento before we left the mountains for the flat coastal Adriatic plain. But we were bound for the Gargano promontory where again the geology produces a dramatic change in the scenery. From flat littoral the most picturesque road begins to wind along a quintessential Mediterranean shore of wooded and rocky coves. We stayed for a night in Vieste, the pretty little town perched on its white chalk cliffs above a small harbour. After this brief experience of the anomalous Gargano, from Manfredonia on it was a coastal drive past many beach places, with olives and other intensive plantations inland, to Barletta where we lunched and viewed. Here one begins to sense the overwhelming mediaeval presence of the Normans and Lombards, with its vast moated fort and imposing if austere cathedral with a pencil-thin campanile, and another major mediaeval basilica, San Sepolcro.

The coast is full of Norman wonders: next was Trani, whose very pure cathedral with its outsize bell-tower almost sits in the sea, then before coming to Bari the little port town of Molfetta. There right beside the harbour the twin towers of its Norman cathedral were bathed in a shaft of sunlight with a backdrop of ominous blue-black cloud. Unfortunately sticking to the coast meant we missed out on Frederick II's great Castel del Monte just inland: but one can't see everything.

We stayed in Bari and explored the old city: a most romantic place of pure white narrow streets with of course another remarkable Norman basilica at its heart. This was constructed to hold the remains of St Nicholas, otherwise known as Santa Claus, and the crypt has his rather spooky tomb. In fact, the whole building is definitely massive, squat and square with low, wide towers on its façade: and inside is a somewhat mystical atmosphere of incense and mosaics. More conventional perhaps is the city's cathedral, spare and vertical in its Romanesque interior.

I remember little of our hotel – probably a chain hotel of some sort, as Apulia was then a region rather short of hotels of style and distinction: the main recourse in the south was the somewhat inaccurately named Jolly Hotel chain, which has provided adequate shelter over the years from Verona to Syracuse. We were certainly to grace its outpost in Lecce, the next stop.

Leaving Bari was delayed. Driving out on the main drag Haruko spotted the Valentino emporium, which demanded investigation. Of course, the merchandise was quite different from that in Sloane Street – and rather more elegant and characterful. So, some hours later after much trying-on we emerged with at least a week's worth of ultra-elegant attire: an efficient way to shop! We turned inland at this point to Alberobello, chief town of the conical white *trulli* dwellings: obviously already a touristy place, but delightful, nonetheless. Invited inside one we could see how climatically efficient these spotless little houses were. We bought nice linen things. The flat countryside of olives and oranges seemed bereft of actual dwellings, as the farmers all seem to live in apartment blocks in small towns such as Martina Franca and Locorotondo (good names!) to commute to their fields. We stopped for lunch in Brindisi but found it a dump, and – perhaps unsurprisingly – somewhat sinister.

Lecce of course is the architectural cynosure of far-southern mainland Italy (in fact Italy's easternmost town also): its Baroque buildings comparable with those of Modica, Ragusa and Noto in Sicily. We checked into the Jolly Hotel. Unfortunately, it was dark and wet, and almost all the best buildings were being restored or refaced and were encased in scaffolding. Nevertheless, one got an idea of the arrangement of the main cathedral square, Charles V's castle, the amphitheatre and the rest. The Baroque exuberance of the façades peeped from under the scaffolding. Rather like Oxford in the 1960s, while one might regret the darkening and crumbling patina of the old stone, the sharpness of detail and the creamy tones of the limestone are probably an improvement.

From Lecce the only viable alternative to – then inaccessible – Albania was to turn west for a leisurely return trip to Naples. First stop was Taranto, rather a surprising place with the shore-side promenade past the naval base, lined with apartment houses, leading to the bridge to the artificial island between the Mare Piccolo (lagoon) and Mar Grande (outer harbour), topped by the Castello Aragonese fortifications, and the city's heart with its cathedral among a maze of narrow streets. On the north side of the island is the gentle curve of the fishing port with endless fish restaurants: we lunched at one and Haruko pronounced it the most delicious seafood ever (not bad praise from one born Japanese!). (In southern Italy with its near-monopoly for *frutti di mare* I found myself more often than not making do – perfectly well – with spaghetti *puttanesca* or otherwise tomatoey.) Taranto of course was the most important city of Magna Graecia in BC times, and the Greek heritage is still in evidence, not so much in actual buildings as in an indefinable atmosphere. More recently it contributed to history with the destruction by the Royal Navy flyers of the Italian fleet: it was greatly interesting for an aficionado of naval history to see the actual site – and indeed to see some modern warships at their latter-day berths.

Starting southwards by the Metaponto coastal plain (Greek

names here), we left before the 'toe' of Calabria and turned into the sinuous road across the very rugged final gasp of the Apennines and drove to the western shore at Maratea. Maratea is a dramatically sited little town, tacked in under a huge cliff and dropping down to a little fishing/pleasure port and beach. We lunched at a most charming hotel high on the 'ledge' at the top of the town, but had to press on, vowing to come back and stay another time. (We haven't yet.) The road took us along the Basilicata coast to the ancient ruins of Paestum: this time, unlike the small-hours episode in 1963, we stopped and had a proper look around. Then through decisively non-touristy Salerno to the Sorrento peninsula, we spent a little time in Amalfi and then along that extraordinary precipitous corniche to Positano. We looked at the 'iconic' San Pietro hotel on its shelf above the town but felt it was perhaps over-iconic and over-priced: 'celebrity' stuff. Thus, we actually stayed in Sorrento, in any case a much better jumping-off point for Capri, and a town not without interest itself, occupying the clifftop above its own beach and offering good views up to Vesuvius and Naples itself.

Naturally, the car had had to be left behind when we set sail for Capri. Arriving at the little harbour we had someone take our luggage to the hotel while we climbed up to the main piazza, then moved over to the other side and found our quarters. It was a pleasant hotel in nice gardens with spacious pool and great views down to the Faraglioni rocks and did us very well. We did also visit the Quisisana which is the 'top' hotel around there; and generally explored that southern side of the island.

The Last of the Eighties: Marrakech

The next year we decided on a restful stay in Marrakech. I hadn't been in Morocco since 1965 and then no further south than Fez. Of course, the Mamounia of Churchill (and many others) fame selected itself. It didn't disappoint: I gather much has been 'updated' (i.e. probably ruined) but it had enormous Art Deco style – lovely olivey-green leather chairs and sofas, all rather reminiscent of the Savoy before it too suffered a fate of style-free tarting-up. From our room we had a great view over the gardens to the high Atlas. The gardens are superlative: overflowing with roses on trellises dividing the space geometrically – giving perhaps fresh meaning to the term 'floribunda'. A fine-sized swimming pool was much enjoyed and beside it *al fresco* lunching on the terrace. Nothing that was not to be expected, but the ensemble had great style.

We lost no time in exploring: the souk with its denizens in brown woolly djellabas and innumerable specialist craftsmen and tradespeople – coppersmiths, spice merchants and the rest. Somehow though it seemed to me to lack quite the atmosphere of Fez, which was more 'indoor'-feeling and concentrated. From the Mamounia to the souk one passes the great Koutoubia minaret tower and then crosses the wide expanse of the Djemaa el-Fna 'square': this comes into its own around sunset when all sorts of gatherings of entertainers and audiences materialise with much colour and weird noises.

Perhaps less contrasted than further north, there is of course a much more modern part of the town, becoming positively suburban (in a pleasing palm grove sort of way) where there is a plentiful supply of 'riad' villas, much in demand for rich tenants and expatriates. Less salubrious but 'genuine' and interesting are the tanneries, outside the city walls and gate to be sure, where the hides are marinated in their vividly coloured and evil-smelling pits.

We did also take a car down some way south into the Atlas foothills: not as far as the celebrated oases such as Taroudant, but far enough to grasp the geology and 'sniff the Sahara' (perhaps). By the roadside were frequent stalls or shops selling mineral fragments: some are on my mantelpiece still. We flew back, changing at Casablanca.

West and East Germanies: Year of Transition

The transition from the 1980s into the 1990s witnessed the seismic events of the collapse of communism in the East, which opened up a whole new dimension to travel in Eastern Europe (not that that had been impossible before – see Hungary in 1971 – but it was now far easier, if less 'romantic'). I first flirted with the then Deutsche Demokratische Republik in a few days of May 1989. I flew to Hamburg, of course briefly saw the centre, stayed at a nice hotel by the inner lake and in the morning in a hired car first set off north towards the Danish border, as far as Schleswig (the question remaining unanswered). Kiel on its fjord and Plön straddling its lakes were next, of especial interest to me as my father had been kept on in Kiel for almost a year at the end of the war, I think as 'town major' or equivalent: he was always good at logistics and practicality, and as a surveyor must have been a real asset in the rebuilding. It was sunny and springlike and felt really 'Balticky'.

That night's destination was Lübeck, always associated primarily with Buxtehude but also a magnet for Bach, Handel and many of the great German composers (Bach memorably walking several hundred miles from Thuringia to see him). Though of course smashed to bits in the war Lübeck has been restored to much of its earlier splendour with the soaring spires of the cathedral, Marienkirche and other churches epitomising the Hanseatic or north German 'brick' Gothic. The very solid Holstentor gate provides the appropriate introduction. The waterside with old-style warehouses and a number of vintage vessels reminds one constantly of the Baltic and the Hanseatic network. I ate at the Ratskeller by the city hall on the main market square and tried hearty local north German specialities. Lübeck of course is also the place for marzipan.

I stayed in the eastern outskirts of the city and was up early on a bright morning for my foray into East Germany. The border was only a mile or two away (where now Schleswig-Holstein gives way to Mecklenburg-Vorpommern). I approached the border totally unsure whether in fact I would be allowed in but had a Plan B should I have been refused (I did have a hotel room in West Berlin booked for that night, so it would just have involved the autobahn). However, after quite a bit of waiting I got a pass allowing me to stay in the DDR until midnight. So, I had better get on with it! Driving east along pretty deserted roads I came first to Wismar, another city of impressive tall brick Gothic buildings, but in contrast to thriving Lübeck almost entirely unreconstructed, and looking as if Marshal Zhukov had just passed through. The town runs downhill through a capacious market square towards the narrow harbour inlet. Trabants, piles of bricks, general smokiness everywhere. Unfortunately, on this chance to see the unreconstructed and 'pure' DDR I could take no photographs: in the west the previous day I had been unable to buy even a single roll of film when I ran out, thanks to their total retail shutdown even on Saturdays.

There followed a leisurely and pleasurable drive east towards Rostock, with occasional hint of the coast. A very welcome surprise was to come across Bad Doberan and its fine church, in a pretty and well-kept park, with chinoiserie bridges and evidence of past glory as a Junker's estate. Turning up towards the seaside, the road behind the dunes near Warnemünde was completely lined by parked cars: mounting the dunes to view the sea I saw a large number of sun-worshippers and bathers, few of them wearing any clothes. Loving as I do the rare opportunities to swim in the nude, and undeterred by silly inhibitions, I was tempted to jump in: but with no towel and wanting to push on forgot the idea.

Nearby Rostock is a serious town and port, just not very interesting to the touristically minded as it was almost totally destroyed in the war and now rebuilt mainly as standard Soviet-pattern apartment blocks. Anyway, Berlin called. The autobahn, I believe one of Hitler's first, was entirely 'original' looking: the two carriageways often far apart, a total (and refreshing, if perhaps inadvisable) absence of safety barriers, overhead gantries, or other modern appurtenances. It being a weekend, families were using the 'central reservation' of grass between the opposing carriageways for their picnics!

The road continued in its pastoral way through pleasant countryside into Brandenburg till it was time to turn onto the western 'bypass' to Potsdam. Late afternoon now, but plenty of time to explore a bit. At that time though many of the main attractions of the park were unrestored and/or closed, and the only one I could enter was the giant Neues Palais – which was in fact very impressive. It had been restored by the Poles who I was shortly to find had performed the same service not only in Berlin, and unsurprisingly Warsaw and Gdansk, but also in Russia. From Potsdam one had to sweep round on the ring road to enter 'West Berlin' through a checkpoint on the south side. The contrast was quite extraordinary: a landscape of vast, bare, dun-coloured treeless fields led up to (as it were) the city walls: passing through was an 'Alice in Wonderland' experience as suddenly one was in a tree-lined boulevard of café terraces, shops, advertisements, traffic…

I had no further authorisation for the East, which did not matter as of course there is so much to see even in the western half – even if much of the interesting and historic centre lies to the east of the Brandenburg Gate. Thus, Charlottenburg and the Zoo and the Kurfürstendamm kept me fully occupied till it was time to hand back the car at Tegel and 'emplane'.

Acquaintance with the Baltic was to be further developed only a couple of months later when on *Ardevora*'s maiden voyage I sailed with Tom and Ellen Winser through the top of Denmark, on to Copenhagen and thence to the Stockholm archipelago; returning in 1990 via St Petersburg, Estonia and Latvia to Gdansk and ultimately Warsaw. All this is covered with the rest of my lifetime sailing experiences in a separate section, so no more now.

'With the unfolding saga of the dismantling of the Berlin Wall and the imminent demise of the Soviet Union, somehow Berlin, Eastern Europe and Russia seemed to have a magnetic attraction in 1989–90…'

Jacques Hennessy and Haruko lunching at a restaurant in Bordeaux.

Cheeses in Burgundy.

Cognac: Jacques preparing white asparagus for supper. 'Will you make Hollandaise?'

Greek scenes: 'Without, really, any say in the matter I specialised all through my academic career: at any stage it seemed inevitable that I should specialise in classics…'

Beach at Tolon.

Egyptian scenes: Cairo, Luxor, Edfu, Aswan…

'In July 2003 I reached the milestone of sixty... Haruko said she would give me a first-class ticket anywhere in the world (return too!)... I had no hesitation in saying I would really like to explore South America…'

Top: Cusco, Peru: procession of the Virgin Mary.

Right: Machu Picchu: 'I could re-enter and enjoy a Machu Picchu early evening in near-complete solitude (except for a few contently relaxing llamas or alpacas).'

'Colchani volcano scrubland... sharply relieved near the summit by a troupe selling a variety of amazingly brightly coloured woollens: a splendid punctuation to the greyness, and a response to it...' *Below*: Uyuni salt flats, Bolivia.

Behind the Iron Curtain (Beginning to Melt)

But I was back in Germany with my mother in the autumn of that year, 1989, just as things were getting interesting. From Munich to Passau to collect Mother from a Danube river cruise we crossed over into Austria, with a stop by a pretty but dark and drizzly lake, to Salzburg for just one night: this time at the elegant Sacher Hotel near the Schloss Mirabell and gardens, by the river and looking across to the old city and the Hohensalzburg Fortress. We went up to the fortress and had a good wander round the cathedral area also. Then – as the weather worsened steadily – we drove east into the Salzkammergut 'lake district'. Pretty little towns – St Gilgen and St Wolfgang – afforded *gemütlich* hostelries like the latter's Weisses Rössl. Plenty of strudel and kalbfleisch. Mist shrouded the hillsides. The next day we were striking north, by the Attersee then over the rather wild and bare plateau country near the Czech frontier; then with the usual formalities through said border – still the Iron Curtain – and into (then) Czechoslovakia. Again, the contrast in the standard of living was pretty evident. The first proper stop was the historic old town of Český Krumlov, immediately dubbed Crumbly Chekhov, for obvious reasons. It's built on a steep hill crowned inevitably by an impregnable-looking castle: though decayed and thitherto neglected, efforts at resuscitation did seem to be being made. It remained wet and grey, which did not improve the somewhat mournful atmosphere. All newish buildings were quite hideous and the usual 'workers and peasants' strident signs obtruded.

Pilsen was the next serious place: a much larger and flatter town, concentrated on a broad main square with dilapidated hotel, cafés, cinema etc. Trams, cobbles, buses, smoke. No doubt the local product adds to general happiness there. Soon we were driving into Prague along the Vltava. There were two 'possible' hotels then and we stayed at the Paris (the other was the

Palace): quite a good Art Deco building of medium size in one of the main streets. The rather antiquated telephone set in the room had a button marked, without irony, 'SECRET.SERVICE'. The newer part of Prague was somewhat drab but not without some pre-war flavour of earlier Czech prosperity. What was very evident was the number of music shops – instruments, sheet music, records, pleasingly testifying to the country's great musical heritage and continuing interest. On that side of the river also lies the celebrated Old Town Square, which already was beginning a renaissance of what I felt had perhaps too much of a 'Laura Ashley' character – too many candy pinks and other cosmetic embellishments. The dark charcoal-grey church of Our Lady of Tyn, with its jagged, spiky spires almost hiding behind buildings in the square, was atmospheric with tombs and intimations of the Thirty Years' War and endless religious conflicts. The broad square offered a site for memorials not only to the proto-Protestant Jan Hus but to other martyrs and victims.

Ahead lay the dramatic skyline crowned by the Hradcány palace and the cathedral; appropriately viewed across the Charles Bridge, itself punctuated by the celebrated Baroque statues but not then, mercifully, plagued by the hordes of vendors, exploiters, inebriated Brit stag party celebrants and other unwelcome features of (as I read) today's liberated Prague. We had some inevitably greasy ham and cabbage or suchlike in an atmospheric den, then started on the long plod up the hill. When one arrives at the space before the palace and cathedral compound everything broadens out, with a succession of imposing palaces of the nobility: Kinsky, Schwarzenberg, Sternberg, Lobkowicz… Also the Baroque Loreto monastery, standing proud: its museum has a most wonderful collection of silver and silver-gilt, mainly monstrances and other churchy items.

From the cathedral and palace courtyard one exits by a curiously intimate little lane and begins the descent to the Malá Strana and the river. This afforded lovely views of a muted roseate roofscape topping faded grey-green buildings; alas one feels that things must have been 'smartened up' with the arrival of capitalism. The French Embassy was already beginning this tarting-up process. The Malá Strana – 'Little Town' – boasts several truly impressive Baroque churches, as well as a plethora of urban palaces.

Leaving Prague, we headed west to the old spa towns of Carlsbad (Karlovy Vary) and Marienbad (Marianske Lazne), celebrated for their patronage by Edward VII and his circle 'taking the waters'. Though clearly no longer the haunts of any aristocracy there seemed still to be quite a lot of spa activity going on, and in general both towns looked well maintained. Carlsbad has some steep slopes above the river on which perch various improbably turreted and gabled turn-of-the-century mansions. Down by the river and near the main baths and casino was the sizeable Hotel Moskva – now unsurprisingly renamed. We had lunch in its imposing mirrored, high-ceilinged dining room; there was no one else there. Marienbad, a smaller place, was nevertheless much more spacious with its buildings set among extensive parks. (Alain Resnais' *Last Year at Marienbad* gives a good idea.)

Cheb was the last little town before crossing back into Germany, where we were to stay the night at a charming little modern hotel just outside Bayreuth. I remember some atypically German cuisine nouvelle (but not what it was). In the morning we had a quick look at the town, opera house laden with Wagnerian *geist* (I approve!) and headed for Nuremberg for our last night.

Nuremberg was impressive in a stolid sort of way: the nucleus on a commanding rock looking down on the river with the newer city centre around the marketplace, city buildings and cathedral. I imagine the Christmas market is quite something. Up high, the main attraction is Dürer's house, though other houses surpass it in their verticality and the number of storeys of dormer windows they can pack into one precipitous roof.

The combination of ashlar masonry at lower levels and a riot of half-timbering higher up is very attractive. One has, alas, to wonder how much of it has been reconstituted after the devastating air raids. Certainly, Nuremberg is the one place in Germany where I have been conscious of a less than enthusiastic welcome as a Briton.

Last stop, of course, Munich, with time for little more than a look around the centre, a quick session in the Löwenbräu bierkeller and a quick visit to the Pinakothek, before passing by Nymphenburg, sadly outside only for a glimpse, before it was time to check in. It was very wet.

CAIXA

France and Spain in May

In May 1984 my mother and I, in my little BMW 3 Series, embarked on the overnight ferry from Portsmouth to St Malo: arriving on a grey morning to breakfast in the old city, later renewing our acquaintance with the fine cathedral, and the ramparts around which she had carried ankle-injured me in 1953! The various treacherous islands were more or less visible on a dead calm grey sea. Of course, it was essential to revisit the scenes of that first 1953 holiday: Dinard and then St Lunaire, where the hotel had long since mutated into flats. No sign any more of the German fortifications on the promontories closing off the wide beach. Nor of the patisserie. But happy memories.

Striking south across Brittany was in fact new to me: the weather cheered up a bit and we stopped to visit the great château at Josselin, its long, regular, Gothic/Renaissance façade overseeing the quay and river. The pinnacled window entablatures were surely an inspiration for a certain David Bryce in nineteenth-century Edinburgh. As usual there was a tiresome little shrimp of a man waiting by the door for us to join his tedious tour, which we would far rather have avoided. A distinct contrast was the next sightseeing stop, the long lines of paleolithic monoliths and the dolmens at Carnac. By now we were on the south coast and took the little bridge at picturesque Auray for the main road past Vannes then down to La Baule.

La Baule had been a resort of my mother's parents in the 1930s and played, not then knowing, a not unimportant part in my life, in that it was there that the Macouats met and became the greatest lifelong friends with the Langsdorffs of New York:

'Aunt Martha', her daughter and grandchildren were frequent visitors to Scotland and London, and it was Kathy's husband Bruce Friedlich who gave me my first job in New York – the most wonderful man. La Baule was of course *hors saison* but with its wide beach and stately hotels one could quite see how vibrant it had been in the previous era.

With limited time and much ground to cover, we didn't dawdle on the way down the Atlantic coast to La Rochelle. Our hotel overlooked the zig-zaggy central city and above all the harbour with its two splendid towers were thoroughly explored, its fine town hall, towers, and stately streets with their arcades redolent of its days as a major French port. La Rochelle was a good starting point for the Gironde and the Médoc and ultimately Bordeaux, passing Rochefort and the rather ordinary-looking Royan.

In Bordeaux we stayed, of course, at the Grand Hotel beside the imposing Théâtre on the Place de la Comédie: Bordeaux's classical symmetry is very pleasing as also is its riverside aspect, broad quays giving a foretaste of the marriage of the Garonne and the Dordogne a kilometre or so further seaward, then the Gironde estuary and the wide Atlantic. Bordeaux of course means, for us anyway, but one thing: and so, we set off the next day for a tour of the Médoc, bottom to top and back again. Pottering through St Julien, Pauillac, St Estèphe and the rest, the labels on the claret bottles came to three-dimensional life as we paused to admire each legendary château. Margaux perhaps takes the palm as grandest and indeed most elegant; Palmer, also in Margaux, close both in architecture and viticulture; Cos d'Estournel perhaps the most quirky; Leóville Las Cases and Barton; Cantemerle, Beychevelle … invidious to continue. The variety of the estates and châteaux is remarkable, and the individuality of each, both in their wines and their architecture – and all concentrated in such a small area. We stayed at the hotel attached to Ch. Margaux – of course!

Relentlessly moving towards Spain, I marked the vernacular

architecture of the southern Bordeaux suburbs, single-storey every house. We passed through the Graves *appellation* and took the long straight road through the pinewoods of the Landes, as painted by Churchill and Lavery before the war, their 'twin' paintings seen in Nancy Westminster's drawing room in Sutherland – last encountered at night, driving back from Spain at Christmas 1965 – to Biarritz. Again, the choice owed much to Macouat memories: Biarritz had been another pre-war watering hole for my mother's family. So, it was important to stay at the same hotel, the Victoria (et du Golf!). This had perhaps seen better days, though indisputably 'grand', but was perfectly comfortable; however, I was woken up in the small hours by the furious rattling of the shutters, the chinks in which were so wide that every minute or so the sweep of the lighthouse beam would illuminate me. So not much more sleep! In the morning there was a full gale, which made my promenade on the walkway towards the large rock in the middle of the bay most exhilarating. Surf and breakers were deafening. A sad postscript is that several mainly British yachts crossing Biscay were lost in that storm.

Yet as we moved on after a rather hasty look at the town things seemed to improve. We lunched in Bayonne, a pleasant town with a fine Gothic cathedral; then to St-Jean-Pied-de-Port and into Spain.

Rather than turn westwards along the Basque and Asturias coasts (which we were to do some years later), we headed southwards for the Castilian heartland, spending a night in Burgos and revelling again in the nobility of the cathedral. While I had been there for a night on my way home in 1965, I had otherwise driven straight through from Madrid to the French border and on to the Charente and the historic cities of Castile had remained unexplored. This was now to be rectified. First was Valladolid, perhaps the least dramatic of these towns but full enough of history. The cathedral frontage filled from top to bottom with statuary is extraordinary and one imagined must have been a prototype for similar edifices I had seen in Mexico and was to see in Peru.

Next, Salamanca, a city I find especially attractive and congenial, perhaps because of many perceived affinities with Oxford: a university town par excellence, of a similar vintage; a city of golden stone, its architecture ranging from Roman to Gothic to Renaissance and Baroque. It has the advantage, which Oxford does not share, though Cambridge does – up to a point – of a river running right by the old town. Also, two cathedrals side by side: the modest old Romanesque one and the soaring Gothic, featuring the dome-topped tower so familiar in Spain and of course the cloisters, omnipresent also in the university colleges and a cathedral-sized convent church. We stayed in the Parador on the south bank, ideal for views of the Roman bridge immediately below and a panoramic view of the city ascending the hillside.

A contrast was the next stop, Ávila: austere where Salamanca had been golden and lively – perhaps a grey day following a sunny one tinged one's perceptions. Ávila has a completeness: an almost square city rising up a hillside and enclosed by wholly intact walls with frequent round towers. This always appeals greatly: when one thinks how many cities destroyed their walls – for obvious practical reasons, but all the same – in the nineteenth century (and most horrendously in Mao's China of the twentieth), one can't help but be sad. Provins and Aigues-Mortes in France have that magic – perhaps Carcassonne still, though rather over-touristy nowadays; and St Malo (*vid. sup.*) with its 'walled beach' and doubtless more. I suppose the prime example is Jerusalem, with on a smaller scale Dubrovnik and (even smaller) Malta's Mdina coming to mind too. (I digress.)

Segovia was not entirely as I had expected from the conventional photos, taken from the valley below the 'prow' of the escarpment which culminates in the pointed and pinnacled Alcázar. These inevitably give the impression that this is the 'summit', whereas the hill climbs steeply behind to the main part of the town, past the cathedral. The Alcázar in fact marks the low point of a wedge-shaped promontory. The cathedral – another fine example of the Gothic-Renaissance genre of Castile, with the typical central dome and especially high tower, apsidal flying buttresses galore, does occupy the highest point of the rock. After it, the ground falls away slightly to the flatter terrain of the old town: where the most striking feature has to be the Roman aqueduct, one of the largest and surely one of the best-preserved extant. Its appearance is dramatic, joining two quite steep little eminences and crossing a wide main road into the city, adjacent to a spacious square. An introduction to the city every bit as dramatic as that from below the Alcázar, in a quite different way.

A homely contrast to these superlative edifices, perfect in its own way, is the little Romanesque and Gothic monastery and church of El Parral, on the northern hillside looking up to the city walls, and thus giving perhaps the best view of the silhouette of the city all the way down to the Alcázar. In a garden setting with a small community adjacent, it must have been the perfect retreat for the contemplative life.

After Segovia, rather than turning south to the attractions of Madrid, we hastened eastward along the *autovia* non-stop to Barcelona: exchanging Castile and León for Catalonia, via Aragon. As the *autovia* sweeps right by Zaragoza we had a fine view – at speed – of the stupendous cathedral: with the multiple domes and four enormous towers, one at each corner, it clearly owes much at least in layout to the Arabist period. The river Ebro with its fine old bridges also runs right past. Sadly, I have never visited Zaragoza properly. I had of course had an unfortunate experience of the Ramblas in November 1965 on my first ever night in Spain, when some urchin broke into my Mini-Cooper right in front of the main police station. Nothing like that this time, though we stayed at the very fine Hotel Colón overlooking the cathedral square in the Barrio Gótico, very near.

The Barrio is a charming small and intimate area contrasting sharply with the grandiosity of later Barcelona, with its radiating broad avenues beginning at the top of the Ramblas by the Plaça de Catalunya with its gigantic column. We really only ventured along the Diagonal to visit Gaudí's Sagrada Familia, which really needs no introduction here: a one-off if ever there was one. Primarily though we stayed within the older town, around the Ramblas (especially the food market with appetising *jamón* of all varieties), the Barrio Gótico (but avoiding the queues of the Picasso Museum) and further down the pleasure port, beach and gardens. It had to be a brief stay, but Barcelona is a city one could revisit many times (as I have done twice more). Another great omission – which has not been rectified – yet – is the famous monastery of Montserrat, high in the hills overlooking the city. But it was time to turn northwards for home.

A coastal road allowed us a glimpse of the Costa Brava and so many of the little resorts which featured so prominently in holiday brochures of old – Lloret de Mar, Tossa de Mar, Blanes, Palamós… It is in fact a surprisingly attractive coastline and in many respects little spoiled: the indented coastline with little coves perhaps the explanation. At any rate we saw more than one hotel of apparent class in extensive pine-clad gardens which looked wholly suitable and enticing.

However, it was now to France by the last very wriggly coastal road, to Portbou and Cerbère and to our hotel at the celebrated artists' retreat of Collioure. While both Matisse and Picasso were attracted by Collioure and spent sojourns there, it is perhaps the Fauves – Signac and Derain especially – who are most linked with the place and who produced the best-loved images. This rather like St Tropez or Portofino is perhaps too pretty to be true, with its waterside church with round-topped tower literally emerging from the harbour water and pastel-coloured houses crowding onto the beach. From the pleasant gardens of our hotel, we could look across the bay to all this before some delicious dinner. Alas, next morning we found that the miscreants of Collioure owed nothing to those of Barcelona two decades earlier and had broken the window of my car parked in the street outside (no 'parking' or garage). I can't remember that anything of value had been taken. The same thing had happened to the other residents' cars, and we soon found ourselves in a queue back in Port-Vendres, to report it to remarkably uninterested and unsurprised police: then to replace the window, I think near Nîmes the next day.

Time running short, the attractions of Perpignan and Narbonne were glimpsed from afar as we sped up the autoroute through the endless Languedoc vineyards. One pause though was to view the poor *Lydia* steamship firmly beached on the equally endless sands of that featureless coast. This time also we eschewed the Camargue and even (despite its pristine city walls) Aigues-Mortes, and after window replacement settled in the elegant Imperator in Nîmes. The Imperator is close beside the extensive and beautiful formal gardens, with their bassins and sculptuary, in which we lingered briefly. The well-travelled autoroute took us north up the Rhône valley and to Tournus where, as before and since, we stayed at the Greuze, revelling in its Michelin stars. I cannot in all honesty recall our route to the Channel – it has been done so many times – nor whether another night was spent in France; but it had been a superb trip with many kilometres travelled and sights seen.

Next Spanish Trip

It was three years later, in March 1987, that we did spend some time in Madrid, this time flying there and hiring a car for our brief excursions around about. We stayed in the Ritz which was quite lovely in an understated way. Its position is ideal, looking over to the older part of town but also convenient for the more recent shopping and residential avenues and of course the Prado. If the Prado is thought of as one of the top three or four galleries in the world, for me it has a strong claim as favourite: not just the incomparable collection of (mostly) the great Spanish painters, and of course the other 'greats' patronised by the Habsburgs, but the sobriety and order of the setting make for a perfectly integrated visual experience. This was the second of the (only) two times I have visited and I long for renewed and extended acquaintance. The other great attraction for art-minded Madrid visitors now, of course, is the Thyssen-Bornemisza collection; negotiations for this were still in progress in 1987, but we had seen it in its original and more intimate setting in Lugano some years earlier.

In a great city, museum and gallery-going is one unmissable experience; but the buildings and streetscape, not to mention the social and commercial life of the city, are to me at least as compelling. Of few cities is this more true than of Madrid, especially perhaps as night draws in and tapas summon. While I was used to rather light 'nibbles' and fino sherry in Andalucia, here further north it is substantial tapas and red wine. The Gran Via was pullulating! I am enthralled by the majesty and space of the Plaza Mayor, prototype I suppose for so many main squares in Spain or Latin America; as by the little streets leading off it, with some interesting churches. Further afield of course are such as the Royal Palace and the Retiro Park: these we viewed when heading out of town in the car.

We went west to the Valle de los Caidos, Franco's grandiose monument to the fallen (of his side, of course) of the civil war he instigated. It is of course very impressive in its way, in its setting of a wooded mountain valley with the ginormous cross. This was of course the post-Franco era of King Juan Carlos (last seen in Rothesay), though changes are doubtless coming. Franco himself was not to stay there long and has been removed in ignominy, if not of course without controversy. Not far is the other stupendous memorial to an autocratic monarch, King Philip II, where he sat and plotted his imperialist adventures; notably the Spanish Armada of 1588 (that did not turn out well!); and of course the amazing conquest of most of Latin America, which was to last until a chap called Bolivar came along – and whose heritage, especially linguistic, remains to this day.

It may be simply that it was the product of a more confident age with better architects, but the Escorial, though again enormous and grandiose in a severe way, is a more acceptable monument to an autocrat than Franco's fascist pastiche. I was immensely impressed not only by the scale of the piece with its inner courtyards but especially by its quite beautiful and mercifully unfussy, though by no means modest, chapel (the architect had worked with Michelangelo and Bramante on St Peter's in Rome). The Escorial was from the start and always has been a monastery – viewed as the centre of Christianity by its founder Philip – and remains one to this day. The Royal Library must be one of the most splendid examples of the genre in the world. After all this Jesuit-imperial grandeur, it is perhaps a relief to move outside to view the equally grand (Versailles meets Granada, Seville, Córdoba?) of the formal gardens stretching into the distance.

The final excursion on this rather brief visit was down south to Toledo. The drive out of Madrid gives one the first sight of the central Spanish plain, the Meseta or La Mancha, with its endless wheatfields and masses of sheep flocks. The stark contrast is provided by Toledo on its steep hill above a bend in the Tagus. Viewing the preserved mediaeval city from the hill on the opposite bank, one has a superlative perspective of the city rising to its summit with the (inevitably grim) Alcázar and the towers, domes, and spires of the cathedral. Hard walking once in the centre! Lower down in both senses, I was surprised to see the river almost entirely choked in white foamy effluent – no doubt this has improved since then.

Toledo of course has a rich multicultural heritage of Jewish, Arabic and Mozarabic inhabitants, still very evident today. The great synagogue compelled our attention. The influence and evidence of perhaps Toledo's most eminent inhabitant, El Greco, is also all-pervasive and not just in the museums. In artisan crafts, Toledo is pre-eminent in metalwork – swords, knives, cutlery, and all – as the souvenir shops will not allow one to forget.

Freedom Pass

Normally, my spirits lift the moment I am on water: whether just a boathouse pontoon on the Thames, a cross-Channel ferry or a gale in a fully reefed offshore sailing yacht. But the voyage which began my last Continental tour with my mama was the one time I have been truly relieved to get off a ship.

Spain, Portugal and France with EABB [Dugald's mother]
This was September 1992 (so strict chronology has now been definitely suspended in the interest of thematic consistency) and I had just been released from the wonderful world of investment management. In my beautiful, and likewise liberated, big Mercedes Coupé, Mother and I embarked on the P&O ferry overnight from Portsmouth to Bilbao. Economy or availability dictated inside cabins, fine for a single night especially as in late evening, after Mother had gone to bed, I sat in the cinema and watched some film. There was some low-frequency rolling and the occasional very slight shudder, but I was most surprised to hear a voice on the tannoy announcing that because of the great gale raging we would be twelve hours late into Bilbao and not get there until late the next afternoon. Nothing for it but bed and sound sleep.

In the morning of course we now had the whole day ahead of us and no desire to remain in our poky cabins. Unfortunately, there was not a lot of 'public space': some rather inadequate sofas and chairs in the enclosed verandahs facing the plate-glass windows. Even more unfortunately, some woman in Ayrshire who had met my mother had been told that 'Mrs Barr and her son would be on that sailing to Bilbao' and relayed that to her own friends with the injunction that they should be sure to seek us out. They proved the most insufferable pair of old bores and attached themselves to us like limpets for the rest of the journey. There was literally no room to escape, until the blessed relief of the car deck, the ramp and – España!

From this point for a while and for a change these are some excerpts from my contemporary diary (a rarity for me):

Thursday 9th September
Bilbao – we arrived some five hours late because of supposed 'gale'. Rather prettier than I expected, with the rio winding inland past a series of breakwaters, the port tidy and modern-looking. Several Polish ships at the coal berth. The ferry berth was inconspicuous until the last moment when a 90° turn to starboard was required. Debarcation was instantaneous and fuss-free, with no passport or other formalities. 99 per cent of the GB cars headed off in the direction of the costas for the winter: good riddance. (Even the very beautiful new dark green Bentley Continental, reg. no. GB 6: upholding the tradition of Robert Maclean's Bentley S1, GB 3, which I knew well.) The Bilbao–Santander motorway was about half complete, in intermittent stretches: some fine views, including Castro Urdiales which looked pretty.

Santander was easy to negotiate: we drove past (in fact under) the Hotel Real, then found it easily enough on its suburban avenue. A great white wedding-cake palais but with Spanish sandstone detail including inevitable heraldic plaques. It began to pour when we arrived: but the porter was helpful. Le tout Santander seemed to be there – someone was obviously 'offering a cocktail' – but they dispersed, and the hotel was left to a handful of residents. In the circumstances it was tiresome to have atticky rooms with a view of the car park: but we were too tired to complain or change. Telly had about twenty-five channels: Sky News seemed surprisingly good. Dining room was hushed and under-occupied: food fine. It rained hard all night.

Friday 10th September
Morning dawned fine and showed what we'd missed with the view. Santander has lovely beaches and a general rentier atmosphere. Intense purple morning glories covered everything.

Santillana del Mar: the location was slightly surprising (no Mar for a start). Parking was 'guarded' and easy, with a 200-yard walk to the 'town entrance' where there were several more or less parallel streets. It's a big village, really, set among the fields – no outskirts – and preserved in aspic. Houses made of good tawny stone with coats of arms as advertised: pillared cedary wood galleries, lots of geraniums: so slightly Swiss in feeling, especially with cow odours omnipresent. Much tourist tat inevitably, but not too bad. The Romanesque church, right at the edge of the fields, had a pretty cloister.

The Altamira Caves of course weren't visitable (the waiting list is now *ten* months), but we went round the nicely kept somewhat Japanese-looking exhibition centre in a pine grove. The prehistoric blurb was frankly rather boring (and all in Spanish) but the video, despite standard portentous music and commentary, was worth watching for a bit.

Comillas turned out to be a very nice place for lunch in a café on the esplanade overlooking a slightly Hulot-type beach with big waves. Croquetes, *jamón*, cheese and much beer (and sherry). After lunch drove up to the pavilion by Gaudí, which is now a restaurant, and met with disapproving glares. It is very peculiar: basically, yellow brick with stripes, eaves, gables of green and yellow tiles, exaggerated red-tiled roof, and a sort of minaret/lighthouse tower studded with more green tile rosettes. The rest of inland Comillas is also rather strange and slightly sinister: a large seminary (pontifical university, no less) and gloomy somewhat Irish-looking church.

It was now dark and grey as we headed inland into the narrow valleys beneath the Picos de Europa: very beautiful, with clear rushing rivers thought likely to contain fine trout. The road was narrow and twisting: the mountain scenery super, with very steep valley walls. After some time down in the gorges we began to climb and soon had stupendous views across the valleys to the Picos: a tormented and spectacular range. The mountain village Arenas de Cabrales is the place for gorgonzola-type cheese, and was preparing for its feria, stringing up light bulbs. Cangas de Onis (the first capital of renascent Spain after the battle of nearby, but alas unvisited, Covadonga), has a so-called Roman bridge, which merited a stop: Roman or not, it is handsome. We returned to the coast for a spell, lingering briefly in Ribadeo and whizzing past Villaviciosa, enjoying the tranquil tidal estuaries: then headed for Oviedo on the motorway, unfortunately choosing the wrong motorway spur and thus wrestling for a while with indistinguishable suburbs. However, once 'central park' was located it was easy enough to get to the hotel and once again surrender the keys.

The Reconquista was grand and a trifle gloomy, the staff pretty offhand. We had identical rooms on the first floor in a patio with a boardwalk the width of the Queen Mary's promenade deck outside: so, communication was simple. It rained. We dined in the excellent cafeteria, fairly lightly, but it was delicious. After dinner I wandered up to the old town, where there was lots of light and noise in front of the Ayuntamiento, with tents, stalls for beer, cider (great local speciality) and eats, and various bands belting out cheerful rackets. Some performance had just finished in the cathedral. The squares looked good floodlit, and the general atmosphere was happy and tipsy. It was wet.

Saturday 11th September

I retraced the itinerary in the morning to capture some of this on film, then we tried to approach the cathedral (which was closed unless you bought a ticket for some exhibition) by car: despite infuriating one-way system we eventually got fairly close, and saw some good, sober, Baroque ecclesiastical buildings (library, archbishop's palace, etc.).

We followed a winding, slow, pretty road to the coast near

Cudillero: lots of Asturian hórreos and picturesque agriculture, mainly cow and apple oriented. Many parallels with Devon suggested themselves: though the vast eucalyptus forests were a surprise. The weather deteriorated again with clouds rolling in from seaward virtually at sea level. Occasionally we glimpsed a super beach or rocky headland. We made the acquaintance of the Gijon-Coruña railway which leaps imperturbably across ravines on spindly viaducts, while the road hairpins around. Oviedo province drivers are very slow and initiative-free. Eventually the road emerges onto an open plateau above the cliffs and runs straight to the Luarca turn-off.

Luarca has an upper district of vaguely Sicilian summer residences or fortified farms of fanciful nineteenth-century design behind high walls, followed by the sudden vista, below the inevitable sailors' church and even more inevitable graveyard of some sailors, of a little port far below on an inner bassin closed off by a series of breakwaters. Negotiating the hairpins, then the quayside (signs said, in effect, drive into the harbour and you're on your own), we ended up in front of the 'Meson del Mar' where, under a canopy (it rained intermittently) we ate resolutely non-maritime things – and drank sherry and beer. The whole episode was punctuated by ear-splitting explosions of maroons – at one point a salvo of four – but the inshore lifeboat, moored at our feet, never moved.

Miraculously, warm sunshine now supervened, and we had some wonderful coastal panoramas, especially near Foz. Before that we had made a brief detour to the beach and estuary mouth at Ribadeo – very fin de saison. That marked the entry into Galicia: it soon felt very different, with more open country, a different kind of hórreo (narrower, slatted, like large granite toast-racks with crosses on gable-ends), four-square low-built granite houses, even terrace cultivation. Echoes of Cornwall or Pembrokeshire – or Brittany or the Cortentin (hydrangeas). A high bridge took us Berwick-style past Viveiro, and shortly we turned off towards Cabo de Bares, the charmingly if inaccurately named northernmost point of Spain, first making an unintended diversion to a minute Port Isaac-type fishing hamlet called Porto do Barqueiro. On the cape there was a wind farm and handsome lighthouse arranged somewhat like a Palladian villa: good views to the west along a grey Galician coast, with fitful shafts of sunlight on the sea as the next lot of weather limbered up. However, as we drove southwest towards Ferrol and Coruña, cutting inland, the weather improved dramatically, and the countryside also became more gracious and civilised. The eucalyptus was back in force, also a lot of maize and general smallholder crops. The evening light was golden and when we breasted a hill and looked down into the Ferrol rio and over to Coruña the view was spectacular. There was a tiresome creep down a hill and over the bridge at Pontedeume, then we took the (toll) motorway for the last dozen miles into Coruña. This takes one right into the city centre through really rather handsome high-rise suburbs: perhaps the golden light flattered them. One debouches into the waterfront gardens, whence there was a fleeting vision of the galleried white façades of the old waterfront, luminous and complex against a slate sky.

The Hotel Finisterre was conspicuous at the end of the promenade, by the ramparts and indeed directly opposite the gardens wherein Sir J. Moore's 'corse' is interred. It proved modern, elegant and comfortable: not 'better' than monastic *paradores*, but there is something to be said for purpose-built hotels. Staff charming.

I moved out to capture the last of the light: a large black cloud beat me to it. However, I had a nice ramble through the town centre: the plaza mayor had the usual animated, cheerful, and well-behaved paseo crowd in and around the al fresco cafes. On this occasion they were watching a troupe of high-wire walkers performing on a wire strung to the roof of the (very splendid) ayuntamiento. We later ate in a small restaurant in the arcade of the plaza: OK, though the service could be described as 'reserved'.

Sunday 12th September
During the night the mother of all gales started up and by morning all was driving rain and spray. We drove out to the Torre de Hercules, Roman lighthouse neoclassically reclad in the eighteenth century. It was difficult to get out of the car. One rather longed there would be a picturesque freighter wreck, and there was. We had a quick look at the 'back bay' where golden sands must be lovely in decent weather and being virtually city centre are a marvellous asset to the city. Coruña impressed us a lot.

The motorway made the drive to Santiago de Compostela easy. Rather to my surprise, parking was easy too, with a well-camouflaged and useful subterranean garage spotted by EABB: it was within easy walking distance of the cathedral. This made its awesome presence felt very soon. *Thousands* of brightly clad people were milling around. We decided to go straight in, mainly because it was still pouring. Marvelled at the portal but gave up any attempt to progress further into the church. At noon several mitred bishops and monsignori processed in, but of botafumeiro-swinging there was no sign. Congas of pilgrims, whose home towns were recited, queued to kiss the saint's robe etc. We exited and enjoyed the cloisters and museum with its sculptures and tapestries, also view of the Plaza de Obradoiro, where a rather bush-league old car rally (most American) was self-importantly assembling.

The time had come to board the Reyes Catolicos and coincidentally have a little something. We parked ourselves in their rather handsome cafeteria but were fortunate not to die of exposure before our wants were satisfied. Immensely grave and important-looking waiters took care to put our importunities in their place – we were at that point almost the only clients – and returned to their vital task of transferring quintuplicates of non-existent orders from one spike to another, with much learned conferring. Eventually various combinations of platos combinados appeared: by some time in mid afternoon, we had persuaded them to accept lots of money, and left.

A gentle walk round the town took us back into the cathedral – now quieter – through various doorways, and through pleasant streets of grey granite houses, with well-kept woodwork of white or dark green, several with galleries or fine iron balconies. Glimpses of dressed-up student troubadour parties were had, to the backing of gallego bagpipe strains. As we came back in front of the cathedral the sun emerged and the façade came alive: the stone pavement steamed.

We took the ordinary road to Padrón where St James's stone boat ties up (I suppose it *would* have floated away…?) then off to the coast of the Ria de Arousa. Vilagarcia is the HQ of the Albariño wine district: but the real find here was Cambados (it sounds like something in the fishy department of the menu), which had a fine, wide, stony main square with a low-built crenellated pazo on one side and a sturdy church – a very mini-Santiago – on a terrace on the other.

We followed the coast as far as we could – ending up in one or two culs-de-sac – heading for the isthmus leading to La Toja and El Grove (or A Toja and O Grove if you prefer Gallego) but contented ourselves with turning back at the vast west-facing Playa de la Lanzada, thanks to time constraints. It was blowing hard, but remained sunny all round the coast through Sanxenxo, a smiling shore where bougainvillea flourished, and one would be very happy to have a little villa.

Despite the apparent complexity, our navigational plan brought us right to the *parador* in Pontevedra, inevitably just as the heavens opened. This was a delightful hotel, quiet and restrained with extremely nice people. It nestles into the hillside and has an entrance courtyard which unfortunately couldn't accommodate the Merc. At dinner we saw – and heard – a dozen Americans, the only ones we saw in three weeks: but they subsequently vanished. After dinner my umbrella and I took a walk up the narrow, but handsome, stone-paved street and decided it would well repay attention in the morning.

Monday 13th September

Indeed, it did. I have a more extended walk, enjoying the Alameda at the top of the town, the Portuguese-looking Casa Consistorial, the fine theatre, and the Gothic sailors' church with its elaborate Plateresque façade. Dropping in at the *parador* briefly, I then sampled the town to the east, including the market, before a sudden downpour of intense violence materialised just as I was re-approaching the *parador*. We took refuge in sherry. The downpour was short-lived, and we had pleasant sunshine for our drive down the ria past Marin, Spain's Dartmouth, to Buau, a pretty little fishing port with crystal-clear water, and Hio, out on the point, where Galicia's finest calvary is to be found. We crossed over to the Ria de Vigo, with good views from the corniche of its eponymous port on the opposite shore, searching in vain for an appropriate café for lunch: but there was nothing appealing. We decided to cut our losses, drove over the new motorway bridge and through Vigo (rather attractive in a workaday way) and after a few miles of very holiday-oriented coast reached Baiona. Here there was no mistaking the *parador*, though it was a slight surprise to find an armed guard at the entrance to the old walled fort within which it lies.

The *parador* is vast – long corridors and no lift, not much good for the infirm – but clearly very popular: this was the only hotel where we were conscious of a lot of people staying. The receptionists lacked charm, but the dining room and the sturdy waitresses therein were fine.

We took the car down to the promenade, where a line of old houses faces a fine sandy beach. Many craft were moored including one very large maxi-type yacht. Quarter-tonners were being lifted out and put on trailers after some championships. It was clearly about to produce a deluge and we just made it back to the car in time. We sat in our spacious monastic rooms and watched the surf pounding the rocks far below.

Tuesday 14th September
Morning broke with another full-scale gale and all hopes of 'bright intervals' removed. We set off down the coast towards A Guarda, where the Miño meets the sea at an acute angle. The coast was rugged and sparsely inhabited, with that unmissable 'west coast' feeling where the prevailing winds meet raised beaches with high hills sloping back. Round the corner all looked different: the wind's fury gone, fertility gone rampant on a narrow alluvial plain. The villages already looked Portuguese. We went down to the Corran ferry-type device which links the two shores, and countries, a mile or two below Tuy and Valença. There didn't seem to be many takers. Tuy looked promising from below and even more so when we had parked. There was a high-level esplanade, then a short further climb to the fine Gothic church-cum-fortress. A clean-looking pub (actually jamóneria) claimed our attention and we turned in. Two teenage boys with dark solemn eyes misunderstood my request for 'fino Jerez' and beer came: their dad corrected it, and produced raciones or porciones of olives, ham and cheese carved with painstaking care. The solemn eyes watched the strange foreigners (there was no one else to watch). The eyes wore immaculately pressed striped shirts.

Tuy was a good place.

We spiralled down, out of the town and onto M. Eiffel's bridge, a box-girder creation with a door at the other end surmounted with the coat of arms and name of **PORTUGAL**. Very Alice in Wonderland. We crossed. Swerved right and were in without further formality.

The ramparts of Valença do Minho were Vauban-like and obviously extensive: nevertheless, we were unprepared for the complete alternative town which was found once we'd negotiated a series of traffic lights and narrow gateways. A bustling little main street crammed with cars and souvenir shops: at the far end a jigsaw of little streets and plazas – the pousada was there somewhere. We stopped on the far side and walked up the redoubt to look over the Minho and back at Tuy.

Driving south in the relentless rain it quickly became evident how much poorer Portugal is than Spain: the comparison between East and West Germany came to mind, and there was something of an Atlantic Hungary about it. The tall eucalyptus trees almost lost themselves in the trailing mists: the whole had a jungle feeling, with high-trellised and evidently improved vinho verde vines running rampant, patches of tall maize interspersed and occasional banana trees mingling bizarrely with the heather, gorse and bracken which also formed part of this curious landscape. The occasional austere Baroque church, whitewashed with granite detailing, presented itself among the vine-ensnared levels: signs pointed to mosteiros which we felt disinclined to visit.

Ponte do Lima looked a cheerful little town, with some 300 yards of Roman bridge across the river and its sandbanks, and the town itself rising in terraces on the south side. The principal streets were festooned with red, white and yellow decorations. Azulejos and crenellated towers reinforced the Portuguese identity.

On we ploughed through the rainforest to Braga. As the guidebook warned, this was not an easy place to navigate. Nor, having found our bearings, could we find anywhere remotely legal to park. I parked on a corner and trudged or sploshed down to the squat twin-towered cathedral: the towers have open crowns like St Giles in Edinburgh. Inside was dark and cramped: it felt slightly like a submarine. As in most churches since Santiago, the organ, which occupied either side of the rear nave, had splayed horizontal pipes like trumpets: these almost met in the middle and produced the effect of a canopy and added to the submarine illusion. Signs forbade photography. In the transepts were four small eighteenth-century chapels whose more sophisticated and worldly colouring lightened the prevailing gloom. I photographed these (unsuccessfully) but didn't linger.

The road to Guimarães was easily found and, unfortunately as it turned out, we headed straight there without making the detour to the Bom Jesus pilgrimage complex. This sounds rather spectacular and beautiful, and it is a shame that we spent time in highly disappointing Braga at its expense.

Guimarães should have been simple but wasn't. We went round in circles with occasional tantalising glimpses of enchanting little plazas. Signs to 'Pousada' mysteriously disappeared just as one thought one must be getting warm. We drove down improbably narrow streets, asked directions from policemen and -women (which cancelled each other out), while other kind people volunteered help. None of this got us any nearer. Having identified the Oliveira church, I parked and set out on pedestrian reconnaissance. Needless to say, the pousada was nearby – as the vulture flies – though a good half mile by car. It was so discreet and tasteful that only a brass plate like a Harley Street specialist's identified it: moreover, it was impossible to approach within 25 yards of it by car, so ESP of some sort would be required to locate it.

Entering, dripping wet, I got a willing and helpful young man to come, insinuate his lanky limbs into the back seat (while EABB was attempting to eject from the front!) and guide us for sure to the hotel. I'd had enough of this Weimar-style activity. The pousada was charming and well-run: we had rooms directly above each other, looking onto a paved alley about a handbreadth wide. It poured. My excursion was brief: dinner was good: sleep was blissful (the promised bong-bongs weren't in the end a major problem).

Wednesday 15th September

Breakfast was especially good and after a short walk around together we embarked to drive around the outlying attractions. A tall Baroque church at the end of the immaculate municipal flower beds was rather cold and atmosphere-free, whether despite or because of the acres of azulejos I couldn't really say. As we drove up to the castle a glimmer of sun appeared. The ducal palace lies below the old castle: it was pastiche Burgundian from the start and has been virtually rebuilt – so it's pastiche pastiche Burgundian. Nevertheless, it's impressive. The layout is simple with a succession of large, well-proportioned rooms appropriately furnished with tapestries, excellent Persian carpets, armour, oak furniture, majolica, etc. Overall impression – un-lived in, but what could one expect?

First stop from Guimarães was Amarante, a delightful little town with a fine arching bridge over the R. Tâmega and a substantial red-cupolaed convent facing into a square the other side. The convent is built into the side of a hill so that the campanile (another crown-steeple item) is but a stump when one has toiled up the road behind.

We soon got onto a good quasi-motorway – shown only as putative even on the 1993 map – and swooped towards Vila Real, climbing into proper mountainous Tras-os-Montes country and stopping occasionally for breathtaking views. No guidebooks recommended pausing in Vila Real, so we didn't: but Mateus, home of the notorious rosé, had a disappointment in store – it was firmly closed. There was just one vantage point from which one could get some idea of its fanciful architecture. I'd like to have seen it close up: one consolation is that one didn't feel obliged to buy a bottle.

From Vila Real we were again on a side road towards Régua and the Douro: very charming too, with the vineyards beginning to show, quite different from the jungles which produce the vinho verde (and indeed the dreaded rosé). Régua was a classic wine town with a nondescript main drag lined with warehouses. We spotted a little restaurant on the quayside, parked, and entered. Very simple, friendly and tasty. No port to be had, only some whisky called 'Highland Glen'. The wine was pretty awful.

Crossing the Doucastilro, inevitably, by another of M. Eiffel's creations we drove along the river, dammed above Régua. The sun shone and the scene was picturesque with the white quintas dotted over the steep hillsides. We left the river and drove through ever wilder country, gradually climbing to a high plateau with 'extensive views'. Despite the wildness of the country, it seemed quite densely populated, with many of the new villas – often only half-finished – reputedly erected by returned expatriates from the Americas. In one little town with a barracks a particularly ugly villoid had a sort of fence of red and black bombs – like a perversion of the RNLI mines. The roads were far better than I'd been led to expect and became almost motorway standard in the direction of Mirandela: we reached Bragança without further help and, mercifully, found it easy to locate the pousada, on a hill overlooking the town.

The pousada seemed very run-down and the people rather dopey – they wouldn't, for example, help us with the luggage. The rooms very subterranean, but OK: good view. The general impression was very East European with flaking concrete, peeling paint, rubbish left around: but there's an element of planning blight as the place is closing for a year for total, and much needed, refurbishment. I didn't feel up to dinner but found the bed comfortable.

At this point the contemporary diary stops, and I have to rely on memory for what will be much more abbreviated accounts: perhaps merciful for the reader who may have been assaulted by too much detail!

From Bragança we drove the short distance next day back into Spain, to Zamora; the Douro having now become the Duero, and the architecture now more distinctly Castilian. The *parador* where we stayed occupies the old castle by the cathedral: a building of great charm and antiquity, elegantly converted with courtyards surrounded by enclosed galleries, and with spacious timbered public rooms. Zamora's cathedral is a squat and sturdy fortress-like Romanesque edifice with a strong square tower: the town apparently has more Romanesque churches than any other in Spain. The streets rise gently from the Duero which, though now far inland, is wide and placid as it flows through.

Through the wide Castilian countryside, next day's stop was León: the Hostal San Marcos, a not dissimilar *parador* formerly a convent: it has a quite extraordinary plateresque stone façade and, as at Zamora, inner courtyards with internal galleries behind the full-width arcaded windows. The convent/hotel also incorporates its own sturdy church. But the ecclesiastical treasure of León is the cathedral – perhaps the best example of French-style Gothic in Spain, with twin symmetrical spires, rose windows on west front and transepts, and above all the best and most complete stained-glass windows in Spain. León of course was a major halt of the pilgrims' Camino de Santiago, which we were now rejoining.

The road of the pilgrims returns eastward over the high and dry meseta of Castile and León into La Rioja, by Burgos which this time we bypassed for the more intimate and domestic charms of Haro (even the name is welcoming!). Haro is one of the principal wine towns of Rioja – a wine I have always found eminently and easily drinkable: the entire town is devoted to the wine trade, with visitable retail bodegas at every turn, and a concentration of wineries around the periphery before reaching the actual vineyards. In the centre of the town there is an information Centro di Interpretacion. We stayed in the hotel Los Agustinos, so its name would suggest yet another former convent, rather smaller than most *paradores* but attractive in an unassuming way: a plainish stone façade with elaborate doorway and coats of arms, a glassed-in internal courtyard, and simple modern bedrooms. It's right beside the town centre of tightly knit streets surrounding a narrow main 'rectangle' (rather than 'square'), given vibrancy by the bodegas.

Next, not far, and last night in Spain, Olite in Navarra (or Navarre). Olite is also very much a wine town but is principally famous for its frankly rather absurd but undeniably striking castle. This is one of these things that rises above lower levels of conical slate-turreted preliminaries to huge, machicolated towers, broad and narrow, tall and squat. The profile seen from afar is spectacular. Though the whole thing might look a pastiche it is in fact a genuine late mediaeval conception, built for his delectation by a fifteenth-century pleasure-loving King of Navarre. Below it in traditional 'castle town' style is a compact town of narrow streets in golden stone. Naturally the *parador* is near the castle and centre and there we stayed.

The last of Spain was a quick drive through and stop in Pamplona: quick partly because it was now absolutely pouring. No bulls to impede progress. It seemed a fine town with substantial classical public buildings and some very complex statuary. But it was then 'adios España' as I drove up through the dense beech forests of the western Pyrenees to the evocative Pass of Roncesvalles and down into France. The road winds down to St-Jean-Pied-de-Port, picturesque old town with galleried houses, white with dark red stonework, rising directly from the river: an important starting point for pilgrims on the Camino, and many houses were and are pilgrims' hostels. Not far was Oloron-Ste-Marie where we took our first night's rest in France (odd not to be entering France from the north as usual!). Oloron – we have moved from the Basque country to the Béarn – is one of these quintessential little French towns descending alongside a narrow river issuing forth from the hills, and now almost reaching the plain. Again, a jumble of old houses borders or in some cases rises directly from the river(s) (two meet): here they are grey or cream-coloured, roofs darker grey. The Alysson Hotel was modern, low-built, on the edge of town looking over meadows and with an enormous piscine – alas too late in the year for that! An ideal 'normal' touring halt and in fact quite a change from historic *paradores*.

It was downhill through typical countryside of woods and small fields, rivers by countless small valleys so less of uphill as well, to the 'big town' of the region, Pau. We stopped long enough for a good look at the assemblage of long, tall château (birthplace of the Vert Galant) and numerous other towers, spires and fortifications, set on terraces and belvederes along and above the river. From these esplanades there was also a great view of the range of the Pyrenees whence we had just come. Pau was of course the place for British army officers 'retired' on minimal pay after Waterloo: it was (just) affordable, as Britain wasn't, and with many kindred spirits must have been pleasant for promenades in the formal gardens.

Pau to Toulouse (next stop) is an easy drive through the low-lying country past names redolent of French rugby football prowess: Tarbes, Auch…

Naval Cruising

Brilliant – *November 1992*

Now liberated from the City, after that autumn Iberian trip I was invited by James Burnell-Nugent ('BN') to join him and his ship's company in HMS *Brilliant* for a prolonged 'cruise' from Greece to Romania and back to Sicily. Haruko and I had already been on *Brilliant* when we drove down to Portsmouth one lovely summer evening for a drinks party on board, with many other friends there too. By now, November, the ship was much further abroad and was taking part in a NATO exercise in the eastern Med, and it was arranged that I would join one morning in Thessaloniki.

I flew to Athens a few days before and shortly hired a car and drove north. I diverted from the motorway to the narrow strait between Attica and Euboea near Chalcis, and then along the Euboean Gulf shores to the historic site of Thermopylae: now of course some distance from the sea, which would have made Leonidas' exploits superfluous had it been the case in 480 BC. When I stopped by the coast a very strong north-west wind was whipping the wine-dark sea with angry crests – rather thrilling. I found a pleasant, rather functional hotel at Volos, on the bayside promenade. The atmosphere was quite different from Athens – simpler, more 'northern'. In the morning I set off for a tour of Pelion, starting with the monastery of Panagia Portarea, a steep drive up the mountain: from the adjacent café and terrace a superb view over the city and bay of Volos, as was the case also from neighbouring Makrinitsa, only slightly higher at around 2,000 feet, where I took refreshments before heading down to the eastern shore. The coast was absurdly pretty, as one descended through the pine forest and wound along past many little sandy or shingly coves. To the east one could see strung out the islands of the Sporades, the nearest being the apparently jet-setting Skiathos. The road, of a West Highland dimension, tended to run out by the shore, and I was picking my way to rejoin the 'circuit' (piling Pelion on Ossa?). Over on the west-facing side were many apple orchards, with the most lovely little ruby-red apples still to pick. So back to Volos for another night.

In the morning it was off on the main road north: familiar from 1964 but now 'improved'. While in 1964 Hamish and I were hurrying home and merely stopped to camp and sleep beneath Mount Olympus, before the one-day drive through Yugoslavia, now I had time to drive up the mountain as far as the road wound: an exhilarating drive on a well-surfaced road through pine woods sufficiently open to give breathtaking views down to the coastal plain. There was hardly anyone else there and with the altitude and the pine scent it was exhilaratingly fresh. Before Olympus I had stopped at the gorge of the Vale of Tempe, leading down to the sea from Larissa between Mounts Ossa and Olympus: again, the first time to wander along the riverside and take in the stunning autumn colours.

Thessaloniki was new to me as last time I came that way we had turned left just before for the long slog up through Yugoslavia. I had hoped to stay at the Elektra Palace, an elegant hotel overlooking the main square a bit up the hill, but it was full: I found a perfectly good hotel more 'downtown' not far from the front. The main priority of course was to visit the museum for all its relics of Philip and Alexander (the Great) of Macedon. The most remarkable in my view were the ultra-delicate gold funeral wreaths with sprung oak clusters: but so much else, pottery, mosaics, silver, more gold. I believe that some things may since have been moved to the tourist site at Vergina, much developed since 1992 – Philip himself? I was fortunate to park right opposite the museum as it seemed to be the only free space in Greece's second city. On the waterfront is the celebrated White Tower – now written with a pang of respect for Fitzrovia's late great restaurant of that name – and a lively promenade. At sunset, the cloudless sky was a brilliant crimson; the anchorage was entirely clear of shipping, civilian or naval.

In the morning I had a quick look round the centre for Roman and Byzantine remains: the Byzantine churches (still in Orthodox operation) surprisingly small. But I was due on board *Brilliant*. It was now a dull grey day, and the roadstead was crammed (not 'rammed', fortunately) from one side to another with equally grey warships at anchor. I took a taxi down to the naval base, to its surprise in through the gates and on to the quayside. HMS *Brilliant*, not to my surprise, was the nearest of all. How to get out to her? I had presumed there might be boatmen who for a few drachmae would oblige – but none. I was about to enter the HQ when accosted by a mad woman who, when I said I was going to Romania on that vessel, said 'the Romanians were the most evil people in the whole world' and the Bible – which she promptly produced – said so; pointing out passages underlined in green ink. Escaping her clutches I entered the operations room, which seemed manned exclusively either by captains or by ordinary seamen, with no ranks in between. I asked how I could get out to *Brilliant* and suggested calling on Channel 16 (the emergency channel all ships listen to). At once a chirpy female voice answered; a few seconds later I heard James – 'Is that you, Barr?' A few minutes later I was on the bridge with a large gin and tonic…

After lunch and some cabin chatting and routine, we went off in early evening for drinks together with some other skippers in the second, smaller and older RN Leander-class frigate. Unlike *Brilliant* which had been one of the first ships with Wrens on board, this was still men only: and it showed, with a distinctly less civilised atmosphere. Later we two went out on the town to dinner and to a piano bar, until late, with two Greek captains: nice intelligent chaps and a most interesting and relaxed evening.

We had challenged – or vice versa? – the Dutch Kortenaer-class frigate, comparable in size and with the same engine configuration of two Olympus and two Tyne gas turbines, to a 'drag race' out of the bay; but, I think because of the weather, this was scrubbed. We had also been invited to lunch on the flagship, the American guided missile cruiser *Leyte Gulf*. Stepping aboard, we were cheerfully greeted by the Captain who said 'Since it's you folks, we thought we should open some wine' (the USN is notoriously totally 'dry'). So, we had some very pink Californian rosé with our pizzas. A gesture of transatlantic solidarity much appreciated!

We sailed up the northern Aegean through the night and on a sunny morning I was on the bridge munching a bacon sandwich as we approached the Dardanelles. BN was explaining their WW1 significance to some of his younger colleagues, and I suggested we should turn hard-a-port and cruise up the Gallipoli shore and view the landing beaches: so, we did. Then through the Dardanelles – also remembering Troy and Çanakkale visited in 1961 – and into the Sea of Marmara. Whereas in the Dardanelles with many twists we'd had to proceed with some care, in the Marmara we could open up. In fact, we had to as under the Montreux Convention of 1936 foreign warships must transit the Dardanelles, Sea of Marmara and Bosphorus (thus both enter and exit Turkish waters) in the hours of daylight. In November these are few. And the Black Sea was still a long way off. From the quarterdeck I marvelled at the immense wave thrown up by the four full-throttle jet engines. Another good diversion was small-arms shooting practice from the upper deck.

In late afternoon, excitement and anticipation as the domes and minarets of Istanbul materialised behind and above a wall of light mist before us. We did slow down a bit but were probably well exceeding the speed limit as we cruised past the Golden Horn and Europe on one side and Scutari and Asia on the other. Sizeable and pleasingly classic-looking ferries crossing were avoided, as also a mass of other craft large and small. A wonderful scene which those lucky enough to be on deck could really enjoy. By nightfall indeed we were out of the Bosphorus and into the appropriately Black Sea. I was given the treat of a ride in the Lynx helicopter on a 'night exercise' of some abstruse kind, which was interesting and fun.

On a grey and drizzly morning we berthed at Constanța, Romania's chief port. This was not quite a state visit, but an important and pioneering 'show the flag' visit to the 'new' Romania. After gun salutes and securing an Embassy party – Ambassador and wife and a half-colonel military attaché – came on board. The Ambassador reminded me of the Englishman '*avec son sang-froid habituel*'. His wife exclaimed 'Are these *guns*??' on passing the AA guns on deck. A little later the home team arrived for midday drinks on the bridge: the C-in-C of the Romanian navy, the port Admiral and one or two others. Hospitably, the chief asked if all the arrangements, ship visits etc. had been satisfactory. 'Of course' said James. 'Just one thing, we had hoped to visit your submarine.' 'No' said the Admiral (several double gins down). 'Unfortunately, we have no submarine.' At which point James pointed out of the window to a long black submergible item alongside a pier. 'Oh, that!' and to an underling, 'See to it for a visit tomorrow.'

In the evening there was another, much larger drinks party in the wardroom for local worthies, the British community, and sundry others. Among these was an American army officer, vastly inebriated, who like others wondered about my status alongside the captain and boozily accosted me: 'You sir, you're a spy, yessir!' 'Well, actually, no…' 'Yessir, you are A SPY!' 'Oh well, how perceptive of you to have noticed…' (The Romanians of course will have simply assumed that I was the political commissar responsible for ensuring the Captain did not stray ideologically.) We went out to dinner at a restaurant with the Embassy party, and dogs, presumably rabid, howled all around in the darkness.

The morning saw the visit to the submarine: rather important, in fact, as we believe it was the first time that a group from

NATO or the West had visited and inspected a Russian-built Kilo-class sub. Joining the diplomats and us was our intelligence officer. The diesel-electric Kilo was and is basic in many ways but is highly effective due to its quietness: a sort of stealth Trabant. I was slightly surprised to find some grubby Turkish rugs on the deck sole. The accommodation seemed pretty spartan. The plastic tags to all the various compartments, lockers, machinery were all in Cyrillic script, Russian language: which the Romanians said they could not read, and as the USSR had failed to provide a proper 'handbook' the sub had never gone to sea! (Make of that what you will…)

There was a wreath-laying ceremony, soon after arrival, at the city's war memorial: greatcoated BN laying it with great dignity as the ship's company paraded. Then another afternoon a more elaborate one at Emperor Trajan's spectacular monument at Adamclisi about an hour's drive away. Mr Ceauşescu having been eliminated a couple of years earlier the successor president, Iliescu, presided over the proceedings, involving much marching and counter-marching by Romanian troops and, eventually, the inimitable RN contingent. Iliescu and his entourage/minders arrived in helicopters: lots of black leather coats. BN had to shake his hand; I was distanced. It was interesting to drive through the countryside, the roads populated by numbers of flat rubber-wheeled horse-drawn carts and lined by metal-roofed wooden houses. That evening (?) we were also driven down the coast to Mangalia on the Bulgarian border, where we saw the fenced-off seaside estate of the communist hierarchy.

In Constanța of course we were 'parked' in the very extensive and very drab commercial port. The city itself had a certain somewhat dilapidated and informal charm. We saw the Orthodox cathedral and visited the archaeological museum, while the department store was specially opened for us after hours: James bought a small carpet. Even more after hours, the great attraction was the casino: a substantial Beaux-Arts (Romanian style) edifice projecting out from the seafront which provided various diversions. I assume there was gaming/gambling but never saw it; the main part was given over to entertainment, mainly floor-shows, eating and dancing. I don't think there was striptease as such though the dancers tended to be scantily clad. They were extremely elegant and lissom and the dances spectacular. The main point of course was as a place of relaxation for parties to eat and (far more importantly) drink together, at tables seating perhaps up to a dozen. We had our 'captain's table' which was regularly graced by increasingly merry visits from other members of the ship's company. All this was taken in very good heart and never exceeded limits: it was a good mode of relaxation. In the morning it was back to work.

In the morning therefore we departed Constanța for the day and night back across the Black Sea, then our reverse-direction daylight sail through Turkey. I was on the bridge for many hours as we sailed through the northern Aegean on an inky night, fascinated by the twinkling lights of so many little Greek fishing boats and by the routines and exigencies of navigation and watchkeeping. When I rose later, we were approaching the entrance to the Corinth Canal. I'd seen this so often from above that it was fascinating to experience it from a ship with the carved-out cliffs towering above us on each side. There was very, very little clearance: in fact, the bow and side waves of the vessel helpfully served to keep it pretty well equidistant from the sides. We had sent up the helicopter despite that not being strictly authorised, and it later got some good photos.

While it had been grey in the canal, out in the Gulf of Corinth it became sunny as we steamed westwards. As it was to be my last night on board, I was going to give a drinks party on the bridge roof, for which the oncoming sunset gave an ideal setting. We slowed to a virtual stop off Cephalonia and my guests – those I'd known best and who had been especially helpful – came and went as their duties permitted. A couple of curious little fishing boats came near alongside but to my slight surprise didn't have the initiative to sell any fish to the matelots.

After a swift night-time crossing of the Ionian Sea, we closed the naval base of Augusta, just north of Syracuse, for refuelling and replenishment. The arrangements were clearly largely in the hands of the local mafia, whose neatly suited boss came to a civilised lunch in the Captain's quarters, together (for whatever reason?) with the Canadian military attaché. Then I departed. It had been a superb and fascinating experience observing how a warship operated day and night and in particular what a 'happy ship' this was under my friend's relaxed, jovial yet firm leadership.

Solo again after such good (ship's) company, I took the little train down to Syracuse. The Grand Hotel on Ortygia island being, sadly, closed for the duration, I checked in at – what other – the Jolly Hotel up on the mainland near the classical remains: the Roman amphitheatre, Greek theatre and other things which I inspected the next day. Naturally, I went down to the already familiar heart of Syracuse on Ortygia, tarrying especially to look at the fleet of little boats of all colours in the harbour by the connecting bridge – and of course the wonderful cathedral, its still-evident history stretching from its Doric columns of the fifth century BC to mediaeval rebuilding and, post-earthquake, eighteenth-century high Baroque.

The Baroque indeed, was what was calling me on this brief Sicilian visit and equipping myself with yet another hire car I set off south and west for the great trio of Noto, Modica and Ragusa, all of them new to me. Noto was still in pretty bad shape after a recent earthquake, but I found it most attractive: on a sort of shelf overlooking the broad coastal plain, the street (which should be called Straight) leads from the pleasant gardens where I parked past the cathedral to the main drag lined with Baroque palaces and churches, all in the marvellous golden limestone. The broad-fronted cathedral with its triple façade is approached by a flight of steps as deep as it is wide: providing a splendid setting for this most theatrical of architectural styles.

Onward to Modica and Ragusa, I was skirting the hills in a bare landscape dominated by rough rock walls and, everywhere, prickly pears. Modica and Ragusa, close together, both lie in steep-sided valleys and again make the best use of their setting to dramatise the buildings, whether in the valley or up high. In both towns the verticality of the façade-crowning towers in particular emphasises the drama; in the case of Ragusa the town was effectively divided into two after the earthquake when the upper town was built, for the nobs.

Back in Syracuse and car returned, it was time for the train towards Naples: past Catania and then the resort zone of Giardini Naxos beneath Taormina, which was later to become so familiar; this time I stopped to look at non-trendy Messina and spent the night, before the next day crossing the straits to Reggio Calabria. This had been an objective for some time since the two Riace bronzes, fifth-century full-size Greek warriors, were recovered from the sea. They are simply wonderful in their classical perfection and – well, statuesque – male beauty, topped incongruously by helmets (but missing their spears). Reggio itself was a complete dump. So onward up the long Calabria/Basilicata coast to Naples. Again, the preferred hotel down on the Riviera di Chiaia beyond the Castel dell'Ovo was closed or full, and instead I stayed a couple of nights at a high-rise hotel up the hill from the central city. This worked well, first because there was a fantastic view across to the islands and because at sunset the most extraordinary evolutions of an aerobatic murmuration of starlings occurred. There must have been tens of thousands, and I have never seen anything comparable before or since (not even in the Glasgow of long ago). Also, I rather concentrated on the denser urban area of 'downtown' Naples: narrow streets pullulating with life, washing hanging from tall buildings, street markets and stalls. Of course, there is so much more to see – but another time! Airport and home.

I had not finished with *Brilliant*, while James BN was still commanding her. Her visit to the Pool of London to moor alongside HMS *Belfast* was scheduled for the beginning of July 1993, neatly coinciding with my 50th birthday: very generously,

James suggested I might like to hold a small midday drinks party on board, which I was delighted to do. It had to be limited to thirty people, which meant that if the chosen people accepted, they should jolly well come. Only one – who shall be nameless – didn't turn up, thus the quota was not fully used. It was a Friday, and many were City people for whom it was quite convenient. I had turned up the day before to supervise the champagne (kept in the Captain's bath) and other arrangements. Luckily, it was a lovely day – July 2nd always is – and people spread over the upper deck, the bridge wings, and the bridge roof – my 76-year-old mother gamely climbing the iron ladder. The German tourists on *Belfast* close beside looked on in bemusement. After the rest had departed, Rosamund, Jamie and I had a relaxed afternoon chinwag with James in his cabin; and the Biffens and maybe a few others 'went down to see the engines' as on a Clyde steamer excursion, with a general tour below decks, ops room etc.

I went to stay with the Woodses at Frilsham for the night, having arranged that Georgie, George and I and others of the family would sail on *Brilliant* down river to Gravesend. Mother duly reappeared at the ship and others of the extended Woods/Benson/BN family. Very interesting to transit Tower Bridge, pass Docklands (familiar from Greenwich riverboats) and pass through the Thames Barrier. All too soon we'd stopped off Gravesend and the pinnace brought Robert and brother Ed Woods, who were to be on board through the night, round to Portsmouth. We others entrained back to London. Shortly after, BN was reassigned to an important shore job at the Treasury. From a later TV documentary on *Brilliant* one successor was hardly a success, given scenes of the crew misbehaving on shore leave in Florida: not something James BN would ever have countenanced.

Invincible – *November 1998*

Running somewhat ahead of myself, it is perhaps convenient to move on here to autumn 1998 and write of 'Naval Cruising, part 2' which took place on board a considerably larger vessel, the aircraft carrier HMS *Invincible*, before returning to chronological sequence. In fact, further muddying the sequence, in that summer I had had a day on board out of Portsmouth at the invitation of her commanding officer immediately before James BN, Roy Clare: a sort of 'open day' of demonstrations of flying, refuelling at sea and other evolutions, for the benefit of one group of invited local worthies and another from the Royal Yacht Squadron (I was neither!). This was interesting, and the Squadron people were agreeable. On another, sunnier summer evening after James had taken over Haruko and I drove down for a very jolly evening party – drinks on deck, dinner on the quarter-deck – at her berth in Portsmouth.

The 'cruise', however, on which I was kindly invited was in November and in sharply contrasting weather. *Invincible* had returned to Faslane after a major NATO exercise west of the UK, and the plan was to return to Portsmouth 'northabout': after some navigational exercises in the Western Isles (including of course the Gulf of Corryvreckan), via Cape Wrath, the Pentland Firth, down the east side of the country and so round into the Straits of Dover and the Channel. I looked forward to that with keen anticipation – especially the West Highland bit. From Newark my sister Fiona drove me up to the Gareloch, on the way picking up our cousin Ronald Sandeman (of naval heritage) who lives at Rhu right by the loch. Having gained access to the naval base and the ship we climbed the endless flights to the bridge and James explained all to an interested audience. Then my relations departed.

Next morning plans began to go adrift. There was still a good Force 9 storm, westerly and pinning the ship against the quay wall: there was no way that any tugs could liberate her for the moment. So, we made the best of the enforced stay, visiting several of the operational and repair areas of the base, mainly submarine-related. The weather hardly relented but among a stream of routine visitors to the Captain's cabin there appeared a diver – to my disappointment not with mask and flippers – who had been doing a routine underwater inspection and informed us that the starboard rudder was about to fall off. The thing of course weighed many tons and there was no question therefore of 'Plan A' going ahead. The following hours and days were filled with telexes to and from the naval engineers at Bath: eventually Plan B was authorised, to proceed slowly down the Irish Sea, round Land's End and so up Channel.

This left several days to kill time in Faslane, all imaginatively filled. A 'reconnaissance exercise' was arranged in which I was fitted into an orange survival suit, in which I dangled from the open door as the Sea King helicopter located Fisherman's College, Machrihanish, giving good photo-opportunities. (Almost as memorable was swooping very low over a large herd of red deer on the mountains of Arran.) On a late afternoon there was excitement as one of the ship's Harrier jump-jets took off vertically and roared away. I took many photographs of the Harriers in their below-deck hangar and was fascinated to climb into the pilot's seat of one.

Even more special, though, was our visit to the deterrent. James had a favour owed by the boss of the nuclear facility and a comprehensive visit was arranged. We set off in the ship's Land Rover for Coulport on Loch Long where the Trident submarines are rearmed. After the appropriate checks we arrived by a little barbed-wire-festooned passerelle into the vast floating pontoon-hangar (configuration similar to an Oxford college barge but on an infinitely larger scale). Entering, to change the comparison, was like entering the Hall of the Mountain King. In the dead still water lay the sinister dark shape of one of the Vanguard class 'bomber' (Trident) submarines. Above it, a huge gantry suspended a missile which it was imperceptibly lowering into the silo. After this somewhat sobering sight we drove up the hill, which was dotted with various silos, tanks, and bunkers – and a great deal of barbed wire in coils. This was where the nuclear warheads were stored, and our chaperone took us close to inspect one in its little house. Memory may be playing me false, but I have a recollection that I patted it. Down the hill again we entered the main control room: a vast space, part theatre and part City dealing room, with rows and rows of desks with computer monitors. Servicing these were mostly police officers, almost all with the silver braid of considerable superior status. As in a City office too there were smaller meeting rooms at the back with floor-to-ceiling glass walls; in one we could see a group of half a dozen Royal Marines taking their ease, but clearly on standby. Our 'guide' was explaining the security measures and the three concentric lines of fences to keep 'peace women' and suchlike out: when he said that breaching the third line invited 'final denial', James asked 'Does "final denial" mean what I think it does?' 'Uh-huh' said the man, nodding…

When we eventually sailed the weather was lovely. Strange to be on this vast ship rather than a sailing boat on these waters which I knew so well – passing the ghosts of the old battleships and aircraft carriers which had been laid up there for so many years. We gave a wave to Ronald and Sylvia at their lochside abode; then through the Narrows – tight! – and out into the Firth. Night was falling as we crept down between Ayrshire and Kintyre (having alerted Fiona) into the Irish Sea: at low speed and on a beautiful afternoon the motion was easy and lethargic. The flight deck was the place to stroll (for the privileged). In the Irish Sea surrounded by Scotland, Irelands North and South, north-west England, and north Wales, not to mention the Isle of Man, one could not help feeling its centrality to the Norse empire of long ago. I was inhabiting the Admiral's cabin – larger than the Captain's but of course a less 'occupied' and active space. I woke well before we rounded the Longships and Land's End, to the Lizard and the long haul up the now very familiar south coast. Off the Isle of Wight approaching the eastern entrance to the Solent the frigate HMS *Montrose* appeared and pirouetted around. So ended that voyage.

Eastern Approaches

After that diversion, a quick reprise of early 1993, which quite by chance includes an earlier return to Romania than I had expected. I had spent the first months of the year finding out that no one wanted a specialist Japanese fund manager or stockbroker – the market was in freefall and my accurate predictions of how much further it had to fall, disbelieved by all, reinforced that situation. However, I was actually much happier looking at newer and more niche investment and occupational opportunities. The apparent 'redemption' of the former Soviet Union was a development of immense hope for a rather short time, and I joined my former colleague Ian Cole and his partner in devising vehicles for investor participation in the potential privatisation of state entities in Eastern Europe, also submitting a proposal to HM Government for establishing/advising on a proper stock market in Russia. The latter, which would have involved a large amount of travel around that vast country, came to nothing: thank goodness, as Russia rapidly descended into kleptocracy, gang warfare, dictatorship and murder: not to mention the safety record of Aeroflot. The other scheme, however, looked quite promising for a while, though it too eventually came to nothing. But it did provide for an interesting little excursion.

Ian had made his headquarters and taken up residence in Hungary – perhaps the most promising then of the former satellites – and I flew to Budapest to join them for ten days or so. I enjoyed revisiting a somewhat more relaxed city, especially the restaurants with gypsy music, the Buda castle complex and above all the opera: I saw *Manon* and loved the whole stylish and uncrowded ambience of the opera house on the spacious avenue (and at very little cost). For the weekend we decided – Ian, his partner Rosemary and her daughter Rebecca, and myself – to visit Romania: that part of Transylvania which had until quite recently been part of Hungary anyway, and which still confuses with double place-names and so on.

We set off on the Sunday morning across the great Hungarian plain eastwards. After an hour or so of Ian's driving, I took over, and kept it that way. It took some time to pass the frontier. Lorries were parked up on either side and one had the impression that they had had and would continue to have a long wait. However, we were eventually off. The frontier town of Oradea, what we saw of it, didn't seem especially interesting. The Transylvanian countryside on the quite long drive to Cluj-Napoca was attractive in a 'different'-seeming way: rolling hills with vertical strip cultivation of different crops, green, pink, brown, fawn; dense woods, mainly beech, some chestnut and oak, often running down to the roadside; silvery little rivers. The same sort of flat carts with four rubber-tyred wheels that I had seen in the east six months earlier, but the peasants' dress and the villages were different. The men mostly wore brimless hats which made them look like Flowerpot Men. Many geese wandering around. The houses mostly had the same shiny metal roofs. A process of 'orthodoxisation' seemed to be going on with forcible replacement of Catholic churches by rather unimpressive Orthodox ones.

Cluj-Napoca, when we got there, was quite a fine and spacious town of broad streets and squares with some eclectic buildings: a fine vertical Gothic church and imposing domed Orthodox cathedral, sundry Habsburg palaces – and of course Soviet-era blocks. We strolled around a bit then moved on – there was nowhere obvious to spend the night. Turning up northwards and more into the hills, though, we came across a rather spooky-looking turretted mini-château beside a swift-flowing river between steep slopes: it advertised rooms. In fact, there was nothing in the main building but there were a few huts up the hillside a way, indistinguishable from chicken coops. The girls shared one and Ian and I the other. We had some sort of vaguely palatable dinner in the main – rather poky – house and afterwards sat with rugs in the woods beside the river while fireworks were let off, bonfires glowed, and people sang and pop music of an antiquated kind – '*Romani-a-a-a!*' – blared. Rather touching and totally surreal. The next day's drive back to the frontier by Baia Mare and Satu Mare was really rather magical, the beech forests at their spring brightest, and a feeling that both bears and boars might be disporting themselves in them. Even more Hungarian-feeling, perhaps, though the lowering presence of the Carpathian peaks contrasts strongly with the Great Hungarian Plain; of which, however, we saw little as we were late and sped through the night to Budapest. I enjoyed a few more days in Budapest; but though it had been aimed at creative financing rather than just fun, eventually nothing came of the scheme. Pity.

RUE
DE
L'HÔTEL-DE-VILLE
Chemins de Saint-Jacques-de-Compostelle
RUE
DU PALAIS
ROYAL
RUE DU
DEPARTEMENT
RUE
DE L'ARBRE
CHERI

La Vie en Suisse

In the autumn of 1993, as I was looking for opportunities for involvement as an 'angel' investor or non-executive director in potentially promising start-ups or projects of interest, I was told of one which in fact did occupy much of my time for much of the remaining decade. This is not the place to tell the whole saga, but it was the development and commercialisation of a vending machine to fry chips, itself something for which the vending machine industry had been urgently calling. The rights to the machine, invented by a Norwegian-American, had been bought by a small mainly Swiss group and, shortly after I had invested, we effected a 'reverse takeover', transforming it into a Swiss stock market-listed company. There were many vicissitudes over the next few years but as a director (the 'non-executive' concept does not really exist there), I was fully involved in its operations: in Britain, France and Italy, but above all at our headquarters in Switzerland beside the lake of Geneva at Montreux for board meetings etc. Thus, I was visiting Switzerland virtually every month, for periods between a night and a week; and, as with Japan in a 'previous life', part of the time was also spent on motoring excursions in and around Switzerland – some of which will be mentioned while recounting the next few years.

For my first visit (in many years) to Montreux I chose to drive my Mercedes 'grand tourer' down via Burgundy and the Jura: not dawdling on the way out, with a night at the Chapeau Rouge at Avallon where I had first experienced true red burgundy over thirty years earlier; then for the first time stopping in Dijon to view the ducal palace and the Musée des Beaux-Arts with the remarkable flamboyant Gothic tombs of the dukes, and of course a superb collection of paintings. Dijon struck me as a spacious and stately city, but of a manageable size. It was very wet through the Franche-Comté and over the Jura but better in Montreux, though spring had not come early.

After fairly quickly disposing of the formalities of the reverse takeover and stock exchange listings, and a quick tour past the eponymous Territet to Glion funicular and nearby Chillon, I was off on a slightly more leisurely homeward trip, expecting to take in some previously unknown areas. First through the vineyards of Yvorne and Aigle where the vines were just beginning to show signs of life, then on up to Gstaad. There seemed to be almost as much snow as I had found on that rather extravagant Christmas and New Year at the Palace in 1973–74: that is, not a lot. However, coming down from the hills the sun shone, and cherry and apple blossoms proliferated.

Leaving Switzerland, the next proper stop was Colmar in Alsace where there is so much to see especially in the altarpiece department; Grünewald's Isenheim altarpiece pre-eminent though much more is to be seen in the museums. Colmar is an especially attractive old town of half-timbered gabled houses, due not least to its canal-side perspectives with gaily painted houses and abundant flowers competing. Luckily for the nostrils tanning no longer goes on in the neighbourhood. In fact, Colmar is almost an 'overture' to the much larger Strasbourg, to which I was shortly bound; but again, has the advantage and charm of a more intimate size. But aiming for Alsace's capital I took a leisurely tour through its famous – and highly photogenic – vineyards and wine villages: Riquewihr, Ribeauvillé, Kaysersberg where I stayed in a charming old hotel. With a capacious boot there was much purchasing of the local *spécialités*, both liquid and solid.

Rather than exploring inland to the Vosges, the Ballon d' Alsace and the spectacular Haut-Koenigsbourg – these were for another time – I stayed nearer the river where the land is flatter and duller, to maximise time in Strasbourg. (Alas, the scenery looks especially boring around Barr, where of course I had to photograph the sign – not that there isn't one in South Ayrshire anyway!) It was my first time in Strasbourg and was a revelation: canals again, but a mix of flowery old vernacular houses and grander classical commercial palaces. The cathedral with its pleasing asymmetry and astounding Gothic detail inevitably steals the show: soaring verticality reinforced by the single offset tower and the upthrust of every finial and pinnacle. Inside is no less astounding: the great organ, perhaps the world's finest and most complex astronomical clock, and a profusion of altarpieces and statuary. The cathedral gains much from being frequently viewed – even the façade – from narrow and lively streets; so many, starting with St Paul's after the fire and ending with St Peter's and Mussolini, to my mind suffer from being stranded in wide open areas. On the right-hand side, however, a wide *parvis* leads across and down to the very grand, and totally contrasted, classical palace of the ducs de Rohan overlooking the river.

Crossing over said river into Germany, it was but a short hop to a very different environment at Baden-Baden, where I was to spend a brief relaxing time at the celebrated Brenners Park Hotel (and Spa, not sampled). This must be one of the finest and most luxurious hotels I have ever stayed at, with immaculate German service. Eating al fresco and strolling in the extensive gardens by the little river brought the spring alive, with rhododendrons, dogwood, and the like now fully flowering. The town – perhaps the quintessential spa town – also received a quick drive around, the neoclassical Kurhaus and the equally elegant other bathing and gaming establishments giving off a flavour of Wilhelmine leisure.

Karlsrühe, next on the route, was quite a surprise. Inevitably associated with Second World War air raids, it was heartening to see how beautifully the palace, which was entirely burnt out, had been restored. It is an extraordinary complex of the mid-eighteenth century, the central pedimented building with tower to the rear, flanked by symmetrical low ranges extending at an angle. These enclose a wide grassy and befountained forecourt which in turn is narrowed in by topiary, till a broad avenue connects the whole thing with the town. The palace is pale yellow with white detailing, tranquil and elegant. The museum – the main one of the Land – was surprisingly good, with an eclectic array of objects from, inevitably, mediaeval altarpieces to Greek vases to Second Empire state beds. The adjoining Karlsrühe town seemed pleasant but unfortunately soulless – the fate of so many German towns which have been carefully and assiduously rebuilt since total destruction in the war, but alas lack something in life and charm.

Speyer, next stop, has something of the same feeling with a broad pedestrianised avenue leading up to the cathedral, flanked by elegant rebuilt classical edifices: pavement cafés of an understated sort but no real 'street life'. But what a cathedral! A red sandstone Romanesque basilica, spare and unified on the outside with four slim towers culminating more in diamond- than pyramidal-shaped finials, best approached (as I did) *a tergo* whence the monumental gabled and apsidal east end and curved transepts are best appreciated. Coming round, the octagonal (pyramid-topped) cupola and then a very much contrasting later-date façade are seen: the latter, still Romanesque in style but of a lighter tone and construction, with pinkish horizontal stripes has a somewhat more Italianate feel than the spare, sombre architecture behind and within.

Looking down the main *platz* or avenue, that façade is pleasingly mirrored by the Baroque off-white and red sandstone town hall. Inside, the cathedral is sober and regular, with soaring round pillars and round-topped windows: the horizontal stripes evident also in these and the doorways.

It had begun raining and by the time I got to Trier was relentlessly wet. There I installed myself in the hotel facing the immense dark-grey Roman gate, the aptly named Porta Nigra, rendered even more forbidding by the weather. Trier appears somewhat more lively than the previous places, an animated market square with florists' stalls and striped canopied, gabled, and pinnacled houses and behind, rather as in Prague's Old Town Square, St Gangolf's Church which with its tower surmounted by a narrow spire with smaller 'arrows' at each corner also recalls Prague. Another highly impressive church is the Liebfrauenkirche, next to the cathedral and entirely circular in plan. The cathedral itself is another excessive and imposing Romanesque structure, built on Roman bases whose brickwork is quite evident: as usual, four towers (not as high as Speyer). Later work is both Gothic and Baroque, notably some very special altars. The general impression was of a choice mixture of supreme objects of worship from many epochs. The somewhat quirky character of this great cathedral – Germany's oldest – is well shown by the side view where, rather as at Aachen, the choir rears up massively higher than the nave, somewhat of a low-rise zone before reaching the west front.

The drizzly *Drang nach Norden* (or was it a *Wacht am Rhein*?) continued through the well-ordered vineyards of the Mosel and Rheingau: Berncastel, crossing the Rhine at Bingen; right at Rüdesheim and up the most dramatic Rhinemaiden-infested stretch towards the Lorelei and (rather too rapidly) through Koblenz and on to Cologne (or should that be through Coblenz and on to Köln – this memoir can be arbitrary!). Again, perhaps too perfunctorily to pay proper respect, we drove through Neuwied just north of Koblenz/Coblenz where my maternal grandfather had been at school in his late teens – together with his elder brother who also succumbed to more deadly lessons at the hands of the Germans a very few years later. (This swift transition from an industrialising, wealth-creating, socially and intellectually aspirant society to the horrors of the World War and its subsequent repercussions and replays is why *J'accuse* the Kaiser every bit as much as the obvious twentieth-century tyrants, and now Putin, as an archetypical megalomaniac monster.)

The replay was pretty evident in Cologne where as usual in the bombed parts of Germany the immaculately rebuilt or restored parts tended to a certain sterility. This was certainly not true of the small riverside towns where, while one would suspect a certain expertise in restoration, the quaint centres featuring an M C Escher-style riot of crazily pointed roofs and indeed – can there be crazy timbering as well as crazy paving? – every vertical surface wore a mediaeval fairy scene, notwithstanding now persistent rain to discourage jollification. But the atmosphere was there.

Cologne notwithstanding is a very fine city. The cathedral is truly astounding: sharing with Strasbourg soaring verticality, but possessing also symmetry of the twin towers, the whole in a fittingly sober charcoal grey. The interior soars too, its early pointed Gothic revealed rather more clearly than that of the French examples it followed, with a relative lack of the stained glass windows which are omnipresent in Paris, Chartres, St Denis, Bourges and so many others. In fact, Cologne was begun in mid-thirteenth century to replace an earlier model, around a century later than its prototypes – and was not completed until the nineteenth century.

The site and aspect of the Kölner Dom must be unique, with a sizeable railway terminus pushing at its apse – little space here though there is a *parvis* higher up one side of which, to my great benefit, is occupied by the Am Dom hotel, whose elegant and spare modern bedrooms give a superb view of the façade and right hand side of the Dom (and railway station). Squeezing into the other side of the square and winding downhill almost alongside the railway station is the Römisch-Germanisches Museum, a true revelation. The rather curious choice of site came from its being built around a vast Roman villa mosaic discovered as air raid shelters were being dug during the war – a small compensation! It covers in remarkable depth the Roman civilisation of the area, with the largest collection of Roman glassware.

To me equally as interesting as Cologne's cathedral, spectacular and perfect as it is, were the much earlier twelve Romanesque churches built between the eleventh and thirteenth centuries, which despite in many cases suffering severe wartime damage had been well repaired and restored. They give a wonderful idea of the post-Carolingian era as Cologne was developing into an important religious and intellectual centre. I didn't have time to 'do' the lot but spent some in three in particular: St Gereon, mid-twelfth to early thirteenth century; the Basilica of the Holy Apostles, early thirteenth, and Great St Martin's, much earlier with its commencement in the tenth century. Others which it would be good to visit sometime are, of the earlier cohort, St Andrew's, St Mary in the Capitol (built on the site of the old Roman Capitol), St Ursula (built on the site of the burial place of the 11,000 virgins – or more likely eleven – martyred by the Romans: they have yet to be disinterred); and last of the group St Kunibert.

The older group tend to have a long single nave and somewhat higher choir ending in a semicircular ambulatory, with a single high pointed tower towards a gabled front (St Andrew's, St Ursula). Great St Martin's, even earlier, has a most elegant spire with lesser spires at each corner. I visited it first; it is conveniently placed not so far from the cathedral. The slightly later buildings tend to a more conventionally High Romanesque form with between two and four high square-edged towers culminating in pyramids with a variety of sub-pyramids below, and low gabled west fronts and a plethora of round-windowed apses to the east end. St Gereon's huge octagonal, pyramid-roofed central lantern was apparently the largest built in Europe between Hagia Sophia in Constantinople and the Duomo in Florence. The Holy Apostle is not far behind in this department and besides two slender and pointed rear towers has near the front a quite enormous and very Germanic-looking multi-faceted single tower. The interiors of all these are calm and serene, typically with what we would call 'Norman' nave arches and near-Byzantine apses: but hints of 'Early English' beginning to appear (the Germans might not call it that) in clerestory and choir, and I believe more so in the later, still Romanesque churches.

Having hurried somewhat in Cologne, I drove pretty well straight on to the final stop, Antwerp (Antwerpen, Anvers…). What a contrast to land- or river-bound Cologne with its somewhat uptight air: driving in, down the streets towards the cathedral and the main square, the city was pullulating with rows of open-air pavement cafés, crowded in the late afternoon sunshine. One sensed immediately – though we had not really come down much across the flat countryside – the presence of the sea, the sea air, and the maritime world beyond. All was clearly decorous gaiety. This immediate impression was quickly succeeded by astonishment at the sheer verticality of the townscape: over all the 400-feet cathedral tower, visible from everywhere, but also from frontages whose often corbelled gables (and some non-corbelled) are again of a remarkable steepness as well as extravagance and inventiveness of ornament.

I drove around the centre for a bit, then a mile or two down to the south to the very nice modern Radisson Park Hotel where I had booked; made myself comfortable then set off again for the centre (and the cafés). Next morning was largely a church crawl, concentrating on two in particular highly redolent of the omnipresent Peter Paul Rubens: the essentially flamboyant St Paulus and the Jesuit Baroque St Charles Borromeo. St Paulus is entered by an offset and detached Baroque gateway which gives an idea of the largely black-and-white Baroque furnishings, monuments etc. within. A particularly fine Baroque organ in the gallery is topped by an assortment of trumpeting angels, eagles taking off or landing, and the like – all black and white of course. The rather intimate grassy churchyard is filled with stone Baroque statuary of angels, prophets, worthies: and a most curious pebbled and crucifix-crowned grotto climbs up the transept side.

Though the whole church is redolent of Rubens and his era, with at least one altarpiece, the real Rubens church is the Jesuit Baroque St Charles Borromeo. Its solid tripartite façade is not far distant from the Gesù in Rome, the original Jesuit church, with a central soaring pedimented entablature with near-Rococo stone carving around the medallion above the door designed by Rubens. Inside again is pure black-and-white harmonious Baroque, with much gilt on the high altar, monuments, etc. The upper storey houses pillared, round-arched galleries: though indubitably Catholic, the church was forcibly Protestantised during the vicissitudes of the wars of religion and retained something of the air of Dutch churches further north, despite an orgy of Catholic ornamentation. The high altar has a Rubens altarpiece, but the church's Rubens heritage has been unlucky: the nearly fifty ceiling paintings were destroyed a century later in a fire, while Marie Theresa of Austria was kind enough to relieve it of a few other large paintings.

Lastly, of things ecclesiastical, to the cathedral interior: vast, both wide with seven aisles, and very tall. It at least has managed to maintain three highly important Rubens triptych altarpieces: the *Assumption of the Virgin* above the main altar, and the not quite companier pieces of the *Raising of the Cross* and the *Descent from the Cross*. There is also above the tomb of the Plantin-Moretuses the smaller *Resurrection* (from the tomb before astonished Roman soldiers), flanked by St John the Baptist and Sta. Martina. Many more by other great Flemish painters, also sculptures (sarcophagi) and a particularly fanciful carved wooden pulpit which seems to have some women trying to climb up the delicately complicated stairs.

The Plantin-Moretus house, of the great printer, is both enchantingly demure (though not by any means small) and interesting: around an interior courtyard the printing machines themselves (many) and the library of sixteenth- and seventeenth-century printed books. The cynosure of course is one of the few Gutenberg bibles. After Plantin it had to be Rubens' house: a rather grander affair, with an elegant three-storey façade of triple windows under a steep roof, the whole of course designed by the maestro, with statuary, balconies, pediments, alcoves and contrasting stonework. Behind this is Rubens' vast studio with numerous paintings including a self-portrait. This looks onto a formal garden, intimate yet elegant.

The final museum was the Maritime Museum inside Het Steen castle, which begins on the riverside as a fairytale turreted castle – indeed the supposed setting of Wagner's *Lohengrin*; and proceeds with ever more fanciful, even absurd, turretry and machicolations of towers and gateways towards a narrow non-square with equally bizarre stripey frontage among the pinnacled gables. These of course are even more prominent and sophisticated in the main Groenplaats and Grote Markt with the classical Renaissance Stadthuys (town hall) and Oude Beurs (Bourse) from the earliest sixteenth century dominating the squares – overlooked inescapably by the immensely tall, elegant and intricate cathedral spire. (A Shard for its times!) This is where we came in…

Alas, no time for the main Royal Museum of Fine Arts, passed near the hotel on the way out of town, along the motorway to Ostend and a nice long sea voyage back to Dover and home.

Next, shorter, visit; and the Montreux scene

The subsequent much briefer drive to Montreux took place shortly afterwards when I was entrusted with returning the BMW 8-series Coupé which had served as the company car for the predecessor president, Dr Prince Michael Peglow. The journey cross-Channel and across eastern France and the Jura was easily accomplished in a day: it would have been quicker still had I not been peremptorily stopped by the gendarmerie at the Reims autoroute toll point, for some reason which remained unexplained. Surprisingly, I was able to give them all the insurance details and otherwise satisfy them: but they were officious and rude, and it wasted an hour or two. It was clear not just from their hostile demeanour but also from overheard remarks that they were determined to 'pin something on me'. Bad luck. (I wrote a letter of complaint to the French Ambassador in London and got a mildly apologetic reply from his deputy claiming that 'routine checks' were just that but should be conducted with civility.) It was a joy – quite apart from the sense of embarking on a new and exciting venture – to find myself once again on the sunny shores of the Lac Léman looking across to the looming Chablais massif, just as in Vevey all those years before.

Most often, of course, I flew to Geneva (forty-six flights in eighteen months from April 1995 to October 1996) and thence along the lakeside by rail: through the various seasons the journeys to Lausanne and beyond through the terraced Lavaux vineyards and the little old lakeside towns with their pleasure harbours were a delight. Often also we would be driving to Geneva for meetings, and from that much broader expanse of lakeside the distant view of Mont Blanc compels: but it is as the lake narrows in towards the upper Rhône, the Dents du Midi shining above, and the brooding Chablais massif opposite, that the real drama sets in.

Montreux was and is a fashionable lakeside resort with remnants of Edwardian leisure alongside modern Swiss efficiency: it reminds me constantly of my Macouat ancestors' vacationing and indeed it was with my grandparents that I had first encountered the place. That (as told earlier) had been at the Montreux Palace, indubitably the town's premier hotel: but there were others of the older days still (some now apartments), also the new Royal Plaza where we mostly stayed. It had the great advantage of being right on the lakeside, unlike the others separated by the main road. It was smart and comfortable, and we were there so often that it was like a headquarters for us visitors. We did sometimes stay at the Montreux Palace too, especially if entertaining. The Montreux Palace also hosted Harry's Bar, which was a frequent after-hours venue for socialising with members of the Vaudois financial aristocracy.

The actual head office of the company, TEGE (in full, La Société de Chemin de Fer Territet-Glion SA, originally operator of said funicular railway), was found up the hill behind at Blonay: so, commuting meant a precipitous drive through the vineyards and some hamlets with superior restaurants up to this commanding new point. Above, the wooded mountain loomed above the road over towards Lausanne or Berne: intrepid paragliders jumped from the summits over us, bound for the lakeside, and in the winter we found ourselves among cross-country skiers when going up the hill for an Alpine lunch.

The company had a car, at first a compact Mercedes saloon, later a larger (and not so nice) BMW for the use of the visiting directors: and apart from 'commuting' up the hill and visits to Geneva and Zurich, I used it quite a lot: both for weekends around the locality and for a couple of longer forays down into Italy. We were having the machine further engineered and developed in Bergamo so had reason to go that way, sometimes via Milan, to inspect progress. Bergamo I had hardly known before: it is distinctly divided between the lower modern town 'on the flat' and the old city up on the hill.

Shorter excursions around Montreux tended to concentrate on the Rhône valley debouching into the lake at Villeneuve: all the way up to Sion with its handsome castle, even beyond to the glacier, its source; to the Great St Bernard, obviously the main route into Italy, but also a fine excursion in its own right – vital though to drive over the top rather than use the tunnel; and to ski places such as Verbier and Villars (the nearest of any class). Beyond there Gstaad beckoned if one were on the way to the Oberland and German-speaking cantons. Also attractive for an indefinably different atmosphere was the opposite shore: France begins a few kilometres beyond Villeneuve, continuing through the rather glossy 'thermal stations' of Évian-les-Bains and Thonon-les-Bains almost to Geneva. Even if one wasn't having a rather pretentious (if delicious) lunch at Évian it provided an alternative to the well-travelled route along the north, Swiss shore. Incidentally, while at the frontier village of St Gingolph near the head of the lake there is a border post with lifting barrier, guards etc., if one drives along the smaller road – lane, really – by the lakeside one eventually notices that one is already in France. Swiss number plates on Audis replaced by French on Peugeots, and other clues. This therefore is one way one can pass without formalities between Switzerland and the European Union. Who knew?

In September of 1996 I again took the TEGE car down to Italy: revisiting some of the circuit of the previous autumn but taking a different route to start with, the Great St Bernard pass. As this had been the site of my first ever visit to Italy in 1960 and several times after, it was familiar. A beautiful day and I enjoyed the Aosta valley before stopping again at the Certosa di Pavia, for a little longer than in 1995 and I think taking rather better photographs. Continuing the reversed route, I spent a night again in Parma, a town I was beginning to know well. The same comments on photography. As well as revisiting the 'sights', I spent rather more time in the shopping zones, particular emphasis placed on the great specialities of the place. Otherwise though, I have already described both Pavia and Parma.

New to me, however, was Lucca, next stop. It was a total delight. It's a compact and entirely coherent town of narrow creamy/grey/brown streets, the houses and other buildings tending to pleasing plainness but with many ornate and striking doorways, windows and balconies penetrating the façades. The town is enclosed by virtually intact mediaeval walls, now a pleasant promenade between bastions overlooking the broad surrounding gardens. Inside among the close-knit streets are several piazzas, the most lively being the Piazza dell'Anfiteatro (shape instantly recognisable), a place of *passeggiata*, cafés, enticing food shops – and often of would-be Puccini opera stars gathering a small crowd.

The cathedral and the basilica of S. Michele in Foro compete for the 'spectacular façade' prize: not dissimilar to Pisa, a basically broad pedimented Romanesque frontispiece adorned with levels of round-headed pillared colonnades. But S. Michele has two extra storeys on a narrower upward extension, culminating in a riot of statuary at the summit. Both have spectacular high square-sided battlemented towers: the cathedral's higher, S. Michele's more elaborate, stone-clad on the top two levels but remaining brick-built below. Another much older (8th-century) S. Michele has a more modest brick tower. In fact, the town is punctuated by several further towers. Of civil buildings, the Teatro del Giglio, an elegant classical building, preserves above all Giacomo Puccini's legacy (his house is nearby); also classical in style is the perhaps over-scale Palazzo Ducale. This is perhaps rather a perfunctory listing but shows what is contained in an approachable and unspoilt framework in a small and charming city. Perhaps my favourite discovery, in the simple and austere Romanesque cathedral interior (but containing many good things), is Jacopo della Quercia's moving marble sarcophagus of Ilaria del Carretto – in fact buried elsewhere, on the property of her husband's family, owners of yet another brick tower which sports at its summit several fully grown oak trees!

Marble of course is omnipresent in that part of Italy, due to the presence nearby of the immense Carrara quarries, largest in the world, to which I was next bound. Entering the town, a long perfectly ordinary street has as its backdrop, high above, the jagged profile of the marble mountains. With great chunks removed, artificial peaks and precipices – squared off with microscopic precision to produce vast vertical slabs in some places, chaotic and strewn with rough blocks elsewhere. As one drives up the twisting road further into this apocalyptic scene stonebreakers' yards line the way, often exhibiting the most bizarre carved products as well as rather more practical blocks for, presumably, funerary monumental masons as well as the Rodins, Moores or Hepworths of this world. From this eminence there was a dizzying view down to the Mediterranean, which I descended on the way back over the passes again to Montreux.

III

Further Travels

Eccentric Route to Paris

... by way of Skagen Head? (June 1999)

To drive from London to Paris, a voyage across the North Sea to the very tip of Denmark, thence down through Germany and eastern France, may not seem the immediate first or satnav choice. Yet I had a few days spare before Paris and a TEGE France board meeting – the last – so why not?

At Harwich I boarded the Scandinavian Seaways ferry for the overnight sailing to Esbjerg and was pleasantly surprised by the spaciousness of the outside cabin with kingsize bed, entertainment and all. I don't remember much about dinner. Oil and gas rigs were intermittently seen far off but the speed contrasted with the long peaceful night on *Ardevora* ten years before, sauntering past oil rigs and wind farms which provided the background for Ellen and myself putting the world to rights. It was a grey morning as the ferryboat negotiated the surprisingly tortuous entry channels to Esbjerg port, then disembarkation was rapid and off I went northwards.

Immediately memories of 1989 were vivid as I passed through the old-fashioned villages and towns. Inescapably I was heading for the Limfjord and its canal exiting past Ålborg to the Kattegat, at whose western entrance, Thyborøn, we had arrived in Denmark in *Ardevora*. This time I headed somewhat further inland, joining the Limfjord eventually at its widest expanse, the Logstørbredning (inevitably christened by us as the 'Lobster Breeding') before crossing the canal as it narrows suddenly at Løgstør itself. (We had spent our idyllic first night east from Thyborøn, anchored off a tranquil bay on the north side, where the endless 'simmer dim' without darkness was a wonder.) Largely described in 'Sailing', this will not be repeated here: it was hardly surprising nevertheless how a passage of some hours on the water would be replicated in a matter of minutes on land (a Ferrari helping, though Danish restraint was observed – 'headlights at noon').

Before heading north though, there were 'new' ancient wonders to explore: first, and as notable as anything in Denmark, its oldest extant town Ribe, which also has the oldest cathedral – in parts, as much rebuilding was done after sundry not-uncommon mediaeval episodes. But the overall impression is of a stately twelfth-century cathedral. One spire is elegant Romanesque, culminating in the usual steep steeple (sorry!) with windows multiplying with height. On the north side, however, the uncompromising square red-brick tower with vertical walls to the flat roof provides more of a contrast, perhaps the sharpest I have seen where non-matching towers are a feature in so many places. The interior is calm and white with round nave arches tastefully finished in pink and white Córdoba-style 'keystones'. A particularly good sailing ship model hangs, as in so many Danish churches: nothing Islamic there! Sadly, iconoclasm lasted well into the nineteenth century with the colourful wall frescoes almost all whitewashed over. Amazingly the façade of the magnificent organ dates from the eleventh century: the 'works', however, are much later and must produce a glorious sound. Elaborately carved wooden holy men balance precariously above the pipes.

Despite its seniority, Ribe never seems to have expanded much and is a pleasant small town of mainly low-built brick houses. Perhaps the best of these contains the museum whose exhibits seem to consist mainly of plastic models somewhat incongruously featuring U-boats, Boeing Stratocruisers and the like.

The virtually empty, straight, beautifully surfaced road took me north through a landscape of marshes, lagoons, cow pastures and endless wind farms, Løgstør and the Limfjord, following it (in no time at all) to its exit at Hals into the (relatively) open sea. North of the canal the terrain gradually becomes more open and heath-like, rimmed by long deserted beaches of white sand. Also white from aeons of whitewashing are the tall, lonely churches with their crow-stepped gables and red-tiled roofs. Eventually one arrives at the actual northern point of Jutland; where the cross-currents, as the two bodies of water meet, the Skagerrak and the Kattegat, suggest that swimming might be inadvisable. So nowhere to turn but south after a long stroll through the low grasses and along the beach a little way.

Striking inland, however, I found a most imposing brick-built Renaissance château: open country now giving way to woodland and parkland with great trees bordering broad stretches of ornamental canals and lakes. Voergaard Slot is generally considered not only Jutland's best castle but even its finest Renaissance building. A wide, brick-built frontage with an unbroken equally wide and almost as high, steep tiled windowless roof, is flanked at either end by sturdy faceted turrets in the same idiom. The whole is approached by a long, low bridge over the wide lake/moat (rather like Moritzburg in Saxony), leading to a fine decorative entrance gateway. I didn't have time – or the 'slot' was unavailable – to see the inside but had to press on for the night in a quite charming but not perhaps quite so imposing château-hotel nearby.

The next morning dawned misty and grey, but not drizzly. The first stop was Ebeltoft, on the eastern peninsula of Jutland a little to the east of Åarhus (which I've never seen). It's a ferry port to Sjaelland and Copenhagen, and I was shortly to take the shorter sail to the narrow Sjaellands Odde peninsula and the scenic route down to Roskilde, rather than the longer main route to the motorways towards Copenhagen. Thus, I would be avoiding the three main Danish cities – Odense on Fyn also bypassed – on my way south to Germany. (Also of course evading the Schleswig-Holstein question!)

But Ebeltoft is a great 'destination' in its own right, with a wonderful maritime museum of ships afloat. The prime exhibit is undoubtedly a nineteenth-century three-masted square-rigged ironclad very similar to Portsmouth's *Warrior* with its squat yellow funnel. Schooners, lightships, tugs and other working vessels all lie alongside, and a fine pair of white-painted whalers clearly used recently for pulling races. Inside is the usual complement of photographs, figureheads and other evocations of nineteenth-century life afloat.

The smart catamaran whizzed me across the strait to Sjaelland, and it was a short hop to the other most historic city on my route, Roskilde. Roskilde is famous for its equally dramatic cathedral: plainer and more architecturally severe and complete than Ribe, all brick-built with a frontage which could be called pure Early English were it not pure Early Danish! A triple window above the front door replaces the rose window perhaps more common in the next century's Gothic masterpieces. Unlike Ribe's remarkable towers mismatch, Roskilde's are perfectly matched and in symmetry with the rest of the façade: from plain brick rectangular towers rise twin pale-grey slate spires of an extraordinary slimness and delicacy. Side chapels – later – are of the typical Danish/north German steep-gabled, lancet-windowed, crow-stepped variety, the other a mélange of that below and a much more Baroque topping, innumerable carved figures reaching heavenwards. A third similar spire marks the crossing; with a fairly hefty plain circular apse and a slightly incongruous Byzantine-styled chapel alongside the north tower. Interiors are both Baroque – a pretty jazzy heavily gilded organ – and earlier, grandiose black, porphyry and white mausolea and sarcophagi from Gothic to empire.

Roskilde is considered the 'capital' of Viking things in Denmark with a fantastic display of restored Viking hulls and impedimenta, and several replicas which are regularly raced, rowed and sailed on the long fjord and beyond (we met one in *Swift* around Fyn some years later). I had seen these before so hurried on to Denmark's grandest castle/palace complex, Frederiksborg.

This grandiose Baroque complex is set around three sides of a vast courtyard: tall brick gabled ranges projecting from a receding centre range, all with the usual steep roofs, this time in lead. The more reticent separate side buildings have equally steep tiled roofs. An ultra-elaborate Baroque tower stands in one corner and a somewhat more modest one in the other: finials, *galerie*, *tempietti* crown them. The courtyard is closed off by a lone balustraded wall leading to an outer courtyard featuring its own selection of towers, including a tapering-from-a-bell somewhat Muscovite one. The castle is approached conventionally from the land side, in fact stands on its own projection into the wide lake/moat on the other three sides.

After Frederiksborg I headed fairly rapidly down the motorway system to the southern point of Sjaelland and over a succession of bridges to Denmark's southernmost point, the island of Lolland, for the last sailing of the day to Germany. In fact, the strait is barely half the width of the Great Belt Bridge, and didn't take long. There were only about half a dozen other cars on the ferry and those which got off first were quickly overtaken in the early minutes after arrival.

I then noted that from the beginning to the exit for my booked night's stay, Travemünde, there were no slip roads onto the autobahn: by definition then the road would be entirely free of traffic in front of me (and it was rather unlikely that anything was coming up behind). And, most important of all, there was no speed limit, in common with most German autobahns. So I opened the throttle. Somewhere near the top of the rev range I remembered to lower the headlights – retractable on the 456 – to remove that slight impediment to the airflow. When the speedometer reached 300 (kph of course: 187 in miles) I eased off. In any case Travemünde was rapidly getting close.

Travemünde has an ancient history as a defence against Baltic raiders penetrating the interior by way of its river, but its later importance has been both as a ferry port for almost the entirety of the Scandinavian Baltic, and as a rather chic beach resort, its heyday perhaps before the war. I stayed at a middling-sized, unostentatious but immaculate hotel beside the wide white 'strand', ate and slept well.

Next morning, alas, I felt I had little time to tarry in Travemünde as I wanted to press on to the rather more substantial Lübeck before venturing further into unexplored parts of the Fatherland. Thus, I missed my normal visiting of a venerable 'tall ship': in this case the *Passat*, a four-masted steel barque of the early twentieth century employed on clipper-style bulk carriage from Chile, Australia, etc. But I was anxious to revisit Lübeck which had been my jumping-off point for my first incursion along the Baltic coast when it was still the DDR – the frontier being just east of where I was staying.

With Hamburg, Lübeck was a founder member of the Hanseatic League and remained one of the most prominent. It shows! It is remarkable how it has been authentically rebuilt after the devastation of the Second World War. In particular it is a city of tall spires, close together on the old town's island. Though the cathedral is sited at the southern end, the hill rising from the waterfront with its steeply gabled warehouses is crowned by Lübeck's most notable church, the Marienkirche: besides the Dom, other major churches nearby are St Peter's, St Jacob's and St Catherine's. All are effectively in the same idiom: tall brick Gothic exterior and towers crowned by pale-green lead steeples in one or other of the regional styles, soaring but sober Gothic naves.

In common with most of the town, of course, the churches were effectively destroyed in Allied air raids and have been most beautifully restored – at a cost including, sadly, Buxtehude's tomb in the Marienkirche, where he was organist for forty years. Famously, Bach walked hundreds of miles from southern

Germany to pay his respects: and when Handel, no less, was one of two candidates to succeed him he lost as he would not fulfil the condition of marrying Buxtehude's daughter! The winner did...

Secular buildings provide no less dramatic profiles. Most famous of them must be the Holstentor, the western entrance gate to the city and now after demolition of the walls isolated on its traffic island and gardens. It very clearly marks the change from modern suburbs to the serried ranks of steep-roofed old houses of the old town. An impressive, solid, squat building radiating defensiveness, the dark red brick Holstentor has an effectively oval footprint as its two great circular towers, with their enormous pointed roofs, effectively merge into the structure at either end. The Holstentor is usually called the 'iconic' building of Lübeck, but the other main civic buildings give it a run for its money: the town hall, hospital and other structures, in and around the spacious main square, all have imaginative skylines of pinnacles, pierced windows etc; and plain brick façades enlivened by highly elaborate stairs and entrances. The Rathaus houses the excellent Ratskeller where I ate in 1990 (though the fare was rather too fishy, as well as heavy, for my taste).

Besides this central architectural melée, the waterfront called inevitably, both for its own display of classic Hanseatic warehouses and for another collection of characterful old craft along the quaysides. The latter principally working boats and barges, mostly with masts and sails; but also tugboats, schooners and at least one three-masted square-rigger (on the opposite bank) which looked ready to sail off for Valparaiso... The riverside buildings, mostly warehouses, displayed much imagination: featuring many variations on the central gable or pediment (appropriate whether or not featuring cranes) and copious fenestration. The brickwork also is varied and imaginative, stripey patterns of black and red bricks common.

It was time for a while to return to the old East Germany, not this time along the Baltic seaboard but briefly to Schwerin and thence to turn south and then west. The change – quite apart from the disappearance of frontier paraphernalia – was still immediately evident though one manifestation was seemingly pointless or premature construction of elaborate road crossings, slip roads, etc. where barely populated main roads met minute side roads.

Am sorry that I had little time for anything other than a quick drive into and around Schwerin: a very historic and incredibly picturesque city which was mercifully spared the bombing experience of its near neighbour Lübeck. Fortuitously (but obviously for defence) sited at a corner of an extensive lake, one first sees the extraordinarily romantic profile of the Schwerin Palace, a largely Renaissance building on its own island endowed with the usual complement of towers, turrets, domes and steeples. This was the seat of the dukes of Mecklenburg – who became grand dukes, no less, only fairly recently. Behind it the Gothic brick cathedral has the usual vertiginous tower and spire pointing to the sky; another church of that period, hardly impressive, is St Paul's. The old town, as mentioned, was largely unscathed and seems almost indistinguishable, as a model, from the restoration of other nearby city centres – from Wismar or Gdansk. The main square (mercifully perhaps) is closed to vehicles so on this quick trip I could not savour it. But a glimpse was enough to get the flavour of this pretty town, capital of Mecklenburg – Vorpommern, among the many lakes of this part of the country.

Pressing on southwards along an ordinary and fairly uninteresting main road, not autobahn, I passed Wittenberge, crossing the Elbe shortly after, and then Stendal: after a brief transit of Brandenburg entering Saxony-Anhalt whose capital city Magdeburg was the next stopping place. (Effectively the road has run close to the Elbe most of the way.) Magdeburg, founded by Charlemagne and 'taken up' by Otto, the first Holy Roman Emperor (buried in the cathedral) has a distinguished but variable history, as an archbishopric, early university town and judicial centre. Martin Luther, who was a schoolboy there, arrived back and converted it from Catholicism: rather unfortunately causing the first of two major catastrophes when during the Thirty Years' War Tilly's Catholic troops sacked the city and massacred the entire population.

The second catastrophe involving the virtually total destruction of Magdeburg (the cathedral, now Lutheran again, almost the only exception) was the British and American bombing raids of early 1945 – but with much lower proportionate loss of life. The cathedral thus stands in a splendidly isolated and conspicuous position surrounded by parks leading down a gentle slope to the river. It is really the oldest Gothic cathedral in Germany, built in the first years of the thirteenth century: and a noble and coherent structure. I spent some time inside and was gratified when, in my limited German purchasing an organ recital CD, the kind woman asked me what part of Germany I came from!

Unsurprisingly, Magdeburg was rebuilt after the war in Ulbricht-style East German functionality: the main streets spacious and created for the ubiquitous towns of Eastern Europe, the façades undistinguished and repetitive. Nevertheless the overall effect of a now prosperous town lining the broad Elbe was not depressing and sad.

From Magdeburg I drove on, over the Harz mountains to the ancient university town of Göttingen and then to the equally historic town of Marburg for the next night. Göttingen possesses another upstanding Gothic/Romanesque cathedral with rear-twin octagonal towers of much later date, topped by pinnacles disappearing into the mist. The innermost town, black and white timbering in the main with red-tiled roofs, seemed distinguished by a wish to cram as many windows as possible onto the façades. In the main market square the principal attraction is the fountain with the statue of the 'little goose girl' (*Gänseliesel*) enclosed in a wrought-iron cage of great complexity.

While Göttingen lies in a narrow plain, Marburg is closely surrounded by hills from which good views of the historic town can be had, dominated by the soaring spires of the cathedral or

Elisabethkirche, now purely Gothic in grey stone and leaving behind the faceted Romanesque steeples of north-west Germany, and the more elaborate wrought-iron finials of some later towers. But the church is early Gothic (first half thirteenth century), the lofty nave uncluttered. It was built by the Teutonic Knights as the burial place of St Elizabeth of Hungary and became an important pilgrimage site. Besides the saint's tomb there is a wealth of sculpture, painting and altarpieces. A more unusual (and possibly sinister) feature is the 'chapel' of Paul von Hindenburg alongside. I enjoyed an evening stroll through the university quarter, drove up the hill for the prospect, and spent a pleasant night in a chic modern hotel (whose name I forget).

At Limburg, next stop and (very much) in the Latin also, cathedral architecture was back to the earlier Romanesque epoch of faceted, pointed culminations of tall fenestrated towers: two in front, one central steeple, four at the rear transepts. What is unusual in Limburg – cathedral as well as town buildings – is the red-and-white colour scheme of most buildings. A particularly 'iconic' view is that of the cathedral on its hill site from the ancient bridge over the Lahn, its multitude of spires crowding the sky. The old town descends from the hill in ultra-picturesque fashion within the area of the old city walls.

Istanbul for Easter

For Easter of 1994 we decided to go to Istanbul. I had of course been there briefly on my first Aegean cruise in 1961, then saw it from seaward in both directions from HMS *Brilliant* in late 1992, breaking the speed limit (as described in 'Naval Cruising'). What was missing was more leisured exploration on land.

I have mentioned earlier how surprised I was in 1961 to find the great walls of Byzantium/Constantinople/Istanbul so prominent and in many stretches almost intact. The airport now lies far to the west of the old triangular walled city and I was surprised to find how long it took to get there. The whole area seemed a desolate wasteland of quarter-finished buildings and it was a relief to come down into the city proper (especially given a manic taxi driver).

We stayed at the Çirağan Palace, a most grand and luxurious establishment on the Bosphorus, one of a line of former palaces some of which have unsurprisingly become hotels. This 'water-front' begins near the entrance to the Golden Horn, becoming the district of Besiktas, and starting with the grandest palace of all, the Dolmabahçe; this became the presidential palace and Ataturk died there. The Dolmabahçe is extraordinarily wide and low: it goes without saying ultra-ornate in the late nine-teenth-century style the Turks embraced, yet managing to retain some harmony and proportion in its seemingly endless façade to the water. The other palaces (of which the Çirağan is one) are in general more compact though fairly massive buildings in their own right, and also well proportioned and detailed. It was good to be staying on this 'esplanade' with wonderful views of the Bosphorus and all the maritime traffic (including a Dutch Kortenaer-class frigate moored directly in front), rather than in the congested city; and the taxi rides back and forth were a pleasure too.

Unsurprisingly we made first for the epicentre of historic Istanbul: Hagia Sophia, the Hippodrome, the Blue Mosque and the Topkapi. Hagia Sophia first. It is of course an awesome building and one I find greatly more satisfying inside than out: the purely architectural arrangement of three-dimensional space is nothing short of miraculous. Would, though, that it had not been blemished when deconsecrated as a Christian church! The remaining mosaic surfaces give some idea what the whole must have been like in the glimmer of numberless lamps; but the Islamification superimposed through 'decorative' frescoes is banal. Ichabod! I have fewer worries with the great circular calligraphic plaques on the chief pillars, or indeed the mihrab and suchlike: after all, if by then secular, it had been a mosque for many centuries.

However, I have never been able really to admire the exterior as it now is: unfair as much of the frankly brutalist reinforcement is due to structural problems, but it becomes an agglomeration of buttresses rather than an elegant edifice. This is no criticism of the original architects who achieved something of a scale not previously envisaged (perhaps though they needed a better chartered surveyor...). The rust-red colouring also perhaps lends a somewhat intimidating aspect: but it exudes power! In fact, I think the greatest contribution of Hagia Sophia's exterior is as viewed from a distance, the great dome and the lesser ones unobstructed by the surrounding buildings, which conceal the lower levels.

Superficially and from a distance, the Sultanahmet or 'Blue' mosque to which we now wended our way might seem rather similar: this in fact because the unmistakable silhouette of a great shallow dome surrounded and supported by numerous smaller ones had been established for Istanbul's major mosques by Hagia Sophia – whose later addition of minarets completed the similarity. Yet the (much newer) structure is very different; as is the atmosphere of internal luminosity and the consistency of filigreed decoration, the blue tiles which give it its sobriquet. As a working mosque of course it has a vast expanse of carpet, sub-divided into prayer mat spaces, which adds immeasurably to the sense of space: enhanced by the presence of lone worshippers at intervals. I find the ensemble of the principal building, the great outer courtyard and the six slender minarets very satisfying.

The space, now somewhat unremarkable municipal gardens, between these two great buildings was the old Byzantine Hippodrome, as a cursory look at the town plan can tell. It was full of tourists and locals enjoying the spring sunshine. The short amble to the (themselves impressive) Topkapi Saray ('Seraglio') main gates opened the way to a most varied and pleasurable descent through that palace's many courts and buildings. In the spring sunshine the greenery of the courts and many trees was refreshing, the high proportion of conifers compensating for the still-bare shapes of the rest. Topkapi is of course all museum now, with several different pavilions containing the magnificent, almost unparalleled exhibits. Invidious to mention but quite apart from superb Turkish ceramics the specimens of diamonds and emeralds are unbelievable. There is a superlative representation of Mughal jewellery, jade, daggers – remember *Topkapi*? These are mainly in the harem which is unsurprisingly a very distinct enclosed area. Many spaces have the most exquisite Islamic decoration, yet it is interesting how – in the courts and on façades especially – more neoclassical motifs sit easily together.

A charming street of old balconied wooded houses led us down nearer the shore, where we found ourselves in agreeable souk territory of carpets, silk and jewels: the Grand Bazaar, itself with its high vaulted ceiling an impressive architectural achievement. Much tea was proffered. Outside the streets teemed with commerce of all kinds, enticing-looking if shambolic shops, clothing racks, barrows…

After the intensity of sightseeing and the bustle of the city a quiet evening by the Bosphorus was indicated. The hotel was quiet, but at dinner in the hotel restaurant we had Sheikh Yamani and a small entourage at the next table. In the morning we were to embark for a cruise the length of the Bosphorus on one of the busy boats plying the straits. Weaving through the traffic – familiar to me from eighteen months earlier – one had a less lofty view of the multiplicity of craft to be avoided. Soon we were up to Rumeli Hisari, the great fortress, and beyond it the first of two suspension bridges – among the half-dozen longest in the world and unique in linking two continents. The ship, essentially a workaday commuter transport, put in frequently at small village piers; in between, a goodly number of enviable-looking villas occupied the waterfront, with woods tumbling down behind. These houses came in a variety of designs, often four-square, pedimented or with overhanging top floors, some wood, some stucco; some virtual palaces and some pleasingly modest. Towards the village centres the waterfront buildings crowded together and at times the effect was almost that of a Venetian quay. It all looked highly desirable.

We got off the boat at Yeniköy for a 'run ashore' and lunch, so in fact this time did not go as far as the Black Sea. Naturally fish are the main *raison d'être* there (commuting apart), and there was a fine selection of eateries for my ichthyophagous girlfriend. The little harbour was as picturesque and paintable as these places always are for me: small boats of all sorts jostling together, while tables and chairs at the quay's very edge indicated 'fast food'. There were also many chairs lining the edge whence the male population (only!) scrutinised the proceedings. Immediately ashore were displays of every weird-shaped fish imaginable, possibly even some recognisable; further inland, a 'proper' covered fish market beckoned. We had a nice al fresco lunch and afterwards strolled around inspecting local street life while waiting for the return voyage, getting back as the sun sank.

Next day I set off by myself for the city. My main objective was the Süleymaniye mosque which I had believed – and was right – I would find the most perfect architecturally. The masterpiece of the great architect Sinan, whose tomb I could see in the graveyard, it seems near perfection in both proportion and detail. The external courtyard with its tall, slightly pointed arches seems the definition of elegance; the view up to the dome puts that summit in perfect perspective. Inside, the pale grey interior is judiciously picked out by brick-red embellishments to the lofty arches, while the whole is suffused by light from the vast multi-windowed lunettes and that provided by the side 'chapels'.

The Süleymaniye's gardens and graveyard are a place where it is delightful to wander, both for their immediate contents and for the changing views of the mosque itself, but above all for the oasis atmosphere. Moving out again, the same (at least as far as framing the mosque goes) was provided by walls and gates of sobriety, solidity and proportion – at least one gate approaching an Italian Renaissance hybrid.

That complex is located around halfway up the slope from the Golden Horn to the 'plateau' containing Hagia Sophia, the Hippodrome and the Blue Mosque. Descending from this calm towards the waterfront bustle I found the last on my 'mosque list'; the Yeni Mosque also the last (mid-sixteenth century) of the great 'classical' mosques. This is effectively 'On the Waterfront', its ablutions court giving directly onto a wide area which in turn gives onto a quay crammed with small boats of every description. Street life in this area seemed to veer between tranquil and hyperactive, artisans and cobblers in evidence. I hadn't managed to get into the Yeni, I think as it was getting late; so after gazing across the Horn at the opposite shore, rising steeply to the somewhat spooky-looking Galata Tower, took a walk over the nearby Galata Bridge and had a good wander up the hill in the fading light. This was Pera, a very distinct and characterful area containing among other attractions the famous Pera Palace Hotel, destination of so many *Orient Express* travellers – and not only in detective fiction! From a clear spot on the eminence I could get a fine panoramic view of the old city with the domes and minarets of all its mosques now silhouetted against the sunset, and the Horn gleaming golden. After closer inspection of the unmistakably phallic Tower I had an easy descent through the steep streets to the bridge again and a taxi back to the Çirağan.

Poland 1996 – Japan Society

Two outings by a small group from the Japan Society took place in the mid-1990s, for me sandwiched between the frequent trips to Switzerland. The rationale for the Society's visiting, first Poland (in 1996) and the next year Germany, was perhaps somewhat tenuous (though some links were found), but on the lines of the OU PG Wodehouse Society's official 'mission statement', 'The Society exists to entertain its members', success was achieved.

Ably arranged by then Secretary Roger Caffrey the group had an unsurprisingly diplomatic emphasis: Hugh and Elizabeth Cortazzi, he the late Chairman of the Society and former Ambassador at Tokyo; Delia Pilcher, widow of the late Sir John; Professor Ian Nish and wife Rhona; Lew Radbourne, now joint Chairman with Haruko, and wife Gillian; Haruko, of course, and myself. A few others too.

I have already described my earlier brief visit to Warsaw six years earlier, so a 'gazetteer' is not required here for the old town centre – the Royal Castle and museum, the cathedral and the Old Town Square. All this had been pretty well rebuilt by 1990. We did explore rather further into the area of the old destroyed Warsaw Ghetto and viewed several churches – the Baroque St Paul's and Gothic St Jacek north of the square, and that of the Virgin Mary, Gothic with a fine Baroque bell tower. Returning down the main avenue the succession of well-restored palaces were a roll-call of the Polish aristocracy: Radziwill, Czartoryski, Pilsudski, Poniatowski – and not least, only alphabetically, Zamoyski.

There was also time to visit the palaces, gardens and parks

further from the Warsaw centre: the Łazienki and Wilanów. Both adjoin the Vistula with extensive parkland dotted with statuary, follies, grottoes, Chinese temples etc. and extensive wooded areas. The Łazienki complex in general has a greater number of somewhat smaller buildings than Wilanów, with pavilions, orangeries and the main palace dispersed around the extensive area. The 'amphitheatre' is in fact a (semi-circular) antique-pattern theatre. Different buildings serve as museums and galleries for paintings, sculptures and prints. The earlier Wilanów, built by a Sobieski king, is in a stronger Baroque idiom, with a square tower rising above the centre section, recesses turning to side wings with emphatic Baroque cupola-topped towers also. Much roofline statuary. The gardens again are extensive: formal pastures near the castle, then stretching down to, but not across, the river.

We drove down to Kraków – not worth a flight, and allowing us a stop at Chopin's birthplace at Żelazowa Wola (in fact not far from Warsaw). Though Chopin never lived there other than in his earliest years the small, pretty (but reconstructed) house was reminiscent of the composer's life with appropriate furnishings and exhibits, notably pianos. On one of the latter a young lady gave a very tuneful recital of ballades and polonaises for us.

In Kraków the Cortazzis and ourselves stayed at the pleasingly old-fashioned and unreconstructed Francuski Hotel, in its great location close to the main market square and almost opposite the Czartoryski Museum. That we promptly visited, above all for its supreme attraction, Leonardo's *Lady with an Ermine* (but see below…). But we joined the others to explore the main Town Square (Rynek Glowny) and the complex there: it is the largest mediaeval urban space in Europe, containing in its centre the enormous Cloth Hall, in Renaissance style, and to the sides the basilica of St Mary with its imposing pair of non-matching towers, and the much older Romanesque church of St Adalbert. St Mary's projects out into the square and a trumpeter sounds every hour. Inside, the cynosure is perhaps the altar triptych by

Veit Stoss (Wit Stwosz in Polish!), framed by the three enormously tall stained-glass windows of the apse. The ceiling vaults are blue, studded with gold stars. All that is left of the old Town Hall is the tower: again, a massive but elegant structure, vertical brick and stone Gothic striping giving way at the summit to a double octagonal cupola and finial of later date.

From the square a long, straight garden leads down to the other main sight of Kraków, the Wawel Royal Castle. This sits on an eminence near the river with gardens, again, dropping away to its banks (from which is obtained the best view of the castle with its spires, gables and turrets). Parts of the old city wall which enclosed it can also be seen. The cathedral, part of the Wawel complex, follows the general rule of an asymmetrical front with one tower incomplete: the completed one, however, is of considerable splendour. The cathedral being dedicated to St Wenceslaus (as well as St Stanislaus), one can imagine looking out from it 'on the feast of Stephen…'

Of course, the whole place is imbued with the memory of Archbishop Karol Wojtyla, later Pope John Paul. We – Haruko and I – had a close reminder of him when we went for a late-evening drink in a basement piano bar with an (older) banker acquaintance of hers. He said that his late father had been on the closest of terms with the Pope, and still called him 'Karol'; but he himself would not quite presume to do that. His other revelation was that the Leonardo displayed was not the real thing, which is kept several floors below ground for safety, and what is shown is an exact copy: whether or not that is true I don't know.

Rather deliberately, we did not make a day trip to Auschwitz-Birkenau; but instead to the nearby Wieliczka Salt Mine. This was the most amazing place: down and down one went on a staircase, arriving at a spacious hall (one of several), entirely carved out of the salt. And not only the space, but the furnishings, accoutrements, things like chandeliers – all made out of salt. Naturally, several chapels or religious groupings featured.

It didn't smell salty and wasn't claustrophobic. It was a relief though to have a lift rather than have to use the stairs to regain the surface.

Berlin and Dresden 1997

In April 1997 the Japan Society pioneers of the previous year's trip to Poland regathered for a second Mitteleuropa expedition, this time to Berlin and Dresden, and with an equally slender connection to things Japanese. The group's composition was not quite identical, the main absentee being Haruko who was on some work trip elsewhere. Cortazzis, Nishes, Radbournes, ambassadress Fujii and of course presiding ambassadorial spirit Delia Pilcher came, though.

I hadn't been in Berlin since the flurry of visits in 1989–90 over reunification and much had changed, though much was still a work in progress. The Wall was long gone except for one or two 'heritage' locations down by the Spree in the east: new big buildings were springing up around the Potsdamer Platz, but the stretch from the Brandenburg Gate down to there was still a wide *glacis*; while where the somewhat complex boundary had run north of the Reichstag by the river was still very much a construction site. Everywhere including across main streets like Friedrichstrasse soared huge pipes in tones of surprising purple or pink, rising and falling over obstacles like pythons. The distinction between old east and west had certainly lessened though major works were still ongoing on the Museumsinsel, Unter der Linden and churches.

Unsurprisingly it was there, in the heart of Berlin proper, that we began our visit – walking around generally, a good visit to the Pergamon Museum, also the Neues Museum and indeed the interior of the Dom. The Marxist palace of desperate dreamers was going and the real Royal Palace being reborn. After the Pergamon Altar and other wonders there, it was naturally time for Charlottenburg and the number one star attraction – Nefertiti. The palace is all white and gold, inside as well as out, and the park was at its spring loveliest. With the Tiergarten and then the woods and lakes leading down by the Havel to Potsdam and Babelsberg, Berlin seemed almost as well served as London in open green spaces.

We did in fact head down that way later, through the pleasant suburbs of Wilmersdorf, Grünewald and Dahlem and eventually to overlook the Wannsee. Somehow while the former places seem as innocent as Bridge of Weir where I grew up, with detached mock-Tudor (German equivalent) or 1930s modernist houses in sizeable gardens, a certain sinister aura seems to hang over the Wannsee: probably imagined, deriving from recent atrocious history, but the odd battlemented glimpse through the trees, slender spires across the water, ironwork towers give it a different atmosphere. The film studio area of Babelsberg – in its day bigger than Hollywood – gives the best panoramic view, including Glienicke Bridge which we would shortly cross.

This seemed unchanged – even the abrupt change of road surface, the only evidence of the old border. Potsdam also was perhaps somewhat smarter but the long *allee* to the centre still had its quota of dreary communist-era blocks and Trabis not yet out to grass. In the centre the obvious first and main attraction in the park was Sanssouci Palace itself. I always think of it as a place of near-perfection. The one (important) change was that Frederick the Great had been brought back and reinterred in the grass of the terrace under a super-simple slab. Descending the river terraces (and not losing each other) we had a long ramble, as ever, through the park to the Chinese tea house, past Schinkel creations and to the Neues Palais – the first thing I saw in greater Berlin in 1989, and something I greatly like. A sort of Prussian Hampton Court (later incarnation).

Considerable reconstruction work still seemed to be going on there (though I don't recollect any Polish signs): grainy black statuary waiting to be cleaned and reattached to posturing attitudes on the roofs. At ground level the half-cleaned figures had a comical aspect – black coats and pale breeches. Potsdam town – so much a garrison town – was again patchy with some fully restored houses and some pretty dismal. Many still fenced-off building sites.

The next stop was to the Cecilienhof, site of the 1945 tri-partite Potsdam Conference (Attlee replacing Churchill halfway through; Stalin staying; Truman replacing the sadly late Roosevelt). Cecilienhof is a rambling complex, rather more pretend English Tudor it seemed – Cheshire perhaps or Sussex – than the mediaeval German of the Rhineland or Bavaria, Brandenburg or the Palatinate. Large gables, mainly half not whole timbering, massed chimneys, oriel windows. Of course, we visited the fateful 'round table' indoors, and strolled round the garden with spring flower beds brilliant.

I believe we drove straight to Dresden down the autobahn – not an exceptionally long drive but exceptionally dreary, through endless cabbage fields and nary a hedge in sight. Doing the same drive in the opposite direction in 1989, though from Weimar, Mama and I had stopped once or twice, though whizzing past Leipzig and Dessau; not this time. While on the previous occasion we'd had to go back to Weimar at night (no room anywhere in Dresden!), by now the smart hotel beside the cathedral and opposite the Opera had been rebuilt; and there we settled. This of course was far more convenient for the very compact city centre and the banks of the Elbe. A night-time stroll across the bridge gave a great view of the floodlit buildings opposite, reflected.

We took the Dresden visit somewhat 'back to front' with an expedition into the surrounding countryside before 'doing' the city centre and museums. First up the interminable Neustadt and on to Meissen. There the Meissen porcelain factory, show-rooms and museum are sited fairly low down near the river, and we spent quite a while there, with helpful guide, and demonstrations of the various phases of manufacture – turning, shaping, painting, firing ... I am very fond of Meissen – much more than, say, of Sèvres – and have some pieces, but didn't buy any there.

Meissen town rises steeply from the river – approaching one sees the serried ranks of houses and crowning all the great grey Gothic twin-spired cathedral. After lunch a climb up the cobbled street though buildings, Baroque or earlier, still tending to the monochrome coloration of the East but generally in good, restored condition, led to the market square – with the imposing *yellow* Markt-Apotheke (chemists are big in these parts) and a handsome grey and white Gothic church (tall Baroque tower). From there, there seems an impenetrable high wall of houses before the cathedral: the street becomes steeper and the houses older. Some good Baroque doorways, and signs: 'Walter Schneider, Fleischermeister' sounds straight out of the *Meistersinger* (wrong city though). Some of the steeper roofs had those ranks of attic windows which always remind me somehow of sting rays.

From Meißen (give German orthography a go!) it was a short drive east to Moritzburg and its imposing castle on its island in the lake (both very regular and artificial). Moritzburg is a hefty dark yellow quadrilateral edifice, russet-roofed with totally disproportionate domed towers at each corner. A causeway bridge leads up to it and its broad terrace, balustrades adorned with a succession of blackened urns and figures, somewhat *à la* Charles Bridge in Prague. The lake is reed-fringed and the wooded surrounds tranquil. A certain hunting ambience prevails throughout.

The next excursion was to Schloß Pillnitz, the country residence some ten miles upstream. To save time and presumably money we were driven there along the north bank: sizeable suburban villas behind high walls hid the vineyards above on the hillsides, and many were impressive structures. Pillnitz is also arranged on three sides around a spacious garden quadrangle with large pool: two principal storeys and curving grey-tiled roof of definitely Chinese characteristics, topped with little finials. In the higher central portion, Corinthian-colonnaded at the entrance, the roof is itself two-storey and more steeply curved. Plainer but still elegant blocks complete the ensemble. Sweeping paths round the pond and through the extensive parterres were gay with spring planting, largely daffodils. From the grassy riverbank a constant stream of the ancient river paddleboats passed: on one of which we were shortly to embark for the return cruise to Dresden. This was one of the smaller craft, with largely open decks and slender black funnel, giving a great view of the riparian activities of grazing, vines, boatyards and light industry. Some serious villas and even palaces hugged the skyline above tiered vineyards: and there was considerable barge traffic. Eventually we tied up at the Terrassenufer quay, highly convenient for hotel rest, alongside vessels of many other lines: the *Dresden*, the *Meissen*, also the *Diesbar*, *Stadt Wehlen*, *Leipzig* and maybe others – all in different liveries.

The area of the Schlossstrasse and the Dresdner Schloss immediately behind had been much restored since I was last there – no more gaunt blackened gables or gaping windows open to the sky. The parade of mounted mosaic figures along the length of the wall always enchants me. Before that, on the higher terrace above the Elbe, we visited the Grüne Gewölbe, Augustus the Strong's greatest legacy and I believe *the* museum of decorative arts of the world. Sadly, I understand a major robbery took place quite recently. The Zwinger, visited next, is not far behind in that category and of course also has (or had? … has there been a relocation?) an amazing collection of all the greatest European painters. The palace itself in its unsurpassable Rococo around its wide courtyard is every bit as much of an attraction as its superlative contents. The bombed Frauenkirche was still in the early stages of reconstruction (financed by the British in expiation, and now happily fully restored), so the rather more playful Zwinger provided the fitting conclusion to this all-too-brief visit to Dresden.

Tunisia

Following an earlier trip to Morocco, we decided for Easter 1998 to move further east along the Maghreb and explore some of Tunisia. We stayed at a new and somewhat architecturally uninspiring large hotel at La Marsa, on the beach about 15 minutes west of Tunis. It was a good base, however. Alas, when we took a stroll on the wide sandy beach after arrival it was grey, windy, and cold. Quite possibly Machrihanish would have been bathed in windless sunshine in April! However, things improved quite quickly.

We went into Tunis to look around the centre: like many large cities of the former French-ruled North Africa there is a clear division between the old Arab medina souk 'n' mosque quarter and the nineteenth- and twentieth-century quadrilineal modern city. Between the two was the main shopping quarter – the main artery north-south and crossing it east-west the broad avenue Habib Bourguiba (who guessed?) connecting the port with the medina. This passes the theatres, French Embassy, etc. as it becomes the true modern 'city centre': culminating at the Porte de France, beyond which at the medina entrance is the strategically placed British Embassy, formerly Consulate-General. We had a good look at that as Sir Alan Williams, father of Haruko's great friend Libet, had been Consul-General while Tunisia was still a French colony. Lady Williams (Masha, a White Russian aristocratic émigrée), wrote a book – one of a series about their diplomatic postings – which most vividly describes their challenging and interesting life as Tunisia moved, by means both violent and negotiated, towards independence. Titled *In the Bey's Palace*, it recounts life in the – separate – residence in said palace with a young family interacting with distinguished visitors, British, French, and Arab.

The best thing in Tunis, or rather a short way out from that centre towards the north-west, is the Bardo Museum. Part of a palace complex dating from thirteenth to nineteenth centuries, it houses a splendid array of Punic, Roman, Byzantine and Islamic artefacts. The pride of the collection, I think, is that of Roman mosaics – as good as any in the world. Scenes of mythology – Orpheus, Europa, Venus, Diana, Hercules – all of them – and of hunting, feasting, Bacchanals and other serious pleasures predominate. Many Roman statues, sarcophagi, portrait busts and architectural fragments are preceded in time by Carthaginian Punic objects – mainly ceramics – and followed by Byzantine and Islamic stuff.

A few miles north of Tunis is Carthage – redolent name! – the ancient sites quite widely spread on a hill overlooking the sea to the east and the more modern town on the flat. Perhaps its most important, though a rather sinister, site is the Salammbo Tophet, down by the sea and the two Punic harbour inlets. This was a sanctuary and burial place and was increasingly used for the ritual sacrifice of young children, who were boiled alive in olive oil and placed in large jars, to be seen to this day. Horrid. (Too much information.) One reason I feel that 'delenda Carthago est' (Scipio Africanus) and the conquest by Rome had some redeeming features. Elsewhere, scattered around, are some Carthaginian but mainly Roman housing remains, and from the Roman period a complex of very large baths, theatre and up-market villas: further north the Roman amphitheatre and circus are entirely levelled. Sundry basilicas dating from early Byzantine times to nineteenth-century French colonial are nearer the centre.

On the way out of Carthage I had the most recent car accident of my existence (1998): a car driven by an Arab lady hit my side on a roundabout as I was observing *priorité â droite* (this being France). Back at the hotel of course I reported it to the rental company, and it was replaced by another; the next day, unexpectedly, the exceedingly nice lady driver responsible came with the rental people and owned up that it was all her fault – so there was no charge or penalty. An odd place for one's motoring mishaps! (*Delenda est…*)

Just next to Carthage is Sidi Bou Said, a very pleasant if unremarkable little resort town on a hill promontory above the sea, now facing more north. A steep flagstoned street lined with mainly whitewashed and blue-detailed houses runs down the hill: masses of bright flowers, artists' studios and tourist tat. Paul Klee came here for a while, but you might not know that from his paintings…

There were two longer car expeditions. Haruko and I drove to the ruined Roman city of Dougga, about a hundred miles southwest of Tunis. It was a very pleasant drive through undulating country of grain and, notably, many mimosa plantations for bark used in the omnipresent and malodorous extramural tanneries of North African cities. One has to drive up a fairly steep hill for the last two or three miles to the entrance of Dougga, which occupies the top of a hill: from which the views were extensive. It's a very well-preserved site, mostly, it would seem, because not over-commercialised nor indeed over-restored. A surprising amount of columns still stand alongside paved streets or at a good number of temples and other important buildings. The Capitol Temple is especially elegant and well-preserved, and to me seemed reminiscent of that at Nîmes with slender tall Corinthian columns supporting a substantial and well-preserved pediment. Others are nearly as well preserved and even where less so rows of columns seem to have lasted longest. Other major features are the arch of Septimius Severus (he, of course, the first African-born Roman emperor), the baths, and most impressively, some way downhill, the great three-storey tower of the mausoleum of a Numidian chief: it was built during the Punic Wars by a Numidian king allied with Rome against Hannibal, dating from 202 BC.

Returning from Dougga we paid a brief visit to the British and Commonwealth war cemetery rising up from the roadside: immaculately maintained as ever by the War Graves Commission. As far as I could see, no relations or known people there (Uncle David did get to Tunis with the Argylls, after a near-death experience at Alamein). As always, thought-provoking, and inspiring.

The next long drive was by myself: down south to another spectacular Roman site, the amphitheatre of El Djem. This is only slightly smaller than Rome's Colosseum, and in rather more original condition – unsurprising as not visited by millions each year in one of the world's tourist hotspots. It lies at the end of a road through a pretty scruffy little village: contrasting with Dougga, it sits on flat land near the coast, has no Roman urban remains around it and is solitary. It's pretty well preserved except for some much later depredations on the upper (third) storey; and the seats have gone.

Returning towards Tunis, the necessary diversion was to the ancient and important port town of Sousse. No Roman remains here, it is a predominantly Islamic centre with a vast walled medina sloping down towards the harbour. Here, unsurprisingly, the principal feature is the Great Mosque: as ever, three colonnaded sides around a great courtyard, and the prayer hall on the fourth side. No conventional tall minaret, but a substantial domed and fortified tower for the muezzin. Just behind the mosque is the Ribat, a fortified enclosure with massive walls surrounding a square courtyard housing cells for warrior monks. Climbing a high tower gives a good view of medina and kasbah, higher up, and port and Mediterranean below. There are several smaller mosques, mostly whitewashed and unpretentious, as one finds one's way through the maze of streets. I particularly enjoyed the sophisticated vernacular architecture of domestic houses, some of considerable size, and featuring spacious courtyards into many of which I peered or could enter. Very sophisticated carved doors, windows, balconies, mostly of dark green contrasting with the white. I was enchanted by these little glimpses into the life of the medina. Unlike, say, Fez or

Marrakech, there did not seem to be concentrated clutter and activity of artisanship and commerce: maybe elsewhere nearby, or maybe (more likely) my memory fails me. It had a more tranquil, more intellectual feel.

My journey homeward took me past, but not into, Enfidaville, and certainly not Hammamet of package-deal *plage* fame. Thence skirting Tunis to La Marsa and the hotel – and shortly home. It had been a good 'follow-up' from Morocco and the Atlas: next, a few years on, was to be yet further eastward to Egypt (*almost* on the tank-tracks of Rommel). That is another story.

Latin America 2003

In July 2003 I reached the milestone of sixty years old: not celebrated afloat as the 'big figure' anniversaries of twenty, thirty and fifty had been (motor yacht at Cannes, a junk in Hong Kong and an RN frigate in the Pool of London respectively), but more quietly in London. However, in a magnificent gesture my darling Haruko said she would give me a first-class ticket to anywhere in the world (return, too!), using her copious collection of air miles (needed also for frequent trips to Japan). So it was that, when that offer was made one beautiful summer day at Creems, I had no hesitation in saying I would really like to explore South America. So, I selected Ultimate Travel to map out for me an itinerary with internal travel, guides, hotels all pre-booked throughout Peru, Bolivia, Argentina and even Uruguay and Paraguay, for a month in September and October.

It was a very different day from that fine summer afternoon when I boarded BA 1 for New York, the interim stop on the way to Lima. It was touch and go whether we could land at JFK as a hurricane was forecast; eventually the risk was deemed acceptable. One of the best things about the sadly missed Boeing 747 'Jumbo' is that the first-class cabin is not just below the flight deck but well forrard of it: and the front row has just one seat each side of the aisle. In 1F to starboard I had none other than Dr Henry Kissinger a few feet to my left in 1A. A few nods and words as we settled in – he changing into pyjamas, me not – and I saw him settle down to an eclectic reading list of the *Neue Zürcher Zeitung*, the *Daily Mail*, and some political biography. After we had (bumpily) landed I thought I should at least shake his hand and we had a brief and pleasant conversation while waiting to disembark. Approaching the baggage carousel, he was surrounded by at least half a dozen impressive plain-clothes bodyguards. Despite this sign of, I presumed, fast-tracking, the baggage of all the other passengers came and went, with their owners: only Dr K's and mine resolutely refused to appear (this is in line with BA's policy of leaving higher-paying passengers' baggage till last, if it appears at all – see Calcutta some pages before). This gave, at least, the opportunity for further somewhat sardonic chat with the great man.

Eventually both lots appeared and off he went with his entourage. Somewhat absurdly, without a transit lounge one has to enter the USA – visa waiver, stamp, and all – for the quarter-mile bus journey to another terminal for the LAN/Chile flight (to Peru of course). The airside waiting zone was shared, improbably, with Aer Lingus and everything was green. Perhaps that was why with a couple of hours to wait I dozed off and only awoke from my slumber to find my flight was boarding. A very comfortable flat berth, however, and I awoke to the thrilling sight of several precipitous Andean peaks – of near-Himalayan scale – passing, isolated above a layer of thick cloud. Then descent to early-morning arrival at Lima.

First impressions of Lima were not wholly favourable. On the streets from the airport (itself not the most welcoming place, except for a cheerful greeting from my dragoman from Ultimate, Aquilino), most houses and shops had iron bars like cages reaching right out to the pavement: hardly encouraging! Things got slightly better as we approached our destination, the Lima Country Club. As its name would suggest this was an archetypal American establishment of the type I had become familiar with in places like New Jersey and California: and very pleasant and welcome too. A sprawling white complex which could well have been in Beverly Hills: room and restaurant excellent. Of course, golf featured strongly so greenery abounded: in fact, the district, San Isidro, is a sort of enclave nearer the centre of Lima than the vaunted Miraflores on the coast.

Having arrived in early morning, there was time after settling in to visit the more central area – the archaeological museum and

Bolivar's house, and to walk around the San Isidro park. Next day we went down to Miraflores first: I was glad not to have stayed there, as many friends have done – I wasn't impressed by the hotel, the shore consists of shelving grey friable cliffs, the ocean also was grey, in fact everything was. It's also a long way from the centre, to which we returned to view the cathedral square (Plaza Mayor) and surrounding central area. The cathedral is an enormous and impressive structure, Baroque with twin towers flanking a somewhat lower porticoed entrance; but the interior is a promiscuous riot of Renaissance, Baroque, Gothic and Neoclassical styles. Altars and monuments of extreme opulence testify to the riches the Spanish conquest of Peru provided. I took my first ever photograph with a digital camera, though such is my tech-conservatism that I relied mainly on 'proper' cameras and slide film on this journey – subsequently digitised and filed on my computer.

Near the Plaza Mayor and cathedral is the fine old Aliaga house, which can be (and was) visited, and the basilica and convent of San Francisco. The site for the Aliaga house, next door to Pizarro's, was given by the latter on Lima's foundation in 1535 and the house is thus almost contemporary with Creems in Suffolk! Rather larger though. It is both magnificent and livable (the same family has lived there through the generations uninterruptedly since 1535) with high well-proportioned rooms, central staircases, virtuoso wooden carving and panelling. The whole house exudes an aura of intricate woodwork, leather and stone: many rooms being painted in a deep yellow increases the ambience of warmth.

San Francisco, a basilica too, is nearly as grand as the cathedral. Its site at the corner of a square of major Renaissance and Baroque ecclesiastical buildings perhaps enhances its impact: it is actually joined at the corner to the nunnery at right angles. Unlike the cathedral and other major churches (as Arequipa, seen the following day), it eschews the long low façade with elegant Baroque towers spaced well apart, for a more punchy front with two very solid towers separated only by an exuberant frontispiece portal of reddish-grey stone. The towers and lower part are in a buttercup-yellow finish. Inside is archetypal Baroque, the chapter house with magnificent artworks including fifteen paintings attributed to Zurbarán. As a convent, a sizeable cloister extends beyond, two-storied, more sober in style with rounded arches and pilasters. Church-crawling ended – though there was much more to see – the day finished with a wander round the San Isidro up-market district and dinner and bed at the Country Club.

Next morning a two-hour flight took me the surprisingly long distance south-east and uphill to Peru's second city, Arequipa. It's a most charming city which belies its size – it has almost the feel of a small yet important town – an Oxford or Salamanca, with the aforementioned basilica-cathedral surmounting the spacious gardens of the Plaza de Armas stretching down the hillside. Before the cathedral I visited the very extensive and ancient Monasterio de Sta. Catalina, a little way further uphill and to the left of the cathedral. It has as one might expect numerous arched patios, grey stone or whitewashed, though an Aegean rather than Iberian reminiscence comes with more than one painted in a brilliant blue. The chapel has a perfectly judged classical altarpiece with the saint ethereal in flowing white raiment.

Not unlike Somerset House in London, one approaches the long façade of the cathedral through a rather substantial Corinthian-pillared archway at either end of the immediate walkway. Contrasting with these rather macho structures are the supremely elegant towers near either end of the façade: again, some hints of London and Wren churches with open arches surmounted by further 'decks' and open bell-chambers below the graceful, pointed finial. The long façade is level with vertical emphases at intervals and a relatively restrained centre pyramid. Inside is cool and spacious, neoclassical (the cathedral having been rebuilt after earthquakes) – in pale yellow and grey with broad arches and a plain yellow vaulted ceiling. A fine Baroque organ precedes the choir where a *slightly* greater mix of plaster ornamentation rules in the apse.

The next church visit was to La Compañia, the Jesuit church and monastery. Again, the original buildings were destroyed, and this allowed the order to rebuild in a pure seventeenth-century Jesuit style, with an impressive tripartite centrepiece 'stuck into' a plain front wall, behind which rises just one plain tower with a rather squat dome on top. In fact, the church is somewhat overshadowed by the Jesuits' living quarters alongside, with a handsome cloister behind with colonnade and pool (Trafalgar Square; Creems…). Inside the church all eyes are naturally drawn to the ultra-ornate reredos, evidence once more of the great golden riches of the conquistadors. The architecture is stone and sober, but adorned with numerous subsidiary altarpieces of considerable complexity, and gilt-framed paintings on the walls.

Many more façades and ornamented doorways were encountered as we gently descended the slope towards the very pleasant Hotel Libertador, a modern terracotta-coloured complex in nice gardens, outside the immediate central area. The final stop on the church crawl was the monastery and church of San Francisco: a solid, square, low-built edifice with one low square tower adjoining a façade of pale grey stone in the upper half and russet red below. Inside is sober plain stonework inevitably with a golden Baroque altar and reredos, but relatively restrained.

I was leaving fairly early with guide Lula and driver Oscar in a faithful Toyota Land Cruiser for the quite long drive to spend the next night at the Colca Canyon, before returning for another night in Arequipa. Not just long but high – over 5,000 metres or well above 15,000 feet at the highest point. Leaving Arequipa, low, entirely arid hills culminate in narrow cultivated bright green strips around dusty villages. Further on as one passes the Colchani volcano scrubland takes over even as one climbs. Strange swirly patterns of cultivation intervene;

and small herds of alpaca rather gratifyingly seem to outnumber llamas in this area. Towering above is the magnificent bulk of the volcano. Weird, eroded rock formations presage the descent of a river to meander through the waterscape of a vast plain, haunt of innumerable exotic camelids and scattered settlements. Strange mosses and fungi were to be seen among the desolate rockscape; nowhere more desolate than near the summit point, where strange pyramids of stones gave the impression that some lunatics had chosen this as a form of entertainment – but that could hardly be. Everywhere grey scree and occasional taupe-coloured grazing land made for a *grisaille* scene, sharply relieved near the summit by a troupe of bowler-hatted ladies selling a variety of amazingly brightly coloured woollens: rugs, jackets, ponchos, shawls: a splendid punctuation to the greyness, and a response to it.

The descent to the small town of Chivay was steep and abrupt. Approaching the town, cultivation is on close-packed terraces, though the ground in the valley is not steep. Chivay is a dun-coloured business-like little market town enhanced by great numbers of street stalls. (The bowler hats by the way are generally white, completing a most colourful attire, for most women anyway, of embroidered blouses and jackets, waist sashes and extraordinarily capacious generally blue skirts. The average female height seems to be about 4' 8".) On the outskirts is a fine mission church in silvery stone: twin square towers with pointy tops flanking an entrance portal with two large arches, one above the entrance proper. A not dissimilar church further on had a broader pediment and beneath it an open galleria, giving a flatter façade but still with enormous entrance arch. This was Yanque, after Coporaque the next small place before reaching the Colca Lodge at the beginning of the Colca Canyon itself. Oxen were ploughing by the river rattling down towards the canyon, terraces climbing the ever-steepening banks. It was nice to arrive at the comfortable lodge for a good sleep – possibly brought on by coca beverage for the altitude!

A good thing too for an early start – 6 a.m. breakfast – for the drive to the canyon to see the condors rising and flying (virtually guaranteed). The condor-viewing spot ('Cruz del Condor') is shortly upon one as the gorge has deepened suddenly and dramatically. A small number of probably American tourists had gathered and were vying for photo positions on the steep slope. The condors, however, were not cooperating and were not to be seen all morning. While that was a pity the breathtaking scenery more than compensated. The canyon is arguably the deepest in the world – the only competitor is also in Peru – and one looks across this stunning fissure to the awesome sharply pinnacled mass of Mismi mountain rising directly opposite. This contains the source of the Amazon (I love locating and viewing the sources of great rivers: the Rhône in its glacier, the Seine from a Baron Haussmann-adorned 'source', the Loire in the Auvergne – our Thames in its marshy Gloucestershire field hardly counts; but to climb up Mismi seemed somewhat impractical).

The return to Arequipa inevitably followed the same route and need not be described again. I did this time venture into the little white church at Yanque and was surprised how ornate with gold all over the walls it was. Otherwise, no change. I didn't stop in Chivay or buy woollens: I probably did imbibe coca tea once more for the altitude... Of course, in the opposite direction, the views are different and as one approached Arequipa the dramatically conical El Misti volcano, which overhangs the city at a perilously close-seeming distance, comes increasingly into the frame. Nice Libertador again, then a 5 a.m. call for the next flight, to Cuzco.

No sooner installed in the historic Monasterio hotel than I had a discussion with my guide and a chap from the tour agency about a fairly drastic change of plan. The original idea had been, after an overnight expedition to Machu Picchu and further more local outings around Cusco (as it can also be spelt), to take the train up to Puno on Lake Titicaca, cross the lake and thence into Bolivia at Copacabana and on to La Paz. However, they explained that there were troubles in Bolivia and the trans-lacustrine crossing would not be possible. So alternative arrangements would have to be made to get to La Paz.

These arrangements set in train, it was time to explore the town. The Monasterio lies at the end of a narrow street, largely built of superb Inca masonry, somewhat higher up than the great Plaza de Armas which is the undoubted epicentre of Cusco. A vast square, sloping gently down amid the amphitheatre of mountains, which contains two massive and splendid Baroque churches: the cathedral and the Jesuit church, higher up, while La Merced monastery and church are just nearby. Built of the reddish granite of the region, both have the exuberant sixteenth–seventeenth-century architecture of twin massive towers crowned by cupolas above the open bell chambers: the interiors are endowed with a stupefying quantity of solid-gold-encrusted decoration (alas, unlike in Lima, one was not allowed to photograph inside). Around the square and in the neighbouring streets, the buildings, many clearly religious, sport colonial-era arches and galleries, to make a most harmonious ensemble. Though these replaced the original Inca structures (if with less accuracy of stonework), examples are to be found from time to time in the surrounding streets.

Though I had not realised it was any particular feast day, there was a surprising amount of religiously oriented processions and gatherings: an image of the Virgin borne aloft, students in red cloaks or waistcoats and breeches, young ladies in fetching mini-kilts and sleeveless pullovers looking as if outfitted at Blair Atholl rather than the Andes; then the army with an even more elevated Madonna. Colour, bands, crowding – all seemed good-humoured, though a mass of helmeted soldiers and police in distinctly non-festive uniforms clearly ensured that it stayed that way. (One procession in fact was of Our Lady of the Policemen.) I wandered around the shopping area with some really good antique emporia among the souvenir shops and the lively street markets, before climbing back past the Jesuits to the Monasterio and dinner – to be the last for some time, as I developed three weeks' worth of food poisoning, happily not kicking in until after breakfast each day.

After buffet breakfast next morning I was off with my lovely guide Christina to explore the newer surroundings of Cusco: first the San Domingo convent, built on the Koricancha, the most important Inca sanctuary. Only a fraction of the Inca buildings remains, but that was soon rectified for me by a quick drive up to Sacsayhuaman, a remarkably complete Inca fortress overlooking the city. Its massive walls of irregular-shaped but closely conjoined limestone blocks rise in tiers; within, the great ceremonial plaza features wide concentric circles. More Inca stuff as we moved along the Sacred Valley to Puca Pucara (the 'Red Fortress') and Tambomachay, which climbs more steeply up the hillside, as usual with massive walls bounding the terraces.

Back down to Cusco, the afternoon was essentially 'make and mend': a snack lunch interspersed with rearranging my schedule as news of further disruptions arrived; then a 'commercial' sally into the town, to download my novel and low-capacity SD card to a CD – contrary to expectation this was both easy and cheap, and became a regular activity as I went along: bought some pullovers and sampled the souvenir and tourist scene; and much enjoyed the Inca museum. The next day was to be the 'big one', to Machu Picchu.

Indeed, breakfast was at 5 a.m. to catch the 06.30 train to MP. As ever it was romantic to be setting forth on this rail journey in pitch darkness with hardly anyone around. I imagine cocks crowed. I thought of Ronda in 1965, but while there was no steam loco a compensation was the means employed to climb the steep ring of hills surrounding Cusco: at the end of each stretch of maximum gradient the front of the train simply became the rear, as direction was reversed. In fact, once over the top it descends to a broad plain before entering the fabled Urubamba river valley. This is very lovely, and the narrow track is often only a few feet from the surging river. Subtropical forest and a mass of epiphytic orchids everywhere: I have no doubt there were also exotic fauna lurking which we didn't see. The train we rode has now I gather been replaced with something much more suitable for observing the passing scene; this one tended to have pillars in all the wrong places. But the 'snapshot' photos weren't too bad.

Of course, the train, whether ancient or modern, doesn't go to Machu Picchu itself, way up the mountain, but terminates at Aguas Calientes (= *onsen* of course). A chaotic-seeming place, backpacker-heavy, the final few hundred yards of the railway line running down the centre of the main street: I don't remember steam rising but there was that indefinable sense of the paraphernalia of tanks and piping I associate with hot spring resorts. An embuscade – would that be the right collective noun? – of buses waited to embark the travellers for the dizzying series of hairpin bends up the near-vertical slope. The views became ever more improbable, and the 'iconic' silhouette of the lost city made its first appearance.

I had been booked at the wonderful Sanctuary Lodge for that night: not only a beautiful little hotel, it has the inestimable advantage of being the only one located up the mountain at the ruins' entrance. Further, not only was my room very nice but I had a broad terrace (the only one) directly overlooking the gates. This conferred a quite unmerited sense of privilege as I watched the masses rush for the last bus down the hill, after which I had the place (almost) all to myself. On arrival I had had a proper tour and introduction with Christina, then a lengthy and well-earned lunch in the Santuario before she sadly had to leave for Cusco. Another bonus was that the last bus leaves some hours before the gates close: thus, after a bit of a rest and waving goodbye to the grockles I could re-enter and enjoy a Machu Picchu early evening in near-complete solitude (except for a few contently relaxing llamas or alpacas).

Likewise, after a good if high altitude night, I was ready to

'Through the night I was afflicted by a great and tender nostalgia for the years I had spent in New York and the eastern seaboard.'

Irrawaddy Bridge at Mandalay in Myanmar.

Iguazu Falls, Argentina, 2003.

Ardevora with Tom Winser.

'With sailing, I have made so many deep and lasting friendships, seen so many exotic places around the world and had so many experiences of wind and weather...'

'… we came across an amazing array of "tall ships" – schooners, barques, brigantines, whatever – engaged in a race or rally…'

Caribbean scenes, 2008.

The hangar on HMS *Invincible*, 1998.

Peter Thistlethwayte, Dugald and Eric Elstob in north-west Japan.

Easter 2005 in Bordeaux.

'An abiding and rather marvellous memory is entering the city from the east at nightfall, climbing to the centre with wonderfully atmospheric lit-up market stalls, food places, shops: a sort of brilliant caravanserai scene.'

Creems, dusk in late summer.

Jura from Post Office Bay, Machrihanish, Kintyre.

repeat this uncluttered experience by being at the gate by 6 o'clock. There were a few others: notably some who had been doing the Inca Trail descended on me from high above in dribs and drabs. They must have been up betimes, for the sunrise! Morning light of course showed structures in different relief but most places I had already seen, so returning to the Lodge I had a relaxed time before the bus and train. Another plus was that this time I had a seat facing forward looking through the windscreen – so could see how exiguous was the track along which we were sauntering. It was night well before we reached familiar Cusco.

The revised schedule for the Altiplano and Lake Titicaca (but not quite yet Bolivia) involved a flight via Arequipa to Juliaca, the main town on the route between Puno on Lake Titicaca and Cusco, as it was not a day the train ran (it transpired later that there were further complications). Juliaca seemed a nondescript little place; but there was a certain grandeur to these high-altitude plains with countless herds of livestock roaming with their picturesque attendants. Gradually, extensive lagoons appeared and then the lake itself. I was in a surprisingly modern hotel on a bluff a mile or two from Puno town: after lunch I went down to the shore to visit Puno's proud attraction, the *Yavari* steamer which was built in London in 1861 and transported in kit form, each piece the size a mule could carry, all the way up to Titicaca from the Pacific. Inevitably, it has suffered vicissitudes but was nearing completion of its restoration when I visited, and I believe now does sail on the lake again. A very fine and interesting old survivor.

Next day it was my turn to go cruising on the lake. First stop were the Uros 'floating islands' near the shore at Puno (relocated some time ago after a particularly vicious Titicaca storm. The ability to float perhaps useful for islands). The islanders – usually one family per island of about half a dozen straw huts – harvest the reeds which grow in great profusion by the mainland shore, and out into the lake. Unsurprisingly tourism and the opportunity for handicraft sales going with it are the main source of income: also of course fishing, tomatoes, etc. The woolly garments, bonnets and suchlike are brilliantly coloured and look well against the equally vivid straw surroundings.

Our distinctly twentieth-century little fast excursion boat sped through seemingly indivisible reed banks and out into the open lake, heading for the steep little island of Taquile. Here a laborious climb on foot takes one up from the little harbour to the small settlement high above. The villagers – farmers and textile handicraft exponents, like the Uros – came and went up and down to the port to market their wares. Apparently, men knit, and women sew and weave. ('Who was then the gentleman?') Men and boys sported either embroidered largely crimson woolly bonnets (some men black trilbies) with elegant black and white working clothes and red sashes, the women normally in flowery wide skirts, blouses and headscarves. An intriguing, self-sufficient little community, grouped inevitably in the plaza before a diminutive squat church, and with homesteads peopling the terraces covering the island.

As we sped back to Puno the altitude and the hour made themselves felt and it turned colder. I retreated inside. Back on land, I went down to wander round the town, including the rather impressive cathedral: then had dinner in the hotel with a nice Dutch couple, Jap and Liliane. News was coming in the whole time of the true reason for travel interruptions in the area: traditional antipathy between Puno and Juliaca had been exacerbated by the result of a football match, and there were reports of the road down to Cusco being liable to imminent closure. After various telephone calls it was arranged that we and a number of French tourists staying at another hotel nearer the town would leave by bus early the next morning.

A minibus took us down to the other hotel: but it became clear that many of the French middle-aged women were far from being ready to leave and had no intention of hurrying. Meanwhile reports of road closures intensified. The Dutch couple and I decided to ask our minibus driver Anastasio if he would drive us to Cusco, and if so for how much. The answer was remarkable: I think less than $100 for a 345 km journey. He would just have to clear it with his boss. With no response from his boss, I offered a small extra amount if the wheels could be turning within five minutes. They were.

The journey was uneventful until the outskirts of Juliaca where there were roadblocks and evidence of stone-throwing and suchlike: nothing too threatening but with admirable *sangfroid* Anastasio merely took to the fields and we bumped around a few estancias and small factories and eventually regained the main street: scruffy and shambolic, but passable. And so we were once again on our way, down and down towards Cusco.

At times it seemed like driving down an endless Glencoe: a pretty good road, the surrounding mountains giving way eventually to the more enclosed scenery of the Sacred Valley. We stopped in one or two places but with Anastasio's excellent fast driving were soon back in Cusco: and dined together at the Monasterio. With another day before my flight to La Paz (the new arrangement), I took another drive with Freddy around the Sacred Valley, north-west: Ollantaytambo with its most impressive terraces, Pisac where I made some textile purchases in the market, and back by Chinchero where it was windy, and we encountered some rain.

At the airport for the Lloyd Aéreo Boliviano flight to La Paz there was some delay as it turned out there were indeed riots and disturbances in Bolivia as well as on the Peruvian Altiplano. On our way, there were good views of the lake where I had just been and then of the Bolivian Isla del Sol and Copacabana where I had hoped to go but couldn't. At La Paz airport there were again delays, for the same reason: it turned out that the main airport road was closed – indeed being partly torn up for missiles – and we had to take a parallel road from which one could see sundry malcontents or idlers wandering around on the empty road.

The airport lies on an endless flat stretch of Altiplano with dun-coloured housing estates, small businesses and factories, agricultural enterprises and so on. 'Over the edge' one descends by whichever road is available down to the city lying in a great basin: opposite there towers the volcano Illimani, over 21,000 feet high. Despite lying in a bowl or basin the centre is quite restricted, with a pair of near-parallel rivers rushing down a V-shaped valley. Into this narrow defile crowd a number of near-skyscrapers, among them my hotel, the Europa, where I checked in and had a high-up room with panoramic views of the nearby high-rise buildings and, across the deep valley, up to the ethereal snow-clad summit of Illimani. Fairly soon though I was in a taxi across to the opposite side where the only neighbourhood of any antiquity is to be found, steep cobbled streets leading up to some old but modest houses which contain the historical museum of La Paz. The exhibits were moderately interesting, rather featuring the various revolts and uprisings of Bolivia's past (models of hangings rather prevalent). But the setting in several courtyards was pleasant.

In the visitors' book I found just one other entry for that day: an Oxford friend, Bill Nimmo Smith, Eton and Balliol classicist and by then Scottish judge Lord Nimmo Smith; he and his wife had been there in the morning. I hadn't seen Bill for many years. So, as I wandered down the main drag observing the local colourful street commerce I dropped in at the one other acceptable hotel, much more 'downtown', on the assumption that Bill and his wife were staying there if not at mine. Indeed, they were: but were out. So, I left a note suggesting dinner. Alas, a little while after I had got back, I had a call from him saying that they had an unbreakable date to give dinner, it being their last night, to the team who had guided them all round Bolivia over the past three weeks. So that was that.

I dined in solitary splendour in the hotel restaurant, deserted except for a party of presumed local bigwigs making merry. From my eyrie not only could I enjoy all-round views but also a ringside seat for intermittent explosions and gunfire as the inhabitants of La Paz strove to make their mark on history like those commemorated in the old quarter. This went on much of the night.

Another early departure for the airport – unimpeded – saw me on the Aero Sur flight to Sucre, appositely southbound. Bolivia has a certain ambiguity when it comes to capital cities as both La Paz (much the bigger) and Sucre (much the prettier) claim and are officially granted the title: Sucre, a fine old Spanish conquest town, of course was the earlier. It is still the *constitutional* capital, has the supreme court etc., the comparison with Washington and New York being not wholly misleading. It was named, displacing the original Aymara or Quechua, after a gallant general of Bolivarian times (and after all New Zealand has Wellington…).

I was leaving exploration of Sucre for later but now was engaging a taxi, which turned out to be driven by a homicidal maniac, for the 200-kilometre drive to the fabled city of Potosí. The drive was scenic and spectacular in the extreme, through arid Andean landscapes of dry watercourses and strange rock formations; vegetation basically desert but with occasional patches of the most vivid green.

Potosí in the late sixteenth century was probably the richest and largest city in the world, entirely due to the Cerro Rico conical mountain nearby which seems entirely made of silver. Countless peons and slaves perished over the centuries – and it is still not mined out, and still dangerous – and producing four-fifths of the world's silver it effectively financed Spain's South American conquest (as well as a monster inflation). A large proportion was exported to China, via the Philippines (the 'Manila Galleon'). Potosí is now hardly a rival to Shanghai or Tokyo, or even London or Johannesburg: an indefinable air of desolation and past glories hangs about a place which, however, is by no means ruined. But it looks sad, especially on a dark and drizzly evening at over 4,000 metres above sea level. I checked into a rather plain but perfectly adequate little hotel – the best in town nevertheless, I believe, and went out to explore, and of course to visit the travel agency to rearrange my itinerary yet again.

Despite the remarks above and general air of decrepitude the glory days of Potosí have left it with some remarkably fine buildings in Spanish Baroque style. The cathedral is in fact among the less impressive, greater honours in my view being taken by San Lorenzo de Carangas or San Francisco: numerous other churches, monasteries, and convents (notably the Convento de Sta. Teresa) all sport hyper-elaborate Plateresque frontal porticos and imaginative bell-towers, often in a carillon of three. The most spectacular must be the terracotta red church of the Compañia de Jesús, with an enormous Baroque tower which one can partly ascend (I did). This to my mind – and not it alone in Potosí – gave hints of Chinese influence in its general mass and all-over ornamentation: pure coincidence, or evidence of an early Belt and Road initiative? Among the most significant and interesting buildings is the Mint or Casa de la Moneda, a natural inhabitant of Potosí. Its main fountain court, with white rounded arches fronting back walls of irregular grey stone, a galleria with slim wooden pillars above, features an extraordinary, almost surreal if not somewhat disturbing, plaque of an androgynous, black-mopped face with an elusively mocking grin. A tribute to the peso? The exterior is somewhat more conventional, for all the world like another whitewashed monastery with golden stone portico.

The old streets, leading down to the Plaza de Armas park square, are generally two-storey and colourful in pink, terracotta, white, lemon or sky-blue: a very prominent feature often being a first-floor enclosed balcony, projecting further than usual in Spain and given further emphasis by the low height above street level. I wandered around the Plaza de Armas where evening paseo activities were taking place around the bandstand: it was getting towards dusk and drizzly, and I found a little restaurant, San Marcos, then retired.

The Land Cruiser turned up at 8 and we were off to Uyuni and the salt flats. Quickly out of town under the looming presence of Cerro Rico there were small mining-related settlements: further on, one looked from a considerable height down on the rail and road connections taking one down to the Pacific, now Chile. All monochrome, sage-brush quasi-desert, mountain ranges afar. But there was a strange geological beauty, and the vistas were awesome. A river appeared and isolated tree clumps of the most vivid green, contrasting with hillsides which were now turning purplish among the grey. Dry watercourses suggested torrents in due season. Brick entrances surrounded tiny settlements, at one of which we paused for refreshment (coca?). The hillsides often adopted stranger striated forms, while the broadening dry river valleys in their whiteness presaged the not-so-far-now salt flats. Eventually a straight descent from the mountains pointed directly to Uyuni – just a 'dry' land – and the vast expanse of the *salar* (salt flats) stretching into the distance.

Uyuni was a surprise to find in such a remote spot: small, but with one or two buildings of some substance; a broad central avenue looking as if also made of salt but presumably hardcore below, with central reservation and all; low, mostly silver-grey, buildings alongside. Among them, we found the single-storey Jardines de Uyuni: a ramshackle but charming little place with a colourful, somewhat internal courtyard and a comfortable, basic but entirely welcome bedroom.

We lost little time in setting off onto the salt flats: first, parallel to the land to view the extraordinary graveyard of many ancient steam locomotives, their final resting place a poignant sight. Next, strange little pyramids of excavated salt, awaiting transport for market. Stretching into the distance, these presented another rather surreal sight. Across the salar expanse the islands on the horizon, to which we were bound, seemed closer and we set off into or onto what might be called 'open sea'. In the salar proper the salt takes on an invariable hexagonal form: it is dazzlingly white. We made for an island called Incahuasi and took a walk ashore. This and the other little islands are densely populated by cacti growing among rounded mossy boulders and low desert plants: growing up to about fifteen feet, at which point they have normally sprouted arms raised in supplication to heaven, they are a wondrous and eerie sight – especially when set off by the pure whiteness of their background beneath the clear blue sky.

Heading back towards Uyuni, it was nearing sunset and the salt took on a strange golden glow. About halfway we stopped for a while at the famous Salt Hotel – entirely built of said substance. It is said to be perfectly warm and comfortable, but I rather wonder. Anyway, I was happy to get back to the Jardines and to find I had some slight appetite, at least, for one meal. It was llama – a first for me – and I thought rather good; however, I couldn't eat it all. Another happy event was that for the first time I was able to talk to Haruko on the phone – in this utterly improbable remote quasi-human place! So, happily, to sleep.

The journey back to Sucre involved a stop in Potosí for lunch but then continuation to Sucre: so, a long drive. As usual the opposite direction and time of day offered new and intriguing perspectives, but these need not be described here. Nevertheless, we arrived in time for one to have a good walk around the centre after checking in at the Capital Plaza. Sucre is a largely white-coloured city of distinctly Spanish colonial architecture. Again, often two-storied and with large 'box' balconies – black against the white, different from Potosí's varied colours. In fact, there is a considerable contrast between Potosí's generally warm colouring and Sucre's white: however, this was somewhat mitigated by the grey drizzle in the former and the clear blue sky at Sucre. Many terraces though have elegant 'normal' balconies – almost like small Chelsea or Kensington houses, except often for ochre window entablatures.

Walking down – Sucre like Arequipa is built on a gentle slope – one soon sees the campanile and towers of the cathedral, its entrance gateway and the archbishop's palace adjoining.

Unfortunately, it was shut, though still not late. The indication was to retire to my room – spacious, off an open gallery looking over an internal courtyard, eschew driver again and sleep.

In the morning, my pretty guide Noelle picked me up for a comprehensive tour of the 'white city': the Casa de Libertad, Sucre's showpiece in the main square, low and wide with triangular stone pediment, Baroque churches, of St Philip Neri and Sta. Clara, market, and parks, and further out the La Recoleta monastery and graveyard. Here unsurprisingly the architecture (tombs apart) is more neoclassical. Still brilliant white. The park has a sort of mini-perverted rusty Eiffel Tower: the (white) fish market looks like an opera house. We returned to the shopping area downtown after lunch beside La Recoleta, finding it lively and interesting (I don't think I bought anything). Many old buses second-hand from Japan – kanji and katakana writing not painted over! The parks were lively with shoeshine 'boys', old chaps yakking on benches, colourful spherical ladies selling cigarettes etc. Cathedral shut.

At 7.30 on my last morning, I tried the cathedral again, but though theoretically open from 7 it was still shut; so, proceeded to the airport for a 10.50 flight to Santa Cruz, where I had a longish wait from 11.30 till a 3.30 departure for Buenos Aires on Aerolineas. So, *adios* Bolivia!

The contrast was dramatic: from the arid steppes of the Altiplano the aeroplane descended with views of the Paraná and the River Plate to a proper metropolis. Sweeping on the urban motorway at half-height to tall buildings we came to the most civilised Alvear Palace Hotel in a classy district of balconised ten or fifteen storey apartments lining the avenues: we felt though that some of the affluence was skin-deep. The hotel could well have been in the Faubourg St-Honoré: Beaux-Arts pale stucco, smart doormen, elegant hall, flowers: breakfast room/café to the side. My room was equally spacious and elegant, though changed after one night in it as it proved unacceptably noisy.

After breakfast I was collected for a comprehensive tour: first to the remarkable La Recoleta cemetery or indeed necropolis. Miniaturised streets lined with impressive grey granite mausolea: neoclassical, Baroque, Art Nouveau, with pediments, porches and pillars, adorned inevitably with winged angels in bronze or stone. Effectively little quasi-cubical 'houses', they line the pavement neatly so there is mercifully no room for the gaudy horrors surrounding, say, French or German tombs. Bronze plaques denoted the 'inhabitants': on the mausoleum of the Familia Duarte, we found that of Eva Peron, with a most unconvincing maquette of 'Evita'.

Like the Museum of Fine Arts, the National Library and indeed the Alvear Palace itself, La Recoleta is in the salubrious Palermo district where the roads cut through parks which at that time of year featured massed jacarandas and other spring blossoms in abundance. From there we passed through the centre to La Boca, its vivid primary colours a contrast to the greenery and pastels of Palermo, then to Puerto Madero, the old docklands area now transforming itself into an entertainment, exhibition and above all eating area: bascule bridges, moored tugboats and other paraphernalia of the docks testified to its heritage.

In the afternoon I wandered round the Alvear zone, window shopping and appreciating the architectural scene – a mix of older Beaux-Arts buildings and multi-storeyed balconised more modern flats. It all looked bourgeois and comfortable, and as written earlier somewhat reminiscent of Paris. Balconies adorned with much greenery; and at street level were many stylish and interesting shops – antiques, handicrafts (often leather), patisseries, delis: the full Rue St Honoré. I wandered further up towards the centre of town, then returning as night fell, flopped.

Next morning, I visited the nearby Virgen del Pilar beside La Recoleta: second oldest church in the city, it is now a relatively chaste, white-painted classical structure, with one tower and one smaller belfry, failing to hint at the riches inside: which are basically (and not unusually) vast altarpieces of Baroque golden ornamentation and expressive sculptures. In particular, the reredos behind the high altar provides a stunning contrast in its magnificence with the restrained white nave. The accompanying museum was interesting for the variety of monstrances, chasubles and other *oggetti religiosi*. After that I walked the short way down through the park to the national art museum: then took a taxi up to the main drag, the Avenida de Mayo, with the Plaza de Mayo fronting the Casa Rosada presidential palace – or 'Pink Palace' familiar from Evita scenes. Vainglorious monuments add to the atmosphere, not wholly vitiated by the one mugging I have seen, outside the opera house. Then the cathedral: the interior impressive, somewhat severe in dark grey; monuments in chapels and under rotundas. A more sprightly and elegant spirit was found nearby at S. Francisco, with twin Rococo towers and gold on white interior more reminiscent of Bavaria at its most playful. Graffiti on an industrial scale outside, however, showed that all was not play.

The highlight of one's first visit to Buenos Aires of course has to be an evening in a tango show and dinner establishment in that evocative district; and my kind guide Cielo took me to the undoubted top place, the Esquina Carlos Gardel, upholding the tradition of the legendary prime exponent of the tango. The place was atmospheric, the music fun, the dinner pretty good – I can't remember if I even tried to do the tango … but it was a good culmination of my *first* trip to Argentina.

For the following day I was off to a new country – Uruguay, just across the broad River Plate. Of course, I had seen the film of the epic naval engagement so many times: it was hard to believe the hydrofoil was taking me across these very waters. Met by a new guide, the first stop was Colonia, a sleepy little riverside town which exactly epitomises its name: low-rise, cobbled streets leading down to a tranquil muddy waterfront, shaded by tall poplar-type trees. Few people around and a general air of amiable lethargy. From Colonia a concrete road, almost deprived of traffic, stretched straight for miles through rolling green countryside looking, dry stone walls and all, as if it could have been in Gloucestershire. Beef herds grazing everywhere gave promise of delights to come. A curious circular structure – looking a cross between a bullring and a gasometer (though probably the former), announced the approach to Montevideo. Its arched entrances for some reason recalled the mosque in Córdoba and other Islamic structures.

Soon we were entering Montevideo proper. (I noted that English-speaking Uruguayans pronounce it MonteVIDeo rather than the MontevidEo perhaps more common with us.) After a preliminary look at the centre and the more immediate residential neighbourhoods we took the coastal corniche – here the various stretches, I think at least as far as Punta del Este, are called Ramblas – *à la* Barcelona but following the shoreline rather than perpendicular to it. Nearer the city centre the corniche is lined by high apartment blocks lacking any but the most exiguous balconies; further out, there's an extensive zone of planned developments with gridded or curving streets and individual houses with sizeable gardens, all very livable-looking. The coastal road sweeps along a succession of curving bays with white sand beaches. At Carrasco we found the pleasant hotel booked for the night: rather English in character, sub-Art Deco white and low-built, good gardens and pure English repro interiors. I settled in for the night.

After a visit to the nearby beach the next morning, I took a taxi back to the centre and had a proper look round. The main drag, the Avenida 18 de Julio, features a splendid elaborate mid-twentieth-century tower which would not be out of place in Madrid: numerous other solidly pedimented and pillared edifices give the avenue some style and gravitas. In general, though, it is lower-rise than Buenos Aires, with two-storey terraces leading away down to the river. I was headed for the Mercado del Puerto, the magnificent old covered market which now houses almost exclusively rotisseries and grills, where the beef cattle seen the previous day meet their destiny. The whole place was teeming with evidently satisfied punters and the cheerful atmosphere enhanced by the fragrant smoke from the grills as well as the calls of the chefs. At last, I felt I would make some headway with a steak – not the whole thing, but it was genuinely superb.

After a bit more walking through the old town I took a taxi back to the hotel, where again I met my guide and after another mini-tour was delivered back to the ferry port. At the harbour, the main item of interest was the enormous anchor of the *Graf Spee*, parked in a little curving enclosure of white tiles. Then the hydrofoil back to BA. The next morning for some reason I wasn't feeling too good – could it have been my first encounter with quite glorious beef? – so got up in leisurely fashion in my so-comfortable room, then took a prolonged and leisurely perambulation through mostly the parks and gardens. Along the Libertador to Palermo, gay with spring-blossoming trees lining the avenue; then the Jardin Japones, a pretty good simulation and to me eerily reminiscent of Tokyo, especially Shinjuku Gyoen. It has the same spaciousness with lawns sloping down to a sizeable curving lake; in the background those apartments of this salubrious quarter lucky enough to have balconies overlooking the garden. Tea houses and the usual accoutrements bordering the lake.

In fact, the analogies do not just stop with Japanalia. Perhaps it was the lovely spring weather but the quarter of medium-height apartment blocks could also remind one of Tokyo. Perhaps now more Bunkyo-ku, home of the Botanic Gardens, echoed here by Buenos Aires' own gardens, next on the itinerary. By this time, I was getting nearer the centre, the buildings, often Beaux-Arts or Art Nouveau, were both lower and more distinguished and the light was perfect for obsessive architectural photography.

After this day of leisurely urban peregrination, and totally refreshed, I left the Alvear Palace once more, this time bound for the airport and flight to the Iguazu Falls. I made my way to the Sheraton Hotel on the Argentine side looking over to the falls about a mile away through the rainforest. I was anxious to lose no time investigating this phenomenon. As one walks through the forest, gently dropping to the level of the falls' brink, one comes across numerous 'mini-falls' emerging from the trees and quietly slipping over the nearby edge to their extinction in the river far below. A semi-circular trek takes one round to the more open space of the main river. There of course a series of wooden bridges is needed to take one across, jumping from islet to islet. Where there are turns there are stupefying close-up views of the thunderous main falls. Among the spume swifts could be seen pirouetting out of and into their caves in the rock behind the waters. Down below, the tourist launches gyrated in the whirlpools.

There comes a point when it becomes another country (as well as a possible quick trip to oblivion), so it was time to turn back. The evening light and opposite direction naturally provided (far too many) photo opportunities. A good dinner in the modern and comfortable hotel was accompanied by a harpist (harp from neighbouring and nearby Paraguay – see next bit). Next morning though it was 'another country'. Minimal formalities crossing into Brazil, passing the imposing and elegant Hotel das Cataratas, and reaching the other side of the falls, with a totally different perspective on Argentina. Perhaps the best view, however, is obtained from lower down, where the Brazilians have built extensive viewing decks – extensive and extended over the boiling river. A good place to take refreshments and take it all in. Into the car again and back to Argentina, with a mini-zoo and some clearings with cattle. I believe one should really take more than part of a morning to see Brazil properly, but for the moment that had had to suffice!

Back on the Argentine side, there was a sort of toy train ride to the Garganta del Diablo, then an 'adventure' through the rainforest on a truck and eventually to the rather muddy shore to embark on the RIB for the main voyage. On the way the usual jungle inhabitants such as toucans, leaf-cutter ants and bush-baby-type teddies could occasionally be glimpsed. The boat manfully ploughed its way up the (very) fast-flowing river to, and indeed briefly behind, the falls. We had capes and sort of sou-westers, and the cameras misted up. The sight was awesome. No white-water rafting. Walk up through the forest to the hotel, vistas of river and waterfalls everywhere, magnificent trees – some especially elegant in spring, not yet in leaf.

I was back in Buenos Aires by early afternoon, the flight giving good views of the terrain and especially the Paraná River opening out into the River Plate basin. I took a taxi up to the centre once more – the famous Teatro Colón in particular – and walked back by now-familiar places to the Alvear Palace. The next morning was to be an early one – breakfast just after 5 for the flight to Asunción in Paraguay, giving a useful morning arrival.

I wasn't sure exactly what to expect in Paraguay, but it hadn't been to find myself in the hottest place I have ever been – feeling hotter, I think, at any rate, than Riyadh where it had been 130F in the shade, or more humid Dubai in July.

Asunción is a pleasant enough city, mainly low-rise and sprawling beside the wide and lethargic-looking Paraguay River, on its long journey from the Mato Grosso to join the Paraná downstream and eventually the River Plate. Some of the more impressive buildings of Asunción are pleasingly situated beside or near the river: notably the Palacio de López, the residence of the president and seat of government. This is a wide white building with colonnade and first-floor long open gallery not untypical of late nineteenth-century colonial architecture: less typical is a central square tower which could come from a Perpendicular church in England. Broad lawns run down to the river – actually inlet – bank.

The Palacio de López sits near the bottom of a main thoroughfare running up to the centre: nearby are other 'serious' buildings including the National Pantheon of [predictable]

Heroes: the cathedral (of the Assumption of the Virgin, unsurprisingly), again a typical low white façade between two slender towers; and the main museum. In general, the streets were low-rise and 'colonial' in feeling: not colourful as in Potosí or white like Sucre, but generally rather grey. My walk up the street led eventually to a pleasant garden square. Further 'inland' some higher-rise buildings were appearing – banks, shopping malls and hotels. I had checked into an acceptable new hotel, the Excelsior, opposite a major shopping centre which I found of interest. At least it was cooler! I tried the cathedral, which was shut; though the next morning I could visit early. There was a 'folkloric' show in the hotel at dinner time, featuring señoritas in flamenco-style costumes, contortions, arpas and guitarras.

After the cathedral I walked to a more unconventional attraction: the old railway station, built (by the British of course) even before 1860. It was right beside a city street and is open at the sides to the platforms: a wide ridged roof of course, wooden roof timbers like a mediaeval English hall, giving a light and airy feel. Improbably, the slender flanking towers were capped with steep triangular roofs which could easily be seen in Bavaria. Inside is to be found a wonderful ancient locomotive, old carriages and other memorabilia.

In early afternoon I was picked up for a very worthwhile 'craft tour' taking in some suburbs and surroundings of Asunción which I'd never have known about otherwise. I'd already read that Paraguay was *the* place for 'arpas y guitarras' and was looking forward to visiting a workshop; these were duly found in the nearby Luque district, as were silver filigree jewellery makers – both fascinating. Other handicrafts encountered were beautiful 'spider lace' at Itauguá, slightly further out, and pottery at Areguá near the river. Driving further inland, we came to the broad and lovely Ypacaraí lake with its San Bernardino resort: some time was enjoyed on the pier extending over the tranquil waters, while when driving uphill and away I marvelled at the most groaningly fecund mango trees I had ever seen.

This last phase was a quasi-pilgrimage – in fact not scheduled for the 'tour' – first to the Jesuit mission church at Yaguarón, San Buenaventura: a long, white-walled, plain rectangular building with again a wide shallow-ridged metal roof. Two main surprises: first that inside, looking down the long nave, one is faced with an elaborate gilt (no gold) altar wall exactly found in more conventionally Baroque Jesuit churches, pulpit, monuments etc. featuring in the same idiom. The incongruity between interior and exterior is further emphasised by the strange three-storey rectangular, open-sided tower free-standing alongside – for all the world like a prison watchtower. Weird. Yet the setting was lovely and the experience quite unexpected.

A much more conventional experience was to the shrine of the Virgen de Caacupé. A total contrast to the spare form of Yaguarón, a massive domed concrete edifice, reached by a broad flight of steps and entered through three tall archways under an over-scaled lunette, contains an image of the Virgin, attired in elaborate white and blue silk robes. Not unlike Lourdes, the shrine attracts hordes of pilgrims, as the main focus for the Guaraní people. A larger, even more sparklingly attired image is carried in procession on festal days. So – despite no ceremonies that day – I returned to central Asunción, for a leisurely day further exploring the inner city, then back to Buenos Aires for dinner at a *parrillada* in Recoleta.

Next day my Buenos Aires social life really began. Ricardo Cinalli had kindly told several friends that I would be in town, and I had made some dates. Around noon Virginia Born turned up at the hotel in her Mercedes, to take me to their house and estate near the river at the San Isidro district. I was somewhat startled to find her bodyguard lying doggo on the rear seat! (Virginia was driving.) When we arrived at the gates of their domain there were at least three more guards, emerging from a little guard-house. Evidently security had to be taken very seriously: the next-door property had been ransacked only shortly before.

All, however, seemed tranquil and prosperous as we drove through the beautifully kept gardens up to the main house: a handsome 1930s building, low and wide with pillared entrance and, inside, spacious and beautifully furnished rooms. In particular I admired walls 'panelled' in palest leather or exotic woods, or (of most interest to me) Ricardo's classical/surrealist frescoes. There I met Virginia's husband Juán and also Adrián and Elena Hope, and some of the younger generation, and a happy lunch and afternoon ensued: featuring a lot of tennis (but not by me). The gardens, with an enormous swimming pool as well as the tennis courts on its spacious lawns, has a fine collection of cypresses, pines, monkey-puzzles and other specimen trees: the whole looking down on a newer residential suburb nearer the estuary which was once part of the estate.

My other introduction was to the Bullrich family, owners of the 'Harrods' of Buenos Aires. A full morning on my last day of ambling around S. Telmo and the antique shop zone, then down to Puerto Madero, led me eventually and appropriately via a light Italian lunch to the Patio Bullrich emporium, quite near the hotel. From there Franciso Bullrich picked me up for dinner in their Recoleta flat, conveniently nearby. So, after a most pleasant last evening with more new friends it was time to go back and pack…

Envoi: BA flies from Buenos Aires to Heathrow twice a week, alternating between stops at São Paulo and Rio de Janeiro. Sadly, this time it was São Paulo's turn: I should so much have liked to fly into or over Rio. It was dark and pouring with rain at São Paulo: we stayed in the plane on the tarmac and looked out at a forest of dark grey skyscrapers.

Tour en Voiture: Diary September–October 2008

16 September – Tuesday
From Boulogne – what memories revived, as it's so long one went anywhere but Calais – on the motorway as far as the Neufchâtel-en-Bray exit (in that respect just like last year). However, this time turned south to cut across to Les Andelys. Not as straightforward as it might be, but I was damned if I was going to take the easy, fast and long route to Rouen then back along the Seine towards Paris. (In fact, the satnav, which had earlier suggested I get from Greenwich to Dover via Gatwick and Brighton, had suggested I actually go to Paris.) Over the rather bare Bray country then suddenly down the wooded valley to the Seine. The Chaîne d'Or (where I last stayed fifty-five years ago with my sore toe!) most welcoming, especially with gravel courtyard for the car, which was admired by a nice old English gent (looked like a retired naval commander). The sun still on the chalk cliffs and the river tranquil and lovely. Went out to take some photos. Dinner soigné but rather tough sweetbreads: a pity. Found I'd left the instructions for the new mobile at home so though I could ring HP [Dugald's nickname for Haruko] I couldn't do anything clever to 'pair' it with the car: an opportunity missed. I shall also have to be careful on call time.

17 September – Wednesday
Set off across the bridge and took a few photographs of Ch. Gaillard: didn't bother to go up to it. A lovely morning – mist on the river at first. Down to Pacy then attempted cross-country:

but a combination of satnav and detailed Michelin proved lethal, and I kept missing turns on country roads. Around Ivry-la-Bataille I decided to go back to Anet rather than get involved with Dreux – a most fortuitous decision as, coming into the centre, I was met first by this classical brick façade of a chapel, then the château. Main feature: stags, and Diana the huntress, as it had belonged to Diane de Poitiers. Killed time till it opened at 2 (20 mins) then paid up and walked in. (Visited the stripped out funeral chapel with D de P's looted tomb in the middle.) The other chapel in the château grounds, previously attached to now-destroyed wing – is a marvellous example of early French Renaissance, down to Philibert de l'Orme: Greek cross, effectively circular, dome, wonderful geometric floor. Saints abbreviated, mostly to 4 letters: S PETR, S ANDR, S BART etc. but curiously the actual 4-letter saint St John gets 6 – S IOANNI! Waited for the tour of the interior: desperately slow and pedantic woman enumerating everything, spending most time on the photo of her employer's daughter in her wedding dress. So much of the day was spent in this amazing place, serendipity indeed!

Whizzed round Chartres stopping only to take a photo by the river, then over the Beauce fast on minor roads towards the Loire E of Orléans. Reminiscent of my rushing for the Auberge des Templiers nearly 2 years ago. I really should have stayed there again but had booked in at Pouilly. That seemed still quite far so after Gien (looking nice along the Lungo-Loire in the setting sun) I got on the autoroute which imperceptibly became N7 and got me to Pouilly. Indeed a 1930s roadside étape: surprisingly scruffy in a plain 50s way, but the room was fine, the people charming and the dinner excellent: a very friendly, feisty little bald chef who is a Meilleur Ouvrier de France and speaks excellent English. Toothache getting really bad. Not a good night.

18 September – Thursday

Rang Walpole Street hoping to talk to Eddie or Shirin. Got receptionist Laura who said neither was in. She was going to try to get Shirin to call me, so I waited. Eventually Laura retailed what S told her which was what I knew already! Asked about dentist in the village but he had no space until 4 hours later, so I moved on to Nevers. Arrived there of course when chemist shut so looked around – château, old streets, dull cathedral with apses both ends! Romanesque OK – then had an omelette in café. At 2 went to chemist who said dentist right next door: but they had nothing till tomorrow. So gave up. Stopped briefly at La Charité and photographed again from the bridge.

Thought I'd go to Decize to revisit old haunts so drove down the minor road alongside the Canal Latéral à la Loire, stopping to view the odd ruined château, Romanesque church etc. Many Charolais. Quite grey and misty. At Decize rang Nicky (got Wiggy) and Ran, who was pleasantly surprised (the barge is sold). From there to Moulins which is a charming medium-sized town: seems quite prosperous too. Wandered around a bit and bought boxes of chocs at the most beautiful Art Nouveau chocolatier near where I parked.

From there only a short drive to Bourbon-l'Archambault. Surprisingly, didn't see the Hotel Montespan Talleyrand the first time I drove past: did eventually, and parked right in front of the Talleyrand's front door. Very charming and welcoming people – a huge room with bed, canopy and antique-looking walnut furniture. Delicious dinner: enormous steak. The whole thing ludicrously cheap. In the morning HP rang as I was going for (rather belated) breakfast: how nice to have great tub of butter, not horrid little packets.

19 September – Friday

Didn't mention that the three houses together belonged to Mme de Montespan, Mme de Sévigné and Talleyrand, all devotees of the cure at Bourbon: quite a pedigree. I walked up to the vast ruined castle through the charming little town: bought Wednesday's *Telegraph* for further news of financial disasters. Furious at not buying gold under $800, let alone $750: it went to $890 overnight! Stopped again at St Menoux and viewed the fine church and charming surrounds – bought honey and bics from charming boulangerie. Headed off to the abbey at Souvigny, another charming little village: the nave was closed for repairs. Saw a chic-looking little bookshop/café and thought a warm goat's cheese salad and apple juice might be nice: it was. Chatted to the v. pleasant girl owner (about thirty-eight?) about bookshop/cafés and think I have arranged a jumelage (I said there were four ruined abbeys near St Boswells and several duchesses came for coffee every morning!).

The town was most pleasant, on a hill and three ways meeting in a big marketplace triangle: 'street' furniture as always excellent. Fine vernacular architecture, stone quoins etc: much photographed. A particularly handsome 'gentilhommière' just by the church overlooking the meadows, with handsome gateway. From there through glorious Virgilian Georgics countryside with many Charolais kipping sub tegmine fagi, endless ruined or not so ruined châteaux and churches. Stopped at a particularly impressive ruined one – hipped roof not circular towers – where a peasant couple were stolidly brambling (there were enough brambles for the entire French nation). Joined the main road to St Pourçain at Châtel-de-Neuve where a tiny old church has a great view over the whole Allier valley.

St Pourçain was another charming town: quite unique in its architecture and 'feel' but with some of the Moulins charm. By Gothic church with eighteenth-century frontage (quite good) hemmed in by picturesque old streets. Elegant faceted and tiled steeple; also, a fine municipal clock tower, where Papa, Maman and the deux enfants strike the hours. Bought more chocs from another elegant shop (a charming girl). After all, I do need presents to give… From there a quick drive over the plain to Lapalisse where the hotel was easily found. Hotel is modest and modern, again making great efforts with the cooking, with young and eager chef/patron. Walked through town, over bridge facing enormous château rearing above the picturesque but dilapidated buildings at its feet. In fact, on closer inspection the town was clearly distressed with premises and businesses for sale, shuttered or simply falling down. Back to delicious and unbelievably cheap dinner and bed.

20 September – Saturday
Because of its being Saturday, decided to book hotel at Thiers and take my time getting there. First a lovely little deserted road across to Billy (have also been to Bert!), a little village with big curtain-wall castle overlooking the Sioule. Went in where a bevy of young women including one touting her (not bad) Primavera-type frescoes were welcoming. Made a tour of the battlements: great views, and the village looked good from above. Weather was glorious again. Back through St Pourçain after brief stop at disappointing Vieille Abbaye St Vincent. Next serious detour was Château de Chareil which was partly covered in scaffolding but is clearly very well run: vineyard perhaps the neatest I have ever seen. Whole scene and countryside quite lovely. Next place was abbey and castle of Chantelle (wonderful name!): first went up a side road on opposite side of a wooded defile to get a view, then back, parked in the village then went down to the abbey slumbering away. Ghastly 'perfect' nineteenth-century neo-Romanesque church in village. Met one young and one older man, both delightful to talk to: discussed vegetables etc. as there was a beautiful monastic-style (but informal) potager. Potirons already. Church numinous. The shop deserved attention after the nuns had been so gracious and I bought some things (mostly honey as usual).

The countryside became more open also hillier – rather like Champagne – and I next stopped at Charroux, which is supposed to be v. pretty. It is, in the way of Les Baux and other ruined mediaeval dorfs (dorves, dorfen?) with dinky shops – artisanat, loisirs, etc. But I was very happy to be lured into a picturesque ivy-clad, wooden-beamed courtyard (of the Prince de Condé's house, no less), by a cheerful sprightly man with whom I took refreshment: tonic water, bramble torte (no shortage of ingredients) and coffee. Afterwards, more serendipity: by the clock tower was a museum of public clock mechanisms (entrée libre). The oldest was sixteenth century. Every single one showed the same, exactly correct time!

Weakened and bought some mustard at the mustard fabricateur next door to the tea courtyard, where I recognised the proprietor as having just had her refreshment next door. We discussed mouse-turdy matters amiably. Appalling lurid grotto of Ste. Bernadette of Lourdes in the church. Then more serendipity: in the previously near-deserted car park (a boulodrome with chestnut trees to drop conkers) there was now an array of 50s and 60s cars belonging to proud owners from the Vichy vintage car club. Citroen Light 12, Simca Arianes, little Renaults, Peugeot 404 – all in the correct colours and taking me right back.

Now for the Gorges de la Sioule. Very pretty but hardly spectacular: not in the Tarn or Verdon class. Thickly wooded so it's difficult to get a glimpse of the river let alone photograph it. One or two castles looming above. The best thing was an old Romanesque bridge: as I left, a whole charabanc-load of oldies came and solemnly processed across, chatting away nineteen to the dozen. Efforts to photograph the river contre-jour were unsuccessful. Free of the gorges, it was a swooping drive over to Riom with the mountains becoming more evident. Riom was a handsome town: must have been a Roman garrison town, with 4-square plan and basilica. The black Volvic stone now evident, mostly as quoins. Idiosyncratic and handsome architecture and good street scapes. Went down to the church with the Vierge à l'Oiseau but shut; however, a good copy at the front door. Swooped on past Châtel-Guyon and Maringues (spelling is correct) to Thiers. Amazingly was just thinking I would telephone

HP when I got in (7.15) when the phone rang, mercifully in a long approach street where I could pull in to the side of the road. The position of the town is rather Tivoliesque. Clinging to a hill after a long approach over the plain (again coincidentally, HP going to Hadrian's Villa tomorrow). Found the hotel and parked in semi-souterrain opposite. Old-fashioned, pleasant again, amazingly good value – four-course menu including foie gras (which I didn't have) €20, and enormous portions.

21 September – Sunday
Was up early and left the hotel just after 9. Parked the car just off the winding road and walked down to the old town: big black church, old streets. Beautiful tranquil Sunday morning. Various poor crones labouring up the steep streets/stairs with club feet. Came on a Jesuit-looking church above the ravine with extraordinary cemetery – not unlike Glasgow Necropolis with ornate mausolea in black (note: not 'blackened') stone. The difference was that everyone has to have a little greenhouse above them! Lots of very rusty ironworks and hideously faded artificial flowers – looking like drowned things. All this on a steep slope – some tombs even had (rusty) iron ladders. Only one tomb – obviously – recent death – had a great cornucopia of flowers: everything else totally neglected for decades.

Thiers is the great cutlery town and the shops had dazzling arrays of knives: cooks' knives of all sorts, also beautiful clasp knives etc. Amusing that if I bought one and took it back, even in the boot of the car, I could go to prison.

Whizzed along the N road to Clermont-Ferrand which for the last few miles became an autoroute gratuite: splendid view of the town lying in a bowl, with the Puy de Dôme beyond. After a missed turn leading me into the middle of the Michelin works – not uninteresting, an old-fashioned survival virtually in the middle of town – was lucky and got a space in pretty, climbing rue de Port just above ND du P. Latter sadly was completely closed for restoration. Very complete and unified Romanesque design in black and white. As is the whole town: distinctly handsome. Turning a corner, the vast and tall charcoal grey cathedral was visible: incongruously Île de France in its high nave and twin spires (think Amiens or Chartres). Impressive inside too. On the N side municipal buildings, classical and almost a dead ringer for Edinburgh (Parliament House, Register House). The Edinburgh resemblance kept reasserting itself with tall houses – still dark grey or black and white – on steep streets. Even the street names in elegant black on white serif looked similar. On S side an extensive square with cafés: I had quick prix fixe (Auvergnat potato/cheese/ham thing, apple tart) in the one which had two distinctly pretty waitresses. A quick visit to the Romanesque expo in the tourist office, then time to go.

Back in the direction of Thiers, then right for Billon and more lovely rural roads across to the valley of the Dore. Olliergues was pretty – much evidence of vanished metiers – came across a paper mill (not stopping for Sunday) with lots of rusty rail engines: somehow a Transylvania theme. Found an atmospheric old church and hamlet. The valley broadened out towards Ambert, and I could have sworn I saw Ayrshires roped in for the production of the Fourme. A big church with a very English-looking tower: Magdalen or Somerset, but with beefed-up circular staircase. Didn't see the famous Roundhouse-style town hall. On to La Chaise-Dieu and was delighted to find the Hotel de l'Echo beside the Abbey, with masses of parking on the square right in front. Went for an amble through the cloisters and down to the W. front, where I found a shop to buy produits, mostly mushrooms (chanterelle for Danielle, hope they last). Dinner was v. good but yet another shy mumbling girl painfully enumerating the dishes and fussing with the cutlery, but slow with service when needed (water!). Another perfectly adequate French 2-star place, rather shabby and old-fashioned, but for 45 euros… Madame rather know-all and irritating and looked like a square fat Wayne Rooney.

Monday 22 September

Grey again when I got up but soon burnt off to be a lovely day: crisp because of altitude (and season I suppose). Breakfast rather disappointing. Repacked cases and rearranged boot, thanks to easy parking. The abbey was wonderful: €5 for choir, tapestries and Danse Macabre. The whole thing is sober and beautiful: five choir stalls and three sides with Brussels tapestries of the life of Christ above – each episode the centre of a triptych with relevant OT episodes either side. Danse Macabre is along wall behind part-hard choir stalls: three bays with lively almost charcoal-sketched frescoes on russet-red ground. More tapestries in rooms upstairs. Effigy and tomb of Pope Clement VI, born in La C-D and came back to be buried. Quite a find. There is a music festival sometime in the summer.

Thence over a most beautiful little road by the river winding through pine and deciduous forests, to rejoin the infant Loire at Vorey, shortly climbing away – fantastic views – then back again at Retournac, along the R bank towards Le Puy. The pretty church at Chamalières was being restored but I sneaked (not 'snuck') in behind workmen. A quick divert to see the Polignac acropolis from a distance then into Le Puy and parked in bay parking. Up steep hills and stairs to back end of cathedral. Cloister very fine and trésor had unexpected wooden martial figures.

Walked round the cathedral itself which somehow lacks atmosphere – too mucked-up – then down to extraordinary internal joined staircase and out the front door at 'sub-basement' level to the steep street. Nearing the car, needed a pee so had an ice cream and coffee in a typical style-free urban café.

One last cross-country trip on (very) minor roads didn't disappoint, over to Salignac, surprisingly high with great views over the Loire valley, then down into same: followed it, getting narrower and narrower, to Arlempdes, a sort of Haute-Loire Meteora. Church and ruined château both closed. Picturesque hamlet. Up and over high country with last views of the rolling

Auvergne to near Pradelles where with startling suddenness joined the main le-Puy–Aubenas–Montélimar road. Saw juggernauts for the first time (outside big towns). This road has been vastly improved since Sarah and I drove down it all one long and boiling hot afternoon in July 1964 (and near the bottom, met the Tour de France starting up a long and hard hairpin bend in broiling July heat!). The Jag behaved beautifully in endless fast S-curves. At Aubenas rang the Colombier and eventually got there just after 8 – dark already. Most welcoming-looking place: soigné and 'classy' in a way not so far experienced. (But again, even €120, though more than twice my norm, is pretty good for first-class room.) Rang Aubrey and discovered it was his birthday. Delicious dinner.

23 September – Tuesday

Lovely sunny morning and fresh. Rang Frilsham as it was RBW's birthday – got Georgie pre-swim as Robert already at LHR on his way to Houston. Got his mobile number and had a quick chat as he was about to board. HP rang just as I was sitting down to breakfast: had a chat in the courtyard. Tempted to linger but remembered things would close in Montélimar at noon. Paid the amiable Cyril and walked around the Colombier where workmen were hard at work improving. Very smart pool with conference room beside and bar etc.: all v. modern expensive chairs and loungers. It would be a nice place for a stop in summer, indeed as a base for exploring Ardèche and mid-Rhône.

Found a place quite easily on the boulevard in Montélimar and walked into the centre. Got a 'today's' *Mail* followed by a *Telegraph* then *Times*: had hoped perversely for yesterday's. Came across a v. smart nougat shop and bought some, also chocs. Not much to see with somewhat blank-walled cathedral and invisible château some way away. Bought chestnut beer for Aubrey in one nice shop and bread in another. Then off on a green road to Grignan, didn't stop, as had been there last year, but on through

Valréas to Nyons, where parked for a little look around and, as it happened, an ice cream and coffee in a café. Then down to Vaison where I hadn't intended to stop but there was a place by the old bridge. So, I photographed it and then went looking for Will Cates' old house by the car park by the river. However, thought I really ought to press on by now so took the road for Malaucène and Carpentras. As usual slow through Carpentras but my big mistake was to take the road through l'Isle sur la Sorgue for Cavaillon (had decided to take the autoroute, rather against my principles). Total jam in l'Isle and I took half an hour to go 300 yards by the canalised bit of the Sorgue. Filled up with diesel at the end of the jam. Then onto the autoroute to S of Cavaillon (ses melons). Whizzed down and saw with displeasure a very black sky E of Aix. Montagne Ste. Victoire looking very non-Cézanneish. Rang Aubrey from E of Aix in a downpour and was given more exact directions. Foolishly tried to input Brue-Auriac to the satnav and as a result had tiresome female voice warning me of non-existent heavy traffic after I turned into the minor road. Spotted the Chemin de le Gde. Bastide exactly as per instructions but couldn't see the house. Went on to the end (a bumpy track), turned and 'phoned again: 45 seconds later drew up beside a welcoming Aubrey.

Was absolutely charmed and impressed by the house which now looks as if they have been there for years, with a mélange of Lawrence and de Froidmont furniture giving it a subtly Continental as well as English look. The ground floor really spacious with a wide progression from room to room. Sleeping in Thomas's room under three well-known engravings of Ch.Ch. Each has a really nice study/workplace (at opposite ends of the house). Books everywhere, Library steps in Thomas's room. Had an excellent dinner of roast veal and the chanterelles I had bought at La Chaise-Dieu. Slept like a log.

Wednesday 24 September

Nice relaxing breakfast and usual continuation of the catching up talk of last night. Had a good inspection of the garden and heard all the plans. Helena and Anthea arrived about 1.45 in their hire car from Nice. It was lovely to see them. Much laughter and fun over lateish lunch of cold meats and excellent cheeses.

In the afternoon much further bathing and enjoying the house, books, computers, etc. In the evening I took them to a nice restaurant chosen by A & D in St Maximin: they all fitted in the Jag. Too late to bed. Woke up at 5 a.m. on

Thursday 25 September

It had already been decided that I would stay tonight too. In the morning A & D and I took a walk along to the village and inspected it thoroughly, including a bit down by the river with an old washing place and a vineyard where they'd never been. Back for lunch of four vast quiches. Afternoon at leisure as far as I remember.

Friday 26 September

Had intended to leave therefore packed up and cleared the room for Dominique (super-efficient daily and general factotum) who duly stripped bed etc. However, I had also expressed willingness to come on trip to Le Thoronet Abbey, and it seemed more companionable to go in the one car, so off we all went in the Citroen with Aubrey driving. V. pretty landscape immediately of pine woods, little rivers, and vineyard, mostly with solitary pairs of gateposts. It made sense to go on to Lorgues (beyond le T) and have lunch: where we found two OK-looking restaurants and chose I think the better one. Two kinds of very superior heaped up salad: Anthea and Helena kindly paid. It was clouding over by the time we left and looking v. ominous by the time we got to the abbey, in thick pine forest the heavens opened when we were in the abbey. Very dark and austere: in fact, to tell the truth a bit lacking in incident and interest. Good stop.

By the time we had emerged, it was 5 and obviously would

have been a bit silly for me to go off and find somewhere to spend the night, so warmly urged to stay. We went back via Brignoles and did some shopping in the shopping centre. Green ravioli for dinner.

Saturday 27 September
After breakfast Anthea and Helena went off to Aix: fond farewells. Aub and I downloaded my pics of there and I was mightily impressed by the Mac. Fond farewells again and this time I genuinely was off. Found I didn't need diesel so instead of going to St Maximin went back to Brue like the previous day – re-taking the photos with greater leisure – then on to the other end of Brue-Auriac, then via Correns to see the Baring zone (found the chais, got an idea where the château is but didn't go up). Desperately pretty area. At Cotignac, just like the previous day, the clouds were massing: at Sillans-la-Cascade, where I went on a 30-minute hike to see the waterfall, the rain began just before I got back to the car. On up via Aups to Aiguines and the beginning of the Gorges du Verdon: now dark, cold, and wet, and very atmospheric. Stopped frequently to snap views. Had phoned hotel in Castellane but forgot from which book and therefore the name: luckily, I chose the right one, and the rain was most welcoming (Hotel du Commerce: comical place). Before that drew out two canvasses of a particularly scenic part of the Verdon at Pont de Soleils, just after the official gorge bit but gorgeous enough. No dinner in the hotel as there was a group so went to the one at the other side of the square: it was fine.

Sunday 28 September
Bright beautiful morning with mist clouding the rocky shore above Castellane and ND slowly unveiling herself. After breakfast, chatted to two German bikers from Tübingen saddling up in the car park: very agreeable, recommended the Bonette road, which I remember in HP's Merc being very narrow. However,

I was headed N via the Col d'Allos to Barcelonnette. Said col was very, very narrow and most spectacular, especially with autumn colours. However, it paled beside the side road to the Lac d'Allos which I had taken as an excursion. This climbed and climbed and eventually, though a beautiful new surface, became 1-car width, with absolutely no passing place, and drops of 1–2 feet at the road's edge (and several thousand feet beyond that). I realised that one was done for if one met another car: no way either of passing or reversing and countless hairpin bends. So I bottled out and turned the moment I could. Just then a car did come from the lake direction. So I never saw the lake.

The Mexican-style villa when found turned out to be an ordinary French-looking (modern) hotel but with Mexican decorations and furnishings. (Everything in Barcelonnette is Mexican as numerous inhabitants emigrated there in the nineteenth century, made good and came back here and built villas.) Walked round pretty town in evening sunlight, and again ate out (hotel only did snacks – sans rest).

Monday 29 September

Started slowly, pottering up the pretty Ubaye Valley to Jausiers (more Mexican villas: old walled village), then up the steepening valley to Colmars where there are Vauban forts and eventually the Col de Vars. This was another steep and narrow one with exhilarating views all round. Stopped above Guillestre for birds-eye view and scopes of Mont-Dauphin fort, with the Écrins massif and glacier beyond (second only to Mt. Blanc in France). Driving on the main road rang Sarah G on the off chance that she was in Briançon – she wasn't, Bill was, but Bill ne mérite pas le detour! On up the main road towards the Col du Lauteret and du Galibier: stopped for a bit in le Monêtier, one of the Serre-Chevalier ski places, this actually a charming village in its own right.

The Galibier didn't disappoint. The views were stunning but so were the subtle colours and the startling geology. At the top panted up to the table d'orientation and identified everything, including Mt. Blanc far to the NE, towering over everything just as Everest does from Katmandu. Sadly no souvenir shops open: no cowhides. I really wanted a new one. On the way down Valloire was confusing to negotiate. A very opulent-looking skiing town, but also not without charm: a proper place. Got onto the autoroute at St Michel-de-Maurienne and whizzed to Albertville, thence to the lac and Talloires. The 'cottage' was perfect and so comfortable. Loved having a stroll beside the lake before dinner. Didn't love hearing from HP about the financial catastrophe in US, then finding telly didn't work, and man's well-meaning effort made it worse. However, he fixed it during dinner so afterwards I could masochistically watch it (instead of writing this) then sleep fitfully and with aching teeth.

Tuesday 30 September
Enjoyed a classy breakfast and when London Footsie began to rally slightly turned that off and headed off! Down the lake again to the bottom then stopped at Duingt and decided to sketch out the castle for a painting. Beginning to cloud over a bit and by Annecy it was grey, but still quite warm and mild. Had a quickish lunch outside in the old town, then a wander round, buying the inevitable chocolates but also scented soap, carved off blocks by two v. charming young ladies. Before lunch had estimated Bourg-en-Bresse as being about right for the night and secured room at H de le Prieuré from friendly sounding man.

After a ring road whizz around Annecy traffic suddenly became frightful because of a series of road works but I stuck to the D road as the autoroute goes miles out of the way. Stopped in Nantua (sa sauce) to look at abbey: a shabby-looking town, obviously not prosperous (great contrast to poncey Annecy). After that more road interruptions were promised so like yesterday got on the autoroute (which I had kept seeing in great viaducts spanning the valley) and took it all the way to

Bourg-en-B. Sweeping around over ridges, with a long, long descent into the plain (I remember that going from Geneva to Lyon, and realising that Switzerland, Savoy, etc. really are on a plateau). The abbey and church of Brou duly pitched up on the right and the hotel, functional and peaceful, just beyond. For third night had to eat out and the Chalet just opposite the church was closing: both the place, the two delightful girls, and the food (I had the chicken). Four course, with perhaps the best cheeses yet, €27. And how can they serve ice cream, random parfums, in just a couple of minutes *at the right consistency*?

Wednesday 1 October

After breakfast walked along to the church. Simply amazing. It is described as flamboyant Gothic in the French style, built by Margaret of Austria, widow of no less than three boy-kings, who finally ended up in Brussels. It's for her tomb and that of his husband, Philibert of Savoy (in pole position naturally) and her mother. Slightly less ornate. The tombs are quite remarkable, as in their carving are the rood screen and altars. Rather spookily there are two gisants for Mags and Philibert, the one below as in death and lit with a lurid blue light. The nave is very sober in design with fore and aft chapels to a uniform plan: the massive pillars very complex. The church is deconsecrated (or just not used?) and the monastery is an art gallery, mostly Flemish but some surprising more modern stuff including two soft porn works by a nineteenth-century orientalist. There are no less than three cloisters, and a fine chapter house and so on. All shown very well.

Found some difficulty parking even in the vast car park in Bourg but realised it was market day taking place in much of the same car park. Mostly closing down as 11.45. Hurried to the centre to try and get a paper. (Absurd that you can't get such a thing between noon and 2.) Got a *Times* and *Mail* and then of course found a chocolatier. Also thought a cup of tea would be nice (for Anadin) and a myrtille tart. Very grey and the town is also rather subfusc – workaday, I should say. But I bought some cheese from a nice couple in what remained of the market.

Stopped outside the Auberge Bressane opposite the Brou church and went in to ask about plates. The atmosphere was super and I really felt like sinking into a really good lunch for the next four hours. The proprietor (chef) was a jolly man of quite senior years: wife charming too. The plates were bloody expensive so bought two each of bowl, large plate and very large plate.

Set off up the Lons-le-Saunier road and turned off at Cuiseaux which looked nice on the map. One of these hyper-picturesque walled villages, with some houses being tarted up and most still very decrepit. Went for an amble around the wooded hill behind, then down to the plain again straight to Louhans. I had remembered this having arcaded streets a la Bolognese so stopped and had a wander. Bought some varieties of apples – two each of four kinds. From Louhans straight to Beaune: parked just outside the walls and walked to the centre by the Hôtel Dieu. Hadn't really meant to but found a nice wine-grocer's shop (mostly Volnay, Beaune, Auxey) and bought a couple of bottles for the commissariat. The D road up out of Beaune was fast and pretty and up the Côte d'Or becomes seriously fast (and virtually unpopulated). Pretty little villages before Pouilly, on the river Ouche; but dusk was falling. The last stretch from Pouilly to Sémur seemed to take a long time, though the road was fast. Thrilling descent down the cobbles of Sémur to the little bridge, up to the top and there was this modern little roadside hotel. Superb view of hundreds of yards of illuminated tours et ramparts. Excellent dinner.

Thursday 2 October

Thinking about where to go next, over breakfast I realised that I was very happy in this modern efficient hotel and could quite happily entertain myself in the area and stay another night, with all the joys of not having to move. (The room was modern in an elegant, efficient Swiss sort of way: thank God no ghastly efforts at 'art' on the walls. Monochrome with tan/fawn tinges: refreshing!) Drove up into the town and parked easily in square behind the church – bought a *Times*. Meandered through the streets of old houses, on the 'prow' (like Segovia). I came to an école matrimoniale with much screaming at break, then France's smallest open house, Siamese-twinned to a round watchtower. Lots of these. Occupying most of the prow was a delightfully tranquil-looking hospital. Walking back to the centre, reflected how many of the old and picturesque houses in these places are 'a vendre' or just near-ruined and abandoned. Went into the church – fine – at one minute to twelve but chased out shortly in a gracious manner.

The countryside ramble took me (after taking the wrong road out of Sémur: no better) past pretty hill village of Grignan and down a steep hill to great view of a fortified manor by the Canal de Bourgogne at Courcelles-lès-Montbard. Walked a bit by the lock – almost paintable but not quite. Montbard was confusing and I left for Fontenay. What a delight. The usual Cistercian site in a forest valley: extensive, also no doubt expensive – privately owned and immaculately kept. It was bright and breezy – the sun kept going in and out. Church plain yet grand: cloisters and chapter house excellent, also dormitory. A good feature was the forge with reconstructed water-wheel-driven hammer: very well displayed.

Alésia next: by now cold and windy, especially on top of the hill. Parked near huge Vercingetorix statue: no one there but an improbable group of a very tall unsmiling black man and a few diminutive middle-aged Japanese tourists. Looking at the table d'orientation one woman said 'aah, Naporeon…' So I said 'Naporeon sanban' and without any surprise she said 'Ah so, samban desho'! Mercifully perhaps the fouilles of the Gallo-Roman town were shut: I could see all I wanted through the chainlink fence.

There had been signs to a walled village called Flavigny which sounded vaguely familiar, so I made a detour. Parked outside the walls and walked past the rather grim looking eighteenth- or nineteenth-century monastery, where I saw a ruined Gothic arch and a sign saying 'Carolingian crypt' – and so it was. As I walked around the village taking pics a horsey-headed son of travail grasped me by the hand and declared that an especially fine house was *à vendre*: '2 millions, pas cher, pas cher'. Of course he was talking francs not new-fangled euros and I agreed with that, but managed to extricate myself from any property purchases. I did go into the abbey shop which of course was all about aniseed balls – their little tins are everywhere. The flavour is mostly disguised all sorts of ways: actually the 'nature' was not bad.

Next a bit of cross-country map-reading to take me to the source of the Seine. It was high sweeping ridge country, just right for a watershed. (The source of the Seine, flowing into the Channel, and the Ignon, flowing via the Saône and Rhône to the Med, are about 2 kilometres apart.) Partage des eaux! The actual source was charming: a little dribble through a field, emanating from a clearly man-made grotto, Stourhead-style (no Fontaine-de-Vaucluse here!) with a pretty marble nymph. A plaque said all done by the Baron Haussmann at the behest of, of course, Napoleon samban. Better than his boulevards anyway. I thought I had better a) following Rhône glacier tradition, pee in the stream – if I didn't anyway cows would shortly; and b) jump across it just by where a dinky little toy bridge had been built. Now wet, cold and getting dark so whizzed back to Sémur through Vitteaux and Clamecy: fast, high, sweeping roads and some good light effects. Came across a line of windmills – almost the first seen in France – and of course they were stock still, in a stiff breeze.

Friday 3 October

Bright and breezy morning again. Paid up, bought another *Times* in the town then felt my way down to the river at the base of the ramparts. Found a paintable bit and went to get canvas and charcoal. Then continued round and up to the Montbard roundabout near the hotel and off northwards, but not by the main Montbard road. Joined the canal just W of Montbard. Its bridges and lockkeepers' houses are nothing like as pretty as on the Nivernais. Saw one barge coming into a lock (a bit later on). Drove into Ancy and found 20 minutes still till I could get in (at 2). Eventually did. The place is most imposing inside and out but incredibly luxurious especially the interior courtyard with its gilt pilaster extensively (completely) refaced. Nice young man with extraordinarily thin face took group of three of us round. No photos of the interior but have some pcs. Privately owned by French aristocrats, as is next place – Tanlay.

Tanlay was quite a contrast – rather like Anet, it is early Renaissance and quirky. Has a large, water-filled moat. I was 3 mins. late for tour but kind woman rushed into the house and made them wait. Instead of the classical pinks of Ancy this was a jumble. Very family: including a number of genuinely good pictures. The family had clearly had a number of diplomats and Chinese porcelain etc. was much in evidence: also foreign orders of chivalry (present owner's father, who married formidable-looking Marquise de Tanlay, had been chef de protocole etc.). An entertaining mix of sixteenth, eighteenth and nineteenth centuries but nonetheless impressive.

From there via Tonnerre – which I drove through but couldn't really see – and a bit of canalside potter to Sens, where I drove straight into the garage of the H. de Paris et de la Poste. No one at desk – eventually a goofy youth appeared and showed me rather shabby room. Insisted on keeping car key, a pain since the garage was virtually empty, no one could have used it anyway, and I kept on having to get it off him (after, of course, summoning him). Extra irritation that the restaurant, which advertised itself with great quantities of certificates, meilleur cuisinier de France etc., toques, you name it, was closed on Friday evening! No warning in Michelin. So wandered along (quite a way) to the 2 Michelin rosette place, but they couldn't have me. However, I did book at their bistro-type establishment next door, went away, came back and had probably a more (to my taste) delicious dinner for 1/3 the price. Sens is rather a distressed-looking place with businesses and shops boarded up and even hotels looking as if they have been abandoned. And this at the end of an unprecedented boom!

Saturday 4 October
A beautiful bright morning. The hotel seemed much more 'alive' and the breakfast was good. The patronne spoke excellent English, was humorous and helpful and had spent seventeen years in New York. Enjoyed the cathedral – pity about the scaffolding on the front – some good glass, a Baroque-style tomb of the Dauphin (of Louis XVI) and another rather clunking neoclassical one which was totally anonymous. A small statue of some saint had come from Thomas à Becket's house in Sens (allegedly). Talked to nice slightly older couple from Herts. who had been breakfasting. Museum across rather fine courtyard (Gothic details, steep pitched roof): contained better than usual trésor including, surprisingly, Napoleon's hat from Waterloo and his coat from St Helena (*Quaere*: why in Sens?).

Time to push on but looking at the map decided against cross-country Troyes/Soissons/Amiens route to Channel and decided to go up autoroute to Paris and round the péripherique. Motorway: empty, day glorious: stuff the awful péripherique, we'll just drive through Paris to get a taste (hadn't been there in 3 years). Arriving at Porte d'Italie and heading down rue Monge, thought it would be most agreeable to stop (if I could park) and have a little luncheon on some terrace in the sun. Not a space, of course – but midday saw a *parc souterrain* and dropped down into it, then after securing the car set off to find lunch. During said (frugal) lunch I thought – 'this is vile – all the champagne socialists of the Left Bank out in force – wouldn't some quai/ bouquiniste hopping be nice – why not stay'? Retrieved the appropriate pages from the red Michelin and approached two little nice-looking hotels on the quai diagonally opposite ND. First was complet, second too but obligingly rang up their 'sister ship' just along the quai which could give me its last room. So I dealt.

The Hotel Notre Dame Maitre Albert turned out to be just the ticket, up rue M A just opposite the chevet of ND. A cheerful middle-aged man on the desk, nice lobby and breakfast room. Said I'd be back later (when I found a v. compact but beautifully fitted little room and bathroom). Wandered along the quai, bought a couple of Arthaud picture books from the 40s–50s (Auvergne–Poitou), then over to Île St Louis, along the main street, Notre Dame, over to Châtelet/Beaubourg/r. St Denis and eventually back. Footsore so rested up till about 8.30 when went over to ND for the free concert: singing then at 9.45 the grande orgue bellowed forth: marvellous. People coming in and going out the whole time. About 11 left and found a café near hotel (and car: the hotel turned out to be 50 yards from the car park!) for supper, v. slow service.

Sunday 5 October

Up early (for me), had quick breakfast and was rolling by 8.35. Foul morning. Reasonably quickly through St Denis etc. and onto the Beauvais/Amiens autoroute. Weather deteriorated even further and when I tried to stop for diesel near Boulogne was almost swept off my feet so abandoned the idea. Obviously a day for the tunnel but was unimpressed to find it cost £160.

8CR
K9

IV

Sailing

SAILING

Rather than adhering to strict chronology, it is probably better to take my sailing activities down the years as one whole, almost preordained progression. It has been a very significant part of my life, ever since when eschewing golf and cricket I had first – metaphorically – 'run away to sea'. In the case of golf, that was almost a family 'religion': I had no objection to it and in fact had enjoyed the occasional (usually part) round with my friends until the start of my teens: we were fortunate in that there were two first-rate courses, both climbing up into the hills behind our village and very scenic; the first of these was not 'ours' though being a mere minute's walk from home was useful for walking the dog; while the other, on which we and everyone we did know played, was all of five minutes' walk away. However, I was bored by endless tedious conversations on the subject and the insinuation that proficiency in golf was required for business or professional success. As for cricket, this was the one school sport in which I was undoubtedly successful – principally as a demon fast bowler. However, having caught the sailing bug I gave mainline cricket up in favour of going sailing on half-holidays and at weekends at school. As I wrote earlier, this attracted the ire of my horrible housemaster who happened to be the master in charge of cricket (and who had no doubt hoped that I would one day grace the First Eleven). In one termly report he deplored that I 'had abandoned the manly sport of cricket, which leads to lifelong friendships, for the solitary pastime of sailing', etc. etc. With sailing, I have made so many deep and lasting friendships, seen so many exotic places around the world and had so many experiences of wind and weather that even a life in an MCC tie at Lord's or on village cricket grounds would find it hard to match. So, sailing it was to be, throughout my life.

Youth in Scotland – Dinghies, Day Sailers and Cruisers

It began, as just mentioned, in my schooldays when I took the precaution of bringing my own GP14 dinghy to school. While most members of the sailing club would be limited to one afternoon a week, this meant I could sail on the weekday half-holidays of Tuesdays and Thursdays, as well as on Saturdays and Sundays. The boat was kept on a mooring in Granton harbour: one ran down there through the rather rough council house area of Pilton, occasionally the object of incomprehensible if unmistakable ribaldry from the inhabitants. It was a most welcome break from the confines of the school grounds – though of course limited to the summer term.

In the holidays, and for the few years I kept the boat thereafter, it was usually kept on the Clyde: either at Gourock, on a trailer at the Royal Gourock Yacht Club – thus needing to be launched or retrieved each time; or when we were at Machrihanish for long enough in the harbour at Campbeltown, again on a mooring buoy but with a rope pulley system enabling one to bring it in to the quay and scramble aboard.

The GP provided much pleasure but also with its quick responses and manoeuvrability really taught me the essential principles of sailing and boat handling. It seems an invariable rule that one progresses in life, if a sailor, from smaller boats to ever larger: from quick-responding dinghies to keelboats of increasing length and stability – and comfort! So it was with me (though I should by now, according to the accepted formulae, be owning or at least crewing on vessels of nearly 100 feet: unlikely!).

The next stage then appeared – while I still had the dinghy – when I had a whole summer at home between Easter and going up to Oxford in October 1961. I was invited to crew for John Grayburn on his 24-foot Gareloch racing keelboat, on the loch of the same name. The Garelochs were built as a class (nicknamed 'Gareloch Goddesses', mostly being named after mythological Greek goddesses or muses, though ours was '*Zephyrus*', a boy) in or shortly after 1924. They had dispersed over the years but by 1961 had mostly reconvened at the Royal Northern on the Gareloch. They were and are most beautiful boats, with classic lines like miniature metre boats, some with vestigial cabin roofs. Unlike the boring universal white of GRP boats, each had a distinctive, usually bright, colour of hull and waterline. *Zephyrus* was royal blue, with a narrow white waterline.

Racing was (like the half-holidays!) on Tuesdays and Thursdays, with a 7 p.m. start within the Gareloch: and on Saturdays for a full day on the open firth outside the Narrows. On the weekdays I motored over to Rhu via the Erskine Ferry in my ancient open MG, enjoyed classic afternoon teas on rugs in the garden with John's mother Lady Young, then down to the club. Most of the other crew were of a similar age, parents having bigger boats, notably the 8-metre Cruiser Racer class which John's stepfather Sir Alastair had created soon after the war. It was a close-knit, friendly but very competitive group, and the racing was close. A bonus was the mothballed battleships (KG V class) and aircraft carriers of the still quite recent war, which were sometimes used as marks in the course!

More frequently than might be thought, though, the wind fell away completely and if we could not finish by 10 p.m. the race was abandoned. In either case, we ended with sustaining bacon and eggs in the clubhouse; then for me it was back on the Erskine, or if too late Renfrew, ferry across the river and home about one.

That year and the next, before the Oxford vacs took me further afield, we also graced the Clyde Fortnight (in these degenerate times, now just a Week), based in the Glenburn Hotel at Rothesay. As with the series in the Gareloch, there was a points championship: we won in the second year. The Glenburn was the social hub: King Constantine of Greece was racing in the Dragon class, and his sister Princess Sophia, later Queen of Spain, was also there and came to have tea with us on Sir Alastair's 8-metre *Sonda*, conveniently moored right opposite the hotel.

As I wrote, there was also a small coterie of the 8-metre CR owners: a brilliantly conceived class which enabled West of Scotland owners both to race on equal (non-handicap) terms during the summer then in August take their families on cruises to the Western Islands and Highlands, or wherever. Sadly, the class never really caught on elsewhere, though there are isolated examples in the south. There were also 'passage races', a mix of the two, both within the Clyde and on from Crinan to Mull, Oban and the like. As *Sonda* was No. 1 and the newest boats were nearly twenty years later she never won: but it was nice to cruise in her with the White Ensign streaming from the stern!

Concurrently, there was cruising – and indeed the occasional race – on *Jura*, the converted Scottish Islander owned by dear Cyril Drew, father of my equally dear then girl friend Sarah. The Islanders were again a local day racing keelboat, a little larger than the Garelochs: just as well as four people at a pinch could sleep aboard, only when a board (sorry!) had been inserted between the side berths. Very friendly!

Jura also 'lived' at Rothesay – Port Bannatyne to be precise – for some time, so we drove down to the ferry at Wemyss Bay to take the CalMac ferry over to Bute. Latterly she was moved further away to Tighnabruaich in Cowal, involving this time the Gourock–Dunoon ferry and a longer drive through Cowal – very scenic.

Jura provided an immense amount of fun. Sometimes I borrowed her and had as crew either Sarah's younger brothers or other friends such as Hamish Aird (*vid. passim*). The most dramatic moment was undoubtedly on reaching the supposed haven of Puilladobhrain, south of Oban, to ride out a fearful storm only to find the anchor would not hold. Eventually it was 'Abandon Ship' (once, hopefully, secured) and we four trudged through the woods, over the hill to the hotel by the 'Bridge over the Atlantic' where lodging was found for the night. The morning dawned clear and beautiful, ideal for a sail. Another 'moment' was when with 12-year-old younger brother David Drew as crew I was returning *Jura* from Bute to Gourock. The engine had been removed for repair (literally sent to Coventry), but I was of course perfectly happy to proceed under sail. However, the wind faded and eventually it became a flat calm – right in the middle of the large ship fairway. Towards midnight more than one large ship – at least one a Cunarder – started heading down-firth for the Atlantic. Becalmed and in pitch darkness and without any navigation lights I felt somewhat exposed! But they missed.

In my North American section I have already described my cruise from Long Island Sound to New England in the beautiful old schooner *White Wing*, and further on the midnight sail on Lake Pontchartrain with Jim Coleman and his friends, so no need to repeat these here.

Tina – '*Ocean*' *Racing*

Having returned from my two years in the States in late 1968, I was eager to get afloat again in summer 1969. A kind friend introduced me to Eddie Stettinius who owned the revolutionary One Ton boat *Tina*, which had won the One Ton Cup the year before. Eddie was a large, genial, humorous American, nephew of the former US Secretary of State of the same name who had played a leading part in establishing the United Nations after the war. He kept *Tina* at West Mersea – which I was later to know so well – and was looking for crew for that season's RORC 'ocean' races in home waters. So I did some of these – the Channel Race, the North Sea Race and the West Mersea–Ostend, which to our surprise we learnt (over our *frites* in Ostend) we had won. The Channel Race had its frustrations as one turning point was the buoy off Cherbourg: I had been aching to go to France after several years, but this was all I was to see of it at that stage. I was going to go on the Fastnet Race but as I was offered a job – after months of searching – to start that week I thought I had better behave in a grown-up fashion.

Tina was a revolutionary boat for her time: designed by Dick Carter, built in steel rather than wood, glass fibre or aluminium; about 35 feet long with a short fin keel keeping water resistance low. Curiously enough it was the French who were keenest on the design and, apart from that season's racing, I have seen several of the small class in French ports over the years.

'The Maid' and the Team: Solent, Dorset, France

The other important event of late summer 1969, however, was the launch of the Blackwells' Nicholson 38, christened *Netherton Maid* after Major Holliday's most successful racehorse. (He was Mrs B's father and the leading racehorse owner for many years.) 'The Maid' was technically a motor-sailer but in fact sailed well: there was a centre cockpit with fixed windscreen (and wipers) and an aft cabin. She made an excellent cruiser; perhaps, though, not exactly the fastest.

'The Maid' lived at Gosport and was looked after by an old boy called, inevitably, the Skipper. The routine wherever possible over the next decade and a half was to drive down on a Friday night, or sometimes very early on the Saturday, and set off westward along the Solent. Generally, the destination was Yarmouth, Isle of Wight; Studland in Dorset if time allowed; Cowes or the Beaulieu River if it was short. We would often find ourselves running downwind past Cowes of a Sunday evening when almost all other boats had disappeared – 'the last Nicholson'. Then after putting the boat to bed, it was often the short drive to the Wessex Hotel in Winchester for dinner, then back to London, tired but happy.

A more westerly voyage was when I took the train then ferry on a Saturday morning to Dartmouth, where some Blackwells and two Fleet Air Arm Buccaneer pilots had tied up *en route* to Cornwall, only to find a certain commotion as a motor boat had just blown up – gas explosion presumably. This did not prevent us from motoring off pretty smartly. The naval airmen's tales of deck landings were far more hair-raising. We drifted past the Eddystone light in its solitary splendour and on to Falmouth – first sight of a place I was to get to know so well – and I entrained home, much enjoying all Brunel's bridges and tunnels.

Going back in time, the first of many cross-Channel trips came that August 1969 bank holiday, just Miles Blackwell and myself and four others: pioneering a night voyage to Cherbourg (and again overnight on return, to maximise time in France), hiring a Peugeot estate car and driving down to Coutances and Mont St Michel. Landfall at Portland Bill on the way back was hardly intended, but gave a good introduction to the strength of the Channel tides, as well as a good day-long view of the Jurassic Coast. This was to become something of a routine, with varying crews, both in May and August. One atypically prolonged passage was committed to 8mm film by Dudley Dodd and myself, aptly titled 'Night of Fear'. On that occasion I remember setting off from Gosport on a fine evening and myself cooking veal Soubise for the team. They having retired replete for the night the weather deteriorated quickly: Nigel and I stayed on watch long after our turn was over, crossing the shipping lanes with a 'green' crew; foolishly I went to take a nap in the leaping forepeak as the wind rose, and shortly afterwards returned on deck to be seasick for the second and last time of my life. A long grey day was spent beating against wind and tide to round Barfleur and tie up at last at Cherbourg. Curiously, the crew recuperated amazingly quickly. At the weekend's end the boat had to be left in Cherbourg because of the weather (which had abated by ferry time – but time pressed) and retrieved the following glorious calm weekend. All that is immortalised for posterity.

Ardevora: *Early Days – to the Baltic*

If *Netherton Maid*'s 'range' had effectively been limited to the

Channel, the next sailing epoch was to be virtually global. My City partners Tom and Ellen Winser, following the takeover of our firm, were due to retire or leave by 1990: in anticipation they had formed a plan to build a boat and sail the globe for several years thereafter. Many hours were spent on her design and then supervising construction at Woodbridge – very convenient for weekend inspection visits from Creems. *Ardevora of Roseland* – named after their house in Cornwall – is a 55-foot ketch, this time with a hull of aluminium, with a centreboard giving shallow draught greatly to expand the places that could be visited; a staysail as well as jib/genoa; a beautiful wooden dinghy built by Tom, subsequently replaced by a rubber one. As experience of ocean voyaging grew of course many features were added. In general, she was solid, seaworthy and surprisingly fast.

The launch took place beside the Tide Mill in Woodbridge on a cold, dark day in early 1989. After a few warm-up sessions on the Orwell we were ready – Tom, Ellen, Richard and myself – in July for the maiden voyage across the North Sea to Jutland. Ellen and I stood watch together that first night and saw the oil rigs come and go throughout.

After another long day and night, oil rigs safely left astern, we cleared the Danish coast and tied up alongside the fishing boat quay at Thyborøn, the western entrance to the Limfjord leading to the Kattegat. (Think of it as slicing off the top of the Danish boiled egg.) The Limfjord was delightful: one sails through classic rustic Danish countryside, it sometimes widening into lagoons or even lakes, occasionally narrowing to places bridged for road traffic. The drill was to fly code flag 'N' – black and white chequers – prominently – and hoot – to show one's intention to pass through; then dawdle while the bridge bascules were readied for raising. One such crossing place was a little town called Løgstør (sounds more like Switzerland!) where the channel swept one right by the quay.

We had spent the first night anchored in the most tranquil spot, off a beach on a sizeable lagoon: at that latitude there was in fact virtually no night and with the 'simmer dim' and no human presence nearby the sense of peacefulness was extraordinary. Next day by contrast we tied up at the quayside in Aalborg and had a further day of sightseeing in the charming old centre. A serendipitous discovery in the fine cathedral was the board of mediaeval bishops, containing the names Rosencrantz and Guildensterna – Shakespeare was here? Then, in the evening, the shorter passage to the open sea at Hals. It was surprising how many larger commercial vessels were traversing that stretch of water.

After a (short) night passage the ethereal shape of Hamlet's Elsinore Castle – Helsingør – appeared out of the mist, but was quickly passed as we navigated the ferry traffic to Helsingborg in Sweden opposite, motoring southbound on the Sound to Copenhagen. In fact, we sailed past central Copenhagen – a complex series of buoys and presumed shallows which reminded us of Nelson not seeing the signal – and berthed in Kastrup marina near the airport. I already knew Copenhagen quite well but think I have usually been there in the winter months: in summer it was transformed with greenery and gaiety. Of course, Kastrup being a suburb we had to take taxis in and out of the city – no great trouble.

Round into the Baltic, our first stop was Ystad in Skåne, known to me by repute as my late great friend Eric Elstob had a summer house there. (Eric, who sadly died young only a few years later, wrote an excellent history of Sweden, in the first sentence of which he dates the origin of Sweden to 6839 BC!) Ystad is somewhat younger than that but nevertheless has a wonderful 'olden-tyme' feel with quaint ochre, yellow and russet houses, and as so often in Scandinavia a church with fine Baroque monuments to bearded worthies, and even more important, suspended models of sailing ships.

Next, sailing round the southern extremity of Skåne where the Swedish version of Stonehenge was clearly visible, we parked in the rather more important town of Kalmar: headquarters of the mediaeval Kalmar Union. Befitting such an historic town, Kalmar has a superlative Renaissance castle on its own islet (obviating the need for a moat) and a dramatic Baroque cathedral standing alone. The streets are wide and rather empty-seeming: buildings seventeenth and eighteenth century with far more of an Eastern European feeling than Ystad, Gothenburg or the Danish towns. We enjoyed dining on a terrace overlooking the capacious harbour – *Ardevora* tied up immediately below – on reindeer, bilberries and other Swedish delicacies (no shrimps for me!).

Kalmar is sheltered from the Baltic by the long island of Öland and we left early for the passage north-east then east to Visby, main town of the island of Gotland. Visby is as redolent of the Middle Ages as almost anywhere I have been: city walls and gatetowers still standing proud, streets with both ruined and very much still inhabited houses climbing the hill from the harbour. In midsummer the wild roses everywhere exhaled scent. The mediaeval atmosphere was enhanced by maypoles around which midsummer celebrations were already starting.

After another night passage the presence of 'continental' Sweden was indicated by the lone Landsort lighthouse: from there we penetrated deeper and deeper into the Stockholm archipelago – the Skerries. Starting with 100 per cent sea, one proceeds to 25 per cent land, then 50 per cent, 75 per cent and eventually through fjords to a hundred per cent mainland. We could not linger in the archipelago, however (that pleasure was to come some years later), but made more or less directly for the mainland inlet of Saltsjöbaden, which is the nearest one can get to Stockholm without an extra 40-mile detour.

There I left the boat and took the little train into Stockholm – my first visit. I don't propose to describe this lovely city now, only to mention that my night (in a somewhat faceless hotel in the main shopping district) was enlivened by a phone call from Nigel Blackwell to say that a godson, Richard, had been born. In the morning, I flew back to London while the Winsers, who were taking three weeks' holiday against my two, were going on to the Nautor yard at Pietarsaari on the Gulf of Bothnia in Finland, to leave the boat for the winter (starting in July!).

This had been a highly enjoyable maiden voyage/shakedown cruise: really nothing had gone wrong except one misjudgement when docking at Ystad. The watch routines worked well; the one evening dram was all the more appreciated; the long evenings at anchor or quayside were glorious. Unsurprisingly, when we were all back in the office, planning for the next year's 'retrieval' from the Baltic began.

Ardevora – *Behind the Iron Curtain*

By that time (summer 1990) both Tom and Ellen had left the firm and were free: so, the return cruise could be much more leisurely, and they were to be joined at various points by a series of (mostly) James Capel youngsters, of varying experience but invariable enthusiasm. With the intention of venturing into Soviet waters, a great deal of bureaucratic preparation was needed.

In due course news came from the Gulf of Bothnia that the voyage south had begun. I was sorry to miss the Åland islands, Turku and the islands of the western Gulf of Finland, and entry to the USSR at Vyborg (I was perhaps not too unhappy to miss these formalities, having from the office dealt with endless bureaucratic paper- or rather telex-work); however, with again a mere fortnight available Leningrad and the still-Soviet Baltic states inevitably took precedence.

With my friend and colleague Theo I flew on a Friday night to Helsinki, arriving around midnight. A stern-looking older customs man waved us and our weighty bags of provisions (clanking audibly: I'd brought a dozen of good claret!) through, and we used the few Finnmarks I had procured from 'Jelly' Lang to take a taxi tour of the handsome centre in the 'white nights' of the small hours. After the briefest ever hotel stay, we were off to the airport for Leningrad. Looking down on the approach,

Theo exclaimed 'Bees!' 'You must have amazing eyesight', I said: but it was the rather more sizeable hives she had spotted…

I imagine the airport for St Petersburg (as of course it now is) is somewhat different: the Pulkovo at which we arrived was a modest and old-fashioned place – rather reminiscent of the Renfrew of my youth. An officer behind etched glass in a high wooden booth gave us complex forms to fill out, seated on a settee with antimacassars. Handing in the comprehensive and dutifully completed customs declaration at the exit, we were pleased to see it put away unscrutinised and 'This Rossiya -- pliz go in' from the officer. With this greeting we already had warm feelings for Russia: it was to get better.

We were now in the fourth largest city in Europe; had no idea where the boat was or where and how we would meet up with the Winsers. However, there they were: together with a small Russian man called Oleg, who had turned up, entirely non-prearranged, to drive them (and us) wherever we wanted to go, in a white Moskvitch car. This made things vastly easier. It was only later that I read that the KGB always used white Moskvitches to keep their foreign visitors under control. So, I have warm memories of the otherwise unlamented KGB as an excellent, and free, taxi service.

We drove for what seemed ages northwards to the Srednyaya Nevka, a wooded branch of the Neva on which was the clubhouse of the St Petersburg Yacht Club, supposedly the oldest in the world. The clubhouse itself was a fine 1930s modernist design but was in appalling repair. Beside it as well as a jetty were structures on pontoons with a 'passerelle' to shore, very similar to Oxford college barges; in fact, they housed trade union rowing clubs. (Same thing?)

It was a quarter-mile walk along the riverside to the few shops and the tram terminus. There was nothing in the shops: the grocer had a pile of mouldy-looking potatoes outside every day, and one (different from day to day) sort of equally mouldy green vegetable. The trams just petered out and more often than not had become disconnected from the overhead wires.

The weather was glorious and after a day or so of the inevitable 'boaty' things Theo and I took aforementioned tram down to the centre, along an endless boulevard. We 'did' central Leningrad pretty thoroughly but on such a lovely day outdoors trumped indoors so we didn't even try to visit the Hermitage. For another time – though alas that time has not yet come. One important visit was to the old cruiser *Aurora*, which had fired the first shots of the 1917 revolution: important as Theo's hometown was Aurora, Illinois. Many places, however, were shut including the nearby Peter and Paul Fortress and cathedral, also St Isaac's Cathedral. Never mind. With some difficulty we found a bottle of vodka to give to Oleg.

Next day the ever-obliging Oleg drove us, first to Petrodvorets (Peterhof) Palace and then to Tsarskoe Selo (the Catherine Palace): both immensely impressive, though much work was still being done at Petrodvorets by Poles. I had already visited Potsdam and later on this trip was to visit both Gdansk and Warsaw, all immaculately rebuilt by Poles – the latter two obviously, but this speciality clearly spread both west and east in the East European bloc. The workmanship was superb. (More on Poland later.)

Catherine Palace could be visited inside: huge slippers of felt provided to protect the beautiful parquet floors. The place is vast and was rather empty. By contrast the lake and gardens were animated, with a string quartet playing in front of a neoclassical pavilion (both mirrored in the lake) and Cameron's rather more modest-scale neoclassical Gallery. (Much of the less overwhelmingly Rococo interior of the main palace is also down to Cameron – makes one proud how these Scots got around, in Russia, Sweden, etc.) Sadly Pavlovsk was a palace too far.

Next day we set off westbound, stopping at the yacht club complex on the point of Vasilyevsky Island and picking up a pilot with a genial, rather monoglot black-bearded friend whose main, well-meant, contribution was to bring us two bottles of milk, which were duly ditched as suspect shortly after we dropped the pilot. We travelled along the channel past the shipyards and then the island of Kronstadt as we entered more open waters. An uneventful but pleasant sail took us along the Gulf of Finland and late in the evening to the bay at whose head lay Tallinn.

It was as dark as it ever gets by the time we tied up at the former Olympic marina in the suburbs. We were boarded by customs and immigration in the form of a dead ringer for Nikita Khruschev whose first words were 'You have cigarettes?' Box duly proffered. 'You have whisky?' 'Why, of course: do have a glass.' (Tom in usual ultra-courteous mode but with a hint of menace.) Our failure to have our passports endorsed for Tallinn (or any Soviet city other than Leningrad) was duly overlooked.

Old Tallinn, as advertised, is totally charming, marred only by the imposition of the usual St Basil's-like Russian Orthodox cathedral: the castle and walls well worth the climb. On the way down a café provided the most delicious chocolate cake and coffee for four for, I think, about five shillings equivalent. Otherwise, the shops were bare.

Centreboard or no, we could not attempt the passage between the Estonian mainland and the island of Saaremaa ('Moon' to Arthur Ransome) – though probably for reasons of bureaucracy rather than draught. As usual it was late evening by the time we reached the entrance of the Gulf of Riga. We were met by a sizeable gunboat flying flag 'L', which on consulting the codebook we found meant 'Stop your engines immediately or I fire without warning'. In fact, as usual the engine had packed up, as we were eventually able to communicate to the coastguard. Eventually the words 'Proceed to Riga' were heard on the radio.

I had a wonderful tranquil night, alone on watch on deck while the others slept. Hard on the wind, I could just aim for the river entrance and Riga; on a reciprocal course, a succession of craft came by, including a few old Baltic ketches. By dawn we were entering the Daugava River with about ten miles to downtown Riga. The crew was now awake, just as well: without an engine it was necessary to short-tack the whole way, going about literally under the branches of the trees lining this pretty river. Again, we were met by a gunboat: this time a much smaller vessel powered by some sort of jet engine which left it little alternative between full speed ahead and total stop. So, though we would normally have appreciated a tow, leaving aside any communication problems, it might have been inadvisable to take it. The craft lingered behind, motionless; then roared up past us at a rate of knots, promptly subsiding again – rather like swans landing on water. Eventually we reached our berth, pleasingly near the city centre.

Already from the river we had been excited by the Riga skyline with a plethora of spires – always admired by Tom in particular. We enjoyed exploring the old town: unfortunately, it was now drizzling, emphasising the all-round greyness. But it is beautiful: the epitome of an old Hanseatic town with mediaeval buildings seguing into the Baroque, and one district and church in the cream and gold Rococo more reminiscent of Rastrelli's Rococo in Russia proper.

In 1990 it was evident that the USSR's days were numbered: though we dutifully flew the hammer and sickle as our courtesy flag, I had also had made small Estonian, Latvian and Lithuanian flags and we flew the Latvian one in subsidiary mode. But the citizens themselves were hardly reticent in covering the 'Monument of the Heroes' in national flags and patriotic slogans. This and other manifestations we could see from the high-rise, ugly Soviet Hotel Latvia where we had an excellent lunch, again for a minuscule amount of money.

We were on our last day and aiming to leave late in the evening. There was the problem of how to cash in or exchange our roubles, which we had been quite unable to spend. Theo returned from an expedition saying that for a few pounds' equivalent she could buy two grand pianos: however, it was felt that it might be difficult to stow them on deck for the return voyage. The outcome was that even when 'checking out' of the USSR in the little yacht harbour we could only get a sort of IOU in exchange: I kept mine in my wallet for some years, but appropriately enough found that it eventually disintegrated.

Our eventual departure – we were scheduled to leave in company with a Swedish yacht – was delayed by a pantomime involving what must have been the first British or Western frogman in a Soviet harbour, at least since the revolution. We had been moored between two buoys, fore and aft: while the others were coping with one, at the helm I saw the boat was heading rapidly for the quay, so instinctively put it in reverse to avoid a sharp collision. I had thought we were free of the buoy astern, but no: the mooring line was now entangled with our propeller. There was a certain amount of profane language but nothing for it but that Tom should don his diving gear and submerge himself and eventually with great skill disentangle the prop (Tom and Ellen had both been divers pre-*Ardevora*: amazing how such talents can come in useful!). So eventually we set off around midnight. Tom, mercifully, did not share the fate of Commander Crabb.

The sail down the east coast of the Baltic was not especially pleasant. Grey, quite windy, short choppy seas which are not really *Ardevora*'s forte. We missed out Klaipėda (former Memel) and Lithuania for lack of time: a pity, as it would have been (eventually) one more country – and one for the courtesy flag! After a hard slog round the Frisches Haff we eventually tied up in Gdynia.

Theo and I were due to leave the boat the next morning and fly back from Warsaw the day after. The only question was how to find transport to see neighbouring and infinitely more interesting Gdansk (Danzig) and on to the airport. Before breakfast I went for a shower ashore and was approached by a most distinguished-looking elderly gentleman (aquiline nose, curly hair) who first addressed me in German. Discovering that English was preferable – for both of us – he asked whether by any chance I was in need of a taxi. So I said 'Indeed, and please come to the boat over there in an hour and take us to Gdansk and anywhere else interesting, and then to the airport'. So, after breakfast and fond farewells we left in the care of Caesar, as I had discovered he was most appropriately called.

Caesar of course knew his stuff and on the way to Gdansk took us past the beach resort of Sopot to Oliwa, where there is a fine papal basilica with the sombre yet elaborate tomb-memorials of many of the Teutonic knights (this was of course former Pomerania, not Poland at all, as Hitler noticed). Next step was an ordinary-looking suburban street, but tree-lined with substantial homes and gardens. 'Would you like to see where Lech Wałęsa lives?' 'Of course,' we said: as he pointed out the house and said he would stay in the car parked opposite. We went across, verified (and photographed) the nameplate by the gate and there viewed through a chink was the leader of Solidarity and soon-to-be President sitting on a garden bench, smoking a pipe with his chum on a Saturday morning! This I did feel inhibited from photographing.

Gdansk is a brilliant example of the total reconstruction of an historic city at which the Poles (as recounted earlier) are past masters. One would not have the slightest notion that it was not totally original (of course much of the existing material will have been reused). The architecture especially of the main square is elaborate and wondrous; the colours gay yet congruent. On the waterfront the great storehouses with their cranes to upper floors testify to the strong Hanseatic heritage. One could have lingered, but it was time to fly to Warsaw.

We stayed in a nice modern Sofitel by the park looking over to the Opera: from there we could walk up the avenue, lined with the great palaces of the former nobility, to the old city with its castle-museum. Again, large over-shoes were the order of the day on highly polished parquet floors. Carrying on northwards we passed through narrower and older streets to the main square: again of course complete and brilliantly rebuilt after total destruction by the Germans in the war. It would repay much more time spent, especially with so many more cultural attractions open now, but though I have been to Krakow since (only shortly later) I have not, alas, returned to Warsaw. Sunday night then saw us emplaning for London and Monday morning in the office…

Ardevora – *Home Waters and High Latitudes*

The next year, 1991, was the last for some time that *Ardevora* was in home or near-home waters. They sailed up the east coast to the Orkneys and on to the Faeroes, where I had planned to meet them for my two-week holiday. Together with my young colleague Jeremy 'Jelly' Lang (of whom much more later) I flew there via Copenhagen: a strange dog-leg caused by the Faeroes' status as a Danish possession. At least this gave us a jolly dinner at a restaurant in the Tivoli gardens, and a stroll later along the Nyhavn.

Landing at the airport perilously placed on a clifftop on one of the subsidiary islands, we took the bus to the capital Tórshavn: we had no difficulty in finding *Ardevora* moored at the quay. I personally had no difficulty either in avoiding the local delicacies of puffin and whale. Though Tórshavn is a pleasant little place – I especially admired the turfed roofs of the houses, being motor-mown by their inhabitants – we were off soon enough for the northwest corner and the crossing to Iceland.

Timing is essential for a passage through the islands, as at certain states of tide a vicious 'rost' or tidal rip occurs: not good for a small boat. We caught glimpses of roaring white water in some adjacent stretches. The passage up to Vestmanna between the main island and Vagar to the west was truly dramatic: the cliffs are supposedly the highest sea cliffs in the world (a claim contested by Molokai in Hawaii; past which – well below their summit – I have flown). Vestmanna was drizzly and dark. Putting to sea again, a fairly bumpy passage took us to the south-east corner of Iceland.

I had just stumbled on watch early and beheld the looming grey shapes of the distinctive striped Icelandic mountains over a grey, troubled sea. A few hours took us into the relative calm of the Seydisfjörd and the little town of Seydisfjördur – the biggest, however, on the east coast. The pier was about a mile from the town. We tied up and made everything shipshape, then the other three headed into town for reconnaissance and provisioning. Alone, I found myself having to move the vessel as that berth was needed for a small coaster approaching. With bow and stern lines and springs there was much cordage to untie and reposition (without letting her escape completely!): but with much pushing and pulling the job was done.

We stayed a couple of days and the weather improved: so much so that in a siesta period I climbed the hill behind as far as a waterfall and decided to take a swim in the (rather icy) pool at its foot. This was the first and only time that while bathing under a waterfall I saw a whale. Said whale was of course in the fjord far below and was breaching impressively. I ran down to the boat and alerted the others. Going into the town, we found a certain stir as some of the inhabitants took some interest in this apparition – a rare but not unknown phenomenon there. The best viewpoint was from the north shore of the fjord opposite *Ardevora* but I think the whale got bored (perhaps not alone in that: the main leisure occupation of the local youth seemed to be driving, alone, headlights on, to the road's end on one side; stopping briefly; returning to the end of the road on the other shore; repeating *ad lib* and *ad infinitum*).

The plan had been for *Ardevora* to circumnavigate Iceland, anticlockwise, thence back to the west coast of Scotland and eventually Cornwall. Jelly and I were to disembark at Iceland's second town, Akureyri, on the north coast and take the car hired by the new arrivals back to Reykjavik. This was not to happen. We set off up the north-east coast for Vopnafjördur. Strange polar effects rendered the compass and DF equipment ineffective, and radar provided the best navigational assistance.

Eventually around midnight we arrived at the Vopnafjördur harbour, to be met by a drunken youth who tried to untie us and, singing hymns the while, to throw Tom into the harbour. (He failed.)

Vopnafjördur was a straggly little village which, however, did boast an unpretentious hotel of reasonable size. We went up for dinner and experienced what must be the slowest service I have ever known – though I think we were the only diners there (I can't remember much about the food). So, the next stage of the journey beckoned.

However, after rounding the point into the more open waters the full force of the gale which was blowing up hit us. As it got to Force 9 – 'severe gale' – Ellen announced that she did not intend to go any further. There being no dissension we turned around and made for Seydisfjördur once more. There Plan B was put into operation.

The 'Akureyri party' were phoned and asked to bring themselves – and the car – to Seydisfjördur instead. However, this would not be for a couple of days. I suggested that we hire some vehicle and spend this time doing some inland touring: often this seems rather attractive when one is otherwise limited to gazing at the coast from seaward. Car was duly hired, itinerary agreed (there is effectively just one road in Iceland so that was not difficult), hotel booked, and we set off for the north-east corner.

Weather in Iceland is extraordinarily fickle, and we moved abruptly from gloom near Seydisfjördur to bright sunshine as we reached Lake Myvatn, a great favourite of UK anglers but notorious for blackflies. I don't think we were troubled. What we did see was forests of lupins. Our destination, Húsavik, was a pretty little fishing town: next stop, the North Pole. After supper I took the car out for an excursion northward: the sun seemed high in the sky and though we were still below the Arctic Circle I wanted to see whether the midnight sun was a myth. I parked above a cliff in a scene of wondrous tranquillity:

ponies gambolled, and curlews peeped, the snow on the mountains across Húsavik grew ever-deeper rose pink. I watched the orb of the sun as it dropped and then started to rise again! I went home to bed tired but happy.

Next day was duller. We felt we should aim for Iceland's northernmost point, which is almost on the Arctic Circle. From a high point we looked down on long, desolate grey beaches; every foot of the shoreline was piled high with logs – either Russian forests autodestruct, or a large proportion of wood-carrying freighters capsize. A mystery. We visited an astounding waterfall – I think Goðafoss – horseshoe-shaped like Niagara or Iguazu. More lupins and back to the boat and next day greet the new crew (Capels youth as usual).

It had been an excellent week, and now of course Jelly and I had the pleasure of a drive to Reykjavik along the southern semicircle of the ring road. The weather was mediocre – it didn't matter, added to the atmosphere. After some attractive if workaday fishing hamlets on the east coast the road bore west. My recollections are of the Blue Lagoon, viewed but not entered, the volcanic Vestmannaeyjar islands (some considerably younger than myself), and above all Thingvellir, the original Mother of Parliaments. The fissure there in fact marks the true boundary between the eastern and western hemispheres: the continental masses collide there. The water in the chasm – only ten feet or so wide – is incredibly clear: as in the Trevi Fountain silver coins were clearly visible in its depths. We drove through Reykjavik on the way to Keflavik Airport: it seemed a well-ordered, pleasant town though I gather that weekends are full of British disco maniacs. And so back to work.

The Winsers duly returned by the west coast of the UK. My spies told me that they had met my American friend John Bockstoce and his Arctic exploration vessel in the Crinan Canal (amazing that it fitted), and that they had next turned up in Troon Marina. I telephoned them there; they were not a little surprised that I was so well informed of their movements! That of course marked *Ardevora en route* to returning to Cornwall after starting from Suffolk: she was never to 'do' the English Channel. This marked the end of her three-year 'running in' before the real thing began with the Atlantic crossing as the trade winds began to blow on the way to far and exotic lands.

Ardevora's *New World: Galapagos*

It was not to be that long before I joined them again, in another hemisphere. There had been constant reports of their transatlantic crossing, arrival in the West Indies, and transit of the Panama Canal *en route* for the Galapagos. Theo (again) and I flew out on a February day to join the three of them (Jelly having been lured away from fund management was now a full crew member). First to Miami where we were in a delightful little Art Deco hotel on South Beach, which in 1992 was only beginning to achieve fame (there were some intimations as it was 'Spring Break' and the promenade was full of college kids). It was bliss after London to wake up early, cross what seemed half a mile of sand and immerse myself in the sea: it was warm and sunny. Our other activity was to visit the Miami Boat Show, on or beside a canal some blocks inland. It was really about motor cruisers and 'sport fishing' vessels. I got a really handsome polo shirt.

Next leg was to Quito: another night, exploration of the very hilly old city, amazement that the street vendors sold items like cigarettes and matches singly. The churches gave a sample of the golden Baroque altars of the conquistadores. I bought Haruko some filigree silver earrings with little rubies, conquistadorette style. A driver took us perhaps thirty miles south on the Pan-American highway towards the mighty volcano Cotopaxi: waking from jet-lag dozing on the way back, I saw collision with a car coming the other way must be imminent (it loomed up in the windscreen); but it was averted.

So, still alive, we flew, stopping at Ecuador's second city Guayaquil, to the Galapagos. There is a short boat ride across from the airport on the small island of Baltra to the main island of Santa Cruz where *Ardevora* lay on a mooring in the little port. It was slightly surreal to see sea lions flopping over dinghies and generally showing adolescent behaviour.

As cruising the Galapagos in one's own boat is effectively forbidden, we were chartering another craft – an old Baltic cutter with cut-down mast, shades of two years earlier – and leaving *Ardevora* in the hands of a helpful Australian couple for the two-week duration. The two weeks were important: most of the commercial cruises of larger vessels are only of one week, which leaves time only for the 'inner circle' of the archipelago. Two weeks, however, permits visiting the outer island ring: as each island differs from its neighbours strikingly, this gives a much more complete impression of the islands than the poor tourists on their bigger ships can obtain.

The skipper was called Pepe and unfortunately he was a disaster: a big, bearded man, he was rude, uncouth and fantastically lazy. Mercifully, after a couple of days, he departed clutching his stomach, assailed by some form of lurgi (certainly not seasickness). His replacement, also called Pepe, thus 'Pepe Dos' as against 'Pepe Uno', was delightful: small, neat, helpful, he could not have been a greater contrast. He stayed the course.

We were a somewhat motley crew: Tom and Ellen and Jelly; Theo and myself; all *Ardevora* as well as James Capel veterans. Also, an elderly couple, the Pullingers. Sir Alan, known to Ellen from governing Benenden, had been a distinguished engineer and mountaineer: Jacqueline, of course French, was frail and perhaps not wholly suited to life on *Suleidae*.

Pepe Dos was the only crew – but didn't we have a cook? In addition, and most important, was Roberto the guide. (It is compulsory to have a licensed guide with every group or charter boat.) He was splendid too: robust and enthusiastic, and famed for his invitations to 'walk over lava'.

The vessel itself was sturdy, but rather dark and cavernous: somewhat claustrophobic, especially my berth, a sort of quarter-berth. So, I normally slept on deck where the night temperature was very agreeable. It was likely to rain for a few minutes in the small hours every day, but this was refreshing and acceptable.

The Galapagos archipelago is surprisingly extensive from one side to the other: indeed – rather as the Shetlands are often shown as an inset on UK maps – the furthest north-west, the two small islands of Wolf and Darwin, are usually shown the same way, and are also too far from the central islands to be included on the commercial one-week cruises. Two weeks makes a huge difference, and we had time to visit these outliers.

One peculiarity is that the islands generally have both a Spanish and an English name. Sometimes it seems more natural to use one rather than the other: for example, 'Hood' rather than 'Española', 'Tower' rather than 'Genovesa', 'James' not 'Santiago'. Conversely no one is likely to call Marchena 'Bindloe', far less Isabela 'Albemarle' or Fernandina 'Narborough'. But the options are there. I have the impression that the Spanish names are increasingly used, whether through anti-imperial political correctness or because of large-scale immigration from the South American mainland, I know not. To add to the confusion the 'Spanish' names can sound very English: including the aforementioned Wolf ('Wenman') and even, remarkably, Darwin ('Culpepper'). (Darwin is perhaps generally better known than whichever Culpep(p)er it was, especially in a Galapagos context.) The English names generally have a fine eighteenth-century Royal Naval ring to them: Hood, Jervis, Duncan; though some so commemorated are lost to posterity.

We set off from Baltra south-easterly and toured the archipelago counter-clockwise. Passages between islands were usually at night: if awake on deck I could enjoy the equatorial darkness and the rhythmic sound of the engines (we never sailed). Then one would wake up anchored off a 'new' island with a day's exploration ahead, if wished. Landing places are strictly limited and controlled and divided into 'wet landings' and 'dry landings'. A modest degree of athleticism was required for some of these: otherwise, it was simply a matter of slipping off the *panga* (rubber dinghy) into the shallow water of a beach – gym shoes in hand (carefully inspected, as the authorities are rightly worried about inter-island contamination of seeds etc.). Each island has its unique eco-system with some species unique to one island, others 'specialising' more or less in the more common species.

The unique attraction of the Galapagos of course is not just the variety but the extraordinary tameness of the animal, bird, and marine life. They are truly fearless and, in many cases, thoroughly inquisitive. Blue-and-red-footed boobies will wander up to one's toes and gaze up hopefully. Sea lions frolic around one when snorkelling: even hammerhead sharks come up close for a look. Marine and land iguanas watch on dispassionately, occasionally shuffling off in search of sex or whatever. (Attenborough though showed some sea-snakes putting a rocket under them!) The two-centuries-old tortoises of Santa Cruz or Isabela of course are not going far.

I don't propose to recount the island itinerary in detail – in any case I would need to consult records and photo albums; but the details could be wearisome. Early on we stopped at Bartolemé where we duly climbed the quite low volcano for the 'iconic' Galapagos view down to the isthmus, beach and Pinnacle Rock. Hood, or Española, was another early call, with cliffs, crashing waves and the only colony of waved albatrosses. Everywhere of course were boobies, masked or unmasked, blue- or red-footed, and frigate birds: these last looking quite absurd perched on spiky little trees self-consciously exhibiting their swollen scarlet front to putative mates. In the sky, they were magnificent; so, no doubt, is the Galapagos hawk, but they are hard to find, and I don't think we saw one flying. Cormorants of course do fly – except, natch, the endemic flightless cormorant. The largest flamingo population is concentrated – wouldn't you guess – on Punta *Cormorant* on Floreana. The finches which inspired Charles Darwin to change our entire concept of the natural world and evolution are of course totally unremarkable little brown birds, which only an obsessed specialist would find the time to observe. Finally, I should mention the Galapagos penguin: a small item which on the equator is several thousand miles further north than one might expect: blame the Humboldt Current!

After lunch was of course siesta time, but also often time for Roberto to announce some naturalist expedition: often 'walk over lava' should whichever island's terrain permit. I was pleased that alone of the company I never missed one of these. One day Roberto promised that the walk on lava would bring us to a sort of waterhole where an especially rare bird was likely to be found. Theo (I think) and I dutifully followed him, keeping silent: as we neared the place we crept along, as stealthily as on any stalk in Sutherland. At the edge of the pool, we saw the bird swimming, then flying off affrighted. It was a common-or-garden coot.

The snorkelling was gorgeous. I don't feel any need despite a Seychelles experience to load myself with aqualungs and compressed air but just to don a mask, snorkel and flippers and submerge myself I feel is to enter a different and magical world – so easily! The coral reefs we encountered around the islands were glorious: no hint of any decay, and extraordinary multi-coloured creatures abundant. The most famous and probably the best reef is the 'Devil's Crown' off Floreana: as its name suggests, as remarkable above the waterline as below. Besides the seals and sea lions – difficult to tell which was which – were the sharks: the hammerheads were perfectly behaved, unthreatening, unfrightening. All sorts of bizarre reef fish – some two-dimensional – abounded. All this is endangered by fishermen from the mainland, if not China.

So, the days passed. I remember one languid siesta afternoon anchored by a cave off Isabela, where even the swing of the anchor took one from north to south hemisphere and back every few minutes (perhaps I exaggerate slightly). I spent the time reading Scott's *Old Mortality*, whose plot was suggested to Sir Walter by my ancestor Joseph Train, 'the antiquarian correspondent of Sir Walter Scott': an act of slightly tedious family piety. I have some of his 'curios' which did not end up at Abbotsford, including Old Mortality's mell or mallet – which in fact I have lent there. Then we anchored off James when Jelly and our guide set off up the steep hillside with a shotgun to reduce the number of wild goats which the eighteenth-century RN seamen had kindly introduced (together with the rats). (This failed.)

As always, the return was anti-climactic: I take away only a memory of Miami International Airport which persuaded me never to set forth in the place again. But this resolve must have been abandoned for a later *Ardevora* episode, Costa Rica.

In the autumn the teenage management of James Capel deemed my services unnecessary, and a new phase unwound. Leaving aside various investment activities and other efforts at gainful employment, I could now spend my time more freely than in commuting daily to the City or Docklands. For the remainder of 1992 the nearest to 'sailing' (in fact 'Sailing' © Rod Stewart) was a trip on an RN frigate, HMS *Brilliant*, courtesy of my good friend James B-N. I described this more fully in an earlier section, but observe only that RN ships make excellent cruise liners: their smooth gas turbine engines are a great improvement on noisy reverberating diesels, and the Captain's cabin makes an excellent retreat. This trip, from Greece to Romania through Turkey, and back to Sicily, is not for now: it and a later voyage when James had been promoted to *Invincible* (and Captain of the Fleet) will be described in the main narrative.

Ardevora *in the Antipodes*

However, in the interim since the Galapagos, I had of course been keeping in touch with the *Ardevora* crew: as much as was possible when they were crossing the Pacific with enviable stops at places such as Easter Island, Pitcairn, Tahiti and Fiji (Tahiti I gather was not a success). But this marathon of long Pacific stretches was due eventually to end in New Zealand and so it was arranged that I would join them in Auckland in February, cruise round New Zealand and eventually cross the Tasman to Australia: two months could now be set aside for this.

So it was that, via Singapore on admirable Singapore Airlines, I arrived in Auckland in early 1994. It's a compact place and *Ardevora* was reasonably close, at a dock with much evidence of America's Cup-related activity. It was great to see them again, quite the tanned, salt-encrusted ocean voyagers. Over the evening refreshment there was a discussion about 'what next?' The intention had been to sail down south, round New Zealand's Cape Horn equivalent and through the Foveaux Strait, then cruise the evidently amazing Fiordland (sic) on the west coast; then across to Sydney.

However, though on the first night we were sticking to this, twenty-four hours later (and perhaps helped by some Laphroaig) we decided we were mice not men and would adopt Plan B. Plan B was to park *Ardevora* for a few weeks, hire a suitable vehicle, see as much of New Zealand as possible, and eventually leave for Australia via Cape Reinga, the northernmost point of North Island. Our reasons were: the yard had been slow, and the ship was not quite ready: the tail-end of a hurricane was still hanging around; and there was probably not enough time – they had some deadline to be in Sydney. To tell the truth, I was delighted by this as Plan A would probably have involved little other than sightings of inhospitable grey capes amid days of mountainous seas; while Plan B offered the chance to see a large proportion of what was touted as one of earth's most beautiful countries. It would have been a shame to come all this way and hardly see it! In fact it was a greatly extended version of the Icelandic road jaunt.

So, having arranged the vehicle and taken an exploratory tour north of Auckland we moved *Ardevora* up the Hauraki Gulf to

Gulf Harbour, and next day started our Grand Tour. The vehicle was ideal: an Isuzu (?) minivan with, behind the two front seats, two benches athwartships and luggage space behind. Height ideal for viewing *en route*, the after part being set higher than the driver's and co-driver's front seats. As on board ship, we had effectively two 'watches': for either morning or afternoon Tom and Ellen would be driver and co-driver, while Jelly and I relaxed on the 'back benches' and in the afternoon the roles were reversed.

Our first day going southwards on North Island was unpropitious: it poured with rain (that hurricane tail-end again), and my impressions of the famed Rotorua were rather negative. Geysers and mud are all very well but perhaps not best viewed in steady drizzle. We spent the night in Wellington and at least felt we were getting somewhere, for the next day brought the ferry over the Cook Strait to Picton on South Island. It was exciting to sail up the long 'sea loch' and on disembarking find our B & B for the night.

There was a certain West Highland feeling with a slight chill in the air in the morning. Picton, an attractive little place, has one special attraction in the form of the old windjammer *Edwin Fox*, the second oldest (barely) surviving merchant sailing ship, which carried in turn emigrants, convicts, troops, livestock, minerals between the Antipodes, Europe and China. It has apparently proved impossible to restore the upper deck but even the 'bowels' are evocative. Nothing more so than a board enumerating the convicts transported to Australia, among whom a Mr Barr from Ayrshire convicted of sheep-stealing. Hmm…

Heading roughly north-west, we were enchanted by the whole Marlborough Sounds area: if I have mentioned the Scottish Highlands, this seemed a mélange of the best of that and the West Indies and Greece. Deeply indented 'sea lochs', wooded, steep-to, lush. A complex array of offshore islands, some sizeable: so it was hard to tell what was mainland and what island. At length we turned towards the west coast and drove through the time-warp little town of Nelson, a complete evocation of the Art Deco Thirties. Thence, cutting off the remote north-west tip, to the aptly named Westport whence the coast road led down through the (as I remember) equally apposite Greymouth. It all had that very 'west coast' feeling that I may have remarked on earlier: indefinable, but high hills tumbling down to (often) raised beaches often feature. Here that applied in spades: there is little higher anywhere than Mount Cook and glaciers from its massif came down virtually to sea level, mingling with the ancient woods. We spent a night in the little village of Franz Josef close under the glacier of that name: then on to Haast where one leaves the coast for the centre and south.

I should mention here our sleeping arrangements: armed with a useful volume of bed and breakfasts we chose and booked the next day's stop, usually the night before. B & Bs in New Zealand are generally quite excellent and often form a large part of a substantial house with a pretty garden, in some tranquil setting. Of course, it was self-catering but even after sailing halfway round the world Ellen was up for the task and produced nourishing meals. (We would stop at local stores for provisions, and it was extraordinary that, though perfectly pleasant, the shopkeepers etc. evinced no curiosity whatsoever about where we might have come from.) The not unrelated quirk with the B & B owners was that they got into a frightful tizzy if we had not arrived by about 5 o'clock, when a good four hours or so of daylight remained. Once wise to this, a precautionary phone call often worked: nevertheless, one sensed that we should not push it, and it did rather curtail our time on the road.

The valley and climb inland I remember was quite gorgeous, on a bright late summer morning. We heard the bellbird, which beats the nightingale every time (and does not have the same compulsion to be 'up with the lark'!). The road rose up through the epic woodland with the river rushing below; and eventually passing above Lake Wanaka on the way to Lake Wakatipu and Queenstown, fun capital of New Zealand. We must have spent two nights in Queenstown as among the many attractions advertised Jelly and I found the 'Awesome Foursome' and signed up for the day.

The 'Foursome' consisted of a drive some way up the Shotover River to a spot where it becomes a true canyon, where we embarked on a 'jet boat' which zoomed up the river, coming alarmingly close to the overhanging cliffs each side, to a gravel spit whence we saw the bridge high above. This was the only stage requiring effort, in climbing the steep hillside to the bridge, whence we were destined to jump in (what was then) the highest bungee jump in the world.

There was a little platform overhanging the river far below, a medley of ropes and a few grinning Kiwis. 'You'll be the first, Dugald,' said the evident leader. Gee, thanks: no one to follow and observe the 'technique'. Nothing for it but to shuffle onto what looked remarkably like a scaffold for a hanging. So, I jumped off it. It was the most remarkable feeling: the free fall (head first: I had assumed it would be like diving), then the rebound which was both very powerful and beautifully smooth. After a few more levitations I was lowered down, and hands guided me into a waiting boat and thence to shore. There one could watch others' technique (there were perhaps half a dozen in our group). Jelly having done the same thing from above had clearly learnt from it and when his turn came stepped off the 'scaffold' feet first, with nonchalance and elegance.

Next, a helicopter ride down-canyon to the white-water rafting station. The thing's rotor blades at times seemed alarmingly close to the canyon walls, but we made it. The rafting was a different sort of experience. A lot of preparation of lifejackets, 'seat belts' etc. What was perhaps surprising was how soft and 'bendy' the thing was. What was not surprising was that we got very wet indeed – as warned. It was good fun but insufficiently terrifying.

Arriving back at our hotel, having had a shower, I had seen a Tiger Moth at the airfield. I thought it might be worth going down to see whether there was a chance of a flight: it would still be light for a while, and I had my pilot's licence with me. To my delight it was possible to take the craft up straight away (I can't remember if I had a chaperone – probably, but I was the pilot). As always it was great to cruise around and view this remarkable scenery of lakes and mountains (the Remarkables – which contain a Ben Lomond: now that is remarkable!). So, the day had seen the achievement of an awesome fivesome…

Our turning point on the tour was to be New Zealand's number one icon, Milford Sound. If we could not get there by sea, we could reach it by land. It is, however, an enormous detour as, though not far as the crow flies, Milford Sound is reached by driving a long way south, then west to Te Anau (town and lake), then north to Milford Sound. Fiordland National Park, as it is called, is like nowhere else I have seen, the descent to the sea covered by the forest principally of southern beech trees clinging to the precipitous mountainside, with a multitude of waterfalls. From the small area of flat land by the shore one can see the awesome or remarkable scenery of the Sound, with Mitre Peak dominant in the centre. Inevitably we took a boat trip out on the Sound, but of course as one gets nearer the peak it itself is lost to view: though the astounding waterfalls close-up compensate. Nevertheless, it was lovely to be out on the water: a foretaste of the Tasman. The other sounds and fjords, such as Doubtful Sound, would have been wonderful to explore: but personally, I was glad to exchange that for the proper tour of the country.

Reversing our tracks, we were approaching the high country of Canterbury and Mount Cook. Apart from the very occasional incurious native the only beings met were about a million sheep: we waited patiently until they swarmed past. Approaching the B & B stop nearest Mount Cook (around 5 p.m.) we saw an airstrip with a few small planes and gliders. Tom and Jelly had already booked a tennis court, but Ellen and I thought we would go and see if we could repeat my recent coup at Queenstown.

Indeed, the glider pilot agreed to take Ellen (first of course) and then myself up for an hour's gliding lesson. I asked whether I could sit alongside the pilot of the towing aircraft to learn how the procedure for towing and releasing worked. He said that unfortunately that wasn't allowed: but then the pilot of the other small plane nearby, overhearing, asked if I would like to go up in it for that hour. Of course, I said yes, but was amazed when he asked whether I would like to be put down as Captain myself: again of course I readily agreed. (The consequence is that, since entries in one's logbook are in Greenwich Mean Time, I entered my early evening flight as being in the small hours of the morning – I have no night rating!) Then we made straight for the imposing mass of Mount Cook and had a good look at it – and mercifully not at any other sightseeing light aircraft, which have a habit of crashing… Then it was time for my gliding: a very enjoyable and interesting contrast. But with the evening coming on the thermals were weakening and my flight was probably less prolonged than Ellen's.

Next, down to the sea by Christchurch (sic) and Akaroa: had we stuck to Plan A this was perhaps as much as we would have seen. Fine city though Christchurch is, and this of course was before the devastating earthquake, a more memorable stop was at Kaikoura further north, which is renowned for its sperm whales. We joined one of the several excursion boats and the whales duly appeared and obliged. An awesome sight up close.

The final South Island experience was the wine-producing area of Marlborough, now renowned the world over especially for its Chardonnays (though I personally prefer the Sauvignons). While the pioneer, at least in achieving worldwide fame (and the most expensive) is Cloudy Bay, we found the people there less than wholly welcoming, perhaps over-visited. Infinitely more friendly and enthusiastic were those at Hunter – and I think the wines were better too.

Traversing North Island again, we dropped off the van and were reunited with *Ardevora*. The last intermediate stop before rounding Cape Reinga and departing New Zealand was the Bay of Islands. This is as 'historic' as it gets in NZ as the earliest treaties were signed there and there are numerous 'heritage' sites. It is also a remarkably beautiful area with its wide expanse of bay with many inlets – and islands. A large German cruise ship, the *Bremen*, lay at anchor.

Cape Reinga left behind, it was a course exactly due west – 270° – to Sydney. There was no wind for two to three days. Alone on watch – one would be fully awake, one could be sleeping nearby but at readiness if desired, the other two fully off-watch in their bunks – all that was needed was to press an autopilot button if straying a few yards off course, then another a minute later to resume. I read *Anna Karenina* in these peaceful conditions. However, the customary Tasman gale did eventually materialise, and we were violently thrown around. When its wind at length abated of course the seas did not: in a lumpy, confused sea the engine was needed, but following tradition refused to start: salt water in the works diagnosed. Eventually of course the sea also decayed to total calm, and we were left becalmed like the Ancient Mariner. For two days we floated up and down on the tide, with the loom of the lights of Sydney tantalisingly close on the western horizon. Occasional fishing vessels gave us curious looks. Then when I was alone on deck, just after dawn I felt the gentlest of breezes: setting some sail I set course too for Sydney Harbour Heads and awakened the rest to the happy news.

After the unaccustomed experience of evading ocean-going vessels while tacking through the harbour entrance, we had to anchor in Watsons Bay for customs and immigration. No problems and a genial welcome, but the Australians are very strict, and one does have to throw away all food – even tinned! When we were free of all that we prepared to up-anchor for the final move up to our berth at the Cruising Club of Australia near the Harbour Bridge. I happened to be in the cockpit when a police launch approached and a copper said, 'Would you loike a tow?' This I most gladly accepted on behalf of the company. So it was that we came to a new continent, towed in by the police…

Shortly after we had tied up and tidied, I ventured ashore to hire a car. Walking up the hill I wondered if we had in fact come to the wrong continent, as everyone seemed to be Chinese or other Asian.

I left *Ardevora* at the hospitable CCA soon after and went up to stay with Warren Hogan in a northern suburb of Sydney. (Warren, an even older friend of Haruko's from Washington days and retired Professor of Economics at the University of Sydney, I also knew well as he came to England almost every year and stayed with us, and he and I used to make museum day trips – submarines at Gosport, RAF at Duxford etc; he was a great expert on these matters, and I greatly miss him.) He showed me all around Sydney and further afield, in particular (later on) a trip out to the Blue Mountains to the west, as well as more obvious city sights like the Opera House and Botanic Gardens. In the latter, on I think Easter Monday, we were walking around and greeted by a friend: 'G'day, Warren!' 'Aw, g'day Bill', followed by inconsequential chat and introduction of self. On parting Warren said, 'That was our revered Governor-General.' So, the only person I met quasi-socially in Australia was the top man! (Bill Hayden.)

I flew up for a few days on Hayman Island for beach R & R in the Whitsundays: of course, I took an excursion to the Great Barrier Reef itself, which I found slightly anti-climactic after the Galapagos (and it was certainly outshone later, by the Bay Islands in Honduras). I suspect it was becoming victim of some sort of coral blight. Apart from a briefish snorkel, we cruised over the reef in a glass-bottomed boat filled mostly with young Japanese honeymooners.

This and at least one other expedition (or transfer) was by De Havilland seaplane. I was in the co-pilot's seat and the transferable control column was handed over to me: unfortunately, there was but one set of pedals, for the pilot, and without these one cannot really fly an aircraft…

In Sydney I also stayed a few nights in a high-rise hotel overlooking the quays and Opera House, Harbour Bridge, naval base *et al.* The views were terrific. I took a fast boat down the harbour to Manly, a worthwhile outing to Sydney's premier beach resort. Bondi Beach, on the open sea to the south of the harbour entrance, I had earlier visited with Warren by car, going round by Botany Bay (where somewhat more willing immigrants now land at the nearby international airport). And from that airport I shortly departed for the long but easy flight to London – SIA again.

Meanwhile *Ardevora* and crew were heading north: I had occasional reports but have no knowledge of the places visited. Ellen later said that the Solomons were the place she had most liked on the entire voyage. There was also New Guinea (where Ellen queued at a bank counter beside a man wearing only a penis gourd) and other Coral Sea places: of interest to Second World War naval historians. At some point, however, I understand Ellen decided to fly home and Tom and Jelly sailed on alone, past the Philippines, to Hong Kong. Then Jelly found some friends he had signed up for the next leg to Japan: Tom flew back.

I had of course rather hoped that I could be with them in Japan but other commitments – and perhaps 'full boat' – conspired against that. So, I wrote a fairly comprehensive practical guide to the place, and especially to the Japan Sea coast which they would be sailing up on the way to points further north. The Winsers came back for Japan, but then left *Ardevora* under Jelly's captaincy for what must have been a fascinating sail to Sakhalin, Kamchatka and eventually the Aleutians and Alaska. The owners rejoined in British Columbia, by all accounts a superb cruising ground. Then down the west coast of USA and Mexico and to Costa Rica, where I was able to rejoin them later and shall write shortly.

Interlude: *Brittany Ferry?*

Rosemary, the lawyer girl friend of my former Capels partner Ian Cole owned a pretty 36-foot Swan which needed to be brought back from La Trinité in southern Brittany. So we caught the Eurostar in time for dinner and a modest night in Paris before the TGV for the holiday regions. I hadn't been there before though familiar with most of Brittany: the characteristic array of restaurants along the quayside were as always a tonic, even though most of their piscine offerings are anathema to me.

We sailed the next morning out through the dangerous Quiberon Bay where the French fleet was pursued and largely destroyed by Admiral Hawke in the battle of that name, the final triumph of 1759, the *Annus Mirabilis* which put paid to France's anti-British ambitions. Leaving Belle-Île to port we were on our way north-west up the southern Breton coast with, alas, no more delightful little stops at the pretty little towns thereon. Meanwhile Ian, no sailor he, had nonchalantly retired to his bunk in which he would remain almost to the end of the voyage at Plymouth. This was apparently expected. It left Rosemary and me to share the deck but of course from time to time one of us would need some sleep. Night came on and the real problem was that the autopilot was inoperative: when alone at the wheel, therefore, one could literally not let go of it for any reason otherwise the boat, very responsive to the helm, would slew all over the place. This did complicate life.

Dawn, however, came on and there were now two of us. We were fast approaching the dreaded Pointe du Raz, the long rocky extremity of Brittany, notorious for wild seas, reefs and shipwrecks. Though there are inshore passages simple enough in settled weather and the right state of tide, we deemed it prudent to wait to turn north far beyond the outlying lighthouse: then up Channel to Blighty, remembering how the Navy had ceaselessly patrolled these waters blockading France in the

Napoleonic wars. We approached Plymouth and Ian appeared, fresh as a daisy and exuding good cheer (and nautical suggestions...). It had been good to have 'a bit of a sail', however brief, at least once that year and feel we had earned it.

Ardevora again: *Central America – Canal Zone and Coral Islands*

Costa Rica I thought – and am clearly not alone in this – an enchanting little country. I stayed a few days in San José – itself not uninteresting with museum of pre-Columbian gold and other artefacts, a generally park-like, laid-back air, no army, and a host of Hemingway-lookalike American retirees. The point, however, is to use it as a base for very varied day expeditions. One was to the Arenal lake and volcano: the latter still spews out brilliant orange lava flows. Then the Manuel Antonio Park (one of many nature reserves) for the bird life, especially the magnificent quetzal: this green bird is, however, very elusive, and I never saw one. However, there were scarlet macaws, at least as colourful; and I know not what else. (I do feel, however, that in these national parks the majority of birds are of the 'small, brown' variety and those one sees from an English garden window – spotted woodpeckers, jays, magpies, pheasants, robins, tits etc. are at least as colourful and 'exotic'.)

There was no 'elusiveness' problem about the sloth viewed hanging from a roadside tree in the banana plantations bordering the Caribbean, on the last excursion. The guide pointed it out; someone asked how he knew it was there; he answered that it had been there the day before last and could hardly have gone far! Compared with the sparkling Pacific coast, the Caribbean was dark, humid and gloomy – rather an unwelcome surprise. But it was only one day. The sloth seemed happy, indeed slothful, and had hardly moved.

I took a taxi the nearly 100 kilometers to Puntarenas where I had arranged to meet the *Ardevora* lot. First impressions were not favourable as all houses in and around the town were encaged in metal bars right to the property's boundaries: implying I presumed a somewhat lawless population. However, the hotel I had booked for one night was very pleasant, in a garden setting. In that garden a company of people at one point started up a dance with a catchy tune and amusing 'steps' – *Macarena*. The tune went round and round in my head and had I realised how it would later catch on in the UK and US I would have put in a bid for the rights!

Afloat again, the passage down the Costa Rican coast was extraordinarily tranquil. For days on end, we motored in a flat calm, anchoring in deserted bays with just the jungle backdrop, and frequently taking swims in the pellucid water. We did make a stop at a little place called Golfito where, after some shopping, we walked around another national park where we saw leafcutter ants and little brown birds ... and even a few scarlet macaws. Resplendent quetzals I believe were not on the menu.

Passing into Panamanian waters, little other than a change of courtesy flag seemed to be called for. Heading up towards the canal, we passed some sizeable and steep-to islands, where more recreational craft were visible. At length, we picked up a mooring at the Panama Canal Yacht Club, which had a pleasant woody clubhouse whence we could view the comings and goings. (I still wear their smart green T-shirt.) There was a longish taxi trip around the outskirts of Panama City in search of something or other for the boat: later I enjoyed walking around the small area of the old town, where a sense of the Spanish Main seemed to linger. Then next morning, having embarked the compulsory pilot, we were off: starting with passing under the Bridge of the Americas, passing a USS Bunker Hill class guided missile cruiser (last encountered, indeed lunched on, two years previously in Thessaloniki); then the first flight of locks. It is quite interesting, as a relatively small yacht, being 'paired' through these with Nissan car carriers, designed with about one foot of clearance from the lock walls each side. It was also a long way to throw up a line. Once through the 'staircase' there is an alternation of narrow stretches (hewn out of the hills at considerable human cost in the building of the canal) and sizeable lakes. These were rather pretty in a surreal sort of way: first that one had only a succession of buoys to distinguish the channel from the shallow lake – it all looked the same; second, that from this isolated trees or islets appeared; third, that one would unexpectedly meet a largish merchant vessel coming the other way; and last, that there were no speedboats, motor cruisers, sailing boats or other recreational vessels on the wide expanses of lakes.

Traversing the canal is forbidden after a certain early evening hour: so, we anchored in a bay of the last lake before the lock 'staircase' down to the Caribbean, and dropped the pilot, who would be replaced by another from Colón, the canal terminal. As usual when anchored one's first priority was to jump in for a swim. The existence of caimans (caimen?) (alligators of a sort) had not been understood, but apparently, they pose little threat; and other people were swimming too.

In the morning, the new pilot embarked, we set off for the last, dead straight, leg to Colón. As we were descending the locks the heavens opened in a way I have hardly known, the sky darkened to inkiness, but at least it was warm. Colón is evidently a frightful place; barred windows, armed guards everywhere, a feeling of menace; more immediately there was the nuisance (principally for Tom who had to deal with it) of the bureaucracy of leaving Panama, with carnets, passes, all sorts of documents required. A visit to the supermarket added to the sense of a town under siege.

Tom and Ellen were now flying home so we saw them off: Jelly now skipper, Robin Dutton who had built *Ardevora* at Woodbridge, and myself making up the three-strong crew. We set off northwards in quite a chop: usually only one on deck, as a result of which I was the only one to claim an extra country. I was on deck one night when the lights of the Colombian island of Providencia began to show ahead. Over the next two hours it came alongside and then dwindled astern to nothingness.

When whichever it was came on deck, I was able to say they had missed an entire country... Another curious episode – I think others may have been on deck too – was when we came across a sort of dugout canoe, with about a dozen dark-skinned men paddling furiously. This must have been at least fifty miles off the Nicaraguan coast: presumably they were fishermen (there were reefs not too far away), but there were big seas and it looked perilous – they were far from home.

Having turned west again, 'rounding' Nicaragua, I was fast asleep but heard the change of engine note, came on deck to a magical still night, with twinkling lights of boats and a village, as we dropped anchor after this long passage, at Roatán island in Honduras. In the morning the necessary check-in procedures took us into the little town: I remember best the charming little wooden houses on stilts, presumably homes of fisherfolk. In succeeding days, we motored around the island to the most recommended snorkelling spots; and indeed, the underwater scene was extraordinary and exotic. But the more ambitious excursion was the best part of a day's sail to the minute archipelago of Los Cochinos, atolls much nearer the Honduran mainland, whose mountains rose sharply from the shore to the south. We anchored off a tiny island, surrounded by sand, with a few palm trees – and a village shop for perhaps half a dozen houses! It was simple and natural just to swim ashore. It was the purest Alexander Selkirk/Robinson Crusoe. We sailed back to Roatán, and I took the plane to New York and home.

Transatlantic: *Ardevora Returns*

The next time I saw *Ardevora* could not have been more different from viewing semi-tropical reef fish underwater. As the aircraft began its descent into St John's, Newfoundland I looked out of the window and thought, surely these large grey things parked in various bays could not be icebergs. But they were.

In the intervening period *Ardevora* had sailed up through the Caribbean via Belize and over-wintered in Fort Lauderdale,

Florida: then in spring up the Intracoastal Waterway and eventually into New York harbour, whence by New England and Canada's Maritime Provinces to St John's. I should have loved to sail into New York, which I know so well; and of course, I have already sailed up Long Island Sound and the Massachusetts coast. I haven't yet seen a detailed account of that East Coast voyage; nor indeed of the West Coast, as I mentioned earlier.

As had become customary, a day or two were spent looking around landside: in and around St John's and a brief tour down further south. Even for one used to Sutherland and the Outer Hebrides, this was the rockiest inhabited landscape I had seen. Especially in St John's, a compact and pleasant town curving round its bay with the residential quarter mainly occupying the heights above the harbour, it was extraordinary how thin the layer of soil was and how mossy rock outcrops were ubiquitous.

Ellen was put on the plane home and four of us – an amiable if somewhat somnolent American had joined us – set off for the eastern hemisphere the next morning. A day out, we did not exactly meet the legendary fogs of the Grand Banks, but visibility was not great. Then the icebergs started to appear: curiously, all to the north and thus on the port side. They were strung out like rugby three-quarters and appeared at regular intervals. Scanning the horizon, one would almost sense, but not see, something which a few minutes later became a small white smudge and then morphed into a definite berg. It was rather thrilling. We gave them monikers in alphabetical order, like hurricanes and storms. When it became night however, we wondered when the icebergs might decide to lie dead ahead for a '*Titanic*' ambush. One of us was posted for a stretch of, I think, an hour at the bow, dressed like the Michelin man (it was extremely cold) and equipped with a walkie-talkie with which, hopefully, to alert the helmsman if and when a berg loomed up ahead. However, the night passed without incident or impact. We may or may not have passed directly over the *Titanic*.

By then of course the engine had performed its habitual role of packing up, so we were sailing; and in quite strong wind, so even with reduced sail we were travelling fast. No sudden reversing in panic! Over the days ahead, however, the wind grew lighter and eventually dwindled to nothing. The weather maps showed we were now in the mid-Atlantic zone, where this happens. No engine, no progress. The (rather early model) satnav at one point showed we would arrive in Cornwall on Christmas Eve (this was mid-July). However, eventually a breath of wind developed into a good wind, and we made good progress towards the Scillies and home, sighting nothing except some porpoises and a fierce-looking leaping shark.

I write 'towards the Scillies' but these were nearly our final, or at least intermediate, destination. Once again, the wind had died completely as we approached the islands. It was a moonless night and, on watch alone, I could do nothing as we got closer and closer to the north-east islands, with no steerage way. I did feel it advisable to call the skipper as we drifted – or indeed were swept – nearer and nearer to St Martin's (not only are the Scillies richly endowed with savage rocks and reefs, but also with fierce tidal streams). Though the radar showed we were barely yards away, we missed and eventually sailed on for Land's End and England. (Ever since, I have had some sympathy for Sir Cloudesley Shovell!)

Past Land's End, round the Lizard, the proximity of the green summer countryside seemed so familiar and yet strange after a fortnight at sea: how much more so to those who had spent over three years sailing to the end of the world and back! The final leg was tacking up into Falmouth Bay, between Henry VIII's castles, and picking up a buoy at St Mawes. Quite a little reception committee was awaiting us. We had strung together the courtesy ensigns of all the countries *Ardevora* had visited: they stretched in the 'dressed overall' mode from stem to stern, over mainmast and mizzen top. It was a remarkable achievement by the Winsers – and indeed by Jelly, from neophyte fund manager to seasoned ocean skipper.

Ardevora – *Final Act: Ireland*

My final *Ardevora* trip was the following year. They had sailed across to Bantry Bay in Ireland to join a 'cruise in company' run jointly by the Royal Cruising Club (Tom and Ellen were members and contributed accounts to their excellent annual *Roving Commissions*), the Cruising Club of America and the New York Yacht Club. I flew from Stansted on a glorious July day: by the time we landed in Cork it was a steady dark drizzle. I drove a hired car down the minor roads to Castletownbere where the boat was: there was a bureaucratic problem about the returning crew member I was replacing, rather than myself who had hired it, returning it to the airport, but the fortuitous appearance of a police car I'd seen earlier outside the (closed) police station solved this by certifying his driving licence. It continued to rain.

The morning dawned absolutely brilliant, and we sailed in light airs up the bay to moor opposite Bantry House, the centre of festivities. The house is a large and distinctly Irish Georgian edifice, and marquees were sited on the lawns high above the bay, where we drank and dined and enjoyed a glorious sunset admiring the assembled yachts at their moorings.

The morning began with heavy rain and a rapid departure from Bantry. However, as we approached the entrance of the bay the sun came out and all was breezy and bright. It was a good sail back. This time the eventual destination was Plymouth where the natural berth was Sutton Harbour, of which Ellen was chairman and Tom, myself and other friends shareholders. We did not stop at the Scillies, either intentionally or unintentionally. Coasting past the Lizard was beginning to become rather familiar (and was to become more so).

Chartering 1:
West Indies

The early years of the millennium were sailing-free: after a major operation in 2004 it was difficult for a couple of years (unless one counts cruising on the Canal du Nivernais in May 2005 in Ran Meinertzhagen's splendid old Dutch barge, together with Nicky Talbot Rice). For several years friend Dick Spooner had invited me to join Laurel and him and Bernard and Anne Jenkin in chartering a boat somewhere in the West Indies: very tempting in January and February, but alas not possible. In early 2007, however, I could see no reason not to accept, and we all (except at first Anne) flew to St Lucia, where we drove over to Marigot Bay, a very pretty harbour and marina/hotel complex halfway up the west coast. After a night in the hotel following an excellent dinner in their separate restaurant across the harbour, we met our boat in the morning and had the customary briefing.

Our planned route was northward, up the western (or leeward) side of the island chain, from St Lucia to Martinique, Dominica, the Saintes, and Guadeloupe – and return. It was pleasant sailing weather throughout: very noticeable though that when traversing the passages between the islands, open to the wind from the east, it really blew. In Martinique we navigated the surprisingly complex and congested bay south of Fort-de-France and anchored in the Mouillage des Trois Îlets. Ashore was pleasingly French: we found a nice café, and Bernard talked to his constituents,who may have thought he was speaking from Essex or Westminster. A more open anchorage, and even prettier place, was St Pierre further north. The Martinique Passage between Martinique and Dominica in fact marks the transition from Windward to Leeward islands: the wind blew hard on each passage in the chain. Dominica was simple and unspoilt: we sailed past Roseau, the capital, and anchored off Portsmouth, the little town in Prince Rupert Bay. (Anchoring is not entirely simple in these parts: the shore is steep-to, so there is a very limited 'band' of the right depth; often with other boats already there it can be hard to find a spot avoiding the risk of collision when swinging.)

The highlight of Dominica was a trip up to and on the Indian River, not far from Portsmouth. Here amazing tall banyan-type trees and lianas overhung the tranquil river: gliding along on a little boat one could sense the jungle life behind. Dominica seemed remarkably unspoilt – I suspect rather more so than its near-namesake the Dominican Republic further north.

Between Dominica and Guadeloupe lie the little islands of the Saintes – scene of Admiral Rodney's decisive victory over the French in 1782. The islands are not unlike subtropical Scillies, grouped around a sheltered body of water, with a good anchorage in front of the main, incredibly picturesque, town, Petite Anse. The Saintes are in fact part of Guadeloupe, which of course is a *Département d'Outre-Mer* of France (like Martinique): it proved an enchanting introduction to the larger territory. They have been colonised by both French and British, twice by each.

The scale of Guadeloupe itself of course is quite different. There was a long reach with Basse-Terre – which is actually quite high – to port. The main marina in which we found a berth is reached through a fairly narrow channel leading to Pointe-à-Pitre, the main town, to which I took a taxi on some errand which now escapes me. Meanwhile the excitement was the arrival of Anne Jenkin: the crew was now complete for the return southwards. I don't think we varied it enormously: on reaching northern St Lucia we anchored for the penultimate night in Rodney Bay, a wide and open anchorage featuring on shore the Sandals resort. Then back to Marigot and handing back the vessel. The others had an earlier flight, so I had a night alone in the hotel, enjoying the atmosphere of the islet, and the next day took a leisurely taxi ride by way of the south-west coast, mainly to view the remarkable and celebrated Pitons, but also from the heights near the airport the view south to St Vincent and the Grenadines. Then airport and home. My first post-op sail had been a real success and I could see how it had become a Spooner/Jenkin habit for the end of the British winter.

While talking 'of shoes and ships and sealing-wax' one day Dick had mused about where in Europe we might repeat the charter experience in the summer. Recalling *Ardevora* a decade earlier I recommended the Baltic with some enthusiasm, with the Stockholm skerries especially in mind. Resulting from this, Dick announced in April that he had organised a boat, not in Sweden, but on Fyn in Denmark.

Chartering 2: Denmark with Nicky

Dick and I embarked on a Ryanair flight to Billund: an otherwise, I believe, unremarkable town of central Jutland which, however, is the headquarters of Legoland, so there I imagine most of our fellow-passengers were bound. However, having picked up a car, we were eastward bound to the island of Fyn where we would find our boat at Kerteminde. The Jutland countryside is pleasantly agricultural, and we stopped in one or two pretty villages with half-timbered houses and great barns before Fredericia and the bridge over the Little Belt to Fyn.

Bypassing Odense – which we were leaving for the return journey – we stopped at the charming little town of Munkebo at the head of the inlet where Kerteminde lies. Munkebo has some remarkable 'longhouse-type' half-timbered edifices, now an enticing-looking restaurant and inn. Nearby, across the lagoon, is one of the most remarkable ancient sites of Denmark, the 'ship grave' at Ladby: this was given due attention also. The skeletal remains of the ship are, of course, under a great earthen mound; there is also a small museum with models, explanations of techniques and so on.

Then to Kerteminde and a night in the hotel before joining ship the next morning. There were atmospheric old streets to explore and, as usual in coastal Scandinavia, a fine church with ship models and Baroque funerary monuments. The combination of austere, white-painted Gothic architecture and elaborate decorative objects I always find most attractive: and most of all of course the nautical connotations. We found a nice restaurant where we ate outside in the courtyard: it was getting distinctly chilly and the provision of blankets for our knees was much appreciated. The locals were certainly determined not to freeze.

Kerteminde straddles what looks like a broad canal which is actually an inlet of the Kattegat, broadening out to the west towards Munkebo. So, activity goes on either side, with a distinct nautical flavour. The second night we dined – inside – a restaurant on the 'far' or southern side and viewed some celebratory spectacle as night fell with lanterns, flares etc. lining the waterside and canoeing and suchlike going on – not to mention genial drinking.

Our boat was a centre-cockpit Hallberg-Rassy named *Antares*: capacious and capable. (The name was perhaps unfortunate for denizens of Kintyre remembering how a fishing boat of that name had been dragged under by a submarine and lost: but the Danes could hardly be expected to know that…) After demonstrations we were off southwards into the Great Belt, planning to circumnavigate Fyn clockwise. (In sailing terms this was perhaps an error, as the wind constantly shifted ahead during the week, thus we were close-hauled virtually the whole time: had we turned left, we would have had the wind behind us… But that would not have fitted our plan, nor indeed been the best choice from a 'touristic' point of view.)

It was a bright and breezy day as we carried on under the Great Belt bridge linking Fyn and Sjaelland (thus Odense and Copenhagen). There was quite a lot of larger traffic, including ferries. Going south the sky darkened and by the time we put in at Rudkøbing, on a smaller island, it was a quieter, drizzlier evening. We had a walk ashore to view another small, maritime-flavoured Danish town. We were then not far from Svendborg, Fyn's second largest town, at its southern point, where we were due to meet up the next day with Nicky Jenkin, coming as the third member of the crew.

Svendborg has a capacious harbour with an impressive array of traditional craft of all kinds – wooden yachts and working boats, 'tall ships', many smart green tugboats, the inevitable ferries. The town was also spacious and tranquil, with an air of perhaps somewhat faded mercantile and shipping glory. Tramlines, weatherboarded warehouses, brick crow-stepped-gabled churches…

Nicky duly arrived the next day and we explored Svendborg a little more before continuing the clockwise voyage. Turning by degrees northward we were now in the Little Belt and made the next night's stop at another little town, Assens on the Fyn side. As we sailed up the Belt, we passed innumerable, mostly small traditional craft: gaff-rigged in the main, but one notable exception was the red-and-white-striped square sail of a replica Viking ship which came past.

The customary evening stroll round the town was agreeable: little rust-coloured wooden houses (probably holiday cottages in the main), wild roses in the gardens; and though a much smaller town, another superb church with monuments to match its larger brethren. But the next day was to provide perhaps the most impressive spectacle of the voyage. The day had dawned much brighter and also calmer: on the northern part of the Little Belt, we came across an amazing array of 'tall ships' – schooners, barques, brigantines, whatever – engaged in a race or rally. The wind having died almost completely they tended to be bunched up together and if it was a race, one would not know who was ahead. I wrote 'we' as Dick was asleep while Nicky and I kept the deck: I put on the engine so as to cruise around and get a good look at the fleet, and we aroused the sleeping Dick lest he miss this magnificent sight. Later we entered the narrower channel leading to the open Kattegat and moored in Middelfart, near the bridge we had lately driven over. It was by now the most beautiful luminous evening and drinks and supper in the marina brought an appropriate end.

The morning dawned clear without a breath of air. We motored under the bridge and along a final, wooded, lovely stretch of water out into the Kattegat. Apart from some coasters and many yachts this stretch out to sea featured platoons of windmills. First stop out at sea was the low-lying island of Samsø; then the much smaller and utterly enchanting Tunø. Getting into these tiny harbours is quite a performance as they are essentially (harbour) wall-to-wall boat. A cheerful scene, though, and everyone most helpful. We had time for some long walks through the village with, as usual, an abundance of grassy lanes, wild roses, hydrangeas, low-built timbered houses, and a handsome whitewashed church with solid crow-stepped gables.

Then the final phase: another glorious day, heading south into the Great Belt and back to now-familiar Kerteminde and returning *Antares*. It had been a highly successful initial Scandi-cruise. The 'tour', however, was not yet over as we now had Odense to inspect on the way back to the airport. Odense of course means one thing – Hans Christian Andersen – and his legacy is everywhere. It is an attractive small city of parks and wide streets: with a cathedral of extraordinary verticality in the brick Baltic style, perhaps more reminiscent of Germany – Lübeck? – than of Denmark. The Baroque monuments were superlative: it was appropriate to see that the last name on a great tablet of bishops was Gyldenstierna. (Again…)

Chartering 3: The Stockholm Skerries with Ann

Having got to the threshold of the Baltic in 2008 in Denmark, the next year was to see us in its heartland. This time we had recruited as the third member of the crew Laurel Spooner's sister-in-law Ann Wallace, who proved a delightful shipmate. Once more Dick arranged a charter, this time starting from Trosa, about forty miles south-west of Stockholm, thus a gateway to the Skerries which I have already described cruising in *Ardevora*. An unassuming little town, Trosa also lies abreast a sylvan canal which to the east and seaward becomes a twisting and eventually widening fjord.

Our plan was to follow the line of the outer islands or skerries up to Sandhamn, the yachting Mecca of the Stockholm archipelago: then to return by a more inshore route. In the islands, the normal practice is to moor bow-to to the rocks, with a bow line ashore and an anchor aft: this takes some practice and also considerable agility in clambering ashore over the bow (I have always thought stern-to would be preferable on several grounds; but no doubt they have their reasons). It helps that most cruising boats in these ports are not much over 30 feet overall. As we were somewhat larger – and perhaps less agile and adept – we tended often to anchor in what were usually tranquil little bays, observing from a little way off the congregation of parked boats.

An early stop, where we did tie to a jetty, was the island of Utö: pretty with pine trees and a sheltered little inlet surrounded by reeds, and a grassy little hamlet with village shops and restaurant in the usual dark red wood. Utö is clearly a day destination from Stockholm and the ferry brought fit-looking youths with bicycles. One is always conscious how short the summer season is and can imagine how different things will look in winter. Back home I did a painting of this pretty spot from photos and sketches on the scene.

From Utö we were more on the edge of the archipelago with the open Baltic to starboard; but innumerable islets and rocks to dodge lurk even in the more open water. An endless procession of craft old and new provided much interest. Approaching Sandhamn we came across the first of many beautiful, old varnished boats – launches, cruisers, speedboats – often cruising in a group. In Sandhamn we could tie up at a pontoon. It was not unlike Cowes.

In fact, of course Sandhamn could be called the Swedish Cowes, filled with craft of all kinds, and dedicated to maritime (and social) pleasures. There were numerous pretty sailing boats, up to 12-metre size (and some larger yawls), but the real joy for me was to see the rally of vintage motor boats. The pontoons were crammed full of these: all in immaculate condition and varnished and polished to perfection. Some were open speedboats – not unlike the Venetian Rivas – others had cabins or cockpits of various configurations. I imagine some dated from pre-war years, while others though doggedly traditional in design would have been more modern. During the day there were races, or perhaps processions and these nut-brown vessels all in company amidst churning wakes were a fine sight.

Sandhamn has an elegant waterfront with an all-purpose town hall (?) with airy restaurant from which to watch the day come to its close – and fairly decorous night-time promenades and imbibing begin. Apart from strolling along the quays to inspect the various craft, we wandered through the more residential bit: as usual, demure little red houses surrounded by roses wild or tame, and with a tendency to exhibit sizeable vintage items such as cartwheels, mangles etc. as ornaments in their little wild gardens.

Returning, we were more aware of the mainland as we followed the 'channel' between that and the string of islands culminating at Sandhamn. The broad expanse of water was a minefield of rocks: the satnav was invaluable in helping us avoid them, sometimes by the narrowest of margins. We anchored in a couple of idyllic bays and saw the sun sink to the west. In one we broadcast a tape of Churchill's speeches to the boats parked round the bay: reaction unknown. Moving down the sound we were leaving the island chain and closing the mainland, passing close by Dalarö which lies on the water along a wooded shore. On the tip of an island in the channel is a fortress well placed to repel intruders heading for Stockholm (efficacy against Russian submarines perhaps doubtful). The weather had turned grey and still: travelling now through tree-clad channels there was the sense of leaving the outer skerries for the mainland – and home.

Our final night at anchor was in fact the one occasion of poor weather: in the final bay (though sheltered) before again navigating the 'fjord' up to Trosa. Our brief stay in that little town before leaving for airport and home was enlivened by a display (presumably after a rally) of American cars of the 1950s and 60s – nostalgic for those of a certain age, and a suitable complement to the wooden boats of Sandhamn.

Chartering 4: Gothenburg and Bohuslän, with Laurel

In 2010 we crossed to the other side of Sweden, and this time Laurel was with us. We drove north from Gothenburg to pick up our vessel, *Regina,* a 36-foot aft-cockpit Hallberg-Rassy, from its home at a yard on the island of Tjörn. From there it was a quick sail round to Marstrand, part of which is on Tjörn and (the main part) on its own island, separated by a narrow channel. Sailing round the bottom of Tjörn we got a real feeling of the open sea, the Skagerrak, to the west. It was a fine, bright, breezy day: coasters and small tankers mixed with the customary succession of pleasure craft, mainly sailing. Endless reefs and rocky islets – not a tree between them – ringed the bigger island behind. We got used to squat miniature lighthouses, on barely visible rocks mid-channel or clinging to the islets' sides, suggesting a rapid change of course.

Marstrand occupies roughly the same role in present-day western Sweden as Sandhamn in the east: the summer capital of boating and evening pleasures. In fact, it is a more impressive town altogether, crowned with the massive stone Carlsten fortress atop a quite steep hill, on the island. Below, streets of handsome wooden houses, red, white, grey often with fretwork balcony balustrades and slender pillars to the porches, tumble down to the broad quayside with pontoons and berths for lucky boats like ours. From there we could join the promenade and eventually eat in the main restaurant/meeting place.

It had been a beautiful evening as we explored the waterside, inspected the ferry coming and going and generally joined in the throng. But the morning dawned grey and drizzly. We climbed up to the fortress which in that light looked more forbidding than ever. From the heights we could see a whole panorama of the small islands fringing the coast: bare rock, but still with a surprising number of little, presumably holiday, houses affixed to them. Descending, we took in another sector of the town, adjoining the passage out to the north. Again, there were some quite substantial houses, also public buildings, in the 'gingerbread house' style mentioned before. (There was also something reminiscent of the Wild West stage settings in Westerns like *High Noon*: one almost expected to see Henry Fonda, James Stewart or Clint Eastwood…)

Sailing up past Tjörn, we were passing or putting in at little settlements with evocative names like Skärhamn, Mollösund and, a night's stop, Käringön. This is an impossibly pretty place with the obligatory rust-red houses crowding around, indeed perched on the harbour, and much evidence of (recreational) fishing activity. It was a short walk up a little hill to get a view of the other side of the island and indeed all around, with numerous little bays often fringed with moored yachts. The houses were more higgledy-piggledy, on irregular plots, often on several levels. Garden ornaments, often of considerable size, included a whale's jawbone and several large anchors. With scarcely a tree in sight and a plethora of granite, naturally the houses are predominantly built of wood. But at the waterside supper was enjoyed viewing the promenade of cheerful youth, ashore and on boats.

We struck out from the immediate coastal island fringe and headed across more open water to a miniature group of islands on their own. Approaching this mini-archipelago it was impossible to distinguish one island from another, the whole being like a tightly closed fist around a narrow body of water. Clusters of mast-tops gave a clue as to where there must be inlets offering mooring places. Penetrating an ever-narrowing inlet we were able to anchor and go ashore to climb up then down to the small settlement by the water's edge. It developed into a still moonlit night – if not for long – and there was a sense of great peace, far from the world.

The world reasserted itself to a certain extent as we closed the main island of Orust, north of Tjörn, and threaded our way through the various channels. Yachts from many countries abounded: Norwegian, Danish, German, Czech, American; but I don't recall any British. There were several sightings of a large ketch whose sides were emblazoned with 'Sailing for Jesus'. (Earlier we had several times met a smaller boat proclaiming 'Jesus for Life'. Presumably these are a worthy YMCA/Sea Cadets/Outward Bound operation.)

Reaching the mainland periphery again, we closed the big island of Orust and put in at Ellös to moor at the Hallberg-Rassy marina and boatyard – our ship's birthplace. It was of course crowded with *Regina*'s relations, complete or incomplete; as a bonus the genial Mr Rassy himself appeared and we had a good talk. Our berth made a good viewpoint for a brilliant sunset viewed through a forest of masts. Alas, red sky at night proved not to be a shepherd's or even sailor's delight and the next morning was again grey.

We were predominantly sailing, in quite a stiff breeze, in the broader waters between these larger islands, Orust and Tjörn, and the mainland: though it was sometimes difficult to distinguish which was which. Folkboats and day racer keelboats seemed to be enjoying the combination of strongish wind and relatively calm sea. The shores were now predominantly wooded, mainly firs and pines. Numerous substantial and enviable houses were often set back above the water, with meadows leading down to the shore and the inevitable 'mini-dock' with sauna cabin, boathouse and jetty. We passed a succession of yellow-coloured ferries, while several imposing single-span bridges soared overhead. Pepperpot lighthouses, on isolated rocks or on wooded rocky shores, guided us through convoluted turns, passing a few waterside villages: we would suddenly find ourselves further to seaward with resumption of the pattern of low, treeless islands improbably hosting what were almost 'housing estates' of near-identical white houses with red roofs. The effect from afar was almost of a crowd of gulls on the rocks. A triangular church spire, a prominent windmill and an inverted-triangle water tower graced the larger of these settlements, at one of which we made a fuel stop before handing the boat back (shades of car hire!).

Our last night was alongside in another of these attractive places, where (unlike Marstrand, Gullholmen and several other little towns which straddle a waterway) there was just a sparsely populated island directly opposite, with a narrow strait between. We dined by the quayside in another very typical terrace restaurant, giving us a good view of the comings and goings (several ferries still, even as the evening wore on). As the sun dipped – a lovely calm evening – young women enjoyed gymnastics or acrobatics on the pier beyond our moored boats. And so ended that Swedish sailing experience; another was to come the following year.

Gothenburg, *and Collecting* Swift

In April 2011, I phoned Dick wondering whether we should arrange another Swedish charter for the coming summer. 'Ah' he said, 'I was in Sweden last week and have ordered a boat: an Arcona 43, being built at Kungshamn, north of Gothenburg, which is due to be ready at the end of June.' I looked it up and this seemed to be an ideal design: a good size, obviously a fast cruiser (which is so important), sensible interior layout and evidently built to high standards of finish. It was elegant with a tall mast with three sets of spreaders. My appetite was duly whetted.

When the time came, I flew alone to Gothenburg and this time had an opportunity to explore that handsome city. After checking in to my hotel – a venerable establishment on one of the main streets – I walked down to the waterfront where I found 'the Swedish Ship': a replica of the East Indiaman *Götheborg* (sic), which had come to an untimely end in 1745 at the entrance to this same harbour returning from a voyage to the Indies, or Cathay... The rather more intimidating *Vasa* seems to have set the precedent for this in Stockholm harbour around a century earlier – not to mention the *Mary Rose*. The replica was launched in 2003 after a long, privately financed period of construction spanning the millennium. She had recently made an epic round-trip voyage to Canton, with the King and Queen of Sweden on board for the final stage; and joined in various 'tall ship' rallies around the world.

She is an impressive vessel, fully rigged three-master: her topsides painted in the Swedish colours of blue and yellow: an imposing Chinese-style figurehead of a *shishi* lion which no doubt impressed the good burghers of Canton. Alas, I was unable to go on board (it was already 7 o'clock, though a fine evening lay ahead). Next along the quay was none other than the old Bohuslän steamship on which I had enjoyed a very wet excursion in the Stockholm archipelago a few years earlier, now of course back in her proper home: it was nostalgic to see her again.

I took my time wandering back along the canals and the wide streets of the city: central Gothenburg is not disfigured by skyscrapers and a pleasing harmony of mainly neoclassical architecture prevails. (Caryatids are big; as are bronze statues, no doubt of naval heroes of past times.) There is also the superb modern opera house; but it does not disrupt the elevations of the quarter. It forms a link between the harbour and the more introspective canalside zone. And so to dinner in my stately hotel and bed.

As seems customary in Sweden (not alone in that!) a lovely evening was succeeded by a grey and damp morning. I made my way past the opera house again to the harbour to see the vessels of what is billed as the world's largest museum of floating ships, nineteen in all. Small passenger steamers, tugboats, a steel barquentine, the Fladen light vessel among them: but the main attraction, at least for me, was the naval ships, the destroyer *Småland*, launched in 1952 and decommissioned in 1979, and the submarine *Nordkaparen*, built ten years earlier. One could go aboard both of these and marvel at how old-fashioned the kit, no doubt state of the art in its day, seems now. There were other, smaller naval vessels too: patrol boats, corvettes, and the like.

My appetite for 'heritage' not yet sated, and beginning to

get wet, I made my way back along the quay where Swiss (!), Norwegian and other cruising yachts were berthed, and empty café terraces, to the Gothenburg Museum. This august institution seemed to 'major' in wooden artefacts: as well as boat skeletons and religious figures of evident antiquity, Nordic warrior figures bearing some resemblance to the Lewis chessmen (if of much greater size), and portraits of Victorian-looking dignitaries. One shrewd-looking fellow went by the name of Alexander Barclay: and a pious-looking, presumably Lutheran, clergyman held (most unconvincingly, between thumb and forefinger) a slip of – paper, cloth? – with the exhortation *ΓΝΩΘΙ ΣΕΑΥΤΟΝ* ('know thyself')! A rabbi could have been painted by Rembrandt (but I don't think was).

Impervious to the rain, I explored further, to a soggy green lakeside park with the largest alchemilla plantation I've ever seen, then around the wide streets of the 'merchant city'. While cities such as Odense, as noted, have a Gothic, somewhat Hanseatic feel, there seemed something of St Petersburg about Gothenburg: canals whose bridges sparked elaborate bronze lamps, equestrian statues, equally bronze, of martial figures, tall classical church towers, wide avenues leading from the internal canals to the quays bordering the wide harbour – itself the final phase of a broad river before the open sea. Beyond the older centre, too, but all too evident is a more industrial presence, specifically of shipbuilding and shipping. (In this respect, as well as some of the architecture, Gothenburg is perhaps somewhat reminiscent of Glasgow – or rather, the Glasgow of old, as the shipyards and ships there have effectively disappeared, and the river has been neutered. Of course, there were many links between the two cities in previous centuries – merely look at the portraits…)

Next day I met Dick and Robert Jenkin (this year's third crew member) at the (other) airport, and we set off on the drive north to Kungshamn. A wide, almost deserted dual carriageway took us via the superstore for provisioning and a homely bakery/

delicatessen for a quick lunch to Kungshamn. The little town lies on a small hill above the harbour: our hotel was perched high, and we could spot the sheds of *Swift*'s birthplace. It was the usual rather simple, airy place of white walls and pine: perfectly adequate – but what we wanted to do was get aboard!

At the yard we inspected, in the sheds, several boats in various stages of construction: then came the great moment of clambering aboard *Swift* moored alongside. We had with us Tony Bottomley, Arcona's man in the UK, who would demonstrate everything on the boat: then we cast off for our first epic demonstration voyage, in fairly local waters among the coastal skerries. These contained, among traditional fishing vessels, at least one handsome German ketch: it was perhaps ironical that at that stage we might also have been taken for German, as the mainsail when hoisted transpired to have the designation GER 5443R applied to it! The red ensign, however, belied this, and the erroneous letter was changed overnight to read GBR. (Just as well as many more Germans were sighted in the coming days – also Norwegians, as we were getting closer to Norway.)

We were shown all the 'tricks' of sail adjustment and familiarised with the technicalities and operation of the boat. It was clear straight away that she was very responsive to the helm and also fast: she would pick up quickly with only a small increase in the wind and could sail very close to the wind. The cockpit is very comfortable and well arranged: it is a joy to have two smallish wheels rather than one big one, and moving from side to side, often via the chart plotter, is exceptionally easy.

After a pleasant evening quayside promenade, with as always a plethora of interesting craft to inspect, we dined by the water, before setting off the next morning on the cruise proper.

Our 'shakedown' cruise was not a long one, but we became better acquainted with the Swedish west coast, further north than the previous year. We had a fine sail northwards by the more open waters of the Skagerrak up to Hunnebostrand, also becoming better acquainted with the capabilities of *Swift*, which were impressive: accelerating fast even in relatively light airs and showing remarkably good close-hauled ability.

Overnight stops this time, apart from Hunnebostrand, were Sotenäs and Smögen: in all of these the gentle festive atmosphere of the brief Swedish summer, as enjoyed by its youth, was all-pervasive. In the narrow inlet of Smögen in particular the boats were rafted up together almost from shore to shore; and every cockpit seemed to contain at least a dozen revellers. So, near the Norwegian border a great many of these were from Norway; but also, many other nationalities (again, the Brits seem unaware of this really joyful midsummer activity). Likewise, the quayside, where as elsewhere we found an entirely agreeable and atmospheric restaurant for our final 'dining experience'. All too soon, then, it was time for the drive south to the airport, leaving *Swift* in the capable hands of her creators at the yard in Kungshamn – shortly to see her proud owner again, of course.

Dick returned later in the season with some younger family members to bring *Swift* back to her new home at Woolverstone: so that was going to be the end of the Baltic for the foreseeable future: it was to be 'Westward Ho' from now on. To achieve this new orientation – or rather occidentation – a voyage from Suffolk down channel was scheduled, the first leg of which from Woolverstone to the Hamble I joined the following year.

Swift*: Down Channel, with Excursion to France*

It seemed almost odd to be sailing in 'home waters' again. The wind farms off the Essex coast had of course proliferated. An easy transit of the Thames Estuary brought us to the North and South Forelands and foreboding black clouds over the White Cliffs. Dover Marina is a confusing and scruffy sort of place: the ferry-bound driver aiming for the East Cliff has little sense of this nor really of the town at all, coming straight off the dual carriageway. However, our run ashore took us up the main street, tucked slightly inland, to a most excellent small Italian restaurant: I gather from Dick from his latest repeat voyage that it is still there, as good, and friendly, as ever.

The sail down Channel proved somewhat frustrating: there are of course strong tides and several major headlands, and it was hard to get the timing right. Thus, I remember making only small progress forward after numerous tacks off Hastings beach (however, it was interesting to inspect the town's seafront from very close to shore). Eventually, however, we did enter the large and soulless marina at Eastbourne. In contrast to what we had come to expect shoreside in Sweden and Denmark, with their partying but essentially decorous – and certainly decorative in the case of the golden-haired girls – youth, the place was dismal and virtually deserted. A trek all around the 'basin' took us to the area of a few of the most plebeian chain restaurants – Nando's and suchlike. I can't remember which one was patronised – vaguely Oriental, I think.

The morning, however, dawned bright and clear, and we were off bright and early. In a discussion the previous night I had suggested that rather than zig-zagging futilely up the English coast (the wind was still westerly) we might take just one tack across to France, enjoy a good dinner and overnight, then another tack back to the Hamble where *Swift* was to be parked for a little while. So that's what we did. There was a superb view of Beachy Head as we headed out to sea. The shipping lanes provided a good variety of large vessels, sadly none of them naval (not even Russian!). Closing the French coast, their Monet-esque cliffs stretched as far as one could see both east and west: Fécamp, whither we were bound, slowly appeared as a gap.

The harbourmaster's team directed us to a suitable spot on a pontoon in the inner harbour: formalities did not include any request for passports, just as well as Dick didn't have one with him (quite by chance, I did). It was refreshing to be in France, and we sauntered along the cobbled *quais* checking out the restaurants and appetising shops. Fécamp is home to the highly elaborate monastery in which is distilled the Benedictine liqueur: but we had no time to visit or sample.

As so often, the weather had worsened overnight and steadily deteriorated during the following day. By the time we were closing the coast past the east point of the Isle of Wight it was pouring with rain and blowing hard. At least that speeded our arrival in the Hamble. Dick's contract with the Woolverstone Marina also allows him to visit other marinas of the same group, which is owned by Robert (Lord) Iliffe. Lo and behold, Robert's impressive motor yacht *Dalvina* (a mini-ship really) was there, occupying the 'T' at the end of the pontoon. Robert is a friend, and I asked the skipper whether he was around, to be told he and Annie would be coming shortly as his nephew William was returning the next day with the last leg of the Whitbread Round-the-World race; Will's father and mother Joe and Mary (even closer friends) would be coming too to cruise around the homecoming fleet the next day. The Iliffes appeared shortly: would I like to join them in the morning? Would I not! Unfortunately, Dick had to leave that evening, so I was left in charge of *Swift* for the night, with arrangements for leaving the keys at the office etc.

A very enjoyable day was spent in great comfort and style aboard *Dalvina* watching the fleet come in. Robert was clearly in his element at the helm in the wheelhouse, dodging in and out of the fleet. William's boat was soon spotted. As ever there was a good feeling with the White Ensign flying at the stern: Robert had only recently stepped down as Commodore of the Squadron.

When all the boats had safely tied up there was the prize-giving ceremony, speeches etc. – and also of course reunion of Joe and Mary with their son whom they had barely seen for the best part of a year: he had done all the stages of the Whitbread. Then it was time to make sure *Swift* was properly locked up, get a lift to Winchester station and thence back to London.

Swift in the Scillies and Racing in Ireland: a Mini-Fastnet

The next summer *Swift* was already positioned in the West Country, at Falmouth beside the National Maritime Museum. I drove down and stayed a night or two with Ellen Winser at Tregony, not far away. She being chairman of the Falmouth NMM, it was not difficult for her to park near to the boat! She came on board for a while and greatly approved of *Swift*. Then Dick and I were alone for a couple of days as Laurel's arrival was indeterminate. When she came, we were going to lose no time in heading for southern Ireland via the Scillies; meanwhile we had a little time, not only to go shopping and eating in Falmouth but also to take an excursion boat up the Fal estuary to visit one of the famous Cornish gardens.

Laurel eventually showed up and the next morning we rounded the Lizard and set course for the Scillies. On the way I spotted an orca killer whale, briefly, some way off to seaward; neither of the others saw it, but I am sure of it. The weather was glorious. We arrived in the wide bay of Hugh Town on St Mary's, largest of the islands, and spent some time motoring around trying to find a suitable mooring buoy. Eventually we had success, but it came at a cost. I was up at the sharp end, perilously leaning over the bow and grappling with an extremely slimy and quite heavy buoy. My varifocal spectacles, which I was quite certain I had zipped properly into the breast pocket of my sailing jacket, promptly decided to fall into the water and were lost to sight. Dick was quite sure he could dive for them in the morning: I was not at all sure, given the enormous height of the tide and thus the force with which it would ebb and flow across the sand. So indeed, it proved: as usual the glorious evening had been followed by a gloomy grey morning, the water must have been impenetrable (I did not volunteer myself!) and the specs were probably halfway to Ireland.

This tragi-comic episode was followed by something much sadder and more sobering. Ashore, we had found a nice pub and were just in time for hurried 'last orders' for supper. Having chosen, I went outside to ring Haruko, whom I hadn't been able to call for the past 36 hours or so through being on the high seas. She was highly upset and worried as she had had news that her mother had collapsed at the Misakiguchi railway station on the way to her retirement home at Aburatsubo with a 'burst aorta'; it was doubtful she would survive, and the pressing question was whether she should have an operation or not. Haruko of course was going to fly to Tokyo in the morning (this was a Sunday evening) and her sisters would be doing the same from New York. I felt immense sympathy but also of course impotent as there was really nothing I could do – she was travelling to Tokyo, and I was needed to help get the boat to Ireland. Thankfully Mother pulled through with great fortitude (and without the dangerous operation) and celebrated her 100th birthday this year, eight years on.

In somewhat Swedish fashion, after a fine day and evening the morning dawned grey and drizzly. The gallant dive, unsurprisingly, found no spectacles, nor anything else of interest. We went into the town, had a good look around the main street and went over to the beach on the other side of the island – Hugh Town, the main settlement on the island, is really on an isthmus (were it in the West Highlands it would undoubtedly be called Tarbert). Memories of Harold Wilson in his shorts relaxing with his pipe, as featured on a *Private Eye* cover long ago…

Later in extending our acquaintance with the islands we sailed across the short stretch of water and anchored off Tresco. Tresco is undoubtedly the most attractive of the islands, just the right size for exploring on foot in leisurely fashion. The great attraction is of course the Abbey (a private house) with its glorious subtropical garden, which is open to visitors. But the island has much more in store: miniature valleys, woods, lake ('Great Pool'), gentle hills and sandy bays, and a pleasant little village of stone with shop and pub – no wonder it's a popular place for repeat holiday visitors. Palm trees and ubiquitous agapanthi ('Beware the agapanthus!') best characterised the landscape. Continuing our anticlockwise walk we followed the western shore on an undulating path, whence we looked across the narrow (and shallow) strait to the even smaller island of Bryher. Then it was more open country as we turned round towards our anchorage bay, leaving the Abbey in its woods to port.

Ahead lay the rather longer crossing of the Celtic Sea to Southern Ireland… If *Swift* has one demerit it is to smash her forefoot into oncoming waves of a certain strength, and there was a lot of that on a night that Laurel and I spent on watch together. We were diverted by the lights and antics of not a few fishing vessels. The Irish coast duly showed, and we sailed up the 'loch' to the fine town of Kinsale.

Sailing past the forts (Charles and James: named for the Stuart kings embroiled in mainly religion-inspired wars involving the English, French, Spanish, Ulstermen, native Irish for starters) guarding the entrance, we proceeded up the winding estuary to Kinsale town. Kinsale means in Gaelic 'Head of the Water' and so very similar to Campbeltown, original name Kinloch or 'Head of the Loch'. In fact, there are other similarities: the size of the town and its buildings, the position as per name, the approach up winding waterway. More distilleries in Campbeltown, though fewer forts! The marina is on the south shore just before the inner harbour, closed off by a promontory on the north side; a short walk along the promenade takes one to the centre of the town, past some pleasant Georgian terraces. The town centre, on a small flat area between the hills on either side, also has some fine old buildings, notably the elegant Market House of the very early seventeenth century, and of course the market etc. With four days there we had good walks some way up the hillside roads, and some good eating in the town.

Retracing our wake seaward, we turned westward for the next stopping point of the voyage, Baltimore. Shortly one passes over the wreck of the *Lusitania*, torpedoed in 1915, so near her destination of Queenstown (Cobh). (The inquest into this tragedy was held in the Market House at Kinsale which we had just admired.) The successive bays between prominent headlands had evocative names which could only be Irish: Courtmacsherry, Clonakilty and Glandore. With a (light) headwind we were taking frequent tacks, well inshore by some of the headlands: the pastoral countryside behind was immensely appealing.

Rounding the promontory to reach Baltimore Bay and harbour, one is first greeted by the extraordinary and frankly phallic Baltimore Beacon high on the clifftop: from there it is no distance to Baltimore itself. Yachts generally anchor some way off the quay, that mostly reserved for fishing vessels and the small ferries destined for the islands and places across the bay, and of course for refuelling and loading. The attractive little village consists of several terraces in tiers above the harbour, watched over by an austere high-gabled castle, thirteenth century in origin but in ruins after the sack of Baltimore by Barbary pirates from Algiers in the mid-seventeenth century. (The inhabitants of Baltimore were evidently no slouches in the piracy game themselves, from the highest in the land to the lowest, so perhaps were getting their just comeuppance.) We visited the courtyard and climbed the wooden stairs to the ramparts, giving a good view over the bay. We also had a good look at the demure little Church of Ireland (i.e., Protestant) church, built about 1800 in what might be called Regency Gothic style. The Catholic church, surprisingly, was much less impressive.

We were reinforced by a fourth new member, a young man from the Cambridge University Yacht Club: Dick most generously offers them berths from time to time to give cruising experience. This particular young man was not, however, backward in giving us the benefit of his experience and advice at every opportunity. He was an engineering graduate, an aerodynamicist with one of the Formula 1 teams.

We were headed for Schull on the far side of the splendidly named Roaringwater Bay, for nearly a week enjoying participation in some races of the annual Schull Week. Rather than take the outside route, we opted for the very narrow and tortuous channel leading round the north of the island opposite Baltimore, thankful for the electronic chart which would give us safe passage through the rocks. I was keeping a keen eye on this while steering when there was an almighty bang and we had hit one. Luckily the tracing function on the plotter showed that our route had been through a supposedly rock-free zone; in fact, it transpired that the chart had totally mis-located the rock. Anyway, no damage was done.

Arriving at Schull, we moored as one of a long line of cruising boats parallel to the shore. It was a bit of a walk up to the town but worth it: festivities were in full swing. Unsurprisingly there was a full complement of public houses and much merriment, though the punters were largely overflowing into the street. An act of two pretty girls – a fiddler and a singer – entertained the populace with much brio and charm (I have a video clip).

But we were there for the racing – handicap of course. There were a couple of shorter races round various points in the bay, or further, round some of the islands: but the big one was the 'round the Fastnet' race. This, admittedly, was rather less arduous than the 'proper' Fastnet starting from Cowes, rounding the Fastnet Rock, and returning to Plymouth (or, in 2021, Cherbourg); nevertheless, to round the Rock *very* close up was a thrilling experience, thankfully also captured by video on my iPad. We had a serious addition to the crew in the shape of a nice Galway GP friend of Laurel's, David Buckley, and his two sons, Donagh and Eoghan. They were expert racing sailors, and their concentration and expertise were a thing to behold; as well of course as their thoroughly helpful and amusing characters.

That was a fine clear day and there was a good strong breeze: under spinnaker reaching along the coast on the return leg there were even some fairly 'hairy' moments. I can't remember where we were placed, but believe *Swift* acquitted herself well, in large degree thanks to our imported experts. She proved herself a fast cruiser-racer, well suited to this sort of event (the vagaries of handicap allotted are crucial to the result). The general atmosphere of the regatta was, unsurprisingly, informal, and friendly, with much congregating in the streets of the town afterwards, and swapping of stories probably as tall as a clipper's mast…

All such festivities must come to an end and leaving the Fastnet and the headlands astern we set course directly for the Lizard and Falmouth, this time missing the Scillies on purpose. There was a certain *déjà-vu* feeling as we cruised along the coast past the Lizard in the early morning; but this time it was only the Celtic Sea and not the Atlantic that had been crossed. I returned to Ellen and my car at Cuby House and eventually home.

Swift *in Galicia*

My final *Swift* excursion took place a year later: this time to north-west Spain where Dick and his friends were to have arrived after an enviable voyage down Channel and cross-Biscay. I had expected to meet them in A Coruña, perhaps better known as La Corunna, after a flight to Santiago de Compostela; but telephone contact revealed that they were ahead of schedule, had gone round the Finisterre 'corner' and were now at Muros, on one of the several 'Rias' on that coast. I was sad not to revisit Corunna where Mother and I had spent a night in 1985 – visiting the grave of the great Glaswegian Sir John Moore ('Not a drum was heard, not a funeral note…'), awaking from a glorious evening to a severe gale in the morning (several yachts were lost in Biscay), also to miss Santiago itself, but pressed on by taxi to Muros, through for the most part densely wooded hilly countryside. Muros is a very attractive little harbour town, largely of course of lichen-enhanced granite. Narrow streets of stone houses give onto a little plaza where the harbour begins. Handsome stone and whitewashed houses line the broad quays with a goodly selection of serious fishing boats as well as smaller craft.

The Ria de Muros – or more properly Ria de Muros y Noia,

the latter at the head of the estuary, is the northernmost of the Rias Baixas stretching south from Cape Finisterre to the Portuguese border. Thus, we were going to 'do' the successive rias (= sea lochs) southward in turn. The next day, however, we tied up at the pretty fishing village of Portosín across the same ria. The following day was grey with low cloud shrouding the mainland coast as we left the Ria de Muros for the next one, the Ria de Arousa. Ribeira and A Pobra do Caramiñal are the little towns on the north-west shore, both with marinas and fishing harbours – very similar in fact to Muros. We tied up at A Pobra: the weather was already improving. Next day dawned gloriously sunny and we headed up the 'loch' to anchor off the wide sandy beach of Boiro and swam and enjoyed a siesta. Then a tour around the (slightly more complex) ria took us to the substantially more important town of Villagarcia de Arousa.

The island of Arousa effectively divides the ria into two halves: beyond it the bay of Cambados and the peninsula topped by the splendidly named town of O Grove separate it from the next ria on the list, that of Pontevedra. Pontevedra, a very fine old town which I have visited on an earlier terrestrial trip, is effectively inland where the river debouches into the ria: on the north shore lies Sanxenxo and the smaller and absurdly pretty Combarro to the east, where we overnighted. Combarro has the usual ancient village giving onto a plaza at the quay head, with a broad quay with the capacious marina beyond. The village boasts a magnificent collection of *horreos*, the stone huts on stilts – proof against rats or what littoral pests? – similar to the grain stores of inland Galicia and Asturias, but here of course for fishermen's impedimenta. A pleasant walk takes one along to the beach, and the pierhead has an agreeable restaurant.

Both Combarro and Sanxenxo possess beautiful sandy beaches, and many more can be glimpsed as one sails around the headland separating these rias. Not so many on the next headland leading into the Ria de Vigo. We sailed or motored up that to the enormous motorway viaduct at the Narrows. Great care was needed to avoid the serried ranks of oyster farms, very close together. Then we found our berth in the very large pleasure port, near the Real Club Náutico de Vigo.

This venerable establishment sits, as usual, by the walkway entrance to the pontoons of the marina; built in the 1930s in the style of an ocean liner of that epoch, with a rounded 'prow' pointing seawards: on the first floor a very elegant restaurant and club premises, on the ground level the workaday premises for repairs, storage, etc., and the marina offices. This complex is sandwiched between quays of the commercial port. One crosses the wider 'via del Porto' to get access to the city proper: at that point on quite a steep hill leading up to the cathedral, and a useful feature is a bright red escalator alongside a particularly steep set of steps. Up top, the town is handsome in a severe, stone-built sort of way. Some very interesting shops including a good second-hand bookshop. One descends at right angles, northwards, to the wide boulevards of the more modern town.

We had had to say *hasta la vista* to Nick and Bianca who were taking the superfast Renfe express down to Porto (no distance away). In return we were reinforced by Gareth Ainsworth, a most pleasant Australian who had just completed a maths PhD at Trinity, Cambridge. That night we found an excellent little restaurant, which indeed we revisited on our return some days after, quite some way along the road out of town.

Our aim and turning point was to be Baiona some way to the south: famous as the starting point for the annual ARC cruise in company across to the West Indies (which set off with the trade winds in November). Baiona – or Bayona – is a very pretty place: the great fort overlooks the harbour mouth on its promontory, and the town stretches out below it along the bay. Near the entrance is the yacht club, from which one descends to a very capacious marina. This is divided into the yacht club sector and the 'other': in which resides a full-scale replica of the *Pinta*, the one of Christopher Columbus' three ships which returned to Vigo following the fortuitous discovery of the New World. Naturally we visited that: it was well done. Tiny of course.

The yacht club became a headquarters for a couple of days for coffee, meals, etc.: of course, we also explored the town proper. The waterside promenade is lined with handsome terraced houses; behind there is a lower-rise older main street with similar streets leading off it. The impression is of stone solidity and coherence: no jarring modernity. A wider and newer street at right angles, in which unsurprisingly nineteenth-century buildings house restaurants, shops and offices, leads up to the solid cathedral.

We had a day sail to have a look at the little Islas Cies, part of a national park (no disembarking there). Lying a few miles off the mainland they are naturally a day-trip destination for small leisure craft of all sorts. It was a glorious breezy day, and we found an anchoring slot near the passage between the islands, anchored, lunched, slept. Then back to Baiona, and the next day we returned to Vigo where a couple more young CUYC people – male and female – joined us in time for our second visit to the restaurant and the next stage of the voyage southwards; I, however, had to fly back from Santiago the next afternoon.

Perhaps I slipped up then. I could have taken the same super-express that evening to Santiago, stayed in the familiar and wonderful Reyes Catolicos *parador*, and had the best part of a day there. However, I opted to stay on board, where it became a bit of a squash for the night. Nonetheless a jolly, if quite pricey, dinner was had – lots of *jamón serrano* – and we all squeezed in happily. But unfortunately, there was not a convenient train for Santiago in the morning, so there was nothing for it but a taxi: rather more expensive than that outbound to Muros. I arrived at the airport only to find it – certainly the check-in desks – deserted. There was a long wait till my flight; however, I reckoned, not enough time to go into the town and view its marvels. An opportunity missed.

And Finally – 'Frostbite' Sailing in Japan!

I could hardly finish without mentioning the two or three occasions when I went down to Aburatsubo, usually on Boxing Day, for a day's sail on Sagami-wan with my good friend (and Haruko's second cousin) Yoshiaki Okami. Yoshiaki lived in Athens for several years for NYK Line and bought and brought back to Japan a small but sportingly lined boat called – amazingly enough in view of my early days with *Zephyrus*, Ζεφυρος or *Zephyrus*! She was parked ashore in a yard at the end of one of the spectacular little mini-fjords on that coastline: a contrivance came and dropped her (him?) in the water and we were 'good to go'. Out in the broader bay there was a marvellous view of Mount Fuji and of Oshima ('Big') Island closing off the approaches to Sagami and Tokyo bays. Also very visible nearer were the distinctive high-prowed fishing boats which moved abruptly and with surprising speed, heedless of any other craft in their way. Clearly the ocean belonged to them! We would anchor, probably in the more sheltered fjord (it was really windy outside and the boat was lively to say the least), and Yoshiaki would brew up some lunch – stew or curry – on the little stove in the remarkably cluttered little cabin. An excellent midwinter day out and a novelty to be sailing these exotic waters!

One time we were joined by a rather large chap called, inevitably, Jumbo, a cook. With immense initiative he later went to England and bought in Essex an even smaller 25-foot yacht, which he was fitting out for a solo voyage back to Japan. Unfortunately that coincided with the onset of the Covid pandemic and borders were closed, visas and travel impossible. He had intended to spend some time on the west coast of Scotland, largely for whisky tasting, but that was off: however, he got over to France for a while and then, somehow, to Spain where he found a very accommodating yard just outside our old friend Vigo. Alas, money and patience ran out and he was forced to abandon his plan – which had involved a long stay with friends in Florida also – sell the boat, and return to Japan, where he is now a sushi chef in Hokkaido. What a tale that would have been for the yachting magazines! I admire him immensely.

Yoshiaki has a maritime pedigree as he, like Haruko, is a great-nephew (she great-niece) of the renowned Admiral Yamanashi, a lifelong friend of the Royal Navy and opponent of Japan's militarism, whose memorial with bust we visited on the *Mikasa*, Togo's flagship at the decisive battle of Tsushima: Yamanashi as a young man had stood by her construction at Barrow-in-Furness in 1902. After our visit we went for a Japanese navy curry, another import from Britain!

Chapter Frontispiece Illustrations